MW00634176

# Spoken Sudanese Arabic:
## Grammar, Dialogues, and Glossary

Elizabeth M. Bergman

## Publications of the African Language Project

Chester Hedgepeth, Project Director
University of Maryland Eastern Shore
Princess Anne, Maryland 21853-1299

*Hausa Newspaper Reader* (1996)
Philip J. Jaggar

*Yoruba Newspaper Reader* (1998)
Antonia Schleicher

*Lingala Parallel Texts* (2002)
David R. Woods

*Spoken Sudanese Arabic: Grammar, Dialogues, and Glossary* (2002)
Elizabeth M. Bergman

# Spoken Sudanese Arabic:
## Grammar, Dialogues, and Glossary

Elizabeth M. Bergman

2002
Dunwoody Press

**Spoken Sudanese Arabic: Grammar, Dialogues, and Glossary**



All inquiries should be directed to:
Dunwoody Press
6564 Loisdale Ct., Suite 800
Springfield, VA 22150, USA

ISBN: 1-881265-92-7
Library of Congress Catalog Card Number: 2002116051
Printed and bound in the United States of America

# Table of Contents

**Acknowledgments** ..... i
**Symbols and Abbreviations** ..... ii
**Glossary of linguistic terms** ..... iii
**Preface** ..... vii
About Sudanese Arabic ..... vii
About this work ..... viii
How to use this work ..... ix
**Key to transcription** ..... xii
Notes to transcription key ..... xiii
**Bibliography** ..... xvi
**Maps of Sudan** ..... xviii-xix
**Grammar**
Introduction ..... 1
1. The sounds of Sudanese Arabic ..... 2
1.1 Consonants ..... 2
1.1.1 The consonants of SA ..... 2
1.2 The vowels of SA ..... 6
1.2.1 The short vowels of SA ..... 6
1.2.2 The long vowels of SA ..... 7
1.2.3 The diphthongs of SA ..... 7
1.3 Syllable structure and stress ..... 7
1.3.1 Syllable structures ..... 7
1.3.2 Word-initial syllable structure ..... 8
1.3.3 Avoidance of word-final consonant clusters ..... 9
1.3.4 Word-final geminate consonants ..... 9
1.3.5 Stress rules ..... 11
1.4 Regular sound changes ..... 13
1.4.1 Assimilation ..... 13
1.4.2 Insertion of /a/ following /ʕ/, /ɣ/, /x/, /ḥ/, and /h/ ..... 13
1.4.3 Deletion of unstressed short vowels preceding a single consonant ..... 13
1.4.4 Devoicing of voiced consonants ..... 13
1.4.5 Devoicing of /ʕ/ (voiced pharyngeal fricative) ..... 14
1.4.6 Elision of /ya-/ and /yi-/ ..... 14
1.4.7 The 3MS and 3P prefixes of the imperfect /ya-/ and /yi-/ ..... 14
1.4.8 Resolution of word-final consonant clusters. See 1.3.3 ..... 15
1.4.9 The definite article and relative pronoun /al-/ ..... 15
1.4.10 Lengthening of short vowels ..... 16
2. Nouns and adjectives: derivation and inflection ..... 16
2.1 Noun morphology ..... 16
2.2 Adjective morphology ..... 17
2.2.1 Adjective pattterns ..... 17
2.3 Gender and number inflection ..... 18
2.3.1 Gender and number inflections for nouns, adjectives, and participles ..... 18
2.3.2 The feminine singular inflections ..... 19
2.3.3 The dual ..... 19
2.3.4 The masculine sound plural ..... 20
2.3.5 The feminine sound plural ..... 20
3. Verb morphology ..... 21
3.1 Affixes of the perfect, imperfect, and imperative ..... 22
3.1.1 Suffixes of the perfect ..... 22
3.1.2 Affixes of the imperfect ..... 23

3.1.3 Affixes of the imperative.....24
3.2 Forms of the verb in SA.....25
3.2.1 Form I verbs.....25
3.2.2 Derived verb forms.....31
3.2.3 Form II verbs.....32
3.3 The true or ablaut passive.....34
3.4 Other forms derived from verbs.....35
3.4.1 Verbal nouns.....35
3.4.2 Active participles.....36
3.4.3 Passive participles.....36
3.5 Uses of the perfect.....37
3.5.1 The perfect expresses the past.....37
3.5.2 The perfect expresses a wish (the optative).....37
3.5.3 The perfect is the act (the performative).....37
3.6 Uses of the imperfect.....37
3.6.1 The simple imperfect.....37
3.6.2 The prefixed imperfect.....38
3.6.3 The future.....38
3.6.4 Pre-verbs.....39
3.7 The use of the active participle.....42
4. Pronouns.....43
4.1 Independent personal pronouns.....43
4.2 Suffixed personal pronouns.....43
4.3 Demonstratives.....43
5. Numbers and number derivations.....44
5.1 Numbers for counting (cardinal numbers) and ordering (ordinal numbers).....44
5.1.1 Cardinal numbers 1 - 10.....44
5.1.2 Cardinal numbers 11 - 20.....44
5.1.3 Cardinal numbers 10 - 100.....44
5.1.4 Cardinal numbers 100 - 1000.....45
5.2 Ordinal numbers.....45
5.2.1 Ordinal numbers 1 - 10.....45
5.2.2 Ordinal numbers greater than 10.....45
5.3 Days of the week and months of the year.....45
5.3.1 Days of the week.....45
5.3.2 Months of the year.....46
6. Prepositions.....46
7. Interrogatives.....48
8. Phrases and sentences.....48
8.1 Nouns and noun phrases.....48
8.1.1 Indefinite and definite nouns.....48
8.1.2 Demonstrative phrases.....49
8.1.3 Expressing possession.....49
8.1.4 The noun-adjective phrase.....50
8.1.5 Gender and number agreement.....51
8.1.6 Counted-noun constructions.....52
8.1.7 Expressions of comparison and superlative.....54
8.2 Sentences and clauses.....54
8.2.1 The verbal sentence.....54
8.2.2 The equational sentence.....55
8.2.3 Expansion of the simple sentence.....56
8.2.4 Conditional sentences.....57
8.2.5 Conjunctions.....58

8.2.6 The negative sentence ..... 59
8.2.7 The question ..... 60
9. Markers of organization and attitude ..... 60
9.1 Markers of organization ..... 61
9.1.1 /allii huu/ 'that is; namely; that would be' ..... 61
9.1.2 /almuhimm/ 'the important thing is; the fact is' ..... 61
9.1.3 /zaat/ 'self' ..... 61
9.1.4 /gaam/ 'so, anyway' ..... 62
9.1.5 /maa/ (adds emphasis or prominence; not negative) ..... 62
9.2 Markers of attitude ..... 62
9.2.1 /alḥagiiga/ 'truly, the fact is that' ..... 62
9.2.2 /balaa/ 'enough of, forget about' ..... 62
9.2.3 /daa … daa/ (exclamatory demonstrative) ..... 63
9.2.4 /kidaa/ 'sort of, more or less' ..... 63
9.2.5 /inta/ 'you' ..... 63
9.2.6 /yimkin/ 'maybe' ..... 63
**Selections**
1. taʕaaluu natʕarraf ʕalaa suudaaniin ..... 66
2. jayyatii lii-waaʃinṭun ..... 70
3. zikraayaat aṣṣibaa ..... 78
4. uɣniyya ʕaaṭifiyya: ɣiyaab yoomeen ..... 86
5. anniẓaam addiraasii fi ssuudaan ..... 92
6. attaṭawwuraat fi ttaʕliim ..... 104
7. ʕaadil wa-hudaa ..... 114
8. albaḥas ʕan waẓiifa ..... 122
9. alḥayaa f -ʔamriikaa ..... 132
10. amriikaa ..... 142
11. lamma tisaafir assuudaan ..... 150
12. warriinii bass alḥaaṣil ʃinuu ..... 158
13. jaziirat ʔartimiirii ..... 168
14. ḥall siyaasii li-muʃkilt ajjanuub ..... 176
15. addastuur alʔintixaabii w-ajjabha lʔislaamiyya ..... 182
16. anʃaṭ ḥiẓib kaan aljjabha lʔislaamiyya ..... 192
17. alḥiṣaar alʔiɣtiṣaadii ʕalaa ssuudaan ..... 200
18. liʔannakum maa dafaʕtuu lfaatuura ..... 206
19. naguul li-nnaas ʃinuu? ..... 214
20. ʕaadaat azzawaaj ..... 224
21. ajarrib ḥaaja zayy dii ..... 238
22. ʃin guulik fiihaa? ..... 244
23. alxalaawii fi ssuudaan ..... 254
24. laakin yoom alʕiid ..... 264
25. karaamaat alʔawliyaa ..... 274
26. maa bi-yuktil ..... 282
27. almuusiɣaa lfulklooriyya fi ssuudaan. ..... 292

## Translations

1. LET'S GET TO KNOW SOME SUDANESE ....... 307
2. HOW I CAME TO WASHINGTON ....... 308
3. CHILDHOOD MEMORIES ....... 309
4. LOVE SONG: TWO DAYS' ABSENCE ....... 310
5. THE EDUCATION SYSTEM IN SUDAN ....... 311
6. DEVELOPMENTS IN EDUCATION ....... 314
7. ADIL AND HODA ....... 316
8. SEARCHING FOR A JOB ....... 318
9. LIFE IN AMERICA ....... 320
10. AMERICA ....... 322
11. WHEN YOU GO TO SUDAN ....... 324
12. JUST TELL ME WHAT'S GOING ON ....... 325
13. ARTIMIRY ISLAND ....... 327
14. A POLITICAL SOLUTION TO THE PROBLEM OF THE SOUTH ....... 329
15. THE ELECTORAL CONSTITUTION AND THE ISLAMIC FRONT ....... 331
16. THE MOST ACTIVE PARTY WAS THE ISLAMIC FRONT ....... 334
17. THE ECONOMIC BLOCKADE OF SUDAN ....... 336
18. BECAUSE YOU DIDN'T PAY YOUR BILL! ....... 338
19. WHAT WILL WE SAY TO PEOPLE? ....... 340
20. MARRIAGE CUSTOMS ....... 342
21. I MIGHT TRY SOMETHING LIKE THIS ....... 345
22. WHAT DO YOU THINK OF HER? ....... 346
23. QUR'AN SCHOOLS IN SUDAN ....... 348
24. BUT ON THE FEAST DAY ....... 350
25. MIRACLES OF HOLY MEN ....... 353
26. HE WOULDN'T KILL ANYONE ....... 355
27. FOLK MUSIC IN SUDAN ....... 358

## Glossary

Introduction ....... 363
Glossary ....... 365

## Acknowledgments

Co-workers, consultants, and colleagues have been generous with their advice and counsel during the process that resulted in this work. This is my opportunity to thank them. The final product, however, remains my responsibility.

Co-workers on Arabic projects at LRC/McNeil Technologies, Inc. have been most closely involved in this work. Azizeh Babaa was instrumental in devising and implementing the Arabic script transcription. Eerik N. Dickinson produced the draft Glossary. Habaka Feghali made important contributions to a preliminary draft of this work, especially collecting and sequencing material. Sanait Tesfagiorgis drafted a preliminary version of the selections and translations.

The Technical Support staff of Alan Downing, Cliff Etheridge, Aung Kyaw Oo, and Mark Jeon is ably led by Stephen Poulos. They provided aid and assistance in audio recording and editing, the use of computer hardware and software, and final production.

I should also thank Ed Whitley for his able editing and keen eye. Dr. David Zorc has provided collegial encouragement, guided by his long experience as a linguist and his fine understanding of practical and theoretical issues.

Tom Creamer, Director of LRC/McNeil Technologies, Inc., has been unfailingly supportive. His knowledge of research and production is matched or exceeded by his sympathetic understanding of the writing process.

I would also like to acknowledge with gratitude the support provided by the African Language Project of the University of Maryland, Eastern Shore, under the directorship of Dr. Chester Hedgepath.

Consultants assisted at various stages. Dr. Aisha Abdel Hamid edited an early version of the selections. Almigdad Gibril brought a love of language, a fine awareness of meaning and nuance, and inexhaustible patience with my questions to his role as consultant on grammar and lexicon. Dr. Catherine Miller's review of the manuscript was all an author could ask for. Her critical judgment and sensitive understanding of the challenges SA poses to the researcher were invaluable aids in the final editing process.

Finally, there is my mother, Joyce O. Bergman. My debts to her would fill another volume.

My thanks to all of you.

Elizabeth M. Bergman
Washington, D.C.
November 2002

## Symbols and Abbreviations

| /text/ | text in SA |
|---|---|
| text | text in a language other than English |
| … | incomplete word or sentence |
| *text* | code-switched text |
| 1 | first-person |
| 2 | second-person |
| 3 | third-person |
| adj | adjective |
| adv | adverb |
| ClA | Classical Arabic |
| conj | conjunction |
| disc marker | marker of organization or attitude |
| f | feminine |
| fp | feminine plural |
| fs | feminine singular |
| imperf | imperfect |
| interj | interjection |
| interrog | interrogative |
| m | masculine |
| mp | masculine plural |
| MSA | Modern Standard Arabic |
| nfp | feminine plural noun |
| nfs | feminine singular noun |
| nmp | masculine plural noun |
| nms | masculine singular noun |
| p | plural |
| particle | particle |
| prep | preposition |
| pron | pronoun |
| prop | proper noun |
| s | singular |
| SA | Sudanese Arabic |
| s.b.i. | supplied by informant |
| u.d. | unpublished data |
| vi | intransitive verb |
| vn | verbal noun |
| vt | transitive verb |

## GLOSSARY OF LINGUISTIC TERMS

**adverbial** – one of a varied group of items that modify the verb

**alveolar** – a sound made by the front of the tongue and the alveolar ridge, which is just behind the teeth

**apical** – a sound made by the apex or tip of the tongue

**bilabial** – a sound made by the coming together of both lips

**broken plural** – in Arabic, a plural formed by change in syllable structure and/or vowel change rather than by the addition of a suffix, (also called ablaut plural) as opposed to the **sound plural**

**cardinal** – of a number used for counting, as opposed to the ordinal

**construct phrase** – in Arabic, a structure in which one noun or nominal immediately follows another, so that the second item modifies the first in relationship generally described as possessive (also called iḍaafa), as opposed to the **possessive adjective construction**

**dental** – a sound made by the tip of the tongue against the upper teeth

**derived verb form** – in Arabic, any verb form other than $C_1vC_2vC_3$

**elative** – in Arabic, a form that expresses the comparative or superlative, depending on the construction in which it appears

**elide** – of sounds, to be omitted

**epenthetic vowel** – an extra vowel that has been added to a word (also called helping vowel)

**flap-trill** – a sound made by rapid contact between two parts of the mouth, where one instance of contact is a **flap** and multiple contacts make a **trill**

**fricative** – a sound in which two parts of the mouth come close together and friction results from air passing between them

**geminate** – doubled

**geminate verb/root** – a verb or root in which $C_2 = C_3$

**glottal** – a sound made by the closure or narrowing of the glottis, the opening between the vocal cords

**homophone** – a word that has the same pronunciation as another word but a different meaning

**imperative** – a verb form used for commands

**imperfect** – a verb form that usually expresses duration or continuity of action (also called the present tense), as opposed to the **perfect**

**information question** – a question that asks for a response more detailed than "yes" or "no", as opposed to the **yes-no question**

**intransitive verb** – a verb that cannot take a direct object, as opposed to the **transitive verb**

**invariable** – a word or form that does not undergo change, for example, of number, gender, or person, or a word or form that does not undergo sound change

**labiodental** – a sound in which one lip is in contact with the teeth

**lateral** – a sound in which air escapes around a closure in the mouth

**moon letter** – a letter of the Arabic alphabet to which the l̲ of the definite article al- does not assimilate, a group that includes non-apical consonants and j, as opposed to the **sun letter**

**morphology** – the word-building system of a language

**nasal** – a sound produced by the flow of air to the nose

**nominal sentence** – in Arabic, a sentence that does not contain a verb, generally a copular or possessive sentence (also called equational sentence), as opposed to the **verbal sentence**

**ordinal**– of a number used for ordering rather than counting, as opposed to the **cardinal**

**palatal** – a sound made when the tongue touches or comes near to the hard palate

**perfect** – a verb form that usually expresses completion or a completed action, sometimes called the past tense in descriptions of Arabic, as opposed to the **imperfect**

**pharyngeal** – a sound made with the pharynx

**possessive adjective construction** – in Arabic, a structure in which a possessive adjective links two nouns or nominals so that the second item modifies the first in a relationship generally described as possessive, as opposed to the **construct phrase**

**post-palatal** – a sound made in any part of the mouth behind the palate, including the velum, the uvula, and the pharynx

**prefixed imperfect** – in SA, the combination of the imperfect /bi-/ prefix and the simple imperfect that is the usual or default form of the imperfect in speech, as opposed to the **simple imperfect**

**pre-verb** – one of a variety of forms, usually a verb or participle in SA, that provides additional information about the time frame of the verb (it is aspectual) or about an attitude towards the action of the verb (it is modal)

**relative pronoun** – in Arabic, a pronoun that introduces a definite relative clause

**semivowel** – a glide, in SA /w/ and /y/

**simple imperfect** – the imperfect verb without the imperfect /bi-/ prefix, as opposed to the **prefixed imperfect**

**sound plural** – in Arabic, a noun plural formed by the addition of suffix (also called suffixed plural), as opposed to the **broken plural**

**stem vowel** – a vowel in a verb or noun that is not part of a prefix or suffix (also called internal vowel)

**stop** – a sound made by a complete blocking of the air flow

**strong verb form** – in Arabic, a verb form in which no root consonant is a semi-vowel, as opposed to the **weak verb form**

**sun letter** – a letter of the Arabic alphabet to which the l̲ of the definite article al- assimilates, a group that includes apical consonants but not j, as opposed to the **moon letter**

**transitive verb** – a verb that cannot take a direct object, as opposed to the **intransitive verb**

**unmarked** – the more neutral or general form (also called default form)

**uvular** – a sound made by the back of the tongue against the uvula

**velar** – a sound made by the back of the tongue against the velum or soft palate

**verb form** – in Arabic, one of a limited number of patterns for verb derivation, conventionally numbered with Roman numerals

**verbal noun** – in Arabic, a noun that names the action of the verb and that is usually but not always derived from that verb (also called maṣdar)

**verbal sentence** – a sentence that contains a verb, as opposed to the **nominal sentence**

**voiced** – a sound characterized by vibration of the vocal cords, as opposed to the voiceless

**voiceless** – a sound characterized by no vibration of the vocal cords, as opposed to the **voiced**

**weak verb form** – in Arabic, a verb form in which one or more root consonant is a semi-vowel, as opposed to the **strong verb form**

**yes-no question** – a question that is best answered by "yes" or "no", as opposed to the **information question**

# Preface

## *About Sudanese Arabic*

The language variety described in this work is called Sudanese Arabic (SA), which, in spite of the name, is not the only variety of Arabic spoken in Sudan. Instead, it is the Arabic of the region of the Sudanese capital. This is the metropolitan area that includes Khartoum, North Khartoum, and Omdurman. Sudanese call this area **/alʕaaṣima almusallasa/** 'the tripartite capital'. SA itself is sometimes called "Khartoum Arabic." Sudanese speakers of Arabic refer to it as "Omdurman Arabic."

As in other parts of the Arabic-speaking world, both unity and diversity characterize Arabic in Sudan. Unity results when language is shared through the use of ClA and MSA. ClA and MSA are used in the media, the mosque, the classroom, and other official settings. Varieties of spoken Arabic are shared because of trade, the migrations of nomadic tribes, and the movements of other groups. This means that varieties of Arabic spoken in Sudan share certain essential features. At the same time, however, settlements can be separated by great distances or may be populated by speakers who have migrated to the Sudan from other Arabic-speaking regions. This makes for linguistic diversity within each region and within the country as a whole.

Arabic-speaking Sudan can be roughly divided into four regions. The central region, which includes the area of the capital, extends south into al-Jazira. The northern region stretches from the Atbara River to Dongola. The western region begins on the western bank of the White Nile and includes Kordofan and Darfur. The eastern region extends from the Blue Nile to the Sudan's eastern borders. Arabic is also spoken in the south of Sudan but is usually a second or other language for people whose first language is not Arabic.

Readers seeking further information on the varieties of Arabic spoken in Sudan will wish to consult Kaye on Sudanese and Chadian Arabic, Reichmuth on the Arabic spoken in Shukriyya, and Roth on the spoken Arabic of Abbeché in Chad. Information on these works appears in the Bibliography. Other possible sources include the wealth of published research on Egyptian Arabic and the following sources:

Owens, Jonathan. "Arabic dialects of Chad and Nigeria." *Zeitschrift für arabische Linguistik* 14 (1985): 45 – 61.

Roth, Arlette. *Lexique des parlers arabes tchado-soudanais* (Lexicon of Chado-Sudanese dialects). Paris: Éditions du Centre national de la recherche scientifique, 1969.

Zeltner, Jean-Claude and Henry Tourneux. *L'arabe dans le bassin du Tchad: le parler des Ulâd Eli* (The Arabic of the Chad basin: the dialect of the Ulâd Eli). Paris : Karthala, [1986].

Other sources, primarily unpublished works in French, are difficult to obtain in the US.

My thanks to Dr. Catherine Miller for suggesting these works.

## About this work

This work is intended for those who are familiar with Modern Standard Arabic (MSA) and with at least one other variety of spoken Arabic. This is not an elementary-level conversation manual or textbook. Listening comprehension is the focus of this work. This is largely because, in our experience, speakers of one variety of Arabic can usually understand and respond to speakers of other varieties, even though this response can be difficult to understand, both for Arabic speakers of another variety and for non-native speakers of Arabic. Hence, the present emphasis on listening rather than speaking.

This work is made up of three parts. The first part is a grammar that describes the distinguishing features of SA. This is a sketch or an outline rather than an exhaustive study. It aims to serve as a brief reference for those who need familiarity with SA and for those whose interest is the comparative study of Arabic dialects.

The second part of this work consists of sample selections transcribed from audio recordings. These recordings were made by consultants, all first-language speakers of SA from the region of the capital, or were broadcast by the Sudanese media. They are transcribed in Latin script, in a modified version of IPA (International Phonetic Alphabet), and in Arabic script. Both transcriptions are largely phonemic, in that they record the primary sounds of SA rather than the specific variations each sound may have in actual speech. They also preserve the starts, stops, and slips of tongue that occur in spontaneous speech. An English translation accompanies the transcriptions. A glossary follows each selection. Words and phrases that may be new to learners of SA are listed and defined in the order in which they occur in the selection. Finally, notes provide information about linguistic and cultural features of the selection that may be unclear to those unfamiliar with SA and Sudan.

The third part of this work is a glossary of items. The glossary is a list of words and phrases that occur in the audio selections, plus other items that may be useful or interesting. The glossary follows Arabic alphabetical order. The headword or main word of each entry appears in IPA and Arabic script.

## *How to use this work*

### Step One: The grammar

It is suggested that the learner begin by reading through the grammar and taking notes of those features of SA that seem most different. We recognize that a grammar is not an easy read. It is, however, the fastest and easiest way to get acquainted with the sounds, the word-building system, and the sentence-forming rules of SA. The grammar is brief. Other than some technical terminology used to orient those with a linguistic background, it describes SA in terms that should be familiar to most readers.

## Step Two: Work through the sample selections in order

We recommend that the learner work through the selections in order. There are two reasons for this recommendation. First, the selections are arranged in order of difficulty (both in terms of SA and in terms of length, complexity, topic, etc.). Second, features of SA are described in the notes the first time they occur. Notes are not repeated. The learner who goes directly to selections of particular interest will find gaps in her or his knowledge of SA. These gaps will make learning more difficult than it need be.

## Step Three: Find out about the selection

The learner will want to begin by getting as much information about the selection as possible. Each selection is introduced by a short paragraph about the subject matter and any noteworthy features of that selection. The learner will also find it helpful to read through the glossary and the notes before reading the selection. This gives the learner some familiarity with new material before encountering it in context.

## Step Four: Listen to the selection

Having finished the orientation, the learner should close this book. Listening to the selection without following the transcription lets the learner get used to the voices and get a general idea of the topic. What may sound difficult on the first hearing becomes easier on the second, third, or fourth repetition. The learner will soon recognize familiar words and phrases. It then becomes possible to guess the meaning of new words.

## Step Five: Work through the selection

The learner can read along in the IPA or the Arabic script transcription while listening to the selection. This is a matter of choice. Some people find it easier to read from left to right in Latin script. This, they say, makes up for the effort involved in learning IPA symbols. Reading the IPA transcription also makes using the glossary and notes easier. Only the main word or headword of each glossary entry appears in Arabic; the notes cite Arabic words and phrases only in IPA. Other people think that reading Arabic in Arabic is a better solution because they can recognize familiar words and phrases more easily. However, some of the sounds specific to SA cannot be written in Arabic. There is, for example, no commonly-used letter to represent the sound /g/.

As the learner works through the selection, the glossary and notes will be a primary resource. The glossary's translations of new words and phrases are the learner's first source for new words and phrases in each selection. Items in the glossary include words and phrases from SA as well as some from MSA. Some MSA items are glossed because the sound changes of SA make them difficult for a learner to recognize. Other MSA items are glossed because they cannot easily or readily be found in Wehr's Dictionary of Modern Written Arabic. The learner should note that words and phrases are glossed the first time they occur; they are not repeated. The alphabetic glossary at the back of this work is a useful way to review items that have occurred in a previous selection.

The notes explain grammatical, linguistic, and cultural features of the selection that may be unclear. They do not provide detailed descriptions of a feature. For further information on a particular grammatical feature treated in a note, the learner will want to consult the grammar. Note that the translation of the selection should be the learner's last resort. Most people learn more when they try to work out answers to their questions than they do when they get the answer without effort.

## Step Six: Learn new words and phrases

By this stage, the learner has developed her or his own ways of learning new words and phrases. These may include making flash cards, writing out lists of new items, repeating new items aloud, using new items in sentences, and other strategies. Of course, learners will want to try new methods of learning, if only to vary learning activities.

## Key to transcription

| Latin | Arabic |
|---|---|
| aa | اَ |
| ee | َيْ |
| oo | َوْ |
| aw | َوْ |
| a | َ |
| b | ب |
| p | پ |
| t | ت |
| θ | ث |
| j | ج |
| ḥ | ح |
| x | خ |
| d | د |
| ð | ذ |
| r | ر |
| z | ز |
| s | س |
| ʃ | ش |
| ṣ | ص |
| ḍ | ض |
| ṭ | ط |
| ẓ | ظ |
| ð̣ | ظ |
| ʕ | ع |
| ɣ | غ |
| f | ف |
| g | ق |
| q | ق |
| k | ك |
| l | ل |
| ḷ | ل |
| m | م |
| n | ن |
| h | ه |
| uu | ُو |
| u | ُ |
| w | و |
| ii | ِي |
| i | ِ |
| y | ي |

## *Notes to transcription key*

Transcription reduces the linear sound-plus-image of spoken language to text on a page. It necessarily requires choices and compromises. The following may clarify some of the choices made in this work.

Liaison and elision in natural speech

Liaison, the pronouncing of two words in sequence without a clear break between them, and elision, the omission of sounds or entire syllables in the flow of speech, are essential elements of natural speech. In fact, at the time of writing, liaison and elision distinguish natural speech from machine-generated speech. The gaps between words, even though minute, and the pronunciation of words in their full form are clearly audible in even the best machine-generated speech.

Because liaison and elision are characteristic of natural speech, we have elected not to indicate these features in transcripts. Our assumption and that of the learner should be that words connect unless there is an indication to the contrary. The resulting pages are, we believe, both more readable and more aesthetically pleasing.

A hyphen indicates liaison or elision only where sound changes cross word boundaries. One example is the phrase /**mim -baʕd**/ 'from where', derived from /**min baʕd**/. A word-initial glottal stop (/ʔ/) indicates a break in the flow of connected speech. One example is the utterance /**ʕinduu, ʕinduu ʔakbar**/ 'it (ms) has, it (ms) has more' (Selection 24), where repetition and hesitation accompany the glottal stop (/ʔ/). All three features are characteristic of unconnected, non-fluent speech.

Punctuation in IPA and Arabic transcriptions

Spoken language has its own punctuation. It includes, among other things, hesitations, pauses, interruptions, and overlaps. The conventions that represent this punctuation in writing, however, are limited to specialists. For the sake of readability, therefore, we chose to use written punctuation.

Commas separate items in a list. They also separate clauses in a sentence.

Periods precede the beginning of a new topic.

Quotation marks indicate direct quotes. Question marks denote questions.

Ellipses (...) follow a word that is cut off in the middle of a sentence. They also complete a sentence that is incomplete at the end of a speaker's utterance or turn.

Italics indicate code-switched material. Code-switched material in this work usually consists of a single non-Arabic word, such as *okay*, that occurs in an Arabic utterance.

Treatment of word-final long vowels in IPA and Arabic transcriptions

Although, generally speaking, long vowels in SA and other varieties of Arabic lose their length in word-final position, they are transcribed as long in this work.

Comparing the IPA and Arabic script versions

Note that the two alphabets used in the transcription in this work are radically different. Readers may therefore note that the IPA transcription is not identical to the Arabic script transcription of a given selection. Any differences are due in part to characteristic differences between the two scripts. They are at the same time due to the decision we made to exploit those differences. We decided to build on the flexibility of IPA, developed by linguists to represent the sounds of the world's languages. The IPA version of a selection is, thus, a more phonemic representation of speech. The Arabic script, in contrast, evolved over time as the writing system for ClA and MSA. It, therefore, provides a visible link between ClA and MSA, on the one hand, and SA on the other.

Homographs in Arabic transcription

A glance at the transcription key reveals that, in several cases, Arabic has a single symbol where IPA has two symbols. There is, unfortunately, no easy way to differentiate the two sounds from one another in Arabic. Specialists, of course, can use any number of diacritical marks in Arabic, but we chose to use Arabic script in a more or less conventional form. These homographs include يْ, which corresponds to the diphthong /ay/ and the monophthongized /ee/, and وْ , represented in IPA by the diphthong /aw/ and the monophthongized /oo/. They also include ظ, which stands for /ẓ/ and /ð̣/.

Diacritical marks in Arabic transcription

Commercially-available fonts for Arabic are designed for general purposes and so lack some of the diacritical marks and combinations of marks needed in this work. This is most noticeable in words that require a short alif in Arabic script. Words such as /al̤laah/ 'God' and /laakin/ 'but' are written in Arabic with a short vowel in place of the short alif: أَللّهْ and لَكِنْ .

Treatment of selected morphological features in Arabic transcription

## the alif

Transcription in this work retains the alif of the definite article ال , as in المدرسه الوسطى /almadrasa lwusṭaa/ 'middle school, junior high school'.

It also retains the alif of the 1S imperfect verb, as in باعرف /b-aʕrif/ 'I know'.

In addition, it retains word-final alif (in forms used in MSA), as in الدنيا /addunyaa/ 'the world' and مستوى /mustawaa/ 'level, stage'

## the taa marbuuṭa

This transcript writes the taa? marbuuṭa as ه when not in construct and not sounded as /t/, as in جامعه /jaamiʕa/ 'university'. In contrast, the taa? marbuuṭa appears as ة when in construct and pronounced /t/, as in جامعة الخرطوم /jaamiʕat alxarṭuum/ 'the University of Khartoum'.

## Suffixed pronouns

The suffixed pronouns 1S, 1P, 2S, 2P are written as pronounced, as in زاتي /zaatii/ 'myself'. The 3MS, 3FS, and 3P suffixed pronouns, however, are written as هُ - هَا - هُمْ respectively. This is because their pronunciation is phonologically conditioned, as in لقاها /ligaahaa/ 'he found her' and بيريدها /b-iiriidaa/ 'he loves her'

## Other features

The glottal stop (/ʔ/) does not occur at beginning of utterance. It may be utterance-internal or word-internal, as in: الراجل ا: داء؟ ب: ايوه. /A: arraajil daa? B: aywa./ 'A: That man? B: Yes.'

When the MSA sound ض is pronounced as /ẓ/, it is written ض, as in غضباً عني /ɣaẓban ʕannii/ 'I didn't mean it'.

The form /w-al̤laahii/ 'by God' appears as وَاللّهِ in Arabic.

# Bibliography

Baalbaki, Rohi. Al-Mawrid: *A modern Arabic-English dictionary*. 7th ed. Beirut: Dal el-Ilm Lilmalayin, 1995.

Badawi, El-Said, and Martin Hinds. *A dictionary of Egyptian Arabic: Arabic-English*. Beirut: Librairie du Liban, 1986.

Cowell, Mark W. *A reference grammar of Syrian Arabic*. Arabic series. 7. Washington: Georgetown UP, 1964.

Crewe, W.J. *The place of Sudanese Arabic: a study in comparative Arabic dialectology*. African and Asian Studies Semin Series 20. Khartoum: Institute of African and Asian Studies, University of Khartoum, 1973.

Crystal, David. *A dictionary of linguistics and phonetics*. 4th ed. London: Blackwell, 1997.

Doniach, N.S. *The Oxford English-Arabic dictionary of current usage*. 5th ed. Oxford: Clarendon, 1983.

Ferguson, Charles A. "The Arabic koine." *Language* 35 (1959): 616-630. Rpt. in *Readings in Arabic linguistics*. Ed. Salman H. al-Ani. Bloomington: Indiana University Linguistics Club, 1978. 49-69.

Harrell, Richard S., ed. *A dictionary of Moroccan Arabic: Moroccan-English*. The Richard Slade Harrell Arabic Series. Washington: Georgetown UP, 1966.

Hava, J.G. *Al-Faraid: Arabic-English dictionary*. 5th ed. Beirut: Dar el-Mashreq, 1982.

Hillelson, S. *Sudan Arabic texts*. London: Cambridge UP, 1935

Lane, E.W. *An Arabic-English lexicon*. London: Williams and Norgate, 1863. Rep. Cambridge: Islamic Texts Society, 1984. 2 vols.

Laye, Alan S. *Chadian and Sudanese Arabic in the light of comparative Arabic dialectology*. Janua Linguarum, Series Practica 236. The Hague: Mouton, 1976.

*Meaning of the Glorious Qur'an, The*. Trans. Muhammad Marmaduke Pickthall. N.p.: Islamic Call Society, n.d.

Miller, Catherine, and Al-Amin Abu-Manga. *Language change and national integration: rural migrants in Khartoum*. Khartoum: Khartoum UP, 1992.

Persson, Andrew, et. al. *Sudanese colloquial Arabic for beginners*. Horsleys Green, UK: Summer Institute of Linguistics, 1979.

Qaasim, ʕAwn al-Shariif. *Qaamuus al-lahja al-ʕaammiyya fii al-suudaan* (Dictionary of the colloquial dialect in Sudan). Khartoum: ʃuʕbat ʔabḥaaθ al-suudaan fii jaamiʕat al-xarṭuum; Al-majlis al-qawmiyy li-riʕaaya al-ʔaadaab wa-al-funuun, 1972.

Reichmuth, Stefan. *Der arabische Dialekt der Shukriyya im Ostsudan* (The Arabic dialect of Shukriyya in east Sudan). Studien zur Sprachwissenschaft, Band 2. Hildesheim: Georg Olms, 1983.

Roth, Arlette. *Esquisse grammaticale du parler arabe d'Abbéché: Tchad* (A grammatical sketch of the Arabic dialect of Abbéché: Chad). G.L.E.C.S. Etudes chamito-sémitiques, supplément 8. Atlas linguistique du monde arabe, matériaux, 4. Paris: Librairie orientaliste Paul Geuthner, 1979.

Taine-Cheikh, Catherine. "Aperçu sur la langue (An outline of the language)." *Dictionnaire ḥassaaniyya français* (Hassaniyya-French dictionary). Vol. I. Paris: Geuthner, 1988.

Trimingham, J. Spencer. *Sudan colloquial Arabic*. 2nd ed. London: Oxford UP, 1946.

Wehr, Hans. *A Dictionary of Modern Written Arabic: Arabic-English*. Ed. J Milton. Cowan. Ithaca: Spoken Language Services, 1994.

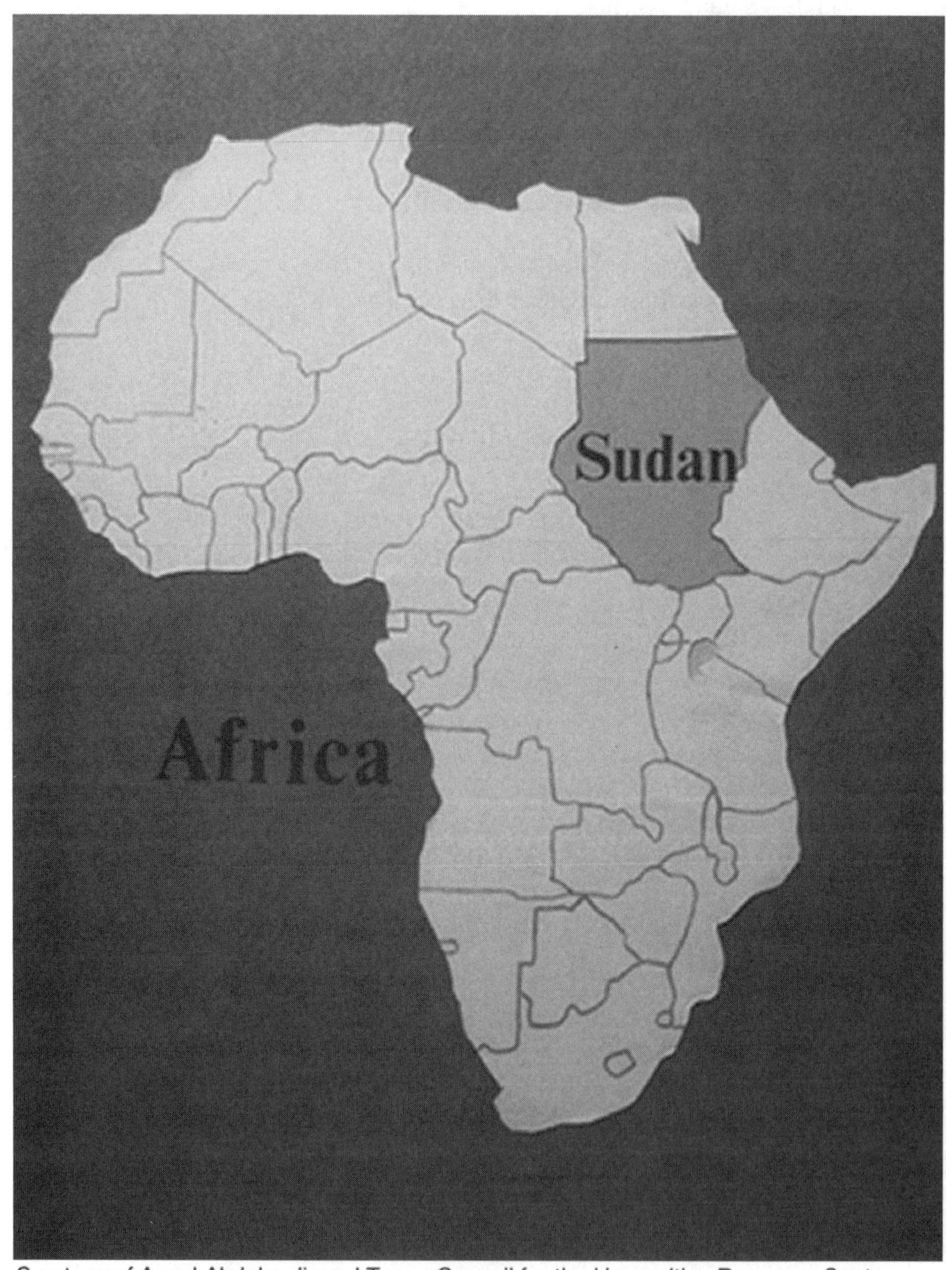

Courtesy of Awad Abdelgadir and Texas Council for the Humanities Resource Center

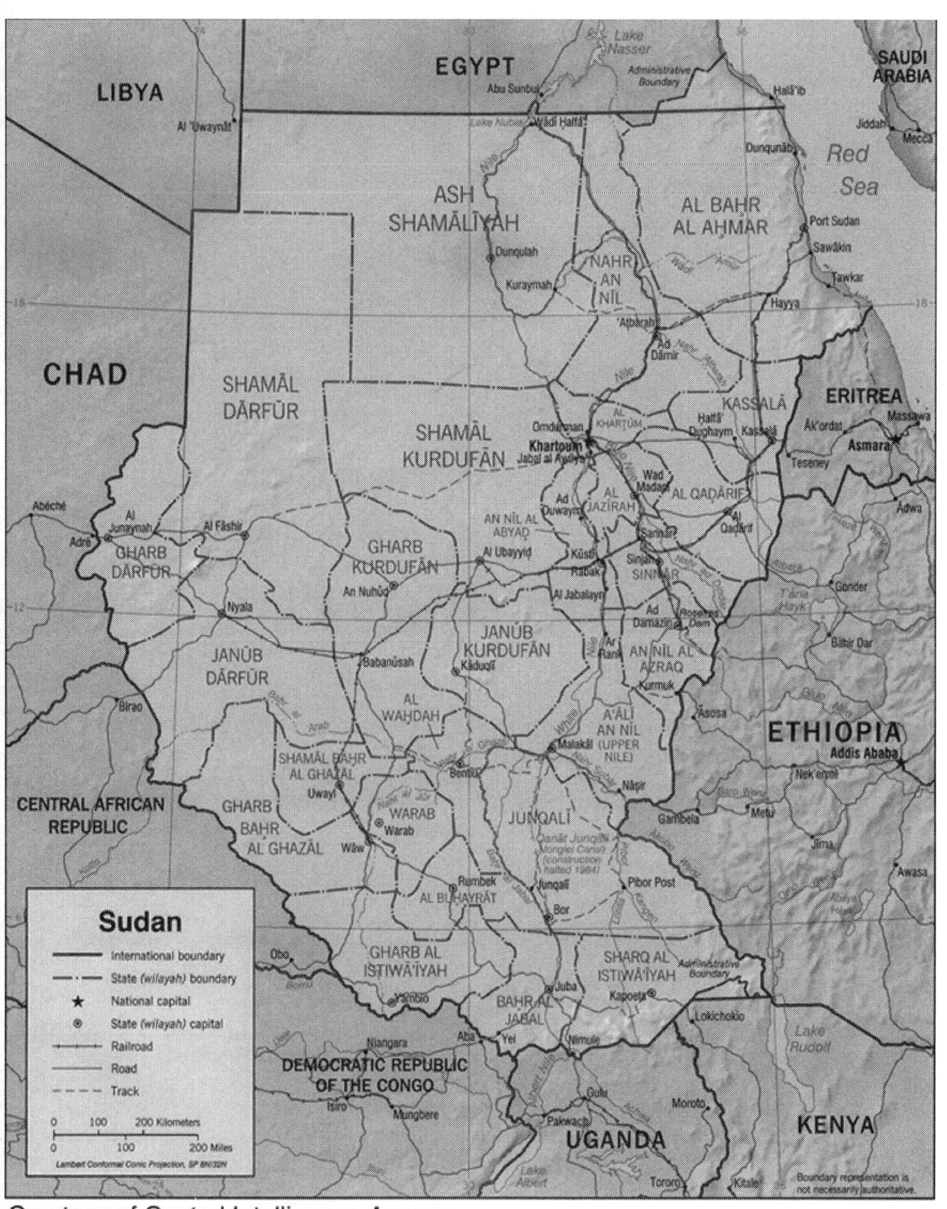


Courtesy of Central Intelligence Agency

# Grammar

The following is a description of Sudanese Arabic (SA). The areas treated here are the SA sound system (phonology), the word-building system (morphology), the structure of phrases and sentences (syntax), and devices that add organization (discourse markers) or emotion. The account of the SA word-building system or morphology begins with nouns and adjectives. It moves on to verbs and the forms derived from verbs. It finishes with the word classes that are based on meaning and function rather than form or derivation: pronouns, numbers, prepositions, and interrogatives.

This is an outline or sketch of SA. A detailed study of this under-described language variety awaits other researchers. Our current goal is to provide a reference for those with a specific focus on SA as well as those with broader interests in Arabic dialectology or in other areas of linguistics. For that reason, our choice of terms aims at those that are widely used or easily understood. Some linguistic terms are provided for the specialist. Similarly, we point out some of the forms and structures shared by SA with other varieties of Arabic. At the same time, the scope of this work imposes restrictions. The use of SA citations is limited because the selections contain numerous examples of the forms and structures described here. Some readers will also note the lack of analysis, also due to restrictions of space.

# 1. The sounds of Sudanese Arabic

## 1.1 Consonants

### 1.1.1 The consonants of SA

| | Bilabial | Labio-dental | Dental | Alveolar | Palatal | Velar | Uvular | Pharyngeal | Glottal |
|---|---|---|---|---|---|---|---|---|---|
| Voiceless Stop | | | t - ṭ | | | k | [q]* | | ʔ |
| Voiced Stop | b | | d - ḍ | | j (IPA ɟ) | g | | | |
| Voiceless Fricative | | f | [θ] | s - ṣ | ʃ | x | | ḥ | h |
| Voiced Fricative | | | [ð] - [ð̣] | z - [ẓ] | | ɣ | | ʕ | |
| Nasal | m | | | n | | | | | |
| Lateral | | | l - [ḷ] | | | | | | |
| Flap-Trill | | | | r | | | | | |
| Semi-Vowel | w | | | | y | | | | |

*Consonants in brackets are limited in their occurrence. See 1.1.1.2 – 1.1.1.3 for details.

#### 1.1.1.1 The palatal realization of the ClA and MSA letter ج

The distinctive SA pronunciation of the letter ج of ClA and MSA, rather than j, is a voiced palatal stop (IPA /ɟ/). That is, the middle of the tongue touches the back of the alveolar ridge (which leads from the teeth to the roof of the mouth). Those unfamiliar with this sound may mistake it for other sounds at first, but learn to recognize it with practice.

Note that the current work represents this sound with the symbol /j/.

#### 1.1.1.2 Other sounds that occur in SA

Consonants other than those listed in 1.1.1 exist in specific environments in SA. For example, /p/ (voiceless bilabial stop) occurs when /b/ (voiced bilabial stop) is found at the end of a word in isolation or before a pause, as in /ʃuraap/ 'shurab (a kind of Sudanese folksong)'. This devoicing of consonants is common in SA and certain other varieties of spoken Arabic (see 1.4.4). Certain other consonants not typical of SA may occur when speakers use non-Arabic words and phrases. This generally takes place in educated SA speech.

#### 1.1.1.3 Correspondences of SA to ClA and MSA consonants

SA and ClA and MSA, of course, share a large amount of vocabulary. The relationship, however, between an SA word and its ClA or MSA equivalent, however, is not always clear at first glance. Consonants change, as do meanings, as words pass from one variety to another. A simple comparison of a list of words shared by SA and ClA or MSA reveals a variety of correspondences between the sounds of SA and those of ClA and MSA. The ClA and MSA letter q, for example, is realized as /g/ and /ɣ/, as well as, more rarely, /q/ and /k/ in SA. For an inclusive list of such correspondences, see the "Introduction" (muqaddima) to Qasim's Dictionary of the colloquial dialect of Sudan (Qaamuus al-lahja al-ʕaammiyya fii al-suudaan).

Correspondences between the sounds of SA and those of ClA and MSA are of three types. One group of correspondences is productive, in that correspondences recur regularly as words pass from one variety to another. A second group of correspondences is, if not productive, at least predictable. A person who knows a word in SA can predict with a fair degree of accuracy how it will sound in MSA. A third group of correspondences is neither productive nor predictable. Correspondences of this type occur only infrequently or sporadically.

##### 1.1.1.3.1 Productive correspondences of SA to ClA and MSA consonants

Words and phrases that come to SA directly or recently from ClA or MSA tend to show productive correspondences between the consonants of ClA or MSA and those of SA. For the most part, these words and phrases deal with "educated" topics or are heard in formal situations. They are the language of politics, economics, government, religion, education, and the media, among other things.

The productive correspondences between SA and ClA or MSA can be briefly described. The ʔ̲ (glottal stop) of ClA and MSA is retained in SA words and phrases of this type. The ʔ̲, in fact, rarely occurs as a phoneme, or basic unit of the SA sound system, except in this context. The dental fricatives of ClA or MSA become alveolar fricatives. That is, θ̲ becomes /s/, ð̲ becomes /z/, and ð̲̣ becomes /ẓ/. Finally, the q̲ of ClA or MSA becomes /ɣ/ or is retained as /q/. The retention of /q/ is rare, however, even in highly formal speech. The following table provides examples:

| ClA or MSA consonant | SA correspondent | ClA or MSA word | SA word | English translation |
|---|---|---|---|---|
| ʔ̲ | /ʔ/ | li**ʔ**anna | /li**ʔ**anna/ | 'because' |
| θ̲ | /s/ | mu**θ**alla**θ** | /mu**s**alla**s**/ | 'three-part' |
| ð̲ | /z/ | **ð**ikraayaat | /**z**ikraayaat/ | 'memories' |
| ð̲̣ | /ẓ/ | ni**ð̣**aam | /ni**ẓ**aam/ | 'system' |
| q̲ | /ɣ/ | al**q**urʔaan | /al**ɣ**urʔaan/ | 'Qur'an' |
| | /q/ | al**q**aahira | /al**q**aahira/ | 'Cairo' |

Correspondences of this type are not limited to words and phrases. The speech of a person speaking in a formal or institutional setting, delivering a political address, giving a classroom lecture, or broadcasting the news will tend to show these correspondences over long stretches of speech. An example is /wa-tanʕam haa**z**ihi jjaziira min ʔal**ʔ**anʃiṭa ʔalka**s**iira minhaa ʔanniʃaaṭ azziraaʕii wa-hiya ʔalḥirfa ʔarra**ʔ**iisiyya lii-muwaaṭiniin haa**z**ihi ʔajjaziira, ḥay**s**u tanʕam ajjaziira bi-maʃruuʕi ziraaʕii kabiir/ 'This island benefits from many enterprises, agriculture among them. That is the main profession of the citizens of this island, inasmuch as the island benefits from a large agricultural project' (Selection 13). Another example of this highly formal style appears in Selection 27.

1.1.1.3.1.1 Other occurrences of /ʔ/ (glottal stop)

As stated in 1.1.1.3.1, the /ʔ/ (glottal stop) rarely occurs in SA as a phoneme or basic unit of the SA sound system. It occurs in items from educated speech or that used in formal contexts. In addition, the /ʔ/ (glottal stop) frequently occurs in careful or hesitant speech. It occurs in word-initial position and separates words from one another. That is, it prevents the elision that is characteristic of spontaneous or non-hesitant speech. Taking the utterance cited in 1.1.1.3.1 as an example of speech that is careful as well as formal, we note that the speaker frequently separates words and phrases with /ʔ/: **/wa-tanʕam haazihi jjaziira min ʔalʔanʃiṭa ʔalkasiira minhaa ʔanniʃaaṭ azziraaʕii wa-hiya ʔalḥirfa ʔarraʔiisiyya lii-muwaaṭiniin haazihi ʔajjaziira, ḥaysu tanʕam ajjaziira bi-maʃruuʕi ziraaʕii kabiir/** 'This island benefits from many enterprises, agriculture among them. That is the main profession of the citizens of this island, inasmuch as the island benefits from a large agricultural project' (Selection 13).

Although the /ʔ/ (glottal stop) is not a phoneme of SA, it may leave traces in the derivational system. This occurs in words shared with ClA and MSA, in nouns (see 1.4.9.2) and verbs (3.2.1.4)

1.1.1.3.2 Predictable correspondences of SA to ClA and MSA consonants

Predictable correspondences of SA to ClA and MSA consonants tend to occur in shared words and phrases in other contexts. These shared words and phrases come from everyday life. Unlike the language of formal or educated settings, in which the process of sharing words and phrases is ongoing, the language of everyday life is relatively stable. For this reason, we refer to the correspondences of SA to ClA and MSA consonants in the language of everyday life as predictable rather than productive.

Like productive correspondences, predictable correspondences can be briefly described. The dental fricatives of ClA or MSA become dental stops. That is, θ̲ becomes /t/, ð̲ becomes /d/, and ð̲̣ becomes /ḍ/. In addition, the q̲ of ClA or MSA becomes /g/. The following table provides examples:

| ClA or MSA consonant | SA correspondent | ClA or MSA word | SA word | English translation |
|---|---|---|---|---|
| θ̲ | /t/ | **θ̲alaaθ̲a** | **/talaata/** | 'three' |
| ð̲ | /d/ | **ð̲aab** | **/daab/** | 'to dissolve; to melt' |
| ð̲̣ | /ḍ/ | **ð̲̣ufur** | **/ḍufur/** | 'fingernail; toenail' |
| q̲ | /g/ | **q̲adara** | **/gidir/** | 'to be able to' |

1.1.1.3.3 Other correspondences of SA to ClA and MSA consonants

Other correspondences of SA to ClA and MSA consonants in shared words and phrases are neither productive nor predictable. They are infrequent or sporadic, showing no recurring patterns. The following table provides examples of some of these correspondences:

| ClA or MSA consonant | SA correspondent | ClA or MSA word | SA word | English translation |
|---|---|---|---|---|
| ʔ | /w/ | ʔayna | /**w**een/ | 'where' |
| ʔ | /y/ | ʔaamiin | /**y**aamiin/ | 'amen' |
| ð | /ḍ/ | ʔuðn | /a**ḍ**aan/ | 'ear' |
| ð̣ | /z/ | hifð̣ | /ḥifi**z**/ | 'memorization' |
| q | /k/ | waqt | /wa**k**it/ | 'time' |
| m | /b/ | makaan | /**b**akaan/ | 'place, location' |
| h | /y/ | ð̣aahir | /zaa**y**ir/ | 'seeming, appearing' |

In addition to the individual correspondences noted above, there are unpredictable correspondences that may take place when two or more of the ClA or MSA consonants j, s, and ʃ occur in a single word. One of these is disimilation, where one consonant becomes less like another, as in ClA and MSA ʃajara and SA /ʃa**d**ara/ 'tree'. Another is assimilation, where one consonant becomes more like another, as in ClA and MSA ʃams and SA /ʃami**ʃ**/ (also /ʃamis/) 'sun'. Yet another is metathesis, or a change in the order of the affected consonants, as in ClA and MSA **dajaaj** and SA /**jidaad**/ 'chickens'.

## 1.2 The vowels of SA

### 1.2.1 The short vowels of SA

SA has three short vowels: /a/, /i/, and /u/. There is considerable variation in the pronunciation of all three short vowels. This variation, however, is non-meaningful phonetic variation. The most variable of the three short vowels is /a/.

### 1.2.2 The long vowels of SA

#### 1.2.2.1 The long vowels /aa/, /ii/, and /uu/

Like the short vowels, the long vowels /**aa**/, /**ii**/, and /**uu**/ show considerable variation. Again, this variation is non-meaninful, phonetic variation. The long vowels, however, tend to retain their length even when a word contains more than one long vowel. For example, where other varieties of Arabic have the pattern /**mafa**tiiḥ/ 'keys', SA has /**mafaa**tiiḥ/ 'keys' (MSA mafaatiih 'keys'). The same long vowels are shortened in word-final position, but retain their quality. That is, they have the same length as short vowels without undergoing any other sound change. For this reason, they are transcribed as long in word-final position throughout this work.

#### 1.2.2.2 The long vowels /ee/ and /oo/

The long vowels /**ee**/ and /**oo**/ most often occur in words where MSA has the diphthongs /ay/ and /aw/ (monophthongization). Examples include /**beet**/ for MSA bayt 'house' and /**yoom**/ for MSA yawm 'day'.

### 1.2.3 The diphthongs of SA

Not all of the diphthongs of SA are replaced by long vowels. The diphthongs /ay/ and /aw/ occur. They are heard most often where the semivowel is doubled or geminate, as in /kwa**yy**is/ 'good' and /**awwal**/ 'first', or where one semivowel follows another, as in /**aywa**/ 'yes'.

## 1.3 Syllable structure and stress

### 1.3.1 Syllable structures

Following are the syllable types that commonly occur in SA (where C = consonant, V = long vowel, v = short vowel):

| | |
|---|---|
| CV | /bag**duu**nis/ 'parsley' |
| Cv | /**ka**biir/ 'large' |
| CVC | /banṭa**loon**/ 'pair of trousers' |
| CvC | /**mad**rasa/ 'school' |
| $C_1VC_2C_2$ (word-final) | /**ḥaajj**/ 'sir, man who has made pilgrimage' |
| $C_1vC_2C_2$ (word-final) | /**bass**/ 'but; only, solely' (see 1.3.4) |

### 1.3.2 Word-initial syllable structure

Word-initial syllables present two apparent exceptions to the syllable structures listed in 1.3.1. These are the word-initial vowel and the initial consonant cluster.

#### 1.3.2.1 Word-initial vowels

Vowels may be transcribed as word-initial, whether in the stream of speech or at the beginning of an utterance. A vowel however, does not begin a word. The explanation for this fact depends on whether a word-initial vowel falls in the the stream of speech or at the beginning of an utterance.

In the stream of speech, syllable structure often crosses word boundaries. A phrase transcribed phonemically includes apparent vowel-initial syllables, as in /fii ḥuduud **al**ɣaanuun w-**i**ḥtiraam **al**ɣaanuun w-**a**nnaas/ 'within the bounds of the law and with respect for the law and for other people' (Selection 10). When syllable divisions are indicated with dots, however, vowel-initial syllables are eliminated: /fii **ḥu•duu•d al•ɣaa•nuun • w-iḥ•ti•raa•m al•ɣaa•nuun** • w-**an•naas**/. This phenomenon, a form of liaison, is a regular feature of spoken Arabic.

At the beginning of an utterance or in isolation, vowels are frequently transcribed as word-initial. Words like /**a**ywa/ 'yes', /**inta**/ 'you (ms)', and /**umbaariḥ**/ 'yesterday' actually have an initial consonant: the /ʔ/ (glottal stop) automatically precedes what appears to be an initial vowel. The word /aywa/, thus, is heard as [**ʔ**aywa], /inta/ as [**ʔinta**], and /umbaariḥ/ as [**ʔumbaariḥ**]. A vowel-initial transcription, however, is conventional in descriptions of spoken Arabic and other languages.

#### 1.3.2.2 Initial consonant clusters

Initial consonant clusters are exceptions to the syllable types listed in 1.3.1. For the most part, they occur in high-frequency words. In some cases, speakers alternate between a cluster-initial variant, such as /**ʃn**uu/ 'what' and a variant in which syllable structure is conventional, as in /**ʃinuu**/ 'what'. The speaker's choice of variant is affected by factors such as speed of speech, style of speech, and the prominence or emphasis given the word in the utterance. In other cases, such as /**kw**ayyis/ 'good, nice', a word has no clusterless variant.

### 1.3.3 Avoidance of word-final consonant clusters

The syllable types listed in 1.3.1 include those containing final geminate consonants. They do not, however, include final consonant clusters where the consonants of the clusters are not identical. In other words, syllables of the types $C_1VC_2C_3$ and $C_1vC_2C_3$ are not typical of SA. Word classes differ in the strategies used to avoid word-final consonant clusters. Nouns have internal epenthetic or helping vowels; verbs have final epenthetic vowels.

#### 1.3.3.1 Avoidance of word-final consonant clusters in nouns

Nouns of the pattern $C_1vC_2vC_3$ often have an epenthetic vowel that is /u/ or /i/, as in /**uxut**/ 'sister' (compare MSA ?uxt 'sister') and /**wakit**/ 'time' (compare MSA waqt 'time'). The epenthetic may also be /a/, as in /**ahal**/ 'relatives, kin' (compare MSA ?ahl 'people'). The internal epenthetic vowels /u/ and /i/ are dropped preceding a suffixed pronoun, as in /**uxtuu**/ 'his sister' and /**waktuu**/ 'his time, its (ms) time'. The internal vowel /a/ is retained in most cases, as in /**ahalak**/ 'your (ms) family'

#### 1.3.3.2 Avoidance of word-final consonant clusters in verbs

1.3.3.2.1 SA avoids word-final consonant clusters in the 1S and 2MS perfect of strong verbs. Avoidance is accomplished through the addition of a final epenthetic /a/ to both forms, as in /**ḍarabta**/ 'I hit' and /**ḍarabta**/ 'you (ms) hit'. The 1S and 2MS perfect forms thus sound the same (are homophonous). The epenthetic vowel is most frequently elided preceding a suffixed pronoun, as in /**ḍarabtuu**/ 'I hit him'.

### 1.3.4 Word-final geminate consonants

Word-final geminate consonants or word-final syllables of the type $C_1VC_2C_2$ and $C_1vC_2C_2$ are typical in SA. These syllable types are unlike word-final consonant clusters or syllables of the type $C_1VC_2C_3$ and $C_1vC_2C_3$, that are not typical of SA (see 1.3.3). The treatment of word-final geminate consonants, in nouns and in verbs, is worth noting.

#### 1.3.4.1 Nouns with word-final geminate consonants

Nouns with word-final geminate consonants are common in SA, as in /**waʃʃ**/ 'face' and /**bitt**/ 'girl; daughter'. In isolation, a noun with word-final geminate consonants does not require an epenthetic vowel. Preceding a suffixed pronoun, except for the 1S /-ii/, the epenthetic short /a/ prevents a sequence of three consonants in nouns with word-final geminate consonants. The result, for example, is /**bittii**/ 'my daughter' and /**bittanaa**/ 'our daughter'. This epenthetic short /a/ may elide preceding the 3S and 3P suffixed pronouns. Speakers vary freely in their use of the epenthetic vowel in such cases, producing /kull**a**hum/ as well as /kullum/ 'all of them'.

1.3.4.1.1 Avoidance of word-final geminates in nouns and other word classes

In general, speakers of SA use nouns and other word classes (except for verbs, see 1.3.4.2) with word-final geminate consonants freely. Speakers occasionally avoid word-final geminate consonants. The most typical avoidance strategy is the addition of an epenthetic vowel, typically /**a**/. The result is, for example, /**muhimma**/ 'important' (compare MSA muhimm 'important'), where the final /-**a**/ is an epenthetic vowel rather than the feminine ending.

Another, less frequent avoidance strategy for a word with word-final geminate consonants is degemination. In degemination, a doubled consonant becomes a single consonant. For example, a variant of /**muhimma**/ 'important', where a geminate consonant is followed by the epenthetic vowel /**a**/, is /**muhim**/, with a degeminate final /**m**/ and no final vowel.

### 1.3.4.2 Verbs with word-final geminate consonants

Verbs with word-final geminate consonants show a lack of regularity. The reasons for this are not clear. The imperfect verb most closely resembles the noun with word-final geminate consonants. The verb with a geminate root resembles the finally-weak Form II verb (of the pattern $C_1vC_2C_2aa$, see 3.2.2.1.1). The active participle of the Form I geminate verb has an unusual form, but only in the MS.

1.3.4.2.1 Imperfect verbs with word-final geminate consonants

Imperfect verbs with word-final geminate consonants most closely resemble nouns with word-final geminate consonants (see 1.3.4.1). That is, in isolation, the imperfect verb with word-final geminate consonants does not require an epenthetic vowel, as in /**yaxuʃʃ**/ 'he enters'. Such verbs take an epenthetic short /a/ preceding the suffixed pronouns of the first and second persons, as in /**yaḥibbanii**/ 'he likes me; he loves me'. Preceding the 3S and 3P suffixed pronouns, however, the epenthetic short /**a**/ is often elided. The result is, for example, that /**yaḥillaa**/ occurs more frequently than /**yaḥillahaa**/ 'he solves it (fs)'.

1.3.4.2.2 Perfect verbs with word-final geminate consonants

Form I verbs with geminate roots (in which $C_2$ = $C_3$) do not occur with word-final geminate consonants. The reason for this is the final epenthetic short /a/ suffixed to the 3MS for in isolation, as in /xatt**a**/ 'to put, place' and /xaʃʃ**a**/ 'to enter'. The rest of the perfect conjugation resembles that of the finally-weak Form II verb, such as /sawwaa/ 'to do, make' (see 3.2.2.1.1). Compare, for example, /xatta/ and /sawwaa/ in the 3FS and 2FS: /xatta**t**/ 'she put' and /sawwa**t**/ 'she did'; /xatt**eetii**/ 'you (fs) put' and /saww**eetii**/ 'you (fs) did'. Preceding a suffixed pronoun, the 3MS perfect verb may retain or omit the epenthetic short /a/ in what appears to be stylistic variation. The result is /xatt**aa**huu/ (with lengthening of the final vowel preceding the suffixed pronoun, see 1.4.9.3) and /xattuu/ 'he put it (ms)'. The same occurrence of the epenthetic vowel is seen in the derived verb forms that have word-final geminate consonants. These are Forms V, VII, VIII, X and it$C_1$a$C_2$a$C_3$ (see 3.2).

1.3.4.2.3 The active participle of geminate verbs

The epenthetic vowel /a/ discussed in 1.3.4.2.2 turns up in another form – but only in the MS active participle of the geminate Form I verb. This MS active participle has a word-final /ii/, as in /laaff**ii**/ 'turning (ms)' (from /laffa/ - /yaliff/ 'to turn'). The final /ii/ of the active participle has apparently been re-analyzed as a finally-weak vowel. The MS active participle, thus, appears to be modeled on the active participle of the finally-weak Form I verb, such as /maaʃ**ii**/ 'going' (from /maʃaa/ - /yamʃii/ 'to walk, go', see 3.2.1.6). Note, however, that the pattern $C_1$aa$C_2$$C_3$ii is not otherwise productive in SA. The FS, MP, and FP active particles of the geminate verb, in contrast, lack this /-ii/: /xaatta/ 'putting (fs)'; /xaattiin/ 'putting (mp)'; and /xaattaat/ 'putting' (fp).

### 1.3.5 Stress rules

The stress rules of SA are largely predictable. Particles and other elements that precede a word and are not themselves words do not take stress. (In this work, most of such particles are transcribed with the following word, as in /**al**kitaab/ 'the book', or are separated from it by a hyphen, as in /**bi-**yarʕif/ 'he knows'.) These elements include the definite article and relative pronoun /al-/, and the imperfect /bi-/ prefix. The rules that follow focus on vowels as the core of the syllable rather than on syllable structure.

1) Only the last three vowels of a word may be stressed.

2) If the word contains a short vowel followed by two consonants (/**sim**sim/ 'sesame') or a long vowel (/ṭam**aa**ṭim/ 'tomatoes'), that syllable is stressed. If the word contains more than one of these patterns, the one closest to the end of the word is stressed (/mustaʃfaay**aa**t/ 'hospitals', with word-final stress).

2a) Note, however, that word-final long vowels are typically not stressed (/**kur**sii/ 'chair', with stress on the first vowel).

3) If the word contains only two short vowels followed by single consonants (/**na**far/ 'person, individual'), the first vowel is stressed. If the word contains three or more short vowels followed by single consonants (/**gi**dirit/ 'she was able'), the third vowel from the end (the antepenult) is stressed.

4) Word stress is not fixed. The addition of suffixes to the end of a word may require a shift in stress to another syllable. Note, for example, the shift in stress from the first vowel of /**ma**kana/ 'engine' to the next-to-last vowel (the penult) in /makana**t**naa/ 'our engine'.

Exceptions to these stress rules occur. The most noticeable of these is the conjunction /laa**kin**/ 'but', with word-final stress.

#### 1.3.5.1 The role of stress in distinguishing homophones

Stress plays a useful role in distinguishing homophones in a sentence. One homophone pair that occurs frequently in SA and other varieties of spoken Arabic is /fii/, the existential particle usually translated as 'there is; there are' (see 8.2.2.4), and the preposition /fii-/ 'at; on' (see 6). Another pair is the negative particle /maa/ (see 8.2.6.1) and the /maa/ that is not negative but adds emphasis or prominence to the phrase that follows (see 9.1.5).

In the flow of speech, the existential /fii/ has regular word stress. That is, it is heard at a pitch and volume similar to that of any one-syllable word in context. The preposition /fii-/, in contrast, is heard as part of the following word and does not take stress. It is cliticized. The homophones contrast in the following example: /**laa**kin **fii ba**ʕḍ al**ʔu**sar **ʔin**nuu **laa**zim yii**kuun fii** **ḥubb** wa-**laa**zim yii**kuun fii** ʔirti**baa**ṭ/ 'But in some families it is the case that there must be love and there must be a relationship' (Selection 20). The first instance of /fii/ is cliticized and is, thus, the preposition. The other instances have word stress and are existential.

The same feature distinguishes the negative particle /maa/ from the /maa/ that adds emphasis or prominence in /anaa **maa** gutta leek **maa** ʕindii ʔahal hinaa/ 'But I told you I don't have family here' (Selection 12). The first instance of /maa/ can only be understood as adding emphasis or prominence because it is cliticized. The second instance takes word stress and is, therefore, the negative particle.

## 1.4 Regular sound changes

### 1.4.1 Assimilation

Assimilation is the process in which one consonant sound becomes like another. It is a frequent process in SA. Assimilation may occur within a word, as in /bi**tt**/ 'girl, young woman' (MSA bi<u>nt</u>). Less frequently, assimilation crosses word boundaries, as in /mi**m** **b**eenum/ 'from among them (mp)' (/mi**n** **b**eenum/ in slow or careful speech). Assimilation is not entirely predictable because it is affected by speed and style of speech. Typically, however, assimilation in SA affects the first of two consonants in a sequence and leaves the second unchanged (regressive assimilation).

### 1.4.2 Insertion of /a/ following /ʕ/, /ɣ/, /x/, /ḫ/, and /h/

When a back consonant such as /ʕ/, /ɣ/, /x/, /ḫ/, or /h/ (a post-palatal fricative) is followed by another consonant in the middle of a word (it is $C_1$ in the sequence $vC_1C_2v$), the short /a/ vowel may be inserted between the two consonants. The result is a word like /ax**a**dar/ 'green', (from SA /axdar/).

### 1.4.3 Deletion of unstressed short vowels preceding a single consonant

An unstressed short vowel preceding a single consonant (in an open syllable) is often deleted in SA. This occurs, for example, when the feminine singular suffix /-at/ is followed by a vowel, either of a suffixed pronoun (as in /madra**st**uu/ 'his school' from /madras**at**uu/) or of a second noun in a construct phrase (as in /madra**st** albanaat/ 'the girls' school' from /madras**at** albanaat/).

### 1.4.4 Devoicing of voiced consonants

The voiced consonants of SA may, in certain environments, be heard as their voiceless counterparts (see 1.1.1). Devoicing can take place when the voiced consonant occurs word-finally, as in /jadii**t**/ 'new' (from /jadii**d**/).

Word-final devoicing is most noticeable when the word is in isolation or before a pause. A voiced consonant may also become voiceless when it precedes a voiceless consonant; that voiceless consonant is most often **/t/**. Devoicing may result from the addition of an inflectional ending. Compare, for example, the SA verb **/twaladat/** 'she was born' with the SA verb **/twalattii/** 'you (fs) were born'. In other cases, however, devoicing is due to word derivation, as in **/iṭṭarra/** 'to be forced, be obliged' (compare MSA u**ḏṯ**iraa).

### 1.4.5 Devoicing of /ʕ/ (voiced pharyngeal fricative)

The voiced pharyngeal fricative /ʕ/ may devoice as described in 1.4.4. Devoicing takes place word-finally, as in **/mastar bitaaḥ kuumbyuutar/** 'a master's degree in computers', (where **/bitaaḥ/** derives from the possessive adjective **/bitaaʕ/** and the following voiceless **/k/** may play a role). Devoicing also occurs when /ʕ/ precedes a voiceless consonant, often /t/. The voiceless consonant may be inflectional, as in **/azzaḥma bitaaḥt annaas/** 'the crowds of people' (where **/bitaaḥt/** derives from the feminine form of the possessive adjective **/bitaaʕ/**). The voiceless consonant may also be derivational, as in **/muḥtamid/** 'depending on, relying on' (compare MSA muʕtamid). In addition, however, /ʕ/ may devoice when it is preceded by and followed by a vowel, as in /aʃʃariiḥa lʔislaamiyya/ 'Islamic law; sharia' (compare MSA ʃariiʕa).

### 1.4.6 Elision of /ya-/ and /yi-/

Where /ya-/ or /yi-/ occur in the sequence vyyvCv, the /ya-/ or /yi-/ elides, as in **/kwaysa/** 'good (fs)' (from **/kwayyisa/**) or **/ḥurriituu/** 'his freedom' (from **/ḥurriyyatuu/**).

### 1.4.7 The 3MS and 3P prefixes of the imperfect /ya-/ and /yi-/

The 3MS and 3P prefixes of the imperfect /ya-/ and /yi-/ show considerable variation in spontaneous speech. The prefix /ya-/ may be heard as /yi-/, as in **/yiktul/** 'he kills' (from **/yaktul/**). See 3.1.2.1 on the forms of the verb for which /ya-/ is preferred.

Both /ya-/ and /yi-/ may be heard as the long vowel /ii/ when they are preceded by a consonant, as in **/b-iiriid/** 'he likes' (from **/bi-yariid/**) and **/b-iitmarrad/** 'he resists' (from **/bi-yitmarrad/**). This long vowel /ii/ may be further reduced to /i/, as in **/b-iwaddii/** 'he takes' (from **/bi-yawaddii/**).

The reasons for this variation are not clear. The generalization of /yi-/ as the imperfect prefix may derive from Egyptian Arabic. Alternatively, it may demonstrate the continuing effect of varieties of Arabic spoken in other parts of Sudan on the Arabic of the capital.

### 1.4.8 Resolution of word-final consonant clusters. (See 1.3.3)

### 1.4.9 The definite article and relative pronoun /al-/

#### 1.4.9.1 Assimilation of the definite article and relative pronoun /al-/

The relative pronoun of SA /al-/ is homophonous with the definite article /**al**-/. Whether /al-/ functions as a definite article or a relative pronoun, the /l/ of /**al**-/ assimilates to the following consonant if that consonant is a "sun letter" or is pronounced with the tip of the tongue (an apical consonant) or is /j/, as in /**assalaṭa**/ 'the salad' and /**ajjaamiʕa**/ 'the university'. The /l/ of /al-/ does not assimilate when the following consonant is a "moon letter" or is not pronounced with the tip of the tongue (is non-apical), as in /**albitt**/ 'the girl'.

#### 1.4.9.2 Doubling or gemination of the /l/ of /al-/

As noted in 1.1.1.3.1.1, the /ʔ/ (glottal stop) rarely occurs in SA. When the /al-/ of the definite article or relative pronoun precedes a word that has an initial /ʔ/ in MSA, the /l/ of /al-/ may be geminate, as in /**all**awwal/ 'the first' (MSA /alʔawwal/ 'first').

#### 1.4.9.3 Lengthening of a word-final short vowel preceding a pronoun suffix

A word-final short vowel that precedes a pronoun suffix is often lengthened. This occurs most often in verbs, as in /**lammaa**huu/ 'he gathered it (ms) up' (from /**lamma**/ 'to gather'), and in the FS form of participles /**kaatbaa**huu/ 'writing (fs) it (ms)' (active participle /**kaatba**/ 'writing (fs)').

### 1.4.10 Lengthening of short vowels

It is not unusual to hear a speaker lengthen a short vowel, whether that vowel is stressed (/**jiiha**/ for /**jiha**/ 'side; direction', with stress on the first syllable) or unstressed (/**biiniyya**/ for /**biniyya**/ 'girlie; little girl', with stress on the second syllable). The reasons for this lengthening are unclear.

# 2. Nouns and adjectives: derivation and inflection

## 2.1 Noun morphology

Nouns in SA, in general, resemble the nouns of other varieties of Arabic. They are derived through similar morphological processes and follow similar syntactic rules. Readers seeking details on, for example, nouns of instance, nouns of place, collective and unit nouns, or diminutives will wish to consult the reference grammar of their choice. (In the absence of a standard reference grammar for MSA or a spoken variety of Arabic, many learners rely on the textbook most familiar to them.)

SA nouns also resemble those of other varieties of spoken Arabic in that they do not inflect for case, as do nouns in MSA. Syntactic relationships are expressed through prepositions, particles, and word order.

In SA as in other varieties of Arabic, nouns have either a sound (suffixed) plural or a broken (ablaut) plural. For details on the sound (suffixed) plural, see 2.3.4 - 5. The broken plural patterns of SA are similar to those of other varieties of Arabic and are equally unpredictable. Note, however, that the broken plural of some nouns of SA differ from the plurals occurring in other varieties of Arabic, such as /**rawaadii**/ 'radios' (singular /**radyuu**/). Readers looking for the plural of a specific SA singular noun or the singular of a specific SA plural are advised that, at the time of writing, no comprehensive dictionary of SA is known to be available. Comprehensive dictionaries of other varieties of Arabic, such as Wehr's Dictionary of Modern Written Arabic or Hinds and Badawi's Dictionary of Egyptian Arabic, may be useful. In consulting these works, however, readers are advised to keep dialect differences firmly in mind.

## 2.2 Adjective morphology

### 2.2.1 Adjective patterns

The adjectives of SA, like nouns, resemble those of other varieties of Arabic. The patterns of adjectives, however, are far fewer in number than those of the noun. The following briefly lists the most common adjective patterns and their associated meaning.

#### 2.2.1.1 The adjective pattern $C_1aC_2iiC_3$

The pattern $C_1aC_2iiC_3$ may be the most commonly-used adjective pattern, as in **/kabiir/** 'large'. It does not change for geminate roots, such as **/jadiid/** 'new'.

#### 2.2.1.2 The adjective pattern $aC_1C_2aC_3$

A specialized adjective has the pattern $aC_1C_2aC_3$ to describe a color (**/aḥmar/** 'red') or a disability (**/aṭraʃ/** 'deaf'). The FS and MP patterns differ from those of other adjectives. The FS has the pattern $C_1aC_2C_3aa$, as in **/ḥamraa/** 'red (fs)' and **/ṭarʃaa/** 'deaf (fs)'; the P has the pattern $C_1uC_2uC_3$, as in **/ḥumur/** 'red (mp)' and **/ṭuruʃ/** 'deaf (mp)'.

#### 2.2.1.3 The adjective pattern $C_1aC_2C_3aan$

The pattern $C_1aC_2C_3aan$ often occurs for adjectives expressing bodily needs or passing states, such as **/ʕaṭʃaan/** 'thirsty' and **/fatraan/** 'tired'.

#### 2.2.1.4 The adjective pattern $C_1aC_2C_2aaC_3$

The pattern $C_1aC_2C_2aaC_3$ is the pattern for adjectives describing a habit (**/ʃaɣɣaal/** 'hard-working; working, employed'), a character trait (**/kaddaab/** 'liar'), or a profession (**/jazzaar/** 'butcher').

#### 2.2.1.5 The nisba or relational adjective

One pattern for adjectives, the nisba or relational adjective, derives from nouns or other adjectives through the addition of the suffix **/-ii/** (**/suudaanii/** 'Sudanese'). The suffix **/-aawii/** also occurs, as in **/ḍungulaawii/** 'from Dongola', as does **/-aanii/**, as in **/foogaanii/** 'upper'.

#### 2.2.1.6 The elative pattern $aC_1C_2aC_3$

The elative (the pattern shared by the comparative and superlative adjective) has the pattern $aC_1C_2aC_3$, like the pattern for colors and disabilities (see 2.2.1.2). Unlike the pattern for colors and disabilities, however, the elative is invariable for number and gender. On the use of the elative adjective, see 8.1.7.

## 2.3 Gender and number inflection

### 2.3.1 Gender and number inflections for nouns, adjectives, and participles

The masculine gender is the unmarked gender for most singular nouns and adjectives. Following are the inflectional endings for the feminine, the dual, and the plural.

| | Noun | Adjective | Participle |
|---|---|---|---|
| FS | /-a/<br>/ʃaaḥ**ba**/<br>'friend (fs)' | /-a/<br>/samh**a**/<br>'nice; pretty (fs)' | /-a/<br>/gaayl**a**/<br>'thinking; saying (fs) |
| | /-at/<br>/ʃaaḥb**at**uu/<br>'his friend (fs)' | /-at/<br>/xafiif**at** addamm/<br>'good humored (fs)' | /-aa-/<br>/ʕaarf**aa**naa/<br>'knowing (fs) us' |
| Dual | /-een/<br>/ʕeen**een**/<br>'two eyes' | | |
| | /-ee-/<br>/ʕeen**ee**haa/<br>'her two eyes' | | |
| MP | /-iin/<br>/ḥiwaar**iin**/<br>'disciples' | /-iin/<br>/kways**iin**/<br>'good (mp)' | /-iin/<br>/maask**iin**/<br>'holding on to (mp)' |
| | (see 2.3.4.1.3) | /-inn-/<br>/kways**inn**um/<br>'their (mp) good ones (mp)' | /-inn-/<br>/ʃaayf**inn**aa/<br>'seeing (mp) her' |
| | | | /-in/<br>/maaʃ**yin** leehaa/<br>'going (mp) to her' |
| FP | /-aat/<br>/sitt**aat**/<br>'ladies' | /-aat/<br>/samḥ**aat**/<br>'nice; pretty (fp)' | /-aat/<br>/ʕaarf**aat**/<br>'knowing (fp)' |
| | | /-aatann-/<br>/baṭṭaal**aatann**uu/<br>'his bad (fp) ones' | /-aatann-/<br>/ʃaayf**aatann**uu/<br>'seeing (fp) him' |
| | | | /-aatan/<br>/maaʃ**aatan** leehuu/<br>'going (fp) to him' |

### 2.3.2 The feminine singular inflection

A feminine noun, adjective, or participle, when it derives from a masculine form, marks feminine grammatical gender with the suffix **/-a/** or one of its other forms.

Certain nouns and adjectives that refer to social roles or biological functions specific to women are not derived from masculine forms. Therefore these do not mark feminine grammatical gender. The best-known of these is /**ḥaamil**/ 'pregnant'.

#### 2.3.2.1 Forms of the feminine inflection

2.3.2.1.1 The form **/-a/** occurs with forms that are independent or isolated. These include the noun (/**ṣaaḥba**/ 'female friend'), adjective (/**samha**/ 'nice; pretty'), and participle (/**gaayla**/ 'thinking; saying'). That is, **/-a/** occurs where there is no suffixed pronoun, no noun following in a construct phrase, or, for participles, no indirect object with the preposition /**bi-**/ or /li-/.

2.3.2.1.2 The form /**-at**/ precedes a suffixed pronoun or a noun in a construct phrase, for nouns (/**ṣaaḥbatuu**/ 'his female friend') and adjectives (/**xafiifat addamm**/ 'good-humored (fs)'). It also occurs with nouns preceding the dual suffix /**-een**/ (/**sanateen**/ 'two years').

The short /**a**/ of /**-at** /may elide when it is unstressed and when /**-at**/ is followed by a vowel, as in /**maktabtaa**/ 'her office' (from /**maktabataa**/).

2.3.2.1.3 The form /**-aa-**/ is used with participles that take a suffixed pronoun as direct object (/**ʕaarfaanaa**/ 'knowing (fs) us'). This long vowel results from the lengthening of the short vowel /**a**/ described in 1.4.9.3.

### 2.3.3 The dual

Only nouns take the dual suffix /**-een**/ to mean "two". The dual is productive in SA and can occur with nearly any noun. It is most often used, however, with nouns that name body parts (/**ʕeeneen**/ 'two eyes') and periods of time (/**yoomeen**/ 'two days').

See 8.1.5.2 on the agreement of adjectives and participles that modify dual nouns.

#### 2.3.3.1 Forms of the dual inflection

2.3.3.1.1 The form /-**een**/ occurs with a noun that is independent or isolated. That is, /-**een**/ occurs in the absence of a suffixed pronoun or of a second noun in a construct phrase (/ʃa**hareen**/ 'two months').

2.3.3.1.2 The form /-ee-/ occurs with a noun that takes a suffixed pronoun (/ʕee**nee**haa/ 'her two eyes') or is followed by a second noun in a construct phrase (/yoo**mee** ʕuṭla/ 'two days of vacation').

### 2.3.4 The masculine sound plural

The suffix for the masculine sound plural of nouns, adjectives, and participles is /-iin/. The forms of the broken or ablaut plural in SA, as in MSA, are not predictable.

#### 2.3.4.1 Forms of the masculine sound plural

2.3.4.1.1 The form /-iin/ occurs with nouns (/ḥiwaa**riin**/ 'disciples'). It also occurs with adjectives (/kway**siin**/ 'good (mp)') and participles (/maas**kiin**/ 'holding on to (mp)') that are independent or isolated.

2.3.4.1.2 The form /-**inn**-/ occurs with adjectives and participles when they precede a suffixed pronoun such as /(kway**sinn**um/ 'their (mp) good ones (mp)' and /ʃaay**finn**aa/ 'seeing (mp) her'.

2.3.4.1.3 A noun that is a masculine sound plural make take either the form /-iin/ or the form /-**inn**-/ preceding a suffixed pronoun. For example, both /ḥiwaa**riin**uu/ 'his disciples' and /ḥiwaa**rinn**uu/ 'his disciples' are acceptable. The tendency, however, is to avoid using a masculine sound plural with a suffixed pronoun. Where an alternative is available in the form of a broken plural, that alternative is preferred, as in /**ḥiwaawiiruu**/ 'his disciples'.

2.3.4.1.4 The form /-in/ occurs with participles preceding indirect object phrases with the prepositions /li-/ or /bi-/ (/maaʃ**yin** leehaa/ 'going (mp) to her').

### 2.3.5 The feminine sound plural

The suffix for the feminine sound plural of nouns, adjectives, and participles is /-**aat**/. Feminine plurals in the SA of the region of the capital are used mostly by women.

#### 2.3.5.1 Forms of the feminine sound plural

2.3.5.1.1 The form /-aat/ occurs with independent or isolated forms. These include nouns (/sitt**aat**/ 'ladies, women'), adjectives (/samḥ**aat**/ 'nice; pretty (fp)'), and participles (/ʕaarf**aat**/ 'knowing (fp)').

2.3.5.1.2 The form /-aatann-/ precedes a suffixed pronoun when an adjective (/baṭṭaal**aatann**uu/ 'his bad (fp) ones') or participle (/ʃaayf**aatann**uu/ 'seeing (fp) him') takes that suffixed pronoun.

2.3.5.1.3 The suffix /-aatan/ occurs when a participle takes an indirect object phrase with the prepositions /li-/ or /bi-/ (/maaʃ**aatan** leehuu/ 'going (fp) to him').

## 3. Verb morphology

The following discussion of verb morphology indicates internal (stem) vowels for verbs in the perfect and imperfect. The vowels indicated here are not definitive. There is some variation between individual speakers. Speed and style of speech may also affect stem vowels.

Note also that the derivation of the verbal noun or masdar and participle are treated here, even though the participle, in particular, also has features associated with the adjective.

## 3.1 Affixes of the perfect, imperfect, and imperative

### 3.1.1 Suffixes of the perfect

| | Singular | Plural | /ʃirib/ 'to drink'<br>Singular | Plural |
|---|---|---|---|---|
| 3M | | /-uu/ | /ʃirib/<br>'he drank' | /ʃiri**buu**/<br>'they (mp) drank' |
| | | /-oo-/ | | /ʃiri**boo**haa/<br>'they (mp) drank it (fs)' |
| 3F | /-at/ | /-an/ | /ʃirib**at**/<br>'she drank' | /ʃirib**an**/<br>'they (fp) drank' |
| | | /-ann-/ | | /ʃirib**ann**uu/<br>'they (fp) drank it (ms)' |
| 2M | /-ta/ | /-tum/ | /ʃirib**ta**/<br>'you (ms) drank' | /ʃirib**tum**/<br>'you (mp) drank' |
| 2F | /-tii/ | /-tan/ | /ʃirib**tii**/<br>'you (fs) drank' | /ʃirib**tan**/<br>'you (fp) drank' |
| | | /-tann-/ | | /ʃirib**tann**uu/<br>'you (fp) drank it (ms)' |
| 1 | /-ta/ | /-naa/ | /ʃirib**ta**/<br>'I drank' | /ʃirib**naa**/<br>'we drank' |

#### 3.1.1.1 The 3MP perfect suffix

The 3MP suffix /-uu/ (/ḍara**buu**/ 'they (mp) hit') may become /-oo-/ when followed by a suffixed pronoun (/ḍara**boo**haa/ 'they (mp) hit her'). Not all speakers regularly make this change.

#### 3.1.1.2 The 3FP and 2FP perfect suffixes

The 3FP suffix /-an/ (/ḍarab**an**/ 'they (fp) hit') becomes /-ann-/ when followed by a suffixed pronoun (/ḍarab**ann**uu/ 'they (fp) hit him'). In the same way, the 2FP suffix /-tan/ (/ḍarab**tan**/ 'you (fp) hit') becomes /-tann-/ when followed by a suffixed pronoun (/ḍarab**tann**uu/ 'you (fp) hit him'). This change does not occur when the suffix is followed by an indirect object in the form of a preposition and suffixed pronoun (/**kataban** leehuu/ 'they (fp) wrote to him').

All speakers distinguish masculine from feminine in the second and third persons singular. Note, however, that only women regularly make those distinctions in the plural, typically when speaking to other women.

### 3.1.2 Affixes of the imperfect

| | Singular | Plural | Example verb /katab/ 'to write' | Plural |
|---|---|---|---|---|
| 3M | /ya-/ | /ya- -uu/ | /**ya**ktib/ 'he writes' | /**ya**ktib**uu**/ 'they (mp) write' |
| | | /ya- -oo-/ | | /**ya**ktib**oo**haa/ 'they (mp) write it (fs)' |
| 3F | /ta-/ | /ya- -an/ | /**ta**ktib/ 'she writes' | /**ya**ktib**an**/ 'they (fp) write' |
| | | /ya- -ann-/ | | /**ya**ktib**annuu**/ 'they (fp) write it (ms)' |
| 2M | /ta-/ | /ta- -uu/ | /**ta**ktib/ 'you (ms) write' | /**ta**ktib**uu**/ 'you (mp) write' |
| | | /ta- -oo-/ | | /**ta**ktib**oo**haa/ 'you (mp) write it (fs)' |
| 2F | /ta- -ii/ | /ta- -an/ | /**ta**ktib**ii**/ 'you (fs) write' | /**ta**ktib**an**/ 'you (fp) write' |
| | | /ta- -ann-/ | | /**ta**ktib**annuu**/ 'you (fp) write it (ms)' |
| 1 | /a-/ | /na-/ | /**a**ktib/ 'I write' | /**na**ktib/ 'we write' |

#### 3.1.2.1 Vowels of the imperfect prefix

The vowels of the imperfect prefix vary. Form I verbs and derived verbs whose stems have an initial single consonant (Forms II and III) typically have **/a/** as the vowel of the imperfect prefix. These are verbs such as Form I /**ya**gfil/ 'he shuts', Form II /**ya**garrii/ 'he teaches', and Form III /**ya**saafir/ 'he travels'. Derived verbs whose stems have an initial consonant cluster typically have **/i/** as the vowel of the imperfect prefix. These are verbs such as Forms V (/**yi**tfassaḥ/ 'he goes for a stroll'), Form VI (/**yi**tgaabaluu/ 'they (mp) meet with one another'), VII (/**yi**nkasar/ 'it (ms) breaks'), VIII (/**yi**stalim/ 'he accepts'). Also among these verbs are verb forms that do not occur in MSA, such as the SA form yit$C_1aC_2iC_3$, as in /**yi**tfatiḥ/ 'it is opened' (see 3.2.2.10).

#### 3.1.2.2 The 3MS and 3P imperfect prefix

The 3MS and 3P imperfect prefix is often heard as /yi-/ (rather than /ya-/), even for verb forms in which /a/ is typically the vowel of the imperfect prefix (Forms I, II, and III). See 1.4.7 on other sound changes to the 3MS and 3P imperfect prefix.

#### 3.1.2.3 The 3MP imperfect suffix

As in the perfect, the 3MP suffix /-**uu**/ (/**yadrusuu**/ 'they (mp) study') of the imperfect becomes /-**oo**-/ when followed by a suffixed pronoun (/**yadrusoohaa**/ 'they (mp) study it (fs)').

#### 3.1.2.4 The 3FP and 2FP imperfect suffixes

Like the FP suffixes of the perfect, the 3FP and 2FP suffix /-an/ (/yaʃuuf**an**/ 'they (fp) see' and /taʃuuf**an**/ 'you (fp) see') becomes /-**ann**-/ when followed by a suffixed pronoun (/yaʃuuf**ann**uu/ 'they (fp) see him' and /taʃuuf**ann**uu/ 'you (fp) see him'). This change does not occur, however, when the suffix is followed by an indirect object in the form of a preposition and suffixed pronoun (/**yaktiban leehuu**/ 'they (fp) wrote to him').

### 3.1.3 Affixes of the imperative

The imperative of all verbs is based on the imperfect verb. The imperative replaces the prefix of the imperfect but retains the plural suffix of the imperfect as described in 3.1.2.

#### 3.1.3.1 The imperative of Form I verbs (excepting medially-weak Form I verbs)

The imperative of strong Form I verbs, initially-weak Form I verbs, and finally-weak Form I verbs replaces the prefix of the imperfect with the prefix /a-/, as in /**a**ʃrab/ 'drink (2ms)' (from /ʃirib/ - /yaʃrab/ 'to drink'), /**a**giif/ 'stop (2ms)' (from /wagaf/ - /yagiif/ 'to stop'), and /**agraa**/ 'read (2ms)' (from /garaa/ - /yagraa/ 'to read').

#### 3.1.3.2 The imperative of medially-weak Form I verbs

The imperative of medially-weak Form I verbs replaces the prefix of the imperfect with zero or no prefix, as in /**guum**/ 'get up (2ms)' (from /**gaam**/ - /**yaguum**/ 'to get up').

#### 3.1.3.3 The imperative of derived verbs

The imperative of derived verbs whose stems have an initial single consonant (Forms II and III) replace the imperfect prefix with zero or no prefix, as in /**ɣassil**/ 'wash (2ms)' (from /**ɣassil**/ - /**yaɣassil**/ 'to wash (s.t.)'). Derived verbs whose stems have an initial consonant cluster (Forms V, VI, VII, VIII, and others) replace the imperfect prefix with /i-/, as in /**itkallam**/ 'speak (ms)' (from /**itkallam**/ - /**yitkallam**/ 'to speak').

#### 3.1.3.4 The negative imperative

The negative imperative is identical in form to the imperfect. The negative particle /**maa**/ precedes the verb, as in /**maa titkallam**/ 'don't speak (2ms)' (from /**itkallam**/ - /**yitkallam**/ 'to speak').

## 3.2 Forms of the verb in SA

### 3.2.1 Form I verbs

#### 3.2.1.1 Strong Form I verbs

The strong Form I verb has one of two perfect stems:

$C_1aC_2aC_3$ /**katab**/ 'to write'

$C_1iC_2iC_3$ /**ʃirib**/ 'to drink'

Stem vowels for the perfect verb in SA, as in other varieties of Arabic, are not predictable.

The imperfect stem of the strong Form I verb has three possible vowel patterns:

$yaC_1C_2aC_3$ /**yaftaḥ**/ 'to open' (perfect /**fataḥ**/)

$yaC_1C_2iC_3$ /**yagfil**/ 'to shut' (perfect /**gafal**/)

$yaC_1C_2uC_3$ /**yamrug**/ 'to go out' (perfect /**marag**/)

Verbs whose perfect stem is $C_1iC_2iC_3$ typically have the imperfect stem $yaC_1C_2aC_3$ (/**simiʕ**/ - /**yasmaʕ**/ 'to hear'). Otherwise, stem vowels for the imperfect verb in SA, as in other varieties of Arabic, are not predictable.

| Strong Form I verb /katab/ - /yaktib/ 'to write' | Perfect Singular | Perfect Plural | Imperfect Singular | Imperfect Plural |
|---|---|---|---|---|
| 3M | **/katab/** | **/katab**uu/ | /ya**ktib/** | /ya**ktib**uu/ |
| 3F | **/katab**at/ | **/katab**an/ | /ta**ktib/** | /ya**ktib**an/ |
| 2M | **/katab**ta/ | **/katab**tum/ | /ta**ktib/** | /ta**ktib**uu/ |
| 2F | **/katab**tii/ | **/katab**tan/ | /ta**ktib**ii/ | /ta**ktib**an/ |
| 1 | **/katab**ta/ | **/katab**naa/ | /a**ktib/** | /na**ktib/** |

### 3.2.1.2 Initially-weak Form I verbs with /w/

There are three possible patterns for the imperfect stem of the initially-weak Form I verb with /w/.

3.2.1.2.1 Retention of /w/ in the imperfect

Some initially-weak Form I verbs with /w/ retain the initial /w/ in the imperfect. They have the perfect stem wa$C_2$a$C_3$ and imperfect stem yoo$C_2$a$C_3$ (/**wa**jaʕ/ - /y**oo**jaʕ/ 'to hurt, pain') or the perfect stem wa$C_2$i$C_3$ and imperfect stem yoo$C_2$i$C_3$ (/**wa**zin/ - /y**oo**zin/ 'to weigh, weigh out').

| Initially-weak Form I verb /wazin/ - /yoozin/ 'to weigh, weigh out' | Perfect Singular | Perfect Plural | Imperfect Singular | Imperfect Plural |
|---|---|---|---|---|
| 3M | **/wazin/** | **/wazin**uu/ | /y**oozin/** | /y**oozin**uu/ |
| 3F | **/wazin**at/ | **/wazin**an/ | /t**oozin/** | /y**oozin**an/ |
| 2M | **/wazin**ta/ | **/wazin**tum/ | /t**oozin/** | /t**oozin**uu/ |
| 2F | **/wazin**tii/ | **/wazin**tan/ | /t**oozin**ii/ | /t**oozin**an/ |
| 1 | **/wazin**ta/ | **/wazin**naa/ | **/oozin/** | /n**oozin/** |

3.2.1.2.2 Elision of /w/ in the imperfect

Other initially-weak Form I verbs with /w/ lose the initial /w/ in the imperfect. They have the perfect stem $waC_2aC_3$ and the imperfect stem $yaC_2aC_3$ (/**wa**gaʕ/ - /yaga**ʕ**/ 'to fall') or the imperfect stem $yaC_2iC_3$ (/**wa**rad/ - /ya**rid**/ 'to fetch water; to take to water').

| Initially-weak Form I verb /wagaʕ/ - /yagaʕ/ 'to fall' | Perfect Singular | Perfect Plural | Imperfect Singular | Imperfect Plural |
|---|---|---|---|---|
| 3M | /**wagaʕ**/ | /**wagaʕ**uu/ | /yaga**ʕ**/ | /yaga**ʕ**uu/ |
| 3F | /**wagaʕ**at/ | /**wagaʕ**an/ | /taga**ʕ**/ | /yaga**ʕ**an/ |
| 2M | /**wagaʕ**ta/ | /**wagaʕ**tum/ | /taga**ʕ**/ | /taga**ʕ**uu/ |
| 2F | /**wagaʕ**tii/ | /**wagaʕ**tan/ | /taga**ʕ**ii/ | /taga**ʕ**an/ |
| 1 | /**wagaʕ**ta/ | /**wagaʕ**naa/ | /aga**ʕ**/ | /naga**ʕ**/ |

3.2.1.2.3 The verb /wagaf/ 'to stop'

The verb /wagaf/ 'to stop' differs from the two patterns for initially-weak Form I verbs described in 3.2.1.2.1 - 2. It loses the initial /w/ in the imperfect, but compensates for that loss by lengthening the stem vowel of the imperfect, /ya**giif**/.

| Initially-weak Form I verb /wagif/ - /yagiif/ 'to stop' | Perfect Singular | Perfect Plural | Imperfect Singular | Imperfect Plural |
|---|---|---|---|---|
| 3M | /wagif/ | /wagifuu/ | /yagiif/ | /yagiifuu/ |
| 3F | /**wagif**at/ | /**wagif**an/ | /tagiif/ | /ya**giif**an/ |
| 2M | /**wagif**ta/ | /**wagif**tum/ | /ta**giif**/ | /ta**giif**uu/ |
| 2F | /**wagif**tii/ | /**wagif**tan/ | /ta**giif**ii/ | /tagiifan/ |
| 1 | /**wagif**ta/ | /**wagif**naa/ | /a**giif**/ | /na**giif**/ |

#### 3.2.1.3 Initially-weak Form I verbs with /y/

Initially-weak Form I verbs with /y/ are less common than those with /w/. They have a single pattern for the perfect and the imperfect. That pattern is yi$C_2$i$C_3$ - yee$C_2$a$C_3$ (/**yibis**/ - /**yeebas**/ 'to be dry; to dry up').

| Initially-weak Form I verb /yibis/ - /yeebas/ 'to be dry; to dry up' | Perfect Singular | Perfect Plural | Imperfect Singular | Imperfect Plural |
|---|---|---|---|---|
| 3M | **/yibis/** | **/yibis**uu/ | **/yeebas/** | **/yeebas**uu/ |
| 3F | **/yibis**at/ | **/yibis**an/ | **/teebas/** | **/yeebas**an/ |
| 2M | **/yibis**ta/ | **/yibis**tum/ | **/teebas/** | **/teebas**uu/ |
| 2F | **/yibis**tii/ | **/yibis**tan/ | **/teebas**ii/ | **/teebas**an/ |
| 1 | **/yibis**ta/ | **/yibis**naa/ | **/eebas/** | **/neebas/** |

#### 3.2.1.4 Hamza-initial or glottal stop-initial Form I verbs

Verbs that have an initial hamza or /ʔ/ (glottal stop) as a root consonant or radical in MSA do not show any sign of that /ʔ/ in the perfect. The imperfect stem, however, has an initial long /aa-/, apparently to compensate for the loss of the /ʔ/. The two most common verbs of this type are /**a**kal/ - /**yaa**kul/ 'to eat' and /**a**xad/ - /**yaa**xud/ 'to take'. Both verbs sometimes have an initial long /oo/ in the imperfect (/**akal**/ - /**yoo**kul/ 'to eat' and /axad/ - /**yoo**xud/ 'to take'). In this, they are similar to initially-weak Form I verbs with /w/ that retain the /w/ in the imperfect, described in 3.2.1.2.1.

| Hamza-initial Form I verb /akal/ - /yaakul/ 'to eat' | Perfect Singular | Perfect Plural | Imperfect Singular | Imperfect Plural |
|---|---|---|---|---|
| 3M | **/akal/** | **/akal**uu/ | **/yaakul/** | **/yaakul**uu/ |
| 3F | **/akal**at/ | **/akal**an/ | **/taakul/** | **/yaakul**an/ |
| 2M | **/akal**ta/ | **/akal**tum/ | **/taakul/** | **/taakul**uu/ |
| 2F | **/akal**tii/ | **/akal**tan/ | **/taakul**ii/ | **/taakul**an/ |
| 1 | **/akal**ta/ | **/akal**naa/ | **/aakul/** | **/naakul/** |

### 3.2.1.5 Medially-weak Form I verbs

Medially-weak Form I verbs have two perfect stems, as in MSA. The perfect stem for 3S and 3P is $C_1aaC_3$. The perfect stem for 2S and 2P, as well as for 1S and 1P, is $C_1vC_3$. The imperfect stem is $yaC_1vvC_3$. In most cases, the short vowel of the perfect stem corresponds to the long vowel of the imperfect stem, as in /ʃaaf/ - /**ʃuf**ta/ - /ya**ʃuuf**/ 'to see' and /ʃaal/ - /**ʃil**ta/ - /ya**ʃiil**/ 'to carry'. In other cases, the two vowels do not correspond, as in /xaaf/ - /**xuf**ta/ - /ya**xaaf**/ 'to fear'.

| Medially-weak Form I verb /ʃaaf/ - /yaʃuuf/ 'to see' | Perfect Singular | Perfect Plural | Imperfect Singular | Imperfect Plural |
|---|---|---|---|---|
| 3M | **/ʃaaf/** | **/ʃaaf**uu/ | /ya**ʃuuf/** | /ya**ʃuuf**uu/ |
| 3F | **/ʃaaf**at/ | **/ʃaaf**an/ | /ta**ʃuuf/** | /ya**ʃuuf**an/ |
| 2M | **/ʃuf**ta/ | **/ʃuf**tum/ | /ta**ʃuuf/** | /ta**ʃuuf**uu/ |
| 2F | **/ʃuf**tii/ | **/ʃuf**tan/ | /ta**ʃuuf**ii/ | /ta**ʃuuf**an/ |
| 1 | **/ʃuf**ta/ | **/ʃuf**naa/ | /a**ʃuuf/** | /na**ʃuuf/** |

### 3.2.1.6 Finally-weak Form I verbs

SA has finally-weak Form I verbs, as does MSA, in which $C_3$ is /y/ or /w/. In SA, however, the distinction between /y/-final roots and /w/-final roots found in MSA does not exist.

All finally-weak verbs in SA have three stems in the perfect. The 3MS stem is $C_1aC_2aa$ (/**garaa**/ 'he read'); the stem preceding vowel-initial suffixes is $C_1aC_2$ (/**garat**/ 'she read'); the stem preceding consonant-initial suffixes is $C_1aC_2ee$ (/**gareet**/ 'I read'). Two patterns occur for finally-weak verbs in the imperfect. Some verbs retain the final /**-aa**/ in the imperfect, as in /**garaa**/ - /**yagraa**/ 'to study; to read'. Other verbs have a final /**-ii**/ in the imperfect, as in /**maʃaa**/ - /**yamʃii**/ 'to go'. The final long vowel of the imperfect elides when the suffix of the imperfect is vowel-initial. One example is /**tagrii**/ 'you (fs) study', from /ta/ (imperfect prefix) + /grii/ (imperfect stem) + /ii/ (imperfect suffix).

| Finally-weak Form I verb /garaa/ - /yagraa/ 'to read' | Perfect Singular | Perfect Plural | Imperfect Singular | Imperfect Plural |
|---|---|---|---|---|
| 3M | /**garaa**/ | /**garuu**/ | /**yagraa**/ | /**yagruu**/ |
| 3F | /**garat**/ | /**garan**/ | /**tagraa**/ | /**yagran**/ |
| 2M | /**gareet**/ | /**gareetum**/ | /**tagraa**/ | /**tagruu**/ |
| 2F | /**gareet**ii/ | /**gareet**an/ | /**tagrii**/ | /**tagran**/ |
| 1 | /**gareet**/ | /**gareen**aa/ | /**agraa**/ | /**nagraa**/ |

### 3.2.1.7 Doubled or geminate Form I verbs

Geminate Form I verbs are those in which $C_2$ and $C_3$ are the same. The perfect stem resembles the imperfect stem with the pattern $C_1vC_2C_3$. Stem vowels vary, of course. Compare /**xatta**/ - /**yaxutt**/ 'to put' with /**ḥabba**/ - /**yaḥibb**/ 'to want, like, love' (see 1.3.4.2 on verbs with word-final geminate consonants). The conjugation of doubled or geminate Form I verbs in the perfect resembles that of the finally-weak Form I verb in SA (see 3.2.1.6). That is, the doubled or geminate consonant is retained throughout the conjugation, and the long vowel /**ee**/ precedes the suffix of the perfect in 2S and 2P, as well as in 1S and 1P (as in /**xatteet**/ 'I put').

| Geminate Form I verb /xatta/ - /yaxutt/ 'to put' | Perfect Singular | Perfect Plural | Imperfect Singular | Imperfect Plural |
|---|---|---|---|---|
| 3M | /**xatta**/ | /**xattuu**/ | /ya**xutt**/ | /ya**xuttuu**/ |
| 3F | /**xatt**at/ | /**xattan**/ | /ta**xutt**/ | /ya**xuttan**/ |
| 2M | /**xattee**ta/ | /**xattee**tum/ | /ta**xutt**/ | /ta**xuttuu**/ |
| 2F | /**xattee**tii/ | /**xattee**tan/ | /ta**xutt**ii/ | /ta**xuttan**/ |
| 1 | /**xattee**ta/ | /**xattee**naa/ | /a**xutt**/ | /na**xutt**/ |

### 3.2.1.8 Irregular verbs

Only one verb in SA is actually irregular. It is the verb /jaa/ - /yajii/ 'to come'.

| | Perfect Singular | Perfect Plural | Imperfect Singular | Imperfect Plural |
|---|---|---|---|---|
| 3M | /jaa/ | /joo/ | /yajii/ | /yajuu/ |
| 3F | /jaat/ | /jan/ | /tajii/ | /yajan/ |
| 2M | /jiit/ | /jiituu/ | /tajii/ | /tajuu/ |
| 2F | /jiitii/ | /jiitan/ | /tajii/ | /tajan/ |
| 1 | /jiit/ | /jiinaa/ | /ajii/ | /najii/ |

The imperative of the verb /jaa/ - /yajii/ is also irregular. It is /taʕaal/.

### 3.2.2 Derived verb forms

The description that follows assumes that weak and geminate stems of derived verb forms behave like strong stems. Weak and geminate stems of derived verb forms are described only where they behave differently from the corresponding strong forms.

This brief description of SA does not include discussion of the meanings associated with each of the derived verb forms. For such information, a reference grammar should be consulted.

### 3.2.3 Form II verbs

Form II is one of the most frequently-used of the derived verb forms. With a geminate $C_2$, it has the pattern $C_1aC_2C_2aC_3$ - $yaC_1aC_2C_2iC_3$, as in **/ɣassal/** - **/yaɣassil/** 'to wash (s.t.)'.

#### 3.2.3.1

Finally-weak Form II verbs have the pattern $C_1aC_2C_2aa$ - $yaC_1aC_2C_2ii$. That is, they have a final **/-aa/** in the perfect and a final **/-ii/** in the imperfect, as in **/garraa/** - **/yagarrii/** 'to teach'.

#### 3.2.3.2 Four-consonant or quadriliteral verbs

Four-consonant or quadriliteral verbs have four, rather than three, root consonants or radicals. They have a pattern similar to that of Form II verbs, except that two different consonants make up the consonant cluster in the middle of the verb. The pattern is $C_1aC_2C_3aC_4$ - $yaC_1aC_2C_3iC_4$, as in **/tarjam/** - **/yatarjim/** 'to translate'.

#### 3.2.3.3 Form III verbs

Form III verbs have a long **/-aa-/** preceding the second root consonant. The pattern of the Form III verb is $C_1aaC_2aC_3$ - $yaC_1aaC_2iC_3$, as in **/saafar/** - **/yasaafir/** 'to travel'.

3.2.3.3.1 Finally-weak Form III verbs have the pattern $C_1aaC_2aa$ - $yaC_1aaC_2ii$. That is, they have a final **/-aa/** in the perfect and a final **/-ii/** in the imperfect, as in **/naadaa/** - **/yanaadii/** 'to call out (to s.o.)'.

#### 3.2.3.4 Form IV verbs

Form IV verbs, with the pattern $aC_1C_2aC_3$ - $yiCC_2iC_3$, such as **/antaj/** 'to produce', occur in SA mainly in words from ClA or MSA. The form is not productive in SA.

#### 3.2.3.5 Form V and Form VI verbs

Form V verbs derive from Form II through the addition of the prefix **/it-/**. Form V has the pattern $itC_1aC_2C_2aC_3$ - $yitC_1aC_2C_2aC_3$, as in **/itfassaḥ/** - **/yitfassaḥ/** 'to go for a stroll'. Similarly, Form VI verbs derive from Form III through the addition of the prefix **/it-/**. Form VI has the pattern $itC_1aaC_2aC_3$ - $yitC_1aaC_2aC_3$, as in **/itgaabal/** - **/yitgaabal/** 'to meet (one another)'.

3.2.3.5.1 Finally-weak Form V and Form VI verbs have a final **/-aa/** in the perfect and the imperfect. Form V has the pattern $itC_1aC_2C_2aa$ -

yit$C_1$a$C_2C_2$aa, as in /itɣaddaa/ - /yitɣaddaa/ 'to eat lunch'. Form VI has the pattern it$C_1$aa$C_2$aa - yit$C_1$aa$C_2$aa, as in /itlaagaa/ - /yitlaagaa/ 'to meet, encounter (one another)'.

#### 3.2.3.6 Form VII verbs

Form VII derives from Form I through the addition of the prefix /in-/. It has the pattern in$C_1$a$C_2$a$C_3$ - yin$C_1$a$C_2$i$C_3$, as in /inkasar/ - /yinkasir/ 'to be broken'.

3.2.3.6.1 Medially-weak Form VII verbs resemble medially-weak Form I verbs because medially-weak Form VII verbs also have two stems for the perfect. The perfect stem for 3S and 3P is in$C_1$aa$C_3$. The perfect stem for 2S and 2P, as well as for 1S and 1P, is in$C_1$v$C_3$. The imperfect stem is yin$C_1$aa$C_3$. The short vowel of the perfect stem of the medially-weak Form VII verb usually corresponds to the long vowel of the imperfect stem of the medially-weak Form I verb. One example is /inʃaal/ - /inʃilta/ - /yinʃaal/ 'to be removed', derived from the Form I verb /ʃaal/ - /yaʃiil/ 'to carry'.

3.2.3.6.2 Finally-weak Form VII verbs have a final long /-aa/ in the perfect and final long /-ii/ in the imperfect. They have the pattern in$C_1$a$C_2$aa - yin$C_1$a$C_2$ii, as in /intahaa/ - /yintahii/ 'to come to an end'.

#### 3.2.3.7 Form VIII verbs

Form VIII derives from Form I through the addition of an infixed /t/ after $C_1$ (and an epenthetic /i/ before $C_1$ to prevent a word-initial consonant cluster in the perfect). It has the pattern i$C_1$ta$C_2$a$C_3$ - yi$C_1$ta$C_2$i$C_3$, as in /istalam/ - /yistalim/ 'to receive, accept'.

3.2.3.7.1 Medially-weak Form VIII verbs have /aa/ as the long vowel of the perfect stem, /i/ as the short vowel of the perfect stem, and /aa/ as the short vowel of the imperfect stem. They have the pattern i$C_1$taa$C_3$ - i$C_1$ti$C_3$ - yi$C_1$taa$C_3$, as in /ixtaar/ - /ixtirta/ - /yixtaar/ 'to choose'.

3.2.3.7.2 Finally-weak Form VIII verbs have a final long /-aa/ in the perfect and final long /-ii/ in the imperfect. They have the pattern i$C_1$ta$C_2$aa - yi$C_1$ta$C_2$ii, as in /iʃtaraa/ - /yiʃtarii/ 'to buy'.

#### 3.2.3.8 Form IX verbs

Form IX verbs, with the pattern a$C_1C_2$a$C_3C_3$ as in /aḥmarra/ 'to be red; to turn red', occur in SA mainly in words from ClA or MSA. The form is not productive in SA.

#### 3.2.3.9 Form X verbs

Form X verbs, with the pattern ista$C_1C_2$a$C_3$ - yista$C_1C_2$i$C_3$ such as /**istaḥamma**/ 'to bathe, take a bath', occur in SA mainly in words from ClA or MSA. The form is not productive in SA.

#### 3.2.3.10 Verb forms that do not occur in MSA

3.2.3.10.1 Verbs of the form it$C_1$a$C_2$a$C_3$ have the pattern it$C_1$a$C_2$a$C_3$ - yit$C_1$a$C_2$i$C_3$, as in /**itfataḥ**/ - /**yitfatiḥ**/ 'to be open, become opened'. The finally-weak verb of this form has a final long /**-aa**/ in the perfect and final long /**-ii**/ in the imperfect, as in /**itlagaa**/ - /**yitlagii**/ 'to allow oneself to be found; to make oneself be found'. This form is very productive in SA.

3.2.3.10.2 The verb form $C_1$oo$C_2$a$C_3$ is not as common in SA in the region of the capital as it is in other areas of Sudan. Among the verbs of this pattern is /**koorak**/ - /**yikoorik**/ 'to shout, cry'.

## 3.3 The true or ablaut passive

The true or ablaut passive voice, familiar from ClA and MSA, derives from an active verb through changes to the prefix and stem vowels (compare the active ḏaraba - yaḏribu 'to hit' with the passive ḏuriba - yuḏrabu 'to be hit'). There are a handful of verbs in SA that can form a true passive voice. These are Form I verbs with the pattern $C_1$i$C_2$i$C_3$ - yi$C_1C_2$a$C_3$, as in /**kitil**/ - /**yiktal**/ 'to be killed' (derived from /**katal**/ 'to kill').

The most commonly-used of these verbs are the following:

| Passive Perfect - Imperfect | English translation | Active Perfect |
|---|---|---|
| /tilif/ - /yitlaf/ | to be destroyed | /talaf/ |
| /ḥirig/ - /yiḥrag/ | to be burned, burnt down | /ḥarag/ |
| /sirig/ - /yisrag/ | to be stolen | /sarag/ |
| /ɣilib/ - /yiɣlab/ | to be conquered | /ɣalab/ |
| /giriṣ/ - /yigraṣ/ | to be bitten (by a snake) | /garaṣ/ |
| /girif/ - /yigraf/ | to be disgusted | /garaf/ |
| /kitil/ - /yiktal/ | to be killed | /katal/ |
| /lidiɣ/ - /yildaɣ/ | to be stung (by an insect) | /ladaɣ/ |

## 3.4 Other forms derived from verbs

### 3.4.1 Verbal nouns

Verbal nouns of Form I verbs in SA, as in MSA, are not predictable. The following list gives patterns and examples of verbal nouns for the derived verb forms. Note that, for many derived verbs, speakers of SA may use the verbal noun of the corresponding Form I verb, if such a verb exists.

| Verb form | Verbal noun pattern | Example |
|---|---|---|
| Form II | $C_ziC_2C_2eeC_3$ | /**girreey**/ (from /**garraa**/ - /**yagarrii**/ 'to teach s.o.') |
| | $taC_1C_2iiC_3$ | /**taḥṣiil**/ (from /**ḥaṣṣal**/ - /**yaḥaṣṣil**/ 'to catch up with, reach') |
| Form III | $muC_1aaC_2aC_3a$ or $maC_1aaC_2aC_3a$ | /**muʕaayana**/ (from /**ʕaayan**/ - /**yaʕaayin**/ 'to look at, stare at') |
| Form IV | (not productive in SA) | |
| Form V | $tiC_1aC_2C_2iC_3$ | /**timallis**/ (from /**mallas**/ - /**yamallis**/ 'to stroke, caress') |
| Form VI | $maC_1aaC_2aC_3a$ | /**maḥaakama**/ (from /**ḥaakam**/ - /**yaḥaakam**/ 'to prosecute, put on trial' rather than /**itḥaakam**/ - /**yitḥaakam**/ 'to be prosecuted, put on trial') |
| Form VII | $inC_1iC_2aaC_3$ | /**inḥilaab**/ (from /**inḥalab**/ - /**yinḥalib**/ 'to be milked') |
| Form VIII | $iC_1tiC_2aaC_3$ | /**istilaam**/ (from /**istalam**/ - /**yistalim**/ 'to receive, accept') |
| Form IX | (not productive in SA) | |
| Form X | (not productive in SA) | |
| SA form $itC_1aC_2aC_3$ | (not predictable and often derived from corresponding Form I verb) | /**fatiḥ**/ (from Form I /**fataḥ**/ - /**yaftaḥ**/ 'to open' rather than /**itfataḥ**/ - /**yitfatiḥ**/ 'to be opened') |

### 3.4.2 Active participles

#### 3.4.2.1 The active participle of Form I verbs

3.4.2.1.1 The active participle of strong Form I verbs has the pattern $C_1aaC_2iC_3$, as in /**ʃaarib**/ 'drinking; having drunk' (from /**ʃirib**/ - /**yaʃrab**/ 'to drink').

3.4.2.1.2 The active participle of medially-weak Form I verbs has the pattern $C_1aayiC_3$, as in /**jaayib**/ 'bringing; having brought' (from /**jaab**/ - /**yajiib**/ 'to bring').

3.4.2.1.3 The active participle of finally-weak Form I verbs has the pattern $C_1aaC_2ii$, as in /**maaʃii**/ 'going; walking' (from /**maʃaa**/ - /**yamʃii**/ 'to go, walk').

3.4.2.1.4 The active participle of geminate verbs has the pattern $C_1aaC_2C_3ii$, as in /**xaattii**/ 'putting (ms)', similar to that of the active participle of the finally-weak verb, such as /**maaʃii**/ 'going; walking' (from /**maʃaa**/ - /**yamʃii**/ 'to go, walk'). The FS, MP, and FP active participles of geminate verbs, however, lack the final long /**-ii**/ and have the pattern $C_1aaC_2C_3$, as in /**xaatta**/ 'putting (fs)'; /**xaattiin**/ 'putting (mp)'; and /**xaattaat**/ 'putting (fp)'.

#### 3.4.2.2 The active participle of derived verbs

The active participle of derived verbs prefixes /**mu-**/ or /**mi-**/ to the 3MS form of the imperfect, as in /**musaafir**/ 'traveling' (from /**saafar**/ - /**yasaafir**/ 'to travel') and /**mingalib**/ 'reversed, overturned' (from /**ingalab**/ - /**yingalib**/ 'to be reversed, overturned').

### 3.4.3 Passive participles

#### 3.4.3.1 The passive participle of Form I verbs

3.4.3.1.1 The passive participle of Form I strong verbs has the pattern $maC_1C_2uuC_3$, as in /**maktuub**/ 'written' (from /**katib**/ - /**yaktib**/ 'to write').

3.4.3.1.2 Medially-weak Form I verbs form their participle on the pattern $maC_1yuuC_3$, as in /**mabyuuʕ**/ 'sold' (from /**baaʕ**/ - /**yabiiʕ**/ 'to sell').

3.4.3.1.3 All finally-weak Form I verbs have a final long /**-ii**/, with the pattern $maC_1C_2ii$, as in /**mabnii**/ 'built' (from /**banaa**/ - /**yabnii**/ 'to build').

#### 3.4.3.2 The passive participle of derived verbs

The passive participle of derived verbs is homophonous with the active participle. Like the active participle, the passive participle of derived verbs prefixes **/mu-/** or **/mi-/** to the stem of the imperfect, as in **/mustaʕmil/** 'used; using' (from **/istaʕmal/** - **/yistaʕmil/** 'to use').

## 3.5 Uses of the perfect

### 3.5.1 The perfect expresses the past

The perfect typically indicates action completed before the moment of speaking, that is, in the past, as in **/akaltuu/** 'I ate it (ms)'. In some cases, however, speakers of SA and other varieties of Arabic use the perfect to refer to events that a speaker of American English thinks of as occurring in the present, such as **/fihimta/** 'I understand'. Usage like this is often explained as referring to the actual moment of comprehension, an event that preceded the moment of speaking.

### 3.5.2 The perfect expresses a wish (the optative)

The perfect sometimes indicates a wish, hope, or desire. This use is called the optative. It most frequently occurs in formulaic language, such as the conventional courtesy **/ʕaaʃat alʔasaamii/** 'may you live long, lit. may the names live'.

### 3.5.3 The perfect is the act (the performative)

In some cases, the perfect occurs in an utterance that is equivalent to an action. A familiar example of the performative in English is the statement "I apologize," where the apology takes place only when the words are said. The performative use of the perfect in SA often occurs in legal or contractual contexts, such as buying, selling, and divorce. It may also occur in other contexts, such as **/xalleetak/** 'I'm leaving you (ms) alone, lit. I have left you (ms)'.

## 3.6 Uses of the imperfect

### 3.6.1 The simple imperfect

The simple imperfect is the imperfect that occurs without the imperfect **/bi-/** prefix (see 3.6.2). The simple imperfect occurs most often following a pre-verb (see 3.6.4), as in **/laazim aḥaṣṣiluu/** 'I have to catch up with him'. The simple imperfect also occurs in isolation. When it does so, it usually refers to a potential rather than an actual event, as in /**leeh taʕmal fiinii kidaa**/ 'why would you (ms) do this to me?' as opposed to /**leeh bi-taʕmal fiinii kidaa**/ 'why do you (ms) do this to me?'

### 3.6.2 The prefixed imperfect

The prefixed imperfect is the imperfect that has the imperfect /**bi-**/ prefix. It is the most usual or default form of the imperfect in speech. If the simple imperfect in isolation usually refers to a potential event (see 3.6.1), the prefixed imperfect refers to an actual event. A prefixed imperfect such as /b-aʃtaɣil/ can be translated as 'I work' or 'I am working'.

The time frame of the prefixed imperfect is not specific. Adverbials of time and place, however, can clarify the time frame of the prefixed imperfect. It may make a general statement, as in /**b-iiriiduu** ʃadiid/ 'he likes him very much'. It may describe repeated or habitual action, as in /**bi-tajii kulla yoom**/ 'you (s) come every day'. It may depict action that takes place at the moment of speech, as in /**b-adrus** hassaʕ/ 'I am studying now'. Finally, it may refer to an event in the near future, as in /**b-aʃuufak** bukra/ 'I'll see you (ms) tomorrow'.

#### 3.6.2.1 The prefixed imperfect of transitive verbs

As stated above in 3.6.2, the time frame of the prefixed imperfect is not specific. Adverbials usually provide details of time that make the time frame of the prefixed imperfect clear. One exception to this rule is the transitive verb. A transitive verb typically takes a direct object, as in /**bi-yibnuu jaamiʕ**/ 'they are building a mosque'. A transitive verb, however, may take an indirect object with the preposition /**fii-**/ rather than a direct object. In this case, the time frame of the verb expands to include action that takes place over a period of time. One example is /**kaan b-ibnuu luuh fii jaamiʕ**/ 'they were building away at a mosque for him' (Selection 25).

### 3.6.3 The future

In many parts of Sudan, the imperfect /**bi-**/ prefix forms the future, as in /**b-aḍrub** leeh **baʕd usbuuʕ**/ 'I'll call him in a week'. In addition, especially in the region of the capital, the prefix /ḥa-/ is added to the simple imperfect to form the future, as in /**ḥ-arjaʕ li-ssuudaan baʕd sanateen**/ 'I will return to Sudan in two years'. Many speakers consider this form, shared with Egyptian Arabic, to be less than authentically Sudanese.

### 3.6.4 Pre-verbs

SA has a variety of pre-verbs. This is a general term for forms, usually verbs or participles, that precede a verb, the main verb. A pre-verb provides additional information about the time frame of the main verb (it is aspectual) or about an attitude towards the action of the main verb (it is modal). The following lists some of the most commonly-used pre-verbs of SA.

#### 3.6.4.1 /kaan/ as a pre-verb

3.6.4.1.1 For the most part, /**kaan**/ marks time in a nominal or verbal sentence. The role of /**kaan**/ is perhaps more clear in verbal sentences. For example, when the perfect of /**kaan**/ precedes the perfect or prefixed imperfect, it changes the time frame of that main verb. It effectively moves the event or action of the main verb into the past or future.

perfect: /ʕaʃaan taʕmil mutaabaʕa wa-taɣyiim li-lmaʃaariiʕ al**kaanat mawwalitaa**/

'in order to do an inspection and evaluation of the projects that they (fs) had funded' (u.d.)

prefixed imperfect: /alwakit daak **kaanuu b-inaggiluu** fiihum ʃadiid/

'At that time, they (mp) used to transfer them (mp) a lot.' (Selection 3)

3.6.4.1.2 The role of /**kaan**/ as a time marker is most prominent where /**kaan**/ does not agree in number or gender with its subject and predicate, as in the sentence /**kaan** ʃaɣɣaal**iin**/ 'At that time, they (mp) were working'. The lack of agreement here shifts focus away from the event or state depicted in the sentence to the time frame expressed by /**kaan**/.

#### 3.6.4.2 /kaan/ as mood- rather than time-marker

3.6.4.2.1 When the perfect of /**kaan**/ precedes the simple imperfect, it affects attitude (mood) rather than time frame. It makes the action of the main verb an obligation, an equivalent of the English "should".

simple imperfect: /maa **kutta** taktuluu/

'You (ms) shouldn't have killed him.' (Selection 26)

3.6.4.2.2 Either the prefixed imperfect or simple imperfect of /**kaan**/ may precede a perfect main verb. In both cases, the combination of /**kaan**/ and the perfect results in an assumption rather than a statement of fact.

| | |
|---|---|
| simple imperfect: | /xaayif **yikuun** tʕawwag ʃadiid/ 'I'm afraid he might have been badly hurt.' (Selection 12) |
| prefixed imperfect: | /alḥalaawaa **bi-tkuun** ʃaalat kull aʃʃaʕar alfii jjisim/ 'The <u>halawa</u> (a traditional cosmetic) will have removed all of the hair on the [woman's] body.' (u.d.) |

### 3.6.4.3 Verbs of motion as pre-verbs

3.6.4.3.1 Verbs of motion frequently function as pre-verbs. They may precede the imperfect, as in /almaa **b-iirjaʕuu yʕiiduu**/ 'those who don't go back to repeat [a year of classwork]' (Selection 6). In verb strings like this, the action of the main verb is the reason for that of the verb of motion. In other words, the relationship between the two verbs can be translated as 'to, in order to'.

3.6.4.3.2 Where a verb of motion precedes the perfect, the relationship between the two verbs is not one of cause and effect. It is simply a matter of sequence, as in /**jaat ʃaafat** ʕaadil fi lʔisbitaaliya/ 'She came and visited Adil in the hospital' (Selection 22). In these cases, the relationship between verbs is best translated as 'and'.

### 3.6.4.4 Other verbs as pre-verbs

3.6.4.4.1 /bigaa/ - /yabgaa/ 'to begin to; to become'

/**biguu** maa ykammiluu taʕliimum/

'They (mp) began not to complete their (mp) schooling.' (Selection 5)

/**bigaa** milyuuneer wi-ḥaggag addaayir yaʕmaluu/

'He became a millionaire and achieved what he wanted to do.' (Selection 9)

3.6.4.4.2 /gaam/ - /yaguum/ 'to up and (do s.t.), to do suddenly; to do (s.t. as a consequence)'

/**gaamuu** nagaluu waaldii lii-januub kurduufaan/

'They (mp) up and transferred my father to Southern Kordofan.' (Selection 3)

/**b-iiguumuu** hum itxawwafuu/

'As a consequence, they (mp) become frightened.' (Selection 5)

3.6.4.4.3 /garrab/ - /yagarrib/ 'to be about to, to be at the point of'

/**garrabta** ʔakammal xamsa sanawaat/

'I have almost finished five years.' (Selection 9)

3.6.4.4.4 /gidir/ - /yagdar/ 'to be able to'

/maa **gdirnaa** nistamtaʕ bii-wuṣuulnaa lii-waaʃinṭun/

'We couldn't enjoy our arrival in Washington.' (Selection 2)

#### 3.6.4.5 Inflecting participles as pre-verbs

3.6.4.5.1 /**daayir**/ 'wanting; needing; intending' (active participle of /**daar**/ - /yaduur/ 'to want')

/bigaa milyuuneer wi-ḥaggag ad**daayir** yaʕmaluu/

'He became a millionaire and achieved what he wanted to do.' (Selection 9)

/**daayrum** ḍaruurii/

'I need them (mp) urgently.' (Selection 26)

/niḥnaa **daayriin** nagṭaʕ almooya dii/

'We're going to cut off the water here.' (Selection 18)

3.6.4.5.2 /gaadir/ 'able to' (active participle of /gidir/ - /yagdar/ 'to be able to')

/maa **gaadira** mʃii fiihuu sariiʕ/

'I can't make progress on it (ms) quickly.' (Selection 21)

3.6.4.5.3 /gaaʕid/ 'keeping on, continuing to' (active participle of /gaʕad/ - /yagʕud/ 'to sit')

/**gaaʕid** taraasil ahalak?/

'Do you (ms) continue to correspond with your (ms) family?' (Selection 11)

3.6.4.5.4 /ʕaawiz/ or /ʕaayiz/ 'wanting, desiring' (active participle of /ʕaaz/ - /yaʕuuz/ 'to want')

/ɣiyam tanʃiʔa ṭayyiba **ʕaawzaak** tasʕad ajjaar/

'The values of a good upbringing want you (ms) to help your (ms) neighbor.' (Selection 27)

#### 3.6.4.6 Invariable forms as pre-verbs

3.6.4.6.1 /mafruuḍ/ 'ought to, should'

/w-**almafruuḍ** almuwaaṭniin yidfaʕuu/

'And the citizens should pay.' (Selection 18)

3.6.4.6.2 /mumkin/ and /yimkin/ 'possible'

/assuudaan biduun diimuɣraaṭiyya maa **mumkin** itgaddam li-giddaam/

'Sudan without democracy cannot make any progress.' (Selection 15)

/maa **yimkin** yaṣalliḥ almakana alleela/

'He cannot fix the engine today.' (u.d.)

## 3.7 The use of the active participle

The active participle is usually translated as 'doing (the action of the verb)'. The time frame of the active participle, like that of the prefixed imperfect (see 3.6.2), is not specific. It may describe action that takes place at the moment of speech, as in /almaʃaakil **alḥaaṣla**/ 'the problems that are occurring'. It may refer to action in the future, as in /hum **musaafriin** li-kasalaa li-ʃahr alʕasal/ 'They (mp) are going to Kasala for a honeymoon.' In addition, the active participle may indicate the result of an action or describe a condition that took place before the moment of speaking and still holds true, as in /anaa **jaaya** min taɣriiban xamsa sanawaat/ 'I came about five years ago'.

In still other cases, the active participle has taken on the meaning and functions of a noun. Active participles that act as nouns (that have been re-lexicalized) usually take a broken plural. Consider, for example, the active participle /raakib/ 'riding', with the masculine sound plural /raakbiin/. In contrast, the noun /raakib/ 'passenger' has the masculine broken plural /rukkaab/.

# 4. Pronouns

## 4.1 Independent personal pronouns

| | Singular | Plural |
|---|---|---|
| 3M | /huwa/ | /hum/ or /hun/ |
| 3F | /hiya/ | /hin/ |
| 2M | /itta/ or /inta/ | /ittuu/ or /intuu/ |
| 2F | /ittii/ or /intii/ | /ittan/ or /intan/ |
| 1 | /ana/ | /niḫnaa/ |

## 4.2 Suffixed personal pronouns

There is a certain amount of variation in the forms of suffixed personal pronouns. In particular, see 1.3.4.1 on nouns with word-final geminate consonants.

| | following v or V | following C | following CC |
|---|---|---|---|
| 3MS | /-huu/ or Ø | /-uu/ | /-ahuu/ or /-uu/ |
| 3FS | /-haa/ | /-aa/ | /-ahaa/ or /-aa/ |
| 2MS | /-k/ | /-ak/ | /-ak/ |
| 2FS | /-kii/ or /-k/ | /-ik/ | /-ik/ |
| 1S (after non-verbal forms) | /-y/ | /-ii/ | /-ii/ |
| 1S (after verbal forms) | /-nii/ | /-nii/ | /-anii/ |
| 3MP | /-hum/ or /-hun/ | /-um/ or /-un/ | /-ahum/ or /-ahun/ |
| 3FP | /-hin/ or /-hun/ | /-in/ or /-un/ | /-ahin/ or /-ahun/ |
| 2MP | /-kum/ or /-kun/ | /-kum/ or /-kun/ | /-akum/ or /-akun/ |
| 2FP | /-kan/ | /-kan/ | /-akan/ |
| 1P | /-naa/ | /-naa/ | /-anaa/ |

## 4.3 Demonstratives

| | 'this, these' (near demonstratives) | 'that; those' (far demonstratives) |
|---|---|---|
| MS | /daa/ | /daak/ |
| FS | /dii/ | /diik/ |
| MP | /deel/ or /dool/ | /deel/ or /doolaak/ |
| FP | /deel/ | /deelaak/ |

# 5. Numbers and number derivations

## 5.1 Numbers for counting (cardinal numbers) and ordering (ordinal numbers)

SA numbers are invariable; they do not undergo changes of gender.

The exception is /waaḥid/ 'one'. The form /waaḥid/ 'one' functions as an adjective in counted-noun constructions and takes gender inflections as do other adjectives.

Numbers in SA compound as in MSA: /waaḥid wa-ʕiʃriin/ 'twenty-one'.

### 5.1.1 Cardinal numbers 1 - 10

| | | | |
|---|---|---|---|
| 1 | /waaḥid/ | 6 | /sitta/ |
| 2 | /itneen/ | 7 | /sabʕa/ |
| 3 | /talaata/ | 8 | /tamanya/ or /tamaanya/ |
| 4 | /arbaʕa/ | 9 | /tisʕa/ |
| 5 | /xamsa/ | 10 | /ʕaʃara/ |

### 5.1.2 Cardinal numbers 11 - 20

| | | | |
|---|---|---|---|
| 11 | /ḥidaaʃar/ | 16 | /siṭṭaaʃar/ |
| 12 | /iṭnaaʃar/ | 17 | /sabʕaṭaaʃar/ |
| 13 | /talaṭṭaaʃar/ | 18 | /ṭamanṭaaʃar/ |
| 14 | /arbaʕṭaaʃar/ | 19 | /tisʕaṭaaʃar/ |
| 15 | /xamasṭaaʃar/ | 20 | /ʕiʃriin/ |

### 5.1.3 Cardinal numbers 10 - 100

| | | | |
|---|---|---|---|
| 10 | /ʕaʃara/ | 60 | /sittiin/ |
| 20 | /ʕiʃriin/ | 70 | /sabʕiin/ |
| 30 | /talaatiin/ | 80 | /tamaaniin/ |
| 40 | /arbaʕiin/ | 90 | /tisʕiin/ |
| 50 | /xamsiin/ | 100 | /miyya/ |

### 5.1.4 Cardinal numbers 100 - 1000

| 100 | /miyya/ | 600 | /suttumiyya/ |
|---|---|---|---|
| 200 | /miiteen/ | 700 | /subʕumiyya/ |
| 300 | /tultumiyya/ | 800 | /tumnumiyya/ |
| 400 | /urbuʕmiyya/ or /rubʕumiyya/ | 900 | /tusʕumiyya/ |
| 500 | /xumsumiyya/ | 1000 | /alf/ |

## 5.2 Ordinal numbers

Ordinal numbers are adjectives that inflect for gender and number.

### 5.2.1 Ordinal numbers 1 - 10

| 1st | /awwal/ (FS /uulaa/) or /awwalaanii/ | 6th | /saadis/ (FS /saatta/) |
|---|---|---|---|
| 2nd | /taanii/ | 7th | /saabiʕ/ |
| 3rd | /taalit/ | 8th | /taamin/ |
| 4th | /raabiʕ/ | 9th | /taasiʕ/ |
| 5th | /xaamis/ | 10th | /ʕaaʃir/ |

### 5.2.2 Ordinal numbers greater than 10

For numbers greater than 10, ordinal numbers are not typically used. The cardinal number is used instead, as in /alʕadad **attalaṭṭaaʃar** bitaaʕ ajjariida dii/ 'the thirteenth issue of this newspaper' (s.b.i.). In informal contexts, an ordering (ordinal) form can be formed with the suffix /-**aawii**/, as in /jiit **alliṭnaaʃaraawii** fi ṣṣaff/ 'I came in twelfth in my class/?' (s.b.i.)

## 5.3 Days of the week and months of the year

The names of most of the days of the week, as well as one version of the month names used in SA, derive from numbers.

### 5.3.1 Days of the week

| Sunday | /yoom allaḥad/ | Friday | /yoom ajjumʕa/ |
|---|---|---|---|
| Monday | /yoom allitneen/ | Saturday | /yoom assabit/ |
| Tuesday | /yoom attalaata/ | | |
| Wednesday | /yoom allarbaḥa/ | | |
| Thursday | /yoom alxamiis/ | | |

### 5.3.2 Months of the year

Two sets of names for the solar months (as opposed to the months of the Islamic lunar or hijra calendar) are used in SA. One derives from European month names; the other numbers the months in order, with January as the first month.

| | | |
|---|---|---|
| January | /yanaayir/ | /ʃahri̤ waaḥid/ |
| February | /fabraayir/ | /ʃahr itneen/ |
| March | /maaris/ | /ʃahri talaata/ |
| April | /abriil/ | /ʃahr arbaʕa/ |
| May | /maayuu/ | /ʃahri xamsa/ |
| June | /yuunya/ | /ʃahri sitta/ |
| July | /yuulya/ | /ʃahri sabʕa/ |
| August | /aɣuṣṭus/ | /ʃahri tamanya/ |
| September | /sibtambir/ | /ʃahri tisʕa/ |
| October | /uktoobir/ | /ʃahri ʕaʃara/ |
| November | /nuufimbir/ | /ʃahri ḥidaaʃar/ |
| December | /diisambar/ | /ʃahri iṭnaaʃar/ |

## 6. Prepositions

Prepositions occur with definite and indefinite nouns, or take suffixed pronouns as objects. A number of prepositions may occur in isolation when they have an adverbial function, as in /giddaam/ 'in front'.

The following lists the most common of the prepositions of SA. The translations given here are general; more precise translations can be found in the general glossary to this work or the glossaries to individual selections.

Prepositions that may not occur in isolation are followed by a hyphen, as in /baraa-/ 'alone, by oneself; oneself'. Those that may occur in isolation do not have a hyphen, as in /barraa/ 'outside of, outside'.

| Preposition | English translation |
|---|---|
| /baraa-/ | alone, by oneself; oneself |
| /barraa/ | outside of, outside |
| /baʕad/ | after |
| /been-/ (also /beenaat-/) | between, among |
| /bi-/ (also /ba-/ and /bee-/) | with (by means of) |
| /tiḥit/ | under |
| /jaay/ | here; this side |
| /jamb-/ | next to |
| /ḥudaa-/ | next to |
| /zayy-/ (also /zeey-) | like, as |
| /ʕalaa-/ (/ʕalee-/ with suffixed pronoun and /ʕa-/ in rapid speech) | on; about |
| /ʕind-/ (also /ʕinn-/ with pronoun suffix) | at (place or person's home) |
| /ɣaadii/ | there; that side |
| /fii-/ | at; on |
| /foog/ | on top; over |
| /gadur-/ | as much as |
| /giddaam/ | in front of |
| /gubbaal/ or /gabli/ | before |
| /guṣaad-/ | opposite; across from |
| /li-/ (also /lee-/ or /lu-/ with suffixed pronoun, and /la/-) | to; for |
| /maʕaa-/ | with (accompanying) |
| /min-/ (also /minn-/) | from |
| /mitil-/ | like, as |
| /muduun/ (also /biduun/) | without |
| /waraa-/ | behind |

Many of these prepositions may occur in compounds, as in **/min baʕad/** 'after'.

## 7. Interrogatives

Following is a list of the interrogatives of SA. See 8.2.7.3 on the use of interrogatives in information questions.

| Interrogative | English translation |
|---|---|
| /**ʃinuu**/ | what? |
| /**kam**/ | how many?; how much? |
| /**keef**/ | how? |
| /**leeh**/ | why? |
| /**miteen**/ (also /**biteen**/) | when? |
| /**min**/ or /**minuu**/ | who? |
| /**ween**/ | where? |
| /**yaat-**/ + suffixed pronoun | which? |

## 8. Phrases and sentences

## 8.1 Nouns and noun phrases

### 8.1.1 Indefinite and definite nouns

SA has a definite article but no indefinite article.

#### 8.1.1.1 The indefinite noun

8.1.1.1.1 The indefinite noun in SA has no special marker. The indefinite noun is a noun that lacks a definite article /**al-**/ or suffixed pronoun, and that is not part of a construct phrase, as in /**ṭarabeeza**/ 'table; a table' or /**wad**/ 'boy; a boy'.

8.1.1.1.2 The word /**waaḥid**/ 'one' may precede an indefinite noun and agree with that noun in gender. This use of /**waaḥid**/ resembles that of an indefinite article. Note, however, that it does not simply indicate indefiniteness. In addition, /**waaḥid**/ 'one' adds emphasis or prominence to the noun that follows, as in /**b-tabkuu ʕalee ʃnuu? waaḥid** kaatil!/ 'What are you all (mp) crying about? A killer!' (Selection 19)

#### 8.1.1.2 A noun is made definite in one of three ways.

8.1.1.2.1 The definite noun may be marked by the definite article /**al-**/, as in /**al**banṭoon/ 'the ferry' or /**ad**dukkaan/ 'the shop'. (The /l/ of the definite article assimilates to /j/ and any "sun letter" or any apical consonant.)

8.1.1.2.2 A noun with a suffixed pronoun is also definite, as in /jeeraan**um**/ 'their (mp) neighbors' or /asnaan**uu**/ 'his teeth'.

8.1.1.2.3 The first noun of a construct phrase (see 8.1.3.1) is definite when the second noun is definite, as in /**madrast albanaat**/ 'the girls' school'. When the second noun is indefinite, the first is also indefinite, as in /**lisaan ʕaṣfuur**/ 'bird's tongue; a bird's tongue'.

8.1.1.2.4 Proper nouns, such as /**assuudaan**/ 'Sudan' and /**faaṭma**/ 'Fatima [a woman's name]', are definite.

### 8.1.2 Demonstrative phrases

A demonstrative phrase consists of a definite noun and a demonstrative that agrees in number and gender with that noun. (See 4.3 for a list of demonstratives.) The demonstrative follows the noun in SA, as in /albanṭoon **daa**/ 'this ferry', /almadrasa **dii**/ 'this school', and /annaas **deel**/ 'these people'.

### 8.1.3 Expressing possession

SA has two ways to express possession and other kinds of close relationships between nouns. One of these is the construct phrase or idaafa familiar from MSA and other varieties of Arabic. The other is the possessive adjective construction, in which an adjective expresses the link between the two nouns.

#### 8.1.3.1 The construct phrase

The construct phrase or idaafa consists of two nouns standing next to one another. The first of these two nouns may not have the definite article /al-/ or a suffixed pronoun. The second noun may be either definite or indefinite. The status of the second noun of the construct phrase determines that of the first noun. That is, when the second noun of the construct is definite, the first noun of the construct is considered to be definite, as in /bitt **al**mudiir/ 'the director's daughter'. When the second noun of the construct phrase is indefinite, the first noun is considered to be indefinite as well, as in /**gamiiṣ guṭun** / 'a shirt made of cotton, a cotton shirt'.

#### 8.1.3.2 The possessive adjective construction

The possessive adjective construction has three elements. The first is the possessed noun, which is modified by the second element, the possessive adjective. The possessive adjectives of SA are **/bitaaʕ/** and **/ḥagg/**.

| MS | /bitaaʕ/ | /ḥagg/ |
|---|---|---|
| FS | /bitaaʕat/ | /ḥaggat/ |
| MP | /bitaaʕiin/ | /ḥaggiin/ |
| FP | /bitaaʕaat/ | /ḥaggaat/ |

These possessive adjectives inflect for gender and number, but do not inflect for definiteness. This is because the possessive adjective, in turn, stands in a construct phrase with the third element of the construction, the possessor noun or pronoun suffix. As is the case with the construct phrase, the possessed noun may be indefinite, as in **/zikraayaat bitaaʕat aṣṣibaa/** 'memories of childhood'. The possessed noun may also be definite, as in **/alʔinɣilaab bitaaʕ nimeerii/** 'the overthrow of Nimeiri'.

Note that speakers in this work use the possessive adjective **/bitaaʕ/** much more often than **/ḥagg/**. Many Sudanese, however, prefer **/ḥagg/**. They may consider **/bitaaʕ/**, also used in Egyptian Arabic, to be less than authentically Sudanese.

#### 8.1.3.3 The use of the construct phrase and the possessive adjective construction

Although the construct phrase and the possessive adjective construction both express a relationship of possession, the two constructions are not used interchangeably by speakers of SA. Only the construct phrase can express relationships of inherent possession. Inherently possessed items are, for example, family members, body parts, one's name and nationality, material from which something comes or is made, and other elements that are permanent or essential, that are inherently possessed. The construct phrase can express other kinds of relationships, but speakers of SA usually use it only for relations of inherent possession. They use the possessive adjective phrase for other relationships, that is, those that are not inherently possessed.

### 8.1.4 The noun-adjective phrase

The noun-adjective phrase is made up of a noun that is followed by an adjective that modifies or qualifies the noun. The adjective agrees with the noun in definiteness as it agrees in gender and number. See 8.1.5 for details of number and gender agreement.

A definite adjective has the definite article /al-/. It can modify a noun that also has the definite article, as in /**al**bitt **as**samḥa/ 'the pretty girl'. It can also modify a noun that has a suffixed pronoun, as in /beet**naa** **al**gadiim/ 'our old house'. Finally, a definite adjective can modify the first noun in a construct phrase that is definite, as in /dustuur assuudaan **al**ʔintiɣaalii/ 'the Transitional Constitution of Sudan'.

### 8.1.5 Gender and number agreement

See 2.3.1 for gender and number inflections for nouns, adjectives, and participles. The following description is a general outline of agreement. Patterns of agreement vary in spontaneous speech. Note that, in the discussion of agreement that follows, "modifiers" includes all elements that usually show agreement in Arabic. These are adjectives, participles, pronouns, and verbal predicates.

#### 8.1.5.1 Agreement of singular nouns

All modifiers of a singular noun are also singular. They agree with the noun in gender, as in /beet jadiid/ 'a new house' and /ʕarabiyy**a** jadiid**a**/ 'a new car'. They also agree with the noun in definiteness, as in /**al**beet **a**jjadiid/ 'the new house' and /**al**ʕarabiyy**a** **a**jjadiid**a**/ 'the new car'.

#### 8.1.5.2 Agreement of dual nouns

Only nouns may take the dual ending /-een/. Modifiers of dual nouns are plural.

8.1.5.2.1 Dual nouns referring to male human beings or to human beings in general have MP modifiers, as in /raajl**een** kubaar/ 'two large men' and /mudarris**een** ʃaaṭr**iin**/ 'two clever teachers'.

8.1.5.2.2 Other dual nouns, those referring to female human beings and to inanimate objects, have FP modifiers, as in /bitt**een** fatraan**aat**/ 'two tired girls' and /beet**een** kabiir**aat**/ 'two large houses'. The use of FP modifiers for inanimate (or non-human) dual nouns is an extension of the use of FP modifiers for inanimate plural nouns (see 8.1.5.3.3).

#### 8.1.5.3 Agreement of plural nouns

8.1.5.3.1 Plural nouns referring to male human beings or to human beings in general have MP modifiers, as in /assawwaa**giin** alʕayyaa**niin**/ 'the tired drivers' and /allawlaad aṣṣuɣaar/ 'the small children'.

8.1.5.3.2 Plural nouns referring to female human beings take plural modifiers. Most SA speakers use MP modifiers for plural nouns referring to female human beings, as in /anniswaan almoojuu**diin**/ 'the women who are present' or /albanaat aṣṣuɣaar/ 'the young girls'. Plural nouns referring to female human beings may also take FP modifiers, as in /albanaat assamḥ**aat**/ 'the pretty girls'. The use of FP modifiers occurs most often among women.

8.1.5.3.3 Plural nouns referring to inanimate objects (or non-human plurals) usually have FS modifiers, as in /alʕarab**aat** albaayẓ**a**/ 'the broken-down cars'.

#### 8.1.5.4 Agreement of /kaan/ in clauses with /fii-/ and /ʕind-/

In SA, unlike certain other varieties of spoken Arabic, /kaan/ generally agrees with the grammatical subject in a nominal sentence of location or of existence with /fii-/ 'there is, there are' (see 8.2.2.4). Agreement of /kaan/ is also common in equational sentences of possession with /ʕind-/ 'to have' and other prepositions (see 8.2.2.5). An example is the clause /kull yoom ʔaḥad **takuun** fiihaa **ʕlaanaat** katiira jiddan/ 'every Sunday it (fs) has a lot of advertisements' (Selection 18), where the simple imperfect /takuun/ 'it (fs) is' agrees with its non-human plural subject /ʕlaanaat/ 'advertisements'.

### 8.1.6 Counted-noun constructions

SA has several structures that combine a number and a counted noun. SA numbers are invariable. They do not undergo changes of gender or sound change. The exception is /waaḥid/ 'one', which functions as an adjective in counted-noun constructions and takes gender inflections as do other adjectives.

#### 8.1.6.1 The number "one"

8.1.6.1.1 The number "one" is most often expressed by an indefinite singular noun, as in /isim/ 'a name; one name' or /ʃamʕa/ 'a candle; one candle'.

8.1.6.1.2 Where a speaker wants to express the number "one" or "a single" with greater clarity or emphasis, the word /**waaḥid**/ 'one' follows the noun. The word /waaḥid/ agrees with the noun in gender and definiteness, as in /gabli **yoom waaḥid** min alʕiris/ 'one day before the wedding' or /min **sulaala waaḥida**/ 'from a single line of descent'.

#### 8.1.6.2 The number "two"

8.1.6.2.1 The morphological dual takes the form of the suffix /-**een**/, as in /yoom**een**/ 'two days'.

8.1.6.2.2 The morphological dual is reinforced or emphasized when the word /itneen/ follows the dual noun, as in /yoom**een itneen**/ 'two days'.

#### 8.1.6.3 Numbers larger than two

8.1.6.3.1 The counted-noun construction for the numbers 3-10 consists of the number followed by a plural noun, as in /**xamsat agsaam**/ 'five sections'. This structure becomes definite when the definite article precedes the number only, as in /**al**ʕaʃara wizaaraat/ 'the ten government ministries'.

8.1.6.3.2 Some expressions of time have a counted-noun construction for the numbers 3-10 that consists of the number followed by a singular noun, as in /talaata **yoom**/ 'three days'.

8.1.6.3.3 The counted-noun construction for numbers over 10 consists of the number followed by a singular noun, as in /ʕiʃriin sana/ '20 years'. This structure becomes definite when the definite article precedes the number only, as in /**al**xamasṭaʃar yoom dii/ 'these 15 days'.

#### 8.1.6.4 Ordinal numbers in phrases

8.1.6.4.1 The ordinal numbers of SA usually function as adjectives. They follow the noun they modify and agree in number and gender, as in /alyoom allawwal/ 'the first day' or /assana attaalta/ 'the third year'.

8.1.6.4.2 The ordinal numbers, plus the word /aaxir/ 'last', also occur as the first noun of a construct phrase where the second noun is indefinite or where the ordinal takes a suffixed pronoun. The resulting phrase is another way of expressing order, as in /awwal yoom/ 'the first day' or /aaxrataa/ 'the end of it (fs)'.

### 8.1.7 Expressions of comparison and superlative

The form that expresses the comparative and the superlative in SA is the elative. It has the pattern $aC_1C_2aC_3$. The elative is invariable for number and gender.

#### 8.1.7.1 The comparative

8.1.7.1.1 Comparison in a phrase consists of an indefinite singular noun followed by an elative, as in /**beet aḥsan**/ 'a nicer house'.

8.1.7.1.2 Comparison in a clause consists of three elements. The first element is an indefinite elative, the second is the preposition /min/, and the third is the noun or suffixed pronoun that is the object or person to which the comparison is made. Examples are /**beetum akbar min beetnaa**/ 'Their (mp) house is larger than our house' or /**axuuy aṭwaal minnii**/ 'My brother is taller than I.'

8.1.7.1.3 Adjectives derived from other forms, including participles as well as adjectives of the form $aC_1C_2aC_3$, do not form an elative. These adjectives form comparatives using the elative /**aktar**/ as an intensifier. The result is an explicit comparative structure, as in /loonaa ʔabyaḍ **aktar** min allaban/ 'Its (fs) color is whiter than milk.'

#### 8.1.7.2 The superlative

8.1.7.2.1 The elative followed by an indefinite singular noun expresses an absolute superlative, as in /**akbar wad**/ 'the oldest boy'.

8.1.7.2.2 The elative followed by a definite plural noun or a suffixed pronoun expresses a relative superlative, as in /**akbar albuyuut**/ 'the biggest of the houses' or /**aḥsankum**/ 'the best of you (mp)'.

## 8.2 Sentences and clauses

### 8.2.1 The verbal sentence

The verbal sentence, in its simplest form, consists of two elements. The subject is a noun or pronoun, and the predicate is a verb. The subject typically precedes the verb, as in /**almuʃkila iṭṭawwarat**/ 'The problem progressed' (Selection 21) or /**hum itxawwafuu**/ 'They (mp) got frightened' (Selection 5).

The pronoun subject of a verbal sentence is usually expressed in the inflected form of the verb rather than as an independent pronoun. When the pronoun subject appears as an independent pronoun it typically conveys emphasis or contrast, as in /ʔawlaad **ʔanaa** b-aʕrifun/ 'boys I (personally) know' (Selection 5).

### 8.2.2 The equational sentence

The nominal or equational sentence has two basic elements. The subject is a noun or pronoun. The predicate may be a noun, a pronoun, and adjective, an adverb, or a prepositional phrase. No verb or other copular element links subject and predicate, and the subject usually but not always precedes the predicate. Equational sentences express a range of relationships.

#### 8.2.2.1 The equational sentence of identification

The equational sentence of identification has a subject and predicate that are both definite, as in /**isimaa hudaa**/ 'Her name is Hoda' (Selection 22) or /**inta aʃʃaahid alwaḥiid**/ 'You (ms) are the only witness' (Selection 26).

Identification can also be expressed in a nominal sentence that uses the presentational particle /yaa-/ or /aa-/. This particle takes a suffixed pronoun whose referent is the predicate, as in /yaa**huu xaalii** lkunta b-afattiʃ fiih/ 'He's my uncle, the one I've been looking for' (Selection 7).

#### 8.2.2.2 The equational sentence of description or attribution

The equational sentence of description or attribution has a definite noun or pronoun as its subject. The predicate, however, is indefinite, as in /daa **mujrim ḥaagid**/ 'That (ms) is a vicious criminal' (Selection 19) or /annaas deel kullahum **faaḍiyyiin**/ 'These people are all at leisure' (Selection 22).

#### 8.2.2.3 The equational sentence of time and place

The equational sentence of time resembles the equational sentence of place. In each case, the subject is a noun or pronoun, as in /**jaamʕat juuba** fii juuba/ 'The University of Juba is in Juba' and /**daa** sanat tisʕa wa-sitteen/ 'That (ms) was in '69.' The predicate is a prepositional phrase or an adverbial, as in /algubba dii **fii ʔumm ʃinaaʃin**/ 'This domed tomb is in Umm Shinashin' or /almuʕaayna **baakir**/ 'The appointment is tomorrow.'

#### 8.2.2.4 The equational sentence of existence

The equational sentence of existence resembles the equational sentence of time and place (see 8.2.2.3). The equational sentence of existence, however, is introduced by the existential particle /fii/. In addition, the grammatical subject of the sentence is an indefinite noun, as in /maa fii **ṭariiga** ɣeer

**innuu** ʔanaa ʔaktuluu/ 'There is no way, except for me to kill him' (Selection 26).

#### 8.2.2.5 The equational sentence of possession

The equational sentence of possession relies on a specialized use of the preposition /ʕind-/ 'lit. at' or /maʕaa-/ 'lit. with'. The possessive use of these prepositions differs from their use in expressing spatial relations in two ways. First, the preposition takes a suffixed pronoun whose referent is the possessor. That pronoun occurs even when a noun phrase in the same sentence names the possessor, as in **/kulla zool fi lʕaalam** ... ʕind**uu** lḥilim **alʔameerikii**/ 'Everyone in the world has the American dream; lit. Everyone in the world he has the American dream' (Selection 9). Second, the prepositional phrase precedes the grammatical subject of the sentence, the item possessed, as in /intii **maʕaaki** ḥagg/ 'You (fs) are right, lit. You (fs), with you (fs) is a right.'

### 8.2.3 Expansion of the simple sentence

The following describes some of the ways in which a simple sentence in SA can be expanded.

#### 8.2.3.1 The topic-comment sentence

The topic-comment sentence consists of a topic that is a noun or a pronoun, and a comment that is itself a complete sentence. Note also that the topic contains a pronoun, suffixed pronoun, or verb inflection whose referent is the topic. The sentence that is the comment may be verbal, as in /**inta maa ḥa-tjiik** ḥaaja/ 'Nothing will happen to you' (Selection 26). The comment may also be a nominal sentence, as in /niḥnaa **ʕamarnaa bi-saaʕaat**/ 'Our lives are counted in hours, lit. We, our lives are by hours' (Selection 4).

#### 8.2.3.2 The relative clause

A relative clause in SA is another kind of sentence embedded in a second sentence. The embedded sentence modifies a noun or pronoun in the main sentence. A relative clause is called definite when the noun it modifies, the head noun, is definite. It is indefinite when the head noun is indefinite.

8.2.3.2.1 The definite relative clause modifies a definite noun. It is indicated by the definite relative pronoun /al-/, homophonous with the definite article /al-/. The relative clause contains a resumptive pronoun. This is a pronoun, suffixed pronoun, or verb inflection whose referent is the head noun, as in /yuktul **arraajil alʔakramuu**/ 'He would kill the man who was good to him, lit. He would kill the man who *he* was good to him' (Selection 19).

8.2.3.2.2 The indefinite relative clause modifies an indefinite noun. There is no indefinite relative pronoun in SA. The indefinite relative clause, like the definite relative clause, contains a resumptive pronoun. This is a pronoun, suffixed pronoun, or verb inflection whose reference is the head noun, as in /yiktul **waaḥid lammaa**huu min aʃʃaariʕ/ 'He would kill someone who took him in off the street, lit. He would kill someone who *he* took him in off the street' (Selection 19).

8.2.3.2.3 Relative clauses in which the resumptive pronoun should or would be an independent pronoun often omit this pronoun, as in /**aḥmad allakbar minnii**/ 'Ahmad, who is older than I, lit. Ahmad who older than I' (Selection 3).

### 8.2.4 Conditional sentences

There are three conditional particles in SA that introduce the condition clause of the sentence: /**loo**/, /**kaan**/, and /**izaa**/. The particle /**izaa**/ occurs mainly in formal or classicized speech. The uses of the particles /**loo**/ and /**kaan**/ overlap to a certain extent, and the verb of the condition clause is typically the perfect. The best indicator of the reality of a conditional sentence in SA is, therefore, the verb of the result clause. The following outlines the three types of conditional sentence in SA.

#### 8.2.4.1 Hypothetical conditions

A hypothetical condition is one that is possible but not guaranteed, or describes in general terms what "someone" might do. Hypothetical conditions tend to have /**loo**/ as the conditional particle. The verb of the condition clause is perfect. The verb of the result clause is the simple imperfect, as in /**loo waaḥid min ajjamaaʕa deel gaam jannan wallaa kidaa yawadduu ṭawwaalii li-nnaas ṣṣaalḥiin**/ 'If someone from this community were to up and go crazy, or something like that, they (mp) would take him right away to the holy people' (u.d.).

#### 8.2.4.2 Real or predictive conditions

A real or predictive condition describes or predicts the event of the result clause. The conditional particle of a real condition can often be translated with 'when' as well as 'if'. Real conditions usually have /**loo**/ as the conditional particle, although /**kaan**/ also occurs. The verb of the condition clause is perfect. The verb of the result clause is the prefixed imperfect, as in /loo alḥaaja dii ṣiḥḥat **b-addiik** gizaaza bitaaʕat samin/ 'If this thing is true, I'll give you (ms) a jar of cooking fat' (u.d.), or the future, as in /loo ʔitgabaḍ **ḥa-ytḥaakam**/ 'If he is arrested, he will stand trial' (u.d.).

#### 8.2.4.3 Unreal or contrary-to-fact conditions

An unreal or contrary-to-fact condition describes a situation that has not or will not take place. The conditional particle **/kaan/** introduces the condition clause and may also introduce the result clause. The verb of the condition clause is the perfect. The verb of the result clause is perfect when the result is in the past, as in **/kaan** maa **ʕaajabatik** maa **kaan guttii** fiihaa kidaa/ 'If she didn't please you (fs), you (fs) would not have said such things about her' (Selection 22). When the result would take place in the future, the verb of the result clause is the prefixed imperfect, as in **/kaan xitiinaa** **rrayyis maa bi-tjiinaa** ʔayya ʕawaja/ 'If we avoid the Boss, no harm will come to us' (Selection 26).

### 8.2.5 Conjunctions

Other expansions of the simple sentence rely on the use of conjunctions. The following lists some of the more common conjunctions of SA.

| Conjunction | English translation |
|---|---|
| /amma/ | but, however |
| /awwal maa/ | as soon as |
| /badal/ | instead of |
| /bass/ | but |
| /baʕad maa/ | after |
| /zayy maa/ | like, as |
| /ʕaʃaan/ | because; in order to |
| /gabli maa/ or /gubbaal maa/ | before |
| /gadur maa/ | as much as |
| /laakin/ | but |
| /lamman/ | when |
| /liʔannuu/ | because; so that |
| /li-ḥaddi/ and /li-ḥaddi maa/ | until |
| /li-ɣayat maa/ | until |
| /mujarrad maa/ | as soon as, no sooner than |
| /miteen maa/ and /miteem maa/ | whenever |

| Conjunction | English translation |
|---|---|
| /mitil maa/ | like, as |
| /min/ | when, at the time of |
| /min/ and /mimmaa/ | since the time that; as soon as |
| /izaa kaan ... aw .../ | whether s.t. be ... or ... |
| /izaa ... wa-ʔizaa .../ | either ... or ... |
| /izan/ | so, therefore |
| /illaa/ | but, however |
| /innuu/ or /annuu/ | that |
| /ween maa/ | wherever |
| /wa-/ | and |
| /wakit/ | when |
| /wallaa/ | or |
| /yaa ... yaa .../ | either ... or ... |

### 8.2.6 The negative sentence

#### 8.2.6.1 The negative particle /maa/

The negative particle /maa/ is the all-purpose negative particle of SA. It occurs in verbal sentences (/**maa xalleetii leey ḥaaja**/ 'You (fs) haven't left me anything' (Selection 10)) and nominal sentences (/**daa ʃakluu maa ẓariif**/ 'That one (ms), his appearance isn't nice' (Selection 7)).

Speakers of SA use /**maa**/ where speakers of certain other varieties of spoken Arabic do not. One conspicuous example of SA usage of /**maa**/ is the negative imperative. The imperative in SA is negated with /**maa**/, as in /inta yaa ʕargala **maa** djaglib!/ 'Argala, don't chicken out!' (Selection 26).

#### 8.2.6.2 The negative particle /muʃ/ (or /miʃ/)

The negative particle /muʃ/ (or /miʃ/) occurs in SA far less often than /maa/. Some speakers believe it is not authentically Sudanese. The negative particle /muʃ/ usually negates non-verbal constructions, as in /**zamaan bi-nguul leeh ḥisaab muʃ riyaaḍiyyaat**/ 'In the old days, we called it "arithmetic," not "mathematics"' (Selection 6). The most frequent use of /muʃ/, however, is in the confirmation question /**muʃ kidaa?**/ 'Isn't that so?' (see 8.2.7.2).

### 8.2.7 The question

#### 8.2.7.1 The yes-no question

The yes-no question in SA is indicated only by intonation. The speaker's voice rises as it approaches the end of the utterance, as in /**daa kaan fii ʔitneen w-sabʕiin?**/ 'That (ms) was in '72?' (Selection 6).

#### 8.2.7.2 The confirmation question

The confirmation question is another kind of yes-no question. It uses the phrase /**muʃ kidaa?**/ 'Isn't that so?' to request confirmation of a statement. The phrase /**muʃ kidaa?**/ occurs after the statement, as in /**maa daayir taguul leey ḥaaja, muʃ kidaa?**/ 'You (ms) don't want to tell me anything, isn't that right?' (Selection 12).

#### 8.2.7.3 The information question

Questions that ask for information rely on interrogatives to do so (see 7 for a list of the most commonly-used interrogatives of SA). In SA, the use of an interrogative does not require movement within the sentence. That is, the question that uses an interrogative typically has the same structure as the response, as in /**alfakii ʕalii wad minuu?**/ 'Alfaki Ali who? lit. Alfaki Ali son of whom?' compared to /**afakkir alfakii ʕalii wad muusaa**/ 'I think Alfaki Ali Wad Musa, lit. I think Alfaki Ali son of Musa' (Selection 25).

## 9. Markers of organization and attitude

In addition to the types of words discussed, SA has a category we call "markers". Markers are words or phrases that differ from other classes in that they are not well integrated into an utterance through agreement (as are adjectives) or dependence (as are suffixed pronouns). In addition, they do not really affect the content or meaning of the utterance. These markers, however, play two very important roles in utterances. One group of markers consists of devices that organize. Another group is made up of devices that indicate the speaker's attitude. In both groups, translation is not the best indicator of function. For that reason, the English translations of markers in the examples cited are given in italics. Following are some of the more common markers of SA.

## 9.1 Markers of organization

### 9.1.1 /allii huu/ 'that is; namely; that would be'

The form /allii/ in the phrase /allii huu/ 'that is; namely; that would be' is not the relative pronoun of SA (which is /al-/). It is instead part of a phrase that precedes and indicates an explanatory comment. The phrase is usually, but not always, invariable, as in /muʕḍ̣am aʃʃaʕb assuudaanii muʕtamid ʕa-lmuɣtaribiin bitaaʕinnuu, annaas yaʕnii **llii huu** gaaʕdiin fi ʔameeriikaa zayyinaa kidaa/ 'Most of the Sudanese population depends on its (ms) expatriates, people, you know, that would be living in America kind of like us' (Selection 17).

### 9.1.2 /almuhimm/ 'the important thing is; the fact is'

The form /almuhimm/ (with variants) 'the important thing is; the fact is' has two functions in discourse. In many cases, it is resumptive. That is, it indicates a return to the topic at hand after a digression. The sentence /**muhimm** yaʕnii ʕan ṭariig almunaẓẓama, ʕan ṭa ... ṭariigtii lxaaṣṣa b-iiḥaawil ɣaaytuu ʔalgaa ṭariiga/ '*Anyway*, you know, through the organization, by a ..., on my own, I'm trying my best to find a way' (Selection 8) follows the speaker's complaints about how hard it is to find work. At this point, he turns back to describe his applications and interviews to date.

In other cases, the form /almuhimm/ 'the important thing is; the fact is' precedes and indicates an evaluative comment. The same speaker quoted above follows a description of an organization he has applied to with his opinion of the position, in /**ʔalmuhim** yaʕnii hiya waẓiifa ẓariifa ʃwiyya laakin alwaaḥid kaan ligaahaa yakuun xaamma ʃadiid yaʕnii/ '*Anyway*, you know, it's (fs) kind of a nice job. But if a person got it (fs), it (fs) would be really great, you know' (Selection 8).

### 9.1.3 /zaat/ 'self'

The form /zaat/ 'self' takes a suffixed pronoun and adds prominence or emphasis to the word that follows. An utterance such as /maa ʕaarif alwaddaanii ʃinuu **zaatuu** wa-maa ʕaarif ʔanaa **zaatii** lwaddaanii leehuu ʃinuu/ 'I don't know *exactly* what led me here. *Even* I don't know what brought me to him' (Selection 12) illustrates the use of this form.

### 9.1.4 /gaam/ 'so, anyway'

The invariable form /gaam/ 'so, anyway' functions like /almuhimm/ (see 9.1.2). It is a resumptive that indicates the return to the main topic. For example, the statement /baʕdeen **gaam** ... **gaam** b-yibnuu fii, ʔay, kubba kidaa/ 'Well, *anyway* ... *anyway*, they (mp) were building a, yes, a kind of domed tomb' (Selection 25) follows a series of questions about details of place and signals that the speaker is getting back to his story.

### 9.1.5 /maa/ (adds emphasis or prominence; not negative)

In addition to the negative particle /maa/, SA has another particle /maa/ that is homophonous with the negative particle. The /maa/ that is not negative is a particle that adds emphasis or prominence to the phrase it precedes.

An utterance like /dii **maa** ḥaaja kidaa, **maa** b-tiʃbah ḥillatnaa/ 'This (fs) is *really* something, it's (fs) *not* like our village' (Selection 11), containing both uses of /maa/ can best be understood by relying on context. In the flow of speech, the two particles are clearly unlike. The first, in the clause /dii **maa** ḥaaja kidaa/ 'this (fs) is *really* something', is pronounced as part of the word that follows (it is cliticized). It is not stressed, as an independent word or particle usually is. In contrast, the second use of /maa/, in the clause /**maa** b-tiʃbah ḥillatnaa/ 'it's (fs) *not* like our village', has the stress, pitch and volume of an independent word or particle.

## 9.2 Markers of attitude

### 9.2.1 /alḥagiiga/ 'truly, the fact is that'

The word /ḥagiiga/ in the phrase /ah, muʕaayanteen **ḥagiiga**/ 'ah, *actually* two interviews' (Selection 8) indicates and softens the speaker's self-correction. In other contexts, /alḥagiiga/ (or /ḥagiiga/) mitigates a speaker's statement, as in /**alḥagiiga** maa ʃuftum/ '*really*, I haven't seen them' (Selection 26).

### 9.2.2 /balaa/ 'enough of, forget about'

The form /balaa/ makes for a strong statement of disapproval, as in /**balaa** xuuk **balaa** kalaam faariɣ/ '*The hell with* your (fs) brother and this nonsense!' (Selection 19).

### 9.2.3 /daa ... daa/ (exclamatory demonstrative)

The use of /daa/ 'this (ms)' in the sentence /daa banii ʔaadam daa?/ 'Is this (ms) a human being?' (Selection 19) differs from the use of /daa/ as a demonstrative. Here, /daa/ modifies an indefinite noun phrase (/banii ʔaadam/) and it both precedes and follows that noun phrase (/**daa** banii ʔaadam **daa**/ 'Is this (ms) a human being?'). These facts, as well as the context in which /daa/ occurs, indicate that it does not function here as a demonstrative. It is rather a marker that conveys a strong reaction. That reaction may be positive or, as in this case, negative.

### 9.2.4 /kidaa/ 'sort of, more or less'

The form /kidaa/ 'sort of, more or less' has a variety of meanings, the most usual of which is 'thus, in this way'. When it functions as a marker of attitude, /kidaa/ follows a word or phrase to mitigate or soften its meaning, as in /nnaas albusaṭaa kidaa/ 'people who are more or less simple' (Selection 16).

### 9.2.5 /inta/ 'you'

The pronoun /ʔinta/ 'you (ms)' does not always refer to the listener. In a context such as /**inta** zzool daa mnuu?/ 'Who's that man?' (Selection 7), /ʔinta/ 'you (ms)' is instead a marker that gets the listener's attention and underscores the urgency of the speaker's question.

### 9.2.6 /yimkin/ 'maybe'

In the phrase /ʔaktar manṭiga **yimkin**/ 'the greatest region, *maybe*' (Selection 3) the form /yimkin/ (also /imkin/) 'maybe' softens or mitigates the sense of the preceding noun phrase /ʔaktar manṭiga/ 'the greatest region'. In this example, /yimkin/ 'maybe' follows the phrase it modifies. In most cases, however, it precedes the modified word or phrase, as in /fi lʔusar **ʔimkin** arraaɣiyya/ 'in families that are, *maybe*, advanced' (Selection 20). The form /yimkin/ also functions as a pre-verb in its literal sense 'it is possible'.

# Selections

# taʕaaluu natʕarraf ʕalaa suudaaniin[1]

*In this first selection, contestants in a television game show introduce themselves. All of the contestants as well as the audience members come from Artimiry Island near Wadi Halfa in northern Sudan. Further information about Artimiry Island appears in selection 12.*

A: tfaḍḍaluu gaddimuu ʔanfuskum.[2]

B: b-ismi llaah arraḥmaan arraḥiim,[3] ruḍwaan ʕalii xarraaj.[4]

A: naʕam?

C: b-ismi llaa arraḥmaan arraḥiim, lubnaa mḥammad sileemaan, jaamaʕat ʔumm durmaan[5] alʔislaamiyya lfiɣra θθaanya ʔiʕlaam, jiziirat ʔartimiirii.

A: ʕaaʃat alʔasaamii.[6] naʕam?

D: b-ismi llaa rraḥmaan arraḥiim, manaal jaabir ʕabbaas, kulliyya ʃarg anniil ajjaamiʕiyya,[7] taalta tijaara w-bunuuk.

A: naʕam?

E: b-ismi llaa rraḥmaan arraḥiim, muðhar sayyid ʕabd algaadir, jaamaʕat alxurṭuum, jiziirat ʔartimiirii.

A: jiziirat ʔartimiirii, ṭayyib.

# تَعالُوا[1] نَتْعَرَّفْ عَلَى سّودَانِينْ

أ: تْفَضَّلُوا قَدِّمُوا أَنْفُسْكُمْ.[2]

ب: بِسْمِ اللّهْ اَلرَّحْمَنْ اَلرَّحِيمْ،[3] رُضْوَانْ عَلِي خَرَّاجْ.[4]

أ: نَعَمْ؟

ت: بِسْمِ اللّه الرَّحْمَنْ اَلرَّحِيمْ، لُبْنَى مْحَمَّدْ سلَيْمَانْ، جَامَعَةْ أُمّ دُرْمَانْ[5] اَلإِسْلاَمِيَّه اَلْفِغْرَه التَّانْيَهْ إِعْلاَمْ، جِزِيرَةْ أَرْتِمِيري.

أ: عَاشَتْ اَلأَسَامِي.[6] نَعَمْ؟

ث: بِسْمِ اللّه الرَّحْمَنْ اَلرَّحِيمْ، مَنَالْ جَابِرْ عَبَّاسْ، كُلِّيَّهْ شَرْق اَلنِّيلْ اَلجَّامِعِيَّهْ،[7] تَالْتَهْ تِجَارَهْ وْبُنُوكْ.

أ: نَعَمْ؟

ح: بِسْمِ اللّه الرَّحَمَنْ اَلرَّحِيمْ، مُظْهَرْ سَيِّدْ عَبْدْ اَلْقَادِرْ، جَامَعَةْ اَلْخُرْطُومْ، جِزِيرَةْ أَرْتِمِيرِي.

أ: جِزِيرَةْ أَرْتِمِيرِي، طَيِّبْ.

## Vocabulary

**taʕaal** تَعَالْ *vi imperative of* **jaa** *'to come'* come one, let's (do s.t.); come, come here {*fs:* **taʕaalii**, *pl:* **taʕaaluu**}

**itfaḍḍal** اتْفَضَّلْ *vt used in imperative* please, go ahead {*fs:* **itfaḍḍalii**, *pl:* **itfaḍḍaluu**}

**umm durmaan** أُمّ دُرْمَانْ *prop* Omdurman (city across Nile River from Khartoum)

**fiɣra** فِغْرَهْ *nfs* period of study, phase of study; paragraph {*pl:* **fiɣaraat**}

**jiziirat ʔartimiirii** جَزِيرَةْ أَرْتِمِيرِي **[jiziirat ʔartiimiirii; jiziirat ʔartimirii]** *prop* Artimiry Island (near Wadi Halfa in Northern Province)

**alxurṭuum** اَلْخُرْطُومْ **[alxarṭuum]** *prop* Khartoum (capital of Sudan)

**ṭayyib** طَيِّبْ *adj* good, well; all right {*fs:* **ṭayyiba**, *mpl:* **ṭayyibiin**, *fpl:* **ṭayyibaat**}

## Notes

**1** The form /taʕaaluu/ 'come (mp)' in the clause /**taʕaaluu** natʕarraf ʕalaa suudaaniin/ 'let's get to know some Sudanese' is an imperative. It is the imperative of the verb /jaa/ - /yajii/ 'to come'. This irregular (or suppletive) form occurs in SA and other dialects of Arabic.

The imperative /taʕaal/ 'come (ms)' occurs both independently and as a pre-verb, as it does here. As a pre-verb, before a simple imperfect, /taʕaal/ 'come (ms)' means 'come on, let's (do s.t.)'.

**2** The verb /itfaḍḍal/ 'please' typically occurs in the imperative, as it does in the clause /**tfaḍḍaluu** gaddimuu ʔanfuskum/ 'please present (mp) yourselves (mp)'. A second verb may follow /itfaḍḍal/. If so, the second verb is also imperative, as /gaddimuu/ 'present (mp)' is here, /tfaḍḍaluu **gaddimuu** ʔanfuskum/ 'please present (mp) yourselves (mp)'.

In spite of its imperative form /itfaḍḍal/ is an invitation. The speaker uses /itfaḍḍal/ to prompt or urge the listener to an action that benefits the listener, such as sitting down, taking a serving of food, or introducing herself. When asking a favor, the speaker instead uses /min faḍlak/ 'please (ms)'.

**3** The invocation of the divine, /bismi llaa rraḥmaan arraḥiim/ 'in the name of God, the merciful and compassionate', begins activities of many kinds.

**4** The three parts are, first, the speaker's given name (/ruḍwaan/), followed by the name of the speaker's father (/ʕalii/), which is then followed by the name of the speaker's grandfather or a family name (/**xarraaj**/). This is one of several naming practices used by speakers of Arabic.

**5** The city of /**ʔumm durmaan**/ 'Omdurman' is located across the Nile River from Khartoum. With Khartoum and North Khartoum, it forms a metropolitan area called "The Three Towns" or "The Tripartite Capital" (al-ʕaaṣima al-musallasa). Within that area, Khartoum has traditionally been viewed as the official and administrative capital of Sudan, North Khartoum the commercial hub, and Omdurman the cultural center.

**6** The phrase /**ʕaaʃat alʔasaamii**/ 'may you live long, lit. may the names live' is the speaker's response to hearing a name or names he recognizes. Conventional courtesies such as this frequently use the perfect to describe a hope, desire, or wish as though it had already happened. This use of the perfect is known as the optative.

**7** This speaker here says /**kulliyya ʃarg anniil ajjaamiʕiyya**/ 'Eastern Nile University College'. She fails to pronounce the final /t/ of /**kulliyya**/ 'college' as would be usual in the construct phrase (/**kulliyyat ʃarg anniil**/).

# jayyatii lii-waaʃinṭun

*The speaker here describes the long trip from Sudan to Washington. Her speaking style is mainly SA, but her pronunciation and vocabulary both show formal or MSA influence. See note 6 for one example of a self-correction that shifts from informal to more formal.*

jayyatii lii-waaʃinṭun[1] kaanat ka-lʔaatii: ʔawwal ḥaaja ʔitḥarraknaa min assuudaan ʃahri tamanya[2] ʔa ... w-maʃeenaa ʔa ... nayruubii, gaʕadnaa fii nayruubii taɣriiban ʃahareen,[3] ʔa ... yoom tizʕa[4] wu-ʕiʃriin tizʕa bi-ẓẓabṭ assaaʕa waaḥda bi-lleel ʔa ... taḥarraknaa lii-waaʃinṭun ʔa ... bii-ʔalxuṭuuṭ alja ... albaljiikiyya ʔa ... ʔa ... nazalnaa fii baljiikaa taɣriiban zayy saaḥteen[5] kidaa dayya, baʕd daaka ʔatḥarraknaa min baljiikaa, nazalnaa fii niiyoork. ʔa ... min niiyoork, waṣalnaa niiyoork zayy assaaʕa waaḥda ḍuhuur ʔa ... gaʕadnaa fiihaa masaafa, mudda yaʕnii,[6, 7] baʕd daaka tḥarraknaa li-waaʃinṭun llii huu waṣalnaahaa zayy assaaʕa sabʕa[8, 9] bi-lleel yaʕnii rriḥla taɣriiban kaanat min assaaʕa waaḥda bi-lleel la-ɣaayat taanii yoom[10] assaaʕa sabʕa bi-lmisaa min nayruubii lii-waaʃinṭun. kaanat riḥla ḥilwa jiddan jiddan ʔa ... bass mutʕiba ʃwayya liʔannuu ṭabʕan almasaafa ṭawiila ʔaxadat zayy taɣriiban ṭamanṭaaʃar[11] saaʕa ʔa ... laakin ʕumuuman yaʕnii kaanat arriḥla ḥilwa. ṭabʕan kaan maʕaay zoojii wa ... ʔaḥlaa fiihaa ḥaaja[12] ʔa ... ʔinnuu yaʕnii nazalnaa fii baljiikaa, baljiikaa kaanat ḥilwa ʃadiid raɣm innuu maa ṭalaʕnaa min almaṭaar laakin ʕumuuman yaʕnii mim -baʕiid kidaa zzool kaan yaʕnii bruksil ʔaxad fikra ʕannaa ʔinnaa balad ḥilwa[13] jiddan jiddan. fii niiyoork barḍuu maa ṭalaʕnaa[14] min almaṭaar laakin ʔa ... ʕirifnaa ḥaaja barḍuu yaʕnii taɣriiban min azzaḥma bitaaḥt annaas[15] u-kidaa daa ʕirifnaa ḥaaja ʕan

# جَيَّتِي لِيوَاشِنْطُنْ

جَيَّتِي لِيوَاشِنْطُنْ[1] كَانَتْ كَالآتِي: أَوَّلْ حَاجَهْ إِتْحَرَّكْنَا مِنْ اَلسُّودَانْ شَهْر تَمَنْيَهْ[2] أَ ... وْمَشَيْنَا أَ ... نَيْرُوبِي، قَعَدْنَا فِي نَيْرُوبِي تَغْرِيبًا شَهَرَيْنْ،[3] أَ ... يَوْمْ تِزْعَهْ[4] وُعِشْرِينْ تِزْعَهْ بِالظَّبْطْ اَلسَّاعَهْ وَاحْدَهْ بِاللَّيْلْ أَ ... تَحَرَّكْنَا لِيوَاشِنْطُنْ أَ ... بِيأَلْخُطُوطْ اَلْجَ... اَلْبَلْجِيكِيَّهْ أَ ... أَ ... نَزَلْنَا فِي بَلْجِيكَا تَغْرِيبًا زَيّ سَاحْتَيْنْ[5] كِدَا دِيَّا، بَعْدْ دَاكَ أَتْحَرَّكْنَا مِنْ بَلْجِيكَا، نَزَلْنَا فِي نِيَّوْرْكْ. أَ ... مِنْ نِيَّوْرْكْ، وَصَلْنَا نِيَّوْرْكْ زَيّ اَلسَّاعَهْ وَاحْدَهْ ضُهُورْ أَ ... قَعَدْنَا فِيهَا مَسَافَهْ، مُدَّهْ يَعْنِي،[6, 7] بَعْدْ دَاكَ تْحَرَّكْنَا لِوَاشِنْطُنْ اللِّي هُو وَصَلْنَاهَا زَيّ اَلسَّاعَهْ سَبْعَهْ[8, 9] بِاللَّيْلْ يَعْنِي الرِّحْلَهْ تَغْرِيبًا كَانَتْ مِنْ اَلسَّاعَهْ وَاحْدَهْ بِاللَّيْلْ لَغَايَةْ تَانِي يَوْمْ[10] اَلسَّاعَهْ سَبْعَهْ بِالْمِسَا مِنْ نَيْرُوبِي لِيوَاشِنْطُنْ. كَانَتْ رِحْلَهْ حِلْوَهْ جِدّاً جِدّاً أَ ... بَسّ مُتْعِبَهْ شْوَيَّهْ لأَنُّهْ طَبْعًا اَلْمَسَافَهْ طَوِيلَهْ أَخَدَتْ زَيّ تَغْرِيبًا طَمَنْطَاشَرْ[11] سَاعَهْ أَ ... لَكِنْ عُمُومًا يَعْنِي كَانَتْ اَلرِّحْلَهْ حِلْوَهْ. طَبْعًا كَانْ مَعَاي زَوْجِي وَ... أَحْلَى فِيهَا حَاجَهْ[12] أَ ... إِنّهُ يَعْنِي نَزَلْنَا فِي بَلْجِيكَا، بَلْجِيكَا كَانَتْ حِلْوَهْ شَدِيدْ رَغْمْ اِنّهُ مَا طَلَعْنَا مِنْ اَلْمَطَارْ لَكِنْ عُمُومًا يَعْنِي مِمْ -بَعِيدْ كِدَا الزَّوْلْ كَانْ يَعْنِي بْرُكْسِلْ أَخَدْ فِكْرَهْ عَنّهَا إِنّهَا بَلَدْ حِلْوَهْ[13] جِدّاً جِدّاً. فِي نِيَّوْرْكْ بَرْضُهْ مَا طَلَعْنَا[14] مِنْ اَلْمَطَارْ لَكِنْ أَ ... عِرِفْنَا حَاجَهْ بَرْضُهْ يَعْنِي تَغْرِيبًا مِنْ اَلزَّحْمَهْ بِتَاحْةْ اَلنَّاس[15] أُكِدَا دَا عِرِفْنَا حَاجَهْ عَنْ

albalad fi lmaṭaar. ʔa … hassa ʔa … yaʕnii fii waaʃinṭun waṣalnaa ssaaʕa tamaanya bi-lleel ʔaw sabʕa w-nuṣṣ ʔa … kaan al … jjaww yaʕnii baarid ʃwayya maa gdirnaa nistamtaʕ yaʕnii bii-wuṣuulnaa lii-waaʃinṭun ʔillaa ʔa … yaʕnii baʕd maa ʔistaɣarreenaa w-kidaa dayya.

اَلْبَلَدْ فِالْمَطَارْ. أَ ... هَسَّهْ أَ ... يَعْنِي فِي وَاشِنْطُنْ وَصَلْنَا السَّاعَهْ تَمَانْيَهْ بِاللَّيْلْ أَوْ سَبْعَهْ وْنُصّ أَ ... كَانْ اَلْـ... الجَّوّ يَعْنِي بَارِدْ شْوَيَّهْ مَا قْدِرْنَا نِسْتَمْتَعْ يَعْنِي بِيوُصُولْنَا لِيوَاشِنْطُنْ إِلاَّ أَ ... يَعْنِي بَعْدْ مَا إِسْتَغَرَّيْنَا وْكِدَا دَيَّا.

## Vocabulary

**jaa** جَا *vt irregular conjugation* to come, arrive {*imperf:* **yajii**, *vn:* **jayya**}

**li-** لِ **[la-; lee-; lii-]** *prep* to, for; to have been for (amount of time)

**ḥaaja** حَاجَهْ *nfs* thing, something {*pl:* **ḥaajaat**}

**itḥarrak** اتْحَرَّكْ *vi* to depart, leave; to go; to move {*imperf:* **yitḥarrak**, *vn:* **ḥaraka**}

**assuudaan** اَلسُّودَانْ *prop nms* Sudan

**ʃahri tamaanya** شَهَرِ تَمَانْيَهْ **[ʃahri tamanya]** August *(lit. month eight)*

**maʃaa** مَشَى *vt* to go; to go to; to leave {*imperf:* **yamʃii**, *vn:* **maʃii**}

**gaʕad** قَعَدْ *vi* to stay, remain; to sit {*imperf:* **yagʕud**, *vn:* **guʕaad**}

**yoom** يَوْمْ *nms* day {*pl:* **ayaam**}

**bi-ẓẓabṭ** بِالظَّبْطْ **[bi-ððabṭ; bi-ḍḍabṭ]** exactly, precisely

**zayy-** زَيّ **[zeey]** *prep* about, approximately, something like; like, as

**kidaa** كِدَا **[kadii]** *adv* sort of, more or less

**daaka** دَاكَ **[daak]** *pron ms* that, far demonstrative {*ms:* **daak**, *fs:* **diik**, *pl:* **deelak**}

**ḍuhur** ضُهُرْ **[ḍuhuur]** *nms* afternoon

**masaafa** مَسَافَهْ *nfs* a long time; a long distance {*pl:* **masaafaat**}

**yaʕnii** يَعْنِي *interj invariable* you know, I mean, that is *(lit. it means)*

**allii huu** اَللِّي هُوَ **[allii huwa]** *disc marker also invariable* that is; namely; that would be (precedes and indicates explanatory comment) {*fs:* **allii hiya**, *mpl:* **allii hum**, *fpl:* **allii hin**}

**taanii** تَانِي *adj* next; another; second {*fs:* **taaniya**, *mpl:* **taanyiin**, *fpl:* **taanyaat**}

**ḥilwa** حِلو *adj* nice; pretty; sweet {*fs:* **ḥilwa,** *mpl:* **ḥilwiin,** *fpl:* **ḥilwaat**}

**bass** بَسّ *conj* but; only, solely

**ʃwayya** شْوَيَّة **[ʃwiyya]** *adv* somewhat, a bit

**liʔannuu** لأنَّهُ **[liyannuu; liʔinnuu; laʔannuu]** *conj invariable* because, on account of; so that

**innuu** انَّهُ *conj invariable* that

**ʃadiid** شَدِيد *adv* very, extremely; frequently; a lot

**ṭalaʕ** طَلَع *vt* to exit, leave; to get up, stand up; to turn out to be; to go up, ascend {*imperf:* **yaṭlaʕ,** *vn:* **ṭuluuʕ**}

**maa** ما *particle* not

**zool** زُول *nms* individual, person; friend, pal, buddy {*fs:* **zoola,** *pl:* **naas**}

**balad** بَلَد *nfs, also nms* country, nation {*pl:* **bilaad**}

**barḍuu** بَرْضُو **[barðuu; barduu]** *adv* also, too; nevertheless, even so

**bitaaʕ** بِتاع *adj possessive* of, belonging to; about, approximately {*fs:* **bitaaʕa,** *mpl:* **bitaaʕiin,** *fpl:* **bitaaʕaat**}

**daa** دا *pron ms* this, near demonstrative {*ms:* **daa,** *fs:* **dii,** *pl:* **deel**}

**wa-kidaa daa** وكِدا دا **[wa-kidaa dayya; wa-kidaa]** *invariable* and so on, etcetera

**hassa** هَسَّة **[hassaʕ; hassii]** *adv* now; just now

**nuṣṣ** نُصّ *nms* half {*pl:* **anṣaaṣ**}

**gidir** قِدِر *vi pre-verb* to be able to {*imperf:* **yagdar,** *vn:* **gudra**}

**istamtaʕ** اِسْتَمْتَع *vt* to enjoy {*imperf:* **yistamtaʕ,** *vn:* **istimtaaʕ**}

**wa-kidaa dayya** وكِدا دَيّ **[wa-kidaa daa; wa-kidaa]** *invariable* or so, something like that

## Notes

**1** Note the preposition used in the phrase /lii-waaʃinṭun/ 'to Washington'. SA, like certain other varieties of spoken Arabic, uses a single preposition /li-/ (also /la-/, /lii-/, and /lee-/) 'to' where MSA has ʔilaa 'to' and li- 'for; to'.

**2** In addition to western names for the months of the solar calendar, SA and certain other varieties of Arabic name months by number, as in /ʃahri tamanya/ 'August, lit. month eight'. The count begins in January with /ʃahri **waaḥid**/ 'month one', making August /ʃahri **tamaanya**/ 'month eight'.

Note also that this speaker says /**tamanya**/ 'eight' here, with a short /a/ in the second syllable, but /**tamaanya**/ 'eight' later, with a long /aa/ in the second syllable. In careful speech /**tamaanya**/ occurs because SA usually keeps a long vowel even in a syllable that ends in a consonant.

**3** The clause /**gaʕadnaa fii nayroobii taɣriiban ʃahareen**/ 'we stayed in Nairobi for about two months' illustrates two of the ways speakers of SA pronounce the Arabic letter ق. They are /**gaʕadnaa**/ 'we stayed' (compare MSA qaʕadnaa 'we sat; we stayed') and /**taɣriiban**/ 'approximately' (compare MSA taqriiban 'approximately'). The letter ق most often has the sound /g/ (voiced velar stop); the sound /ɣ/ (voiced velar fricative) tends to occur in recent borrowings from MSA. The variant /k/ (voiceless velar stop) sometimes occurs, and /q/ (voiceless uvular stop) may occur in careful or formal speech.

**4** The word /tizʕa/ 'nine' is an example of assimilation, one sound becoming like another. In rapid speech, as here, /tisʕa/ 'nine' may be pronounced /tizʕa/, with /z/ in place of /s/. The influence of /ʕ/ (voiced pharyngeal fricative) on the preceding /s/ (voiceless alveolar fricative) causes /s/ to be pronounced /z/ (voiced alveolar fricative).

**5** The form /saaḥteen/ 'two hours' derives from /saaʕateen/ 'two hours' as a result of two sound changes. One sound change eliminates a short unstressed vowel in an open syllable (/**saaʕateen**/ > /saaʕteen/). In the other, assimilation occurs when /ʕ/ (voiced pharyngeal fricative) becomes its voiceless counterpart /ḥ/ (/saaʕteen/ > /saaḥteen/).

**6** This speaker corrects herself in the phrase /**masaafa, mudda yaʕnii**/ 'a long time, a period of time, you know'. She replaces the less common usage /**masaafa**/ 'long time' with the more common /**mudda**/ 'period of time'. Note, however, that SA and certain other varieties of Arabic use /**masaafa**/ for time as well as space.

**7** The speaker's use of /yaʕnii/ 'you know, lit. it (ms) means' here is typical of SA and certain other varieties of spoken Arabic. For the most part, this form covers up hesitations, fills in gaps in talk, and holds the speaker's turn in conversation. That is, it functions like the phrases "you know" and "I mean" do in American English. In other cases, /yaʕnii/ indicates a clarification, as it does in /**yaʕnii rriḥla taɣriiban kaanat min assaaʕa waḥda bi-lleel la-ɣaayat taani yoom assaaʕa sabʕa bi-misaa**/ 'this means that the trip was, approximately, from one o'clock in the morning until the next day at seven o'clock in the evening'.

**8** The item /(a)llii/ (or /illii/) in /**waaʃinṭun llii huu waṣalnaahaa zayy assaaʕa sabʕa**/ 'Washington, which we reached at about seven o'clock' looks like the relative pronoun occurring in certain other varieties of spoken Arabic. Speakers of SA may, in fact, use /**allii**/ as a relative pronoun in more formal speech. The use of /**allii**/ in informal speech, however, is limited to explanatory comments such as this one. The phrase /**allii huu**/ here is invariable; it does not agree in gender with its referent, the grammatically FS proper noun /**waaʃinṭun**/ 'Washington'. In other cases, the pronoun following /**allii**/ agrees in number and gender with the referent, as in /**kaaduglii** llii **hiya** **maɣar ʕamal alwaalid ḥaaliyyan**/ 'Kadugli, which is where my father works now'.

**9** SA and certain other varieties of spoken Arabic typically tell time as the speaker does here, /**assaaʕa sabʕa**/ 'seven o'clock'. The number has its invariable cardinal (used in counting) form and is indefinite. In contrast, MSA tells time with a noun-adjective phase, where the number is an ordinal (number used for ordering) that modifies the noun that is the unit of time (for example, al-saaʕa al-saabiʕa 'seven o'clock').

**10** The word /**taanii**/ 'second' in the phrase /**taanii yoom**/ 'the next day' looks like the elative in a phrase like /**ʔaḥlaa ḥaaja**/ 'the nicest thing'. That is, the modifier does not inflect for gender or number. It also precedes the noun, which is indefinite. In other words, the ordinal here acts as the first noun of a construct phrase. This use of ordinal numbers (used for ordering) occurs in SA and certain other varieties of spoken Arabic.

**11** The number /**ṭamanṭaaʃar**/ 'eighteen' illustrates how the numbers 11 – 19 in SA and certain other varieties of spoken Arabic differ from those of MSA. The numbers of spoken Arabic are compound words, not two distinct words as in MSA (θamaaniya ʕaʃar 'eighteen'). These compounds have lost some sounds present in the MSA numbers and, in addition, have pharyngealized sounds where MSA does not. Finally, the numbers 11 – 19 in spoken Arabic are invariable; they do not inflect for gender.

**12** The phrase /**ʔaḥlaa fiihaa ḥaaja**/ 'the nicest thing about it (fs), lit. the nicest about it (fs) thing' is unusual because of the position of the prepositional phrase /**fiihaa**/ 'about it (fs)'. The elative /**ʔaḥlaa**/ 'nicest' and the noun it modifies, /**ḥaaja**/ 'thing', together form a construct phrase, /**ʔaḥlaa ḥaaja**/ 'the nicest thing'. The construct phrase is typically an unbroken unit. Here, however, /**fiihaa**/ 'about it (fs)' intrudes on the construct phrase in what appears to be a slip of the tongue.

**13** In the phrase /**balad ḥilwa**/ 'a nice country', a grammatically F adjective /**ḥilwa**/ 'nice' modifies the noun /**balad**/ 'country'. The noun /**balad**/ 'country' belongs to a small group of nouns that SA and varieties of Arabic treat as either grammatically FS or grammatically MS.

**14** The particle /**maa**/ in the statement /**maa ṭalaʕnaa**/ 'we did not leave' is a negative particle. It may negate a verb in the imperfect as well as the perfect; it also negates non-verbal structures. SA differs from MSA and from certain other varieties of spoken Arabic in that /**maa**/ is the most-used negative particle.

**15** The possessive adjective /**bitaaʕ**/ 'of, belonging to' (see selection 2, note 5 on the sound change that results in /**bitaaḫt**/) links two nouns, as in /**azzaḥma bitaaḫt annaas**/ 'the crowds of people'. Note that the possessive adjective agrees in number and gender with the noun it modifies, that is, with the thing possessed, although it does not agree in definiteness. The possessive adjective construction exists in SA alongside the construct phrase familiar in MSA (<u>zaḥmat al-naas</u> 'the crowds of people').

# zikraayaat aṣṣibaa

*In this selection, the speaker talks about his childhood. The somewhat formal language he uses draws on MSA as well as SA. The influence of MSA is especially noticeable in the pronunciation of /θ/, /ð/, and /ð̣/ (interdental fricatives) and in the use of words like /ḥaaliyyan/ 'presently'.*

ʔa … ʔanaa ṭabaʕan[1] naʃ … ʔa … naʃʔatii, twalatta[2] fii ʔa … alxurṭuum haaðaa ʔalf u-tisʕumiyya w-sittiin, ʔalwaalid ṭabʕan kaan ʃaɣɣaal fi lxurṭuum fii … ka-musaaʕid ṭibbii. ʔalwakit daak kaanuu b-inaggiluu[3] fiihum ʃadiid.[4] baʕad maa twalatta ṭawwaalii gaamuu nagaluu waaldii[5] lii-januub kurdufaan fii ḥitta ʔismaa[6] haybaan yaʕnii madiina ṣaɣiira kidaa. fa … fi lmadiina dii ṭabaʕan ʃaahitta l … bi-jadd annaʃʔa bitaaʕtii kaanat hinaak llii hiya ɣarya sukkaanaa zeey θalaaθa ʔarbaʕa ʔalf nasma kidaa. fa … yaʕnii kaanat fatra jamiila jiddan jiddan u-lwaalid ṭabʕan kaan ʃaɣɣaal fil … fil … ʃʃafaxaana hiya ṭabaʕan kaanat akbar wiḥda ṣaḥḥiyya fi lmanṭiga ṭabʕan u-huwa kaan ʕalaa raas aʃʃafaxaana[7] dii. fa-lmuhim kaanat ʔayyaam jamiila[8] yaʕnii wu-fi lmanṭiga nafsaa hii … yaʕnii ʔa … twaladuu mu … ʔaxwaanii kullum taɣriiban ʔallii huu ʔal … ʔaḥmad allakbar minnii[9] kaan mawjuud w-itwalad ʔiibraahiim w-itwaladat θuriyyaa w-ʕawaaṭif u-ṣalaaḥ u-ballaa w-ajjeelii.[10] ʔa … lmuhim yaʕnii kunnaa ʔusra zayy maa taguul mutmaaska ʃadiid ʔa … laakin ṭabaʕan ḥasab ð̣uruuf al … al … ʔalḥarb u-lmaʃaagil alḥaaṣla fi ssuudaan ṭabʕan ʔiṭṭarruu ʔalwaalid ʔitnagal li-lʔubayyiḍ. u-naʃʔatnaa barð̣uu kaanat, ʔaxadnaa fatra ṭawiila fi lʔubayyiḍ wu-rajaʕnaa li-lmanṭiɣa taanii wa-ḥaaliyyan hassii lwaalid ṭabʕan wa … w-alʔusra mustaɣirra fii, been alxurṭuum wa … ʔa … kaaduglii llii hiya lma … maɣar ʕamal alwaalid ḥaaliyyan. ʔa

# زِكْرايَاتْ الصِّبَا

أَ... أَنَا طَبَعًا[1] نَشْ... أَ... نَشْأَتِي، تْوَلَتَّ[2] فِي أَ... اَلْخُرْطُومْ هَذَا أَلْفْ أُتِسْعُمِيَّهْ وْسِتِّينْ، أَلْوَالِدْ طَبْعًا كَانْ شَغَّالْ فَالْخُرْطُومْ فِي... كَمُسَاعِدْ طِبِّي. أَلْوَكِتْ دَاكْ كَانُوا بِنَقِّلُوا[3] فِيهُمْ شَدِيدْ.[4] بَعَدْ مَا تْوَلَتَّ طَوَّالِي قَامُوا نَقَلُوا وَالْدِي[5] لِيجَنُوبْ كُرْدُفَانْ فِي حِتَّهْ إِسْمَهَا[6] هَيْبَانْ يَعْنِي مَدِينَهْ صَغِيرَهْ كِدَا. فَـ... فَالْمَدِينَهْ دِي طَبَعًا شَاهِتَّ لْـ... بِجَدّ اَلنَّشْأَهْ بِتَاعْتِي كَانَتْ هِنَاكْ اللِّي هِيَ غَرْيَهْ سُكَّانْهَا زَيّ ثَلَاثَهْ أَرْبَعَهْ أَلْفْ نَسْمَهْ كِدَا. فَـ... يَعْنِي كَانَتْ فَتْرَهْ جَمِيلَهْ جِدّاً جِدّاً أُلْوَالِدْ طَبْعًا كَانْ شَغَّالْ فَالْـ... فَالْـ... الشَّفَخَانَهْ هِيَ طَبَعًا كَانَتْ اَكْبَرْ وِحْدَهْ صَحِّيَّهْ فَالْمَنْطِقَهْ طَبْعًا أُهُوَ كَانْ عَلَى رَاسْ اَلشَّفَخَانَه[7] دِي. فَالْمُهِمْ كَانَتْ أَيَّامْ جَمِيلَهْ[8] يَعْنِي وُفَالْمَنْطِقَهْ نَفْسْهَا هِي... يَعْنِي أَ... تْوَلَدُوا مُـ... أَخْوَانِي كُلّهُمْ تَغْرِيبًا أَللِّي هُو أَلْـ... أَحْمَدْ الأَكْبَرْ مِنِّي[9] كَانْ مَوْجُودْ وِاتْوَلَدْ إِيبْرَاهِيمْ وِاتْوَلَدَتْ ثُرِيَّا وْعَوَاطِفْ أُصَلَاحْ أُبَلاَّ وَالجَّيْلِي.[10] أَ... الْمُهِمْ يَعْنِي كُنَّا أُسْرَهْ زَيّ مَا تَقُولْ مُتْمَاسْكَهْ شَدِيدْ. أَ... لَكِنْ طَبَعًا حَسَبْ ظُرُوفْ اَلْـ... اَلْـ... أَلْحَرْبْ أُلْمَشَاكِلْ اَلْحَاصْلَهْ فَالسُّودَانْ طَبْعًا إِطَّرُّوا أَلْوَالِدْ إِتْنَقَلْ لِلأُبَيِّضْ. أُنَشْأَتْنَا بَرْظُهْ كَانَتْ، أَخَدْنَا فَتْرَهْ طَوِيلَهْ فَالأُبَيِّضْ وُرَجَعْنَا لِلْمَنْطِغَهْ تَانِي وَحَالِيّاً هَسِّي الْوَالِدْ طَبْعًا وَ... وَالأُسْرَهْ مُسْتَغِرَّهْ فِي، بَيْنْ اَلْخُرْطُومْ وَ... أَ... كَادُقْلِي اللِّي هِيَ الْمَـ... مَغَرَ عَمَلْ اَلْوَالِدْ حَالِيّاً. أَ

... ʔalmanṭiga llii naʃaʔta fiihaa ṭabʕan manṭiga zayy maa tguul yaʕnii ʔaktar manṭiga yimkin[11] la-ḥaddii llaḥza dii b-adzakkaraa kulla yoom yaʕnii.[12] w-ʔaktar ʔumniyya ʕindii hassii bass ʔatmannaa ʔinnii ʔaḥaggigaa ʔinnii ʔazuur almanṭiga dii liʔannahuu yaʕnii ʔirtabaṭat fiihaa zikraayaat bitaaʕat aṣṣibaa w-ʔaṣdigaa w-annaʃʔa. w-alwaaḥid[13] awwal maa tfataḥ fii ddunyaa dii tfataḥ fii lmanṭiga dii w-ʃaafaa w-ʕirif alḥayaa fiiyaa w-ḥattaa nnaas yaʕnii ʔal ... ʔal ... ʔalʔusra w-alʔahal alhinaay fa ... ʕaʃaan kidaa yaʕnii ʔatmannaa ʔinnii ʔazuuraa yaʕnii.

... أَلْمَنْطِقَه اللِّي نَشَأْتَ فِيهَا طَبْعًا مَنْطِقَهْ زَيّ مَا تْقُولْ يَعْنِي
أَكْتَرْ مَنْطِقَهْ يِمْكِنْ[11] لَحَدِّي اللَّحْزَهْ دِي بَادْزَكَّرْهَا كُلَّ يَوْمْ يَعْنِي.[12]
وْأَكْتَرْ أُمْنِيَّهْ عِنْدِي هَسِّي بَسّ أَتْمَنَّى إِنِّي أَحَقِّقْهَا إِنِّي أَزُورْ
اَلْمَنْطِقَهْ دِي لأَنَّهُ يَعْنِي إِرْتَبَطَتْ فِيهَا زِكْرَيَاتْ بِتَاعَتْ اَلصِّبَا
وْأَصْدِقَا وَالنَّشْأَهْ. وَالْوَاحِدْ[13] اَوَّلْ مَا تْفَتَحْ فِي الدُّنْيَا دِي تْفَتَحْ
فِي الْمَنْطِقَهْ دِي وْشَافْهَا وْعِرِفْ اَلْحَيَاهْ فِيِيَا وْحَتَّى النَّاسْ يَعْنِي
أَلْ...  أَلْ...  أَلأُسْرَهْ وَالأَهَلْ اَلْهِنَاي فَ...  عَشَانْ كِدَا يَعْنِي
أَتْمَنَّى إِنِّي أَزُورْهَا يَعْنِي.

## Vocabulary

**itwalad** اِتْوَلَدْ *vi* to be born {*imperf:* **yitwalid**, *vn:* **wilaada**}

**ʃaɣɣaal** شَغَّالْ *adj* working {*fs:* **ʃaɣɣaala**, *mpl:* **ʃaɣɣaaliin**, *fpl:* **ʃaɣɣaalaat**}

**ka-** كَ *prep* in the capacity of

**wakit** وَكِتْ *nms* time; period of time; point in time {*pl:* **awkaat**}

**daak** دَاكْ **[daaka]** *pron ms* that, far demonstrative {*ms:* **daak**, *fs:* **diik**, *pl:* **deelak**}

**bi-** بِ **[b-; bii-]** *particle* prefix of imperfect verb indicating simple present, habitual present, or future, depending on context

**ṭawwaalii** طَوَّالِي *adv* immediately, right away; always, continuously

**gaam (gumta)** (قُمْتَ) قَامْ *vi pre-verb, agrees in number, gender, and tense with main verb* to up and (do s.t.), suddenly (do); to get up (in order to do s.t.); to wake up, get up; to do, go ahead and do (as a consequence or result of a previously described event); to get up, stand up {*imperf:* **yaguum**, *vn:* **goom**}

**januub kurdufaan** جَنُوبْ كُرْدُفَانْ *prop* Janub Kordofan, Southern Kordofan Province

**ḥitta** حِتَّهْ *nfs* place, locale; situation, condition; portion, piece {*pl:* **ḥitat**}

**haybaan** هَيْبَانْ *prop* Hayban (town in Southern Kurdufan Province)

**dii** دِي **[diyyat; diyya; dih]** *pron fs* this, near demonstrative {*ms:* **daa**, *fs:* **dii**, *pl:* **deel**}

**ʃaahad** شَاهَدْ **[ʃaahid]** *vt* to experience, witness {*imperf:* **yaʃaahid**, *vn:* **muʃaahada**}

**hinaak** هِنَاكْ *pron* there

**zeey** زَيّ **[zayy]** *prep* approximately, about

**ʃafaxaana** شَفَخَانَةْ *nfs* clinic {*pl:* **ʃafaxaanaat**}

**wiḥda** وِحْدَةْ *nfs* regional center, local center; unit, basic unit {*pl:* **wiḥdaat**}

**almuhim** اَلْمُهِمْ **[(al)muhim(ma); (al)mihimm]** *disc marker* the important thing is; the fact is (indicates return to topic after digression; precedes and indicates evaluative comment)

**al-** اَلْ *pron; invariable relative pronoun* who, which, that

**mawjuud** مَوْجُودْ **[moojuud]** *adj* present; alive; available {*fs:* **mawjuuda**, *mpl:* **mawjuudiin**, *fpl:* **mawjuudaat**}

**zayy-** زَيّ **[zeey]** *prep* like, as; about, approximately, something like

**zayy maa** زَيّ مَا **[zeey maa]** *conj* as

**zayy maa taguul** زَيّ مَا تَقُولْ as they say *(lit. as you would say)*

**iṭṭarra** اِطَّرّ *vt* to force (s.o. to do s.th.) {*imperf:* **yiṭṭarr**, *vn:* **iṭṭiraar**}

**itnagal** اِتْنَقَلْ *vi* to be transferred, moved {*imperf:* **yitnagil**, *vn:* **nagliyya**}

**alʔubayyiḍ** اَلأُبَيِّضْ *prop* al-Ubayyid (capital of Northern Kordofan Province)

**barḍ̱uu** بَرْظُو **[barḍuu; barduu]** *adv* also, too

**axad** اَخَدْ *vt* to take, spend (time); to take up to use; to take, receive {*imperf:* **yaaxud**, *vn:* **axid**}

**taanii** تَانِي *adv* again, another time; also, as well

**hassii** هَسِّي **[hassaʕ; hassa]** *adv* now; just now

**kaaduglii** (كَادُجْلِي) كَادُقْلِي *prop* Kadugli (city in Southern Kordofan Province)

**maɣarr** مَغَرّ *nms* site, place; headquarters {*pl:* **maɣaar**, **maɣarraat**}

**maɣar ʕamal** مَغَرْ عَمَلْ work place {*pl:* **maɣaar ʕamal**, **maɣaaraat ʕamal**}

**illii** اِلّي *pron invariable relative pronoun* who, which, that

**yimkin** يِمْكِنْ *disc marker invariable; also variable pre-verb* maybe *(lit. it is possible)*

**li-ḥaddi** لِحَدّ **[la-ḥaddii]** *conj* until, up to

**bass** بَسّ *adv* only, solely; but

**itfataḥ** اِتْفَتَح *vi* to be opened, opened up {*imperf:* **yitfatiḥ**, *vn:* **fatiḥ**}

**itfataḥ fii ddunya** اِتْفَتَح في الدُّنْيا to grow up; to become aware of the world around one *(lit. to open up to the world)* {*imperf:* **yitfatiḥ fii ddunya**, *vn:* **fatiḥ fii ddunya**}

**ʃaaf (ʃufta)** شَاف (شُفْتَ) *vt* to see; to find, get; to understand, get, see {*imperf:* **yaʃuuf**, *vn:* **ʃoof**}

**ahal** أهَل *nmpl* family, relatives, kin *(lit. people)* {*pl:* **ahaalii**}

**hinaay** هنَاي *nms* thingamabob, what do you call it; what's his name; etcetera {*fs:* **hinaaya**, *pl:* **hinaayaat**}

**ʕaʃaan** عَشَان *conj* because, because of; to, in order to

**kidaa** كدَا *pron* this, that

## Notes

1 The second /a/ of /ṭabaʕan/ 'of course' is an epenthetic or helping vowel. It may be inserted between two consonants where one of them is /ʕ/, /ɣ/, /x/, /ḥ/, or /h/.

2 The verb /twalatta/ 'I was born' derives from /itwaladta/, with assimilation of /d/ (voiced dental stop) to /t/ (voiceless dental stop). The derived form of this verb, it$C_1$a$C_2$a$C_3$, occurs in SA and certain other varieties of spoken Arabic. As it does here, this form has a passive meaning, where the subject of the verb undergoes rather than performs an action.
Note also that the final /a/ makes /twalatta/ 'I was born' homophonous with /twalatta/ 'you (ms) were born'. The final /a/ of /twalatta/ does not indicate number, person, or gender; it is not an inflection. It is a helping or epenthetic vowel that prevents this word from ending in a sequence of two consonants.

3 The imperfect usually occurs with the imperfect /bi-/ prefix, as it does here in /**b**-inaggiluu/ 'they (mp) transfer, they (mp) are transferring'. The meaning of the prefixed imperfect depends on context. Here, it indicates ongoing action: 'they (mp) transfer' or 'they (mp) are transferring'. In contrast to the prefixed imperfect, the simple imperfect has no prefix (/yinaggiluu/ 'they (mp) transfer, they (mp) are transferring'). It occurs most often in SA as the main verb that follows a pre-verb.

4 The clause /b-inaggiluu **fiihum** ʃadiid/ 'they (mp) transfer them (mp) a lot' contains an indirect object with the preposition /fii/. The verb /naggal/-/yanaggil/ 'to transfer, move (s.o. or s.t.)' usually takes a direct object, as in /b-inaggiloo**hum**/ 'they (mp) transfer them (mp)'. The use of the indirect object here suggests that the

action of the verb took place over a period of time. This is supported by the use of the intensifying adverb /ʃadiid/ 'a lot; very, much'.

**5** In a verb string like /**gaamuu** nagaluu waaldii/ 'they (mp) up and transferred my father', the pre-verb /**gaam**/ indicates the launching of an action. It can be translated as 'to up and do (the action of the main verb)' or 'to suddenly do (the action of the main verb)'. The verb /**gaam**/ in general means 'to get up; to undertake'. As a pre-verb, /**gaam**/ is unlike other pre-verbs because /**gaam**/ and the main verb have the same morphological tense. That is, if one is perfect, so is the other.
Note also that the speaker uses the Form I verb /**nagal**/ rather than the Form II /**naggal**/ that occurs in the previous sentence. In this context, both verbs mean 'to transfer'.

**6** The item /ʔismaa/ 'its (fs) name' is made up of /ʔisim/ 'name' and the possessive suffixed pronoun /-**haa**/ 'her; its (fs)'. In careful speech, the item is pronounced /ʔi**si**maa/, with retention of the second short /i/. In this case, however, the unstressed short vowel is deleted in an open syllable.
Note that the 3S and 3P suffixed pronouns (/-**huu**/ 'his; its (ms)'; /-**haa**/ 'her; its (fs)'; /-**hum**/ 'their (mp)'; and /-**hun**/ 'their (fp)') are pronounced without /h/ following a consonant. The /h/ of these suffixed pronouns is sounded only following a vowel.

**7** The construct phrase or <u>idaafa</u>, such as /**raas** aʃʃafaxaana/ 'the head of the clinic', exists in SA alongside the possessive adjective construction that uses /bitaaʕ/ or /ḥagg/ 'of, belonging to' (as in /azzaḥma **bitaaḥt** annaas/ 'the crowds of people'). The construct phrase and the possessive adjective construction share a function: they link two (or more) nouns in a relation of possession. They are not, however, interchangeable. Only the construct phrase can link nouns that name family members, body parts, or certain other categories (all considered to be inalienably possessed or permanently belonging). The possessive adjective construction is usually limited to linking other kinds of nouns.

**8** The form /almuhim/ 'anyway' often precedes and indicates an evaluative comment, as it does here in /fa-**lmuhim** kaanat ʔayyaam jamiila/ 'so, anyway, those were good times'. In other cases, it occurs in its literal sense of 'the important thing', as in /bass **almuhimm** yakuun azziik bitaaʕuu turkwaazii/ 'but the important thing is that its (ms) edge be turquoise'.

**9** The element /al/ is not the definite article in /ʔaḥmad **al**lakbar minnii/ 'Ahmad who is older than me'. It is /al-/ 'who; that', the definite relative pronoun of SA. This relative pronoun is identical in sound to the definite article of SA /al-/ 'the' and undergoes the same sound changes that the definite article does. However, the definite article only precedes a noun or adjective; the relative pronoun may precede

any word. Where there is no apparent difference between the two structures, the best translation is the one that sounds most natural.
In slow or formal speech, the form **/allakbar/** 'who is older' is pronounced **/alʔakbar/**. Other frequently-used words like **/awwal/** 'first' also show loss of **/ʔ/** together with doubling of the **/l/** of the relative pronoun or definite article **/al-/** in rapid speech.

**10** The speaker places the verb **/itwaladat/** 'she was born' at the start of this clause, **/w-itwaladat θuriyyaa w-ʕawaaṭif u-ṣalaaḥ u-ballaa w-ajjeelii/** 'and Thuriya was born [there], and Awatif, and Salah, and Balla and al-Jeeli'. This verb has 3FS agreement. In effect, it takes **/θuriyyaa/** 'Thuriya (woman's name)' as its grammatical subject rather than the whole string of names that is the logical subject of the clause.

**11** In the phrase **/ʔaktar manṭiga yimkin/** 'the greatest region, maybe' the invariable form **/yimkin/** 'maybe' functions as a marker of attitude. It softens or mitigates the sense of the preceding noun phrase **/ʔaktar manṭiga/** 'the greatest region'. In this example, **/yimkin/** 'maybe' follows the phrase it modifies. In most cases, however, it precedes the modified word or phrase, as in **/fi lʔusar yimkin arraaɣiyya/** 'in families that are, maybe, advanced'. The form **/yimkin/** also functions as a pre-verb in its literal sense 'it is possible', as in **/ʔimkin maa tittafig maʕaay/** 'it's possible you do not agree with me'.

**12** This clause, **/ʔaktar manṭiga yimkin la-ḥaddii llaḥza dii b-adzakkaraa kulla yoom yaʕnii/** 'the area maybe that until this moment I remember most every day, you know', is an indefinite relative clause. It looks complex because of the additions to it: **/yimkin/** 'perhaps'; **/la-ḥaddii llaḥza dii/** 'until this moment'; **/kulla yoom/** 'every day'; and **/yaʕnii/** 'you know'. The first two additions separate the indefinite noun phrase that is the head (**/ʔaktar manṭiga/** 'lit. the greatest area') from the relative clause itself (**/b-adzakkaraa/** 'I remember it'). Note that the clause that follows this one, starting with **/ʔaktar ʔumniyya/** 'the greatest wish', has a similar structure.

**13** Although **/alwaaḥid/** means, generally, 'a person', here it is another way for the speaker to refer to himself. His use of **/alwaaḥid/** 'a person' instead of the 1S pronoun can be understood in several ways. In particular, it makes the experiences he describes generally applicable rather than purely personal. Speakers of SA and certain other varieties of Arabic may use **/alwaaḥid/** 'a person' to stand in for a variety of personal pronouns.

# uɣniyya ʕaaṭifiyya: ɣiyaab yoomeen

*In this selection, the speaker recites the words of a popular love song. Note that the beloved addressed here is a woman, although grammatical references are masculine. Love songs and poetry in Arabic often use masculine forms to address or describe women. References to the beloved's eyes, cheeks, and long, flowing hair, however, call up conventional images of feminine beauty.*

taɣiib yoomeen wu-maa taḏhar
    wa-niḥnaa ʕamarnaa bi-saaʕaat[1]
tasiibnaa waraaka[2] saharaaniin
    naʃiil alleel bukaa wu-ʔahaat

wa-ḥaatak[3] ʔinta muʃtaagiin[4]
    natuuh fii xuduudak alḥilwaat[5]
titfattaḥ zuhuur arreed
    tanassiinaa lʕaðaab alfaat

natuu fi rmuuʃak alḥilwiin
    wa-fooɣ -xuṣlaatak aʃʃaaridaat[6]
wa-nansaa nnaas wu-kull alkoon
    naɣiib fii rawʕat alkalmaat

# أُغْنِيَّهْ عَاطِفِيَّهْ: غِيابْ يَوْمَيْنْ

تَغِيبْ يَوْمَيْنْ وُمَا تَظْهَرْ
وَنِحْنَا عَمَرْنَا بِساعَاتْ[1]
تَسِيبْنَا وَرَاكَ[2] سَهَرَانِينْ
نَشِيلْ اَللَّيْلْ بُكَا وُأَهَاتْ

وَحَاتَكْ[3] إِنْتَ مُشْتَاقِينْ[4]
نَتُوهْ فِي خُدُودَكْ اَلْحِلْوَاتْ[5]
تِتْفَتَّحْ زُهُورْ اَلرَّيْدْ
تَنَسِّينَا الْعَذَابْ اَلْفَاتْ

نَتُوهْ فِرْمُوشَكْ اَلْحِلْوِينْ
وَفَوْغْ -خُصْلاَتَكْ اَلشَّارِدَاتْ[6]
وَنَنْسَى النَّاسْ وُكُلّ اَلكَوْنْ
نَغِيبْ فِي رَوْعَةْ اَلْكَلْمَاتْ

wakit tanḍam yagiif[7] nabḍii

    w-ansaa lfaat w-ajjaayaat

w-axaaf alleel yafarrignaa

    ʔaduub fi lḥurga w-alʔahaat

wa-leeh yaa siidnaa, maa tarḥam

    ʕuyuun malyaana bi-damʕaat

taʕaal yaa siidnaa, maa -ṭṭawwil

    wa-niḥnaa ʕamarnaa bi–saaʕaat

وِكِتْ تَنْضَمْ يَقِيفْ[7] نَبْضِي
وَانْسَى الْفَاتْ وَالجَّايَاتْ
وَاخَافْ اَللَّيْلْ يِفَرِّقْنَا
أَدُوبْ فِالْحُرْقَهْ وَالأَهَاتْ

وَلَيْهْ يَا سِيدْنَا، مَا تَرْحَمْ
عُيُونْ مَلْيَانَهْ بِدَمْعَاتْ
تَعَالْ يَا سِيدْنَا، مَا -طَوِّلْ
وِنِحْنَا عَمَرْنَا بِسَاعَاتْ

## Vocabulary

**niḥnaa** نِحْنَا *pron* we

**saab (sibta)** (سِبْتَ) سَابْ *vt* to leave behind; to leave alone {*imperf:* **yasiib**, *vn:* **sayabaan**}

**ʃaal (ʃilta)** (شِلْتَ) شَالْ *vt* to carry; to take {*imperf:* **yaʃiil**, *vn:* **ʃeel**, *vn:* **ʃeyalaan**}

**aha** اَهَهْ *nfs* sigh {*pl:* **ahaat**}

**wa-ḥaat-** وَحَاتْ by the life of s.o. (oath or exclamation)

**inta** اِنْتَ **[itta; itt]** *pron ms* you

**taah (tuhta)** (تُهْتَ) تَاهْ *vi* to get lost, go astray {*imperf:* **yatuuh**, *vn:* **tawahaan**}

**reed** رَيْدْ *nms* love

**faat (futta)** (فُتَّ) فَاتْ *vt* to have passed in time, be in the past {*imperf:* **yafuut**, *vn:* **fawaataan**}

**rimiʃ** رِمِشْ *nms* eyelash {*pl:* **rumuuʃ**}

**xuṣla** خُصْلَة *nfs* lock of hair {*pl:* **xuṣlaat**}

**rawʕa** رَوْعَة *nfs* beauty; splendor

**wakit** وَكِتْ *conj* when, at the time that

**naḍam** نَضَمْ *vt* to speak {*imperf:* **yanḍum,** *vn:* **naḍam**}

**nabaḍ** نَبَضْ *nms* pulse, heartbeat {*pl:* **nabḍaat**}

**jaay** جَايْ *adj* coming; having arrived {*fs:* **jaaya,** *mpl:* **jaayiin,** *fpl:* **jaayaat**}

**daab (dubta)** دَابْ (دُبْتْ) *vi* to dissolve {*imperf:* **yaduub,** *vn:* **dawabaan**}

**ḥurga** حُرْقَة *nfs* agony {*pl:* **ḥurgaat**}

**leeh** لَيْه *interrog* why

**siid** سِيدْ *nms* master; possessor, owner {*pl:* **asyaad**}

**ṭawwal** طَوَّلْ *vi* to take a long time (doing s.t.); to be away for a long time {*imperf:* **yaṭawwil,** *vn:* **taṭwiil**}

## Notes

**1** The topic-comment sentence /**niḥnaa ʕamarnaa bi-saaʕaat**/ 'our lives are counted in hours, lit. we, our lives are by hours' introduces a new character to this love song. The new character is the lover who uses 1P pronouns and inflections to speak on behalf of all those infatuated with the beloved. The topic-comment sentence has two elements. The topic of a topic-comment sentence is an independent pronoun (here, /**niḥnaa**/ 'we') or a noun phrase. The comment contains a noun, a pronoun (here, /**ʕamarnaa**/ 'our lives'), or a verb whose referent is the topic.

**2** The form /**-ka**/ occurs in SA, as it does here in the form /**waraaka**/ 'behind you (ms)'. Following a vowel, however, the 2MS suffixed pronoun is more often /**-k**/, as in /**waraak**/ 'behind you (ms)'.

**3** In the utterance /**wa-ḥaatak ʔinta**/ 'by your (ms) life', the form /**wa-ḥaatak**/ is an oath. It occurs in SA, as does the full form /**wa-ḥayaatak**/ 'by your (ms) life'. The independent pronoun /**ʔinta**/ 'you (ms)' follows the oath to add force or emphasis to the statement. Oaths like these and others that invoke the deity are common in everyday speech; few speakers take them at face value.

**4** The context of /**muʃtaagiin**/ 'we yearn, lit. yearning (mp)' makes it clear who the speaker longs for: it is the beloved. This usage of /**muʃtaag**/ 'yearning (ms)' is common in SA and other certain varieties of spoken Arabic. Note also that in SA generally, a predicate may occur with no expressed subject, if that subject would be an independent pronoun.

**5** Non-human P nouns in SA may take agreement with FP modifiers, pronouns, and verb inflections, as in /**xuduudak alḥilwaat**/ 'your (ms) lovely cheeks'. That is only one of several agreement patterns that regularly occur. Most often, agreement for non-human P nouns is FS, as in MSA. MP agreement for non-human P nouns also occurs. Note that all three agreement patterns are demonstrated in this short verse.

**6** In careful speech, the phrase /**w-fooɣ -xuṣlaatak aʃʃaaridaat**/ 'in addition to your (ms) loosened locks' would be pronounced /**w-foog xuṣlaatak aʃʃaaridaat**/ 'in addition to your (ms) loosened locks'. The /**g**/ of /**foog**/ (voiced velar stop) is pronounced /**ɣ**/ (voiced velar fricative) because of the influence of the /**x**/ of /**xuṣlaatak**/ (voiceless velar fricative). This example shows that assimilation (one sound becoming like another, first discussed in selection 2) is not limited to the sounds of a single word. Assimilation also crosses word boundaries, as it does here.

**7** The imperfect /**yagiif**/ 'it (ms) stops' has a long /**ii**/ vowel even though it has as its perfect /**wagaf**/ 'to stop'. This verb is unusual. Some SA Form I verbs with /**w**/ as the first root consonant (initially-weak roots) have a regular conjugation that retains /**w**/ in the imperfect, as in /**wajaʕ**/ - /**yawjaʕ**/ or /**yoojaʕ**/ 'to hurt (s.o. or s.t.)'. In other cases, SA Form I verbs with /**w**/ as the first root consonant lose the /**w**/ in the imperfect, as in /**wagaʕ**/ - /**yagaʕ**/ 'to fall'.

# annizaam addiraasii fi ssuudaan

*The more formal language used by both speakers in this selection may be due to the topic, the effect of government policy on education. The specifics of formal language in this selection differ from those of selection 3. Here, the use of /**kaan**/ in the imperfect is the most striking marker of formality. A contrasting marker of informality is variation in the 3M imperfect prefix. It occurs as /i/(**b-imʃuu**/ 'they (mp) go'), /**ii**/(/**iimʃuu**/ 'they (mp) go'), /**yi**/(/**yikuunuu**/ 'they (mp) are'), /y/(/**ydduuhum**/ 'they (ms) send them (ms)'), and /**ʔi**/(/**ʔidxuluu**/ 'they (mp) enter').*

A: fi zzaman daak la-ɣaayat zamannaa niḥnaa lamman xaʃʃeenaa[1] jjaamiʕa sitta wa-tizʕiin[2] wa-daa wallaa kidaa kaanat al … ajjaamiʕaat fi ssuudaan hii jaamʕat alxarṭuum wa-yaadoob al … al … ʔaa … baduu yanʃuu fii jaamʕat juuba[3] ʔaa … fii jjanuub ʔallii hiya fii juuba wa-fiʕlan kaanat jaamʕa gawiyya jiddan jiddan wa-naajaḥa wa-jaamaʕat ajjaziira[4] wa-kaan fii jaamiʕa waaḥdii[5] ʔillii hiya jaa … ʔala … dii kaanat b-imʃuu leeyaa[6] naas attaʕliim almaṣrii[7, 8] w-kidaa dii jaamʕat alqaahira farʕ alxarṭuum.[9]

B: allii hii hassii magfuula.

A: ay …

B: laakin ʕaarif[10] hassii fi lwaḍaʕ alḥaalii ʕaʃaan taṣal ajjaamaʕa …

A: haa …

B: ɣeer al … al … al … al … al … almustawaa lʔaakaadiimii mafruuḍ ta … ta … yaʕnii tasajjiluu ʔinta ʔiku … b-iikuun fil …. fil … fil … annatiija bitaaḥtak[11] …

A: ay, ikuun fii[12] xidma ʕaskariyya.[13]

# اَلنِّظَامْ اَلدِّرَاسِي فِالسُّودَانْ

أ: فَالزَّمَنْ دَاكْ لَغَايَةْ زَمَنَّا نِحْنَا لَمَّنْ خَشَّيْنَا[1] الجَّامِعَهْ سِتَّهْ وَتِزْعِينْ[2] وَدَا وَلاَّ كِدَا كَانَتْ اَلْـ... اَلجَّامِعَاتْ فِالسُّودَانْ هِي جَامْعَةْ اَلْخَرْطُومْ وَيَادَوْبْ اَلْـ... اَلْـ... آ... بَدُوا يَنْشُوا فِي جَامْعَةْ جُوبَهْ[3] آ... فِي الجَّنُوبْ أَللِّي هِيَ فِي جُوبَهْ وَفِعْلاً كَانَتْ جَامْعَهْ قَوِيَّهْ جِدّاً جِدّاً وَنَاجْحَهْ وَجَامْعَةْ اَلجَّزِيرَهْ[4] وَكَانْ فِي جَامِعَهْ وَاحْدِي[5] إِللِّي هِيَ جَا... أَلَـ... دِي كَانَتْ بِمْشُوا لَيَّا[6] نَاسْ اَلتَّعْلِيمْ اَلْمَصْرِي[7, 8] وْكِدَا دِي جَامْعَةْ اَلْقَاهِرَهْ فَرْعْ اَلْخَرْطُومْ.[9]

ب: اَللِّي هِي هَسِّي مَقْفُولَهْ.

أ: اَيْ...

ب: لَكِنْ عَارِفْ[10] هَسِّي فِالْوَضَعْ اَلْحَالِي عَشَانْ تَصِلْ اَلجَّامَعَهْ...

أ: هَا...

ب: غَيْرْ اَلْـ... اَلْـ... اَلْـ... اَلْـ... اَلْـ... اَلْمُسْتَوَى الآكَادِيمِي مَفْرُوضْ تَـ... تَـ... يَعْنِي تَسَجِّلُهْ إِنْتَ إِكُـ... بِيكُونْ فِلْـ... فِلْـ... فِلْـ... اَلنَّتِيجَهْ بِتَاحْتَكْ[11]...

أ: اَي، اِكُونْ فِي[12] خِدْمَهْ عَسْكَرِيَّهْ.[13]

B: barḍuu laazim takuun[14] fii xidma ʕaskariyya ʔilzaamiyya lii-muddat sana.

A: haa ...

B: hii, takuun baʕiid xaaliṣ ʕan alḥaɣl addiraasii wal ... w-almadaaris wa-kidaa.

A: haa ...

B: takuun bass maʕa lxidma lʕaskariyya w-alxidma lʔilzaamiyya ...

A: ṣaḥḥ.

B: waḥadd ... wa-loo maa ʕamaltahaa[15] ...

A: maa b-takuʃʃ ...

B: maa bi-txalluuk,[16] maa b-idduuk ʃahaada.

A: ṣaḥḥ.

B: aʃʃahaada ssuudaaniyya[17] baʕda maa ta ... tagraa θθaanawii lʕaalii[18] maa b-idduuk aʃʃahaada ssuudaaniyya.

A: haa ...

B: w-bi-ttaalii huruuban alaṭ ... al ... al ... alʔawlaad ʔaw albanaat, albanaat maa b-ikuun ʕinduhum muʃkila fii ḥaaja zayy dii laakin alʔawlaad, muʕẓam ʔalʔawlaad alb-imtaḥanuu ʃʃihaada maa ʕaawziin imʃuu lxidma lʔilzaamiyya walaa ʕaawziin iimʃuu ʔaa ... m ... yikuunuu maa mudarrabiin wa-ydduuhum maḥallat alḥarb.

ب: بَرْضَهْ لاَزِمْ تَكُونْ[14] فِي خِدْمَهْ عَسْكَرِيَّهْ إِلْزَامِيَّهْ لِيمُدَّةْ سَنَهْ.

أ: هَا...

ب: هِي، تَكُونْ بَعِيدْ خَالِص عَنْ اَلْحَغْلْ اَلدِّرَاسِي وَالْـ... وَالْمَدَارِسْ وكِدَا.

أ: هَا...

ب: تَكُونْ بَسّ مَعَ الْخِدْمَه الْعَسْكَرِيَّهْ وَالْخِدْمَه الإِلْزَامِيَّهْ ...

أ: صَحّ.

ب: وَحَدّ... وَلَوْ مَا عَمَلْتَهَا[15]...

أ: مَا بْتَكُشّ...

ب: مَا بِتْخَلُّوكْ،[16] مَا بِدُّوكْ شَهَادَهْ.

أ: صَحّ.

ب: اَلشَّهَادَه السُّودَانِيَّهْ[17] بَعْدَ مَا تَـ... تَقْرَا الثَّانَوِي الْعَالِي[18] مَا بِدُّوكْ اَلشَّهَادَه السُّودَانِيَّهْ.

أ: هَا...

ب: وْبِالتَّالِي هُرُوبًا اَلطْ... اَلْـ... اَلْـ... اَلأَوْلاَدْ أَوْ اَلْبَنَاتْ، اَلْبَنَاتْ مَا بِكُونْ عِنْدُهُمْ مُشْكِلَهْ فِي حَاجَهْ زَيّ دِي لَكِنْ اَلأَوْلاَدْ، مُعْظَمْ أَلأَوْلاَدْ اَلبِمْتَحَنُوا الشِّهَادَهْ مَا عَاوْزِينْ اِمْشُوا الْخِدْمَه الإِلْزَامِيَّهْ وَلاَ عَاوْزِينْ ايمْشُوا آ... مـْ... يِكُونُوا مَا مُدَرَّبِينْ وَيْدُّوهُمْ مَحَلَّةْ اَلْحَرْبْ.

A: aa ...

B: miyyaat minnuhum b-iimuutuu laʔannuhum maa mudarrabiin attadriib al ... al ... b-iiguuluu ʕaleehuu al ... alkaamil aw attaktiikii ʕaʃaan yiwaajhuu masalan ḥitta bitaaʕat ḥarb.

A: haa ...

B: yibgaa b-iiguumuu ymuutuu fi ḥaala zaay dii b-iiguumuu hum itxawwafuu min innum imʃuu lxidma lʔilzaamiyya ...

A: ṣaḥḥ.

B: albi ... ʔa ... fa-taxawwufum daa b-ixalliihum ma -ymtaḥnuu ʃʃihaada.

A: ṣaḥḥ.

B: liʔannuu ʃʃihaada dii waraahaa ḥaaja zayy dii.

A: ṣaḥḥ.

B: yibgaa w-bu ... bi ... bi ... bigat fii ʃʃaariʕ fii kimmiyya kabiira jiddan jiddan min alʔawlaad ʔanaa b-aʕrifun[19] ʔinnuu mustawaahum ʃuṭṭaar laakin mutxawfiin innahun iikammiluu ʔimtaḥanuu ʃʃihaada ssuudaaniyya ʕaʃaan maa ʔidxuluu fi lwaḍaʕ zaayyi daa.

A: ṣaḥḥ.

B: aw muḥtamal yimuutuu.

A: ṣaḥḥ.

أ: آ...

ب: مِيَّاتْ مِنُّهُمْ بِيمُوتُوا لأَنُّهُمْ مَا مُدَرَّبِينْ اَلتَّدْرِيبَ اَلْـ... اَلْـ ... بِيقُولُوا عَلَيْهُ اَلْـ... اَلْكَامِلْ اَوْ اَلتَّكْتِيكِي عَشَانْ يِوَاجْهُوا مَسَلاً حِتَّهْ بِتَاعَةْ حَرْبْ.

أ: هَا...

ب: يِبْقَى بِيقُومُوا يْمُوتُوا فِحَالَهْ زَاي دِي بِيقُومُوا هُمْ اِتْخَوَّفُوا مِنْ اِنّهُمْ اِمْشُوا الْخِدْمَه الإِلْزَامِيَّهْ...

أ: صَحّ.

ب: اَلْبِـ... أَ... فَتَخَوُّفْهُمْ دَا بِخَلِّيهُمْ مَ -يْمْتَحْنُوا الشِّهَادَهْ.

أ: صَحّ.

ب: لأَنّهُ الشِّهَادَهْ دِي وَرَاهَا حَاجَهْ زَيّ دِي.

أ: صَحّ.

ب: يِبْقَى وْبُـ... بِـ... بِـ... بِقَتْ فِي الشَّارِعْ فِي كِمِّيَّهْ كَبِيرَهْ جِدّاً جِدّاً مِنْ اَلأَوْلاَدْ أَنَا بَاعْرِفْهُنْ[19] إِنّهُ مُسْتَوَاهُمْ شُطَّارْ لَكِنْ مُتْخَوْفِينْ اِنّهُنْ يْكَمِّلُوا إِمْتَحَنُوا الشِّهَادَه السُّودَانِيَّهْ عَشَانْ مَا إِدْخُلُوا فِالْوَضَعْ زَايّ دَا...

أ: صَحّ.

ب: اَوْ مُحْتَمَلْ يِمُوتُوا.

أ: صَحّ.

B: fa-biguu maa ykammiluu taʕliimhum, biguu yaaxaduu[20] waẓaayif haamiʃii,[21] ʔaa … ʔaa … ʔaa … maa ʕindahaa maʕnaa.

A: yaʕnii ʕaarif …

B: bi-tḥiss bi-yannuu[22] fii mustaɣbal ḍaayiʕ fii … fii ʃariiḥa kabiira jiddan min alʔawlaad …

A: laa xa … ay ṣaḥḥ …

B: wa-ḥassaʕ ʕaʃaan kidaa talgaa masalan ʔaɣlabiyyat …

A: laakin ʔanaa …

B: … alʔawlaad ʔa … fii jjaamiʕaat wa-kidaa talgaa nizbat albanaat ʔaʕlaa min alʔawlaad.

ب: فَبِقُوا مَا يْكَمِّلُوا تَعْلِيمْهُمْ، بِقُوا يَاخْدُوا[20] وَظَايِفْ هَامِشِي، [21] آ... آ... آ... مَا عِنْدَهَا مَعْنَى.

أ: يَعْنِي عَارِفْ ...

ب: بِتْحِسّ بِيَنّهُ[22] فِي مُسْتَقْبَلْ ضَايِعْ فِي... فِي شَرِيحَهْ كَبِيرَهْ جِدّاً مِنْ اَلأَوْلاَدْ...

أ: لاَ خَـ... اَي صَحّ...

ب: وَهَسَّعْ عَشَانْ كِدَا تَلْقَى مَسَلاً أَغْلَبِيَّةْ ...

أ: لَكِنْ أَنَا...

ب: ... اَلأَوْلاَدْ أَ... فِي الجَّامِعَاتْ وَكِدَا تَلْقَى نِزْبَةْ اَلْبَنَاتْ أَعْلَى مِنْ اَلأَوْلاَدْ.

## Vocabulary

**lamman** لَمَّنْ **[lammaa]** *conj* when

**xaʃʃa** خَشّ *vt* to enter {*imperf:* **yaxuʃʃ**, *vn:* **xaʃaʃaan**}

**wallaa** وَلاَّ *conj* or

**wallaa kidaa** وَلاَّ كِدَا or something like that

**hii** هِي **[hiya]** *pron* she

**yaadoob** يَادوْبْ **[yaadaab]** *adv* barely, just

**juubaa** جُوبَا *prop* Juba (capital of Bahr al-Jabal Province)

**jaziira** جَزِيرَهْ *nfs* island {*pl:* **juzur**, **jazaayir**}

**ajjaziira** اَلجَّزِيرَهْ *prop* al-Jazira (region and province of Sudan)

**fii** فِي *particle invariable* there is, there are (existential); to be going on, be wrong, be a problem

**waaḥid** وَاحِدْ *adj* single, sole {*fs:* **waaḥda**, *mpl:* **waaḥdiin**, *fpl:* **waaḥdaat**}

**ay** أَيْ **[ayya; aywa; iywa]** *interj* yes

**ʕaʃaan** عَشَانْ *conj* to, in order to; because, because of

**mafruuḍ** مَفْرُوضْ *adj invariable; pre-verb* should, ought to

**natiija** نَتِيجَةْ *nfs* grade, result {*pl:* **nataayij, nataaʔij**}

**xaaliṣ** خَالِصْ *adv* very, extremely

**wa-kidaa** وكَدَا and so on, etcetera

**ṣaḥḥ** صَحّ *adj invariable* correct

**loo** لَوْ **[law]** *conj* if

**xallaa** خَلَّى *vt* to let, allow; to cause to be; to leave alone, let be; to leave (behind) {*imperf:* **yaxallii,** *vn:* **xilleey**}

**addaa** أدَّى *vt* to give {*imperf:* **yaddii,** *vn:* **iddeey**}

**ʃahaada** شَهَادَةْ **[ʃihaada]** *nfs* diploma, degree {*pl:* **ʃahaadaat**}

**garaa** قَرَا *vt* to study; to get an education {*imperf:* **yagraa,** *vn:* **giraaya**}

**θaanawii ʕaalii** ثَانَوِي عَالِي **[saanawii ʕaalii]** *nms* high school

**imtaḥan** امْتَحَنْ *vt* to take an exam (in a field or at a level); to give an exam (in a field or at a level) {*imperf:* **yimtaḥin,** *vn:* **ʔimtiḥaan**}

**ʕaawiz** عَاوِزْ **[ʕaayiz]** *adj pre-verb* wanting, desiring {*fs:* **ʕaawza,** *mpl:* **ʕaawziin,** *fpl:* **ʕaawzaat**}

**maḥalla** مَحَلَّةْ *nfs* place; location; seat {*pl:* **maḥallaat**}

**yibgaa** يِبْقَى *adv invariable* then, that's it

**xallaa** خَلَّى *vt* to cause to be; to leave alone, let be; to leave (behind); to let, allow {*imperf:* **yaxallii,** *vn:* **xilleey**}

**bigaa** بِقَى *vt pre-verb* to get to the point that; to begin (inchoative action); to be; to become {*imperf:* **yabgaa,** *vn:* **bagayaan**}

**yannuu** يَنُّهْ **[annuu; ʔannuu]** *conj* that

**ʃariiḥa** شَرِيحَةْ *nfs* section, division, sector {*pl:* **ʃaraayiḥ**}

**ligaa** لِقَى *vt* to find, discover {*imperf:* **yalgaa,** *vn:* **lagayaan**}

## Notes

**1** The verb /**xaʃʃeenaa**/ 'we went in' is the 1P perfect of the verb /**xaʃʃa**/ - /**yaxuʃʃ**/ 'to enter'. Doubled verbs (or geminate verbs, where the second and third root consonants are identical) in SA resemble those of certain other varieties of spoken Arabic. Doubled verbs have two perfect roots. The root seen here, /**xaʃʃee-**/ occurs only where the suffix of the perfect begins with a consonant. The root /**xaʃʃ-**/ occurs in all other cases.

**2** This date, /**sitta wa-tizʕiin**/ 'ninety-six', appears to be a slip of the tongue. The founding of the new universities the speakers names later pre-dates 1996. The phrases that follow, /**wa-daa wallaa kidaa**/ 'and that, or so', suggest that the speaker is aware of his slip but chooses not to correct himself. See selection 2, note 4 for a discussion of the sound change that produces /**tizʕiin**/ 'ninety' rather than /**tisʕiin**/.

**3** The University of Juba or /**jaamʕat juuba**/ was founded in the mid-seventies primarily to serve southern Sudan. It was moved to Khartoum in 1983 because of hostilities in the region but returned to Juba in the late eighties.

**4** Al-Jazira University or /**jaamaʕat ajjaziira**/ in Wad Madani, capital of al-Jazira province, was founded in the late seventies.

**5** The form /**waaḥdii**/ with a final long /**ii**/ in the phrase /**jaamiʕa waaḥdii**/ 'one university' is a slip of the tongue, apparently for /**waaḥda**/ 'one (fs)', with a final short /**a**/.

**6** The speaker here says /**leeyaa**/ 'to it (fs)', with /**y**/ in place of /**h**/, as in /**leehaa**/. As seen in note 6, selection 3, the general rule is that the 3S and 3P suffixed pronouns (/**-huu**/ 'his; its (ms)'; /**-haa**/ 'her; its (fs)'; /**-hum**/ 'their (mp)'; and /**-hun**/ 'their (fp)') are pronounced without /**h**/ following a consonant. The /**h**/ is sounded only following a consonant.

**7** Grammatical agreement is mixed in the clause /**dii kaanat b-imʃuu leeyaa naas attaʕliim almaṣrii**/ 'this (fs) was, people with an Egyptian education used to go to it (fs)'. It indicates that the speaker is changing the topic. The clause begins /**dii kaanat**/ 'this (fs) was', a reference to the university mentioned previously. It continues with the verb /**b-imʃuu**/ 'they (mp) [used to] go', where the grammatical subject looks ahead to the noun phrase /**naas attaʕliim almaṣrii**/ 'people with an Egyptian education'. Occurrences like this in the flow of fluent, grammatical language are not uncommon in natural speech. Unless they interfere with communication, listeners tend to ignore them.

**8** The fact of /**attaʕliim almaṣrii**/ 'Egyptian education' was a holdover from the Anglo-Egyptian Condominium of 1899 – 1955. Because of the Egyptian presence, both governmental and private, Egyptian schools were opened in Sudan. Children of Egyptian nationals and of Sudanese citizens who worked for Egyptian organizations attended these schools and, later, the Khartoum branch of Cairo University.

**9** As the female speaker says in the next utterance, the Khartoum branch of /**jaamʕat alqaahira**/ 'Cairo University' closed during a period of poor relations between Sudan and Egypt.

**10** The active participle /**ʕaarif**/ can be translated as 'knowing'. In contexts like this one, however, /**ʕaarif**/ is equivalent to the prefixed imperfect /**bi-taʕrif**/ 'you (ms) know' or the simple imperfect /**taʕrif**/ 'you (ms) know'. Note that the exact meaning of an active participle depends on usage as much as grammar.
Note also that, where the context makes the subject of a clause obvious, the use of an independent pronoun as the grammatical subject is unnecessary.

**11** In the phrase /**annatiija bitaaḥtak**/ 'your (ms) results', the speaker talks about /**annatiija**/ 'results' rather than 'grades' or 'marks' for classes taken. One of the most important criteria for university admission is the student's score on the high school graduation exam, /**aʃʃahaada assuudaaniyya**/. This phrase names the Sudanese School Certificate Examination itself as well as the Sudanese School Certificate that documents student results.

**12** The form /**ikuun**/ 'it is' is the simple imperfect of /**kaan**/. This variant of /**yakuun**/, in which the imperfect prefix is /i-/, occurs in rapid speech following a consonant. Another common variant is /ii-/ as in /**iikuun**/.

**13** As part of the educational reforms enacted by General Umar Hassan Ahmad al-Bashir in the nineties, /**xidma ʕaskariyya**/ 'military service' became a requirement for high-school graduation and university admission. Some military conscripts received only brief training before being sent into combat.

**14** The verb string /**laazim takuun**/ 'you (ms) have to be' consists of two parts. They are the active participle /**laazim**/ 'necessary', with no change for gender or number agreement, and the simple imperfect /**takuun**/ 'you (ms) are'. In SA and other varieties of spoken Arabic, verb strings provide additional information about the time frame of the main verb (as in /**gaam**/, see note 5, selection 3) or an attitude towards the reality or truth value of the verb, as here.

**15** The clause /**wa-loo maa ʕamaltahaa**/ 'if you (ms) don't do it (fs)' is a conditional clause. Conditional sentences in SA differ from those of MSA and certain other varieties of spoken Arabic. In SA, the conditional particle /**loo**/ (or /**law**/) 'if' introduces situations that could occur (hypothetical conditions) or do occur (real conditions). Except in formal or classicized speech, /**loo**/ rarely occurs where the situation has not or will not take place (contrary-to-fact conditions).

**16** Both speakers make false starts in the exchange /A: **maa b-takuʃʃ** ... B: **maa bi-txalluuk**/ 'A: You (ms) won't ... B: ...you (mp) won't let you (ms) ...'. It is tempting to guess what happened, but speakers themselves may not know why they said what they did. Disfluencies like this are not uncommon in natural speech. Listeners can ignore them, but in writing they become noticeable.

**17** These speakers use the phrase /**ʔaʃʃahaada ssuudaaniyya**/ or simply /**ʔaʃʃahaada**/ for the Sudanese School Certificate, the Sudanese equivalent of a high-school diploma, and for the Sudanese School Certificate Examination, the high-school graduation and university entrance exam.

**18** The phrase /**θθaanawii lʕaalii**/ is the conventional SA term for 'upper secondary school' or 'high school', is M in gender. According to some speakers of SA, the phrase is M in gender because it modifies a noun that is M and has been omitted, such as /**mustawaa**/ 'level'.

**19** The 3MP suffixed pronoun /-**hun**/, as in /**b-aʕrifun**/ 'I know them (mp)', sometimes occurs as a variant of /-**hum**/. The 2MP form /-**kun**/ also occurs in place of /-**kum**/. Note, however, that listeners cannot assume that /-**hun**/ or /-**kun**/ are P forms for both M and F, as some varieties of spoken Arabic in Sudan use these suffixed pronouns for the FP.

**20** The form /**yaaxaduu**/ 'they (mp) take' has as its perfect /**axad**/ and as its imperfect /**yaaxad**/ 'to take'. The hamza or glottal stop of the perfect does not appear in the imperfect. Instead, the first short /**a**/ is lengthened. The verb /**akal**/ - /**yaakul**/ 'to eat' has a similar conjugation.

**21** The speaker here cuts off the phrase /**waẓaayif haamiʃii**/ 'marginal jobs' before pronouncing the final /**a**/ that is the FS inflection. Had she completed the phrase, the adjective /**haamiʃii**/ would have shown FS grammatical agreement: /**waẓaayif haamiʃiyya**/ 'marginal jobs'. As seen in selection 4, note 5, FS grammatical agreement is one of the several ways that SA modifies non-human P.

**22** In careful speech, the speaker would retain the hamza or glottal stop in /**bi-ʔannuu**/, rather than saying /**bi-yannuu**/ as occurs here.

# attaṭawwuraat fi ttaʕliim

*The male speaker in this selection descsribes his early education. This took place in the context of the educational reforms undertaken by the Nimeiri-led government of Sudan in the 70s. Note that the personal topic leads to a more informal, more markedly Sudanese style of speaking than in previous selections.*

A: anaa loo kallamtik ʕan ... yaa rajaaʔ, ʕan al ... ʔa ... ʕan al ... giṣṣit attaʕliim bitaaʕtii yaʕnii ʔum ... ya ... ya ... ḥaaja kidaa kaanat fiihaa mutʕa yaʕnii w-anaa xamsa sniin wallaa rbaʕa sniin wa-ʔummii ʃaalatnii, waddatnii ʔalxalwa.[1] maa tʕallamta leey, yaʕnii fiʕlan maa b-azzakkar[2] kammalta juzuu ʕamm[3] wallaa maa kammaltuu. waa ... ʔalkalaam daa bi-ḍḍabṭ sanat ʔarbaʕa wa-sittiin. yaʕnii fiʕlan attaʕliim kaanat zamaan leehuu kiima[4, 5] w-attaʕliim kaan fiʕlan yaʕnii ʃii muriiḥ bi-ʃakili maa ʕaadii[6] yaʕnii liʔann almudarrisiin zaatum kaanuu naas ʔa ... yaʕnii fiʕlan ʔa ... muʔahhaliin taʔhiil fiʕlan kwayyis jiddan jiddan.[7] fa-ʔarbaʕa wa-sittiin xaʃʃeet almadrasa, ʔisimmaa[8] lmadrasa lʔawwaliyya zamaan[9] ʔa ... yaʕnii lʔawwaliyya wa-b-taaxud[10] fiihaa rbaʕa sniin. laakin fii naas kutaar jiddan jiddan yitxarrajuu min alʔawwaliyya dii mumkin yiʃtaɣaluu mudarrisiin liʔannuu xilaal lʔarbaʕa sniin dii[11] ʔinta fiʕlan bi-tkuun lmuɣarraraat bitaaʕaatak ʔa ... yaʕnii l ... wallaa lḥaajaat alb-iidarrisuuk leehaa bi-tkuun fiʕlan taʔahhilak bi-ṣuura kwaysa jiddan jiddan[12] min naaḥiyat ʔimlaa min naaḥiyat ḥifiz[13] min naaḥiyat ḥisaab,[14] yaʕnii zamaan bi-nguul leeh ḥisaab niḥnaa muʃ riyaaḍiyyaat. fa ... ʔarbaʕa wa-sittiin la-ɣaayat ʔa ... tamaanya wa-sittiin wallaa yaʕnii tisʕa wa-sittiin kidaa

# اَلتَّطَوُّرَاتْ فِالتَّعْلِيمْ

أ: اَنَا لَوْ كَلِّمْتِكْ عَنْ... يَا رَجَاءْ، عَنْ اَلْ... أ... عَنْ اَلْ... قِصِّةْ اَلتَّعْلِيمْ بِتَاعْتِي يَعْنِي أُمْ... يَ... يَ... حَاجَهْ كِدَا كَانِتْ فِيهَا مُتْعَهْ يَعْنِي وَانَا خَمْسَهْ سْنِينْ وَلاَّ ارْبَعَهْ سْنِين وَأُمِّي شَالِتْنِي، وِدِّتْنِي أَلْخَلْوَهْ.[1] مَا تْعَلِّمْتَ لِيّ، يَعْنِي فِعْلاً مَا بَازَّكَّرْ[2] كَمِّلْت جُزُو عَمّ[3] وَلاَّ مَا كَمِّلْتُهْ. وَا... أَلْكَلاَمْ دَا بِالظَّبْطْ سَنَةْ أَرْبَعَهْ وَسِتِّينْ. يَعْنِي فِعْلاً اَلتَّعْلِيمْ كَانِتّ زَمَان لَيْهُ كِيمَهْ[4, 5] وَالتَّعْلِيمْ كَانْ فِعْلاً يَعْنِي شِي مُرِيحْ بِشَكِلْ مَا عَادِي[6] يَعْنِي لأنَّ الْمُدَرِّسِينْ زَاتْهُمْ كَانُوا نَاسْ أ... يَعْنِي فِعْلاً أ... مُؤَهَّلِينْ تَأْهِيلْ فِعْلاً كْوَيِّسْ جِدّاً جِدّاً.[7] فَأَرْبَعَه وَسِتِّينْ خَشَّيْتْ اَلْمَدْرَسَهْ، إِسِمّهَا[8] الْمَدْرَسَه الأَوَّلِيَّهْ زَمَانْ[9] أ ... يَعْنِي الأَوَّلِيَّهْ وَبْتَاخُدْ[10] فِيهَا ارْبَعَهْ سْنِينْ. لَكِنْ فِي نَاس كُتَارْ جِدّاً جِدّاً يِتْخَرَّجُوا مِنْ اَلأَوَّلِيَّهْ دِي مُمْكِنْ يِشْتَغَلُوا مُدَرِّسِينْ لأَنُّهُ خِلاَلْ الأَرْبَعَهْ سْنِينْ دِي[11] إِنْتَ فِعْلاً بِتْكُون الْمُقَرَّرَاتْ بِتَاعَاتَكْ أ... يَعْنِي لْ... وَلاَّ الْحَاجَات اَلْبِيدَرِّسُوكْ لَيْهَا بِتْكُونْ فِعْلاً تَأَهِّلَكْ بِصُورَهْ كْوَيْسَهْ جِدّاً جِدّاً[12] مِنْ نَاحِيَةْ إِمْلاَ مِنْ نَاحِيَةْ حِفِزْ[13] مِنْ نَاحِيَةْ حِسَابْ،[14] يَعْنِي زَمَانْ بِنْقُولْ لَيْهْ حِسَابْ نِحْنَا مُشْ رِيَاضِيَّاتْ. فَ... أَرْبَعَهْ وَسِتِّينْ لَغَايَةْ أ... تَمَانْيَهْ وَسِتِّينْ وَلاَّ يَعْنِي تِسْعَه وَسِتِّينْ كِدَا

wa-xallaṣnaa min alʔibtidaaʔiyya dii wa-ṭawwaalii yamtaḥnuunaa fa-lḥamdi li-llaa najaḥt anaa wa-xadduunii fi lmadrasa ʔa ... wusṭaa. w-almadrasa lwusṭaa barḍuu kaan ʔarbaʕa sniin, yaʕnii lʔawwaliyya rbaʕa sniin[15] w-almadrasa lwusṭaa ʔarbaʕa sniin waa ... assaanawii lʕaalii ʔarbaʕa sniin. ʔanaa fii sana ʔuulaa wusṭaa ʔa ... ḥaṣal alʔinɣilaab bitaaʕ nimeerii[16] tisʕa wa-sittiin fa-gaamuu gaaluu, ‘laa ʔanniẓaam daa fiʕlan niẓaam ʕaqiim[17] w-annaas alb-iiṭlaʕuu hum ʔitxarra ... ʔuwa ... w-annaas al ... yaʕnii ʔa ... almaa b-iirjaʕuu yʕiiduu[18] deel wa-ʔitxarrajuu[19] leehum ʔarbaʕa sniin bass b-iikuunuu naas maa muʔahhaliin ʃadiid.’ fii ḥiin ʔannuu fiʕlan kaanuu mumtaaziin jiddan jiddan[20] laakin muhim dii siyaasa dii w-anaa fii sana ʔuulaa wusṭaa gaamuu ɣayyaruu gaaluu, ‘laaʔ ʔalʔibtidaaʔiyya dii tabgaa sitta sniin.’ w-iisammuuhaa yaahuu ʔa ...

B: alibtidaaʔii.

A: alibtidaaʔii ...

B: badal lʔawwaliyya.

A: ay, badal lʔawwaliyya w-almadrasa lwusṭaa ysammuuhaa ssaanawii lʕaam[21] fa-ʔanaa fa-yaʕnii ʔaa ...

B: daa kaan fii ʔitneen wa-sabʕiin?

وَخَلَّصْنَا مِنْ اَلإِبْتِدَائِيَّهْ دِي وَطَوَّالِي يَمْتَحْنُونَا فَالْحَمْد لِلَّهْ نَجَحْتْ اَنَا وَخَدُّونِي فَالْمَدْرَسَهْ أَ... وُسْطَى. وَالْمَدْرَسَه الْوُسْطَى بَرْضُهُ كَانْ أَرْبَعَهْ سْنِينْ يَعْنِي الأَوَّلِيَّه ارْبَعَهْ سْنِينْ،[15] وَالْمَدْرَسَه الْوُسْطَى أَرْبَعَهْ سْنِينْ وَا... اَلسَّانَوِي الْعَالِي أَرْبَعَهْ سْنِينْ. أَنَا فِي سَنَهْ أُولَى وُسْطَى أَ... حَصَلْ اَلإِنْغِلاَبْ بِتَاعْ نِمَيْرِي[16] تِسْعَهْ وَسِتِّينْ فَقَامُوا قَالُوا، «لاَ أَلنِّظَامْ دَا فِعْلاً نِظَامْ عَقِيمْ[17] وَالنَّاسْ اَلْبِيطْلَعُوا هُمْ إِتْخَرَّ... أُوَ... وَالنَّاسْ اَلْـ... يَعْنِي أَ... اَلْمَا بِيرْجَعُوا يْعِيدُوا[18] دِيلْ وَإِتْخَرَّجُوا[19] لَيْهُمْ أَرْبَعَهْ سْنِينْ بَسّ بِيكُونُوا نَاسْ مَا مُؤَهَّلِينْ شَدِيدْ.» فِي حِينْ أَنّهُ فِعْلاً كَانُوا مُمْتَازِينْ جِدّاً جِدّاً.[20] لَكِنْ مُهِمْ دِي السِّيَاسَهْ دِي وَانَا فِي سَنَهْ أُولَى وُسْطَى قَامُوا غَيَّرُوا قَالُوا، «لاَءْ أَلإِبْتِدَائِيَّهْ دِي تَبْقَى سِتَّهْ سْنِينْ.» وِيسَمُّوهَا يَاهُ أَ ...

ب: اَلابْتِدَائِي.

أ: اَلابْتِدَائِي ...

ب: بَدَلْ الأَوَّلِيَّهْ.

أ: اَيْ، بَدَلْ الأَوَّلِيَّهْ وَالْمَدْرَسَه الْوُسْطَى يْسَمُّوهَا السَّانَوِي الْعَامْ[21] فَأَنَا فَيَعْنِي اَ...

ب: دَا كَانْ فِي إِتْنَيْنْ وَسَبْعِينْ؟

A: laa, laa, fii tisʕa w-sittiin ʔanaa badal gareetii diik ʔarbaʕa sniin, alwusṭaa badal ʔagreeyaa[22] ʔarbaʕa sniin ʔa ... gareetaa xamsa sniin. wa-ʔimtaḥanta baʕd alxamsa sniin wa-barḍuu lḥamdi llaa yaʕnii kunta muwaffaɣ jiddan jiddan najaḥta minn awwal marra wa-xaʃʃeet fiʕlan fii ʔaʕẓam madrasa saanawiyya ʔa ... fii ʔassuudaan ʔallii hii madrasat ḥantuub assaanawiyya.[23]

أ: لاَ، لاَ، فِي تِسْعَهْ وسِتِّينْ أَنَا بَدَلْ قَرَيْتِي دِيكْ أَرْبَعَهْ سِنِينْ، اَلْوُسْطَى بَدَلْ أَقْرَيَّا[22] أَرْبَعَهْ سِنِينْ أَ... قَرَيْتْهَا خَمْسَهْ سِنِينْ. وَإِمْتَحَنْتَ بَعْدْ اَلْخَمْسَهْ سِنِينْ وَبَرْضُهُ الْحَمْدُ اللَّهْ يَعْنِي كُنْتَ مُوَفَّغْ جِدّاً جِدّاً نَجَحْتَ مِنّ اَوَّلْ مَرَّهْ وَخَشَّيْتْ فِعْلاً فِي أَعْظَمْ مَدْرَسَهْ سَانَوِيَّهْ أَ... فِي أَلسُّودَانْ أَللِّي هِي مَدْرَسَةْ حَنْتُوبْ اَلسَّانَوِيَّهْ.[23]

## Vocabulary

**ḥaaja kidaa** حَاجَهْ كِدَا something (difficult to describe)

**waddaa** وَدَّى *vt* to send; to take (s.o. or s.t. to a place), convey; to put, place {*imperf:* **yawaddii,** *vn:* **widdeey**}

**xalwa** خَلْوَهْ *nfs* Qur'an school {*pl:* **xalaawii**}

**juzuu** جُزُو **[juzuʔ]** *nms* juzuʔ (one-thirtieth portion of the Qur'an); part, portion {*pl:* **ajzaa**}

**juzuu ʕamm** جُزُو عَمّ juzuʔ ʕamm (last portion of the Qur'an, first portion learned by heart)

**kalaam** كَلاَمْ *nms* situation; event; gossip; talking, speech {*pl:* **kalaamaat**}

**zamaan** زَمَانْ *adv* long ago

**kiima** قِيمَهْ **[giima]** *nfs* value, worth {*pl:* **kiyam**}

**ʃii** شِي *nms* thing; something {*pl:* **aʃyaaʔ**}

**ʃakil** شَكِلْ *nms* type, form, way; outward appearance, form, shape {*pl:* **aʃkaal**}

**zaat** زَاتْ *nfs* self

**kwayyis** كْوَيِّسْ *adj* good, nice {*fs:* **kwayyisa,** *mpl:* **kwayyisiin,** *fpl:* **kwayyisaat**}

**mumkin** مُمْكِنْ *adj also pre-verb* possible {*fs:* **mumkina,** *mpl:* **mumkiniin,** *fpl:* **mumkinaat**}

**muɣarraraat** مُغَرَّرَاتْ *npl* curriculum

**muʃ** مُشْ **[miʃ]** *particle* not

**alḥamdi li-ḷḷaa** اَلْحَمْدِ لِلَّهْ **[alḥamdi li-llaa; lḥamdi llaa; ḥamdi llaah]**

thank God *(lit. praise belongs to God)*

**deel** دِيْل *pron mp* these, near demonstrative {*ms:* **daa**, *fs:* **dii**, *pl:* **deel**}

**muhim** مُهِم [**(al)muhim(ma); (al)mihim(ma)**] *disc marker* the important thing is; the fact is (indicates return to topic after digression; precedes and indicates evaluative comment)

**laa?** لاءْ [**laa?a; laa**] *interj* no

**bigaa** بِقَى *vt also pre-verb* to be; to become; to begin; to get to the point that (inchoative action) {*imperf:* **yabgaa**, *vn:* **bagayaan**}

**yaa-** يَا [**aa-**] *particle takes suffixed pronoun* he/she/it is, they are {*ms:* **yaahuu**, *fs:* **yaahaa**, *mpl:* **yaahum**, *fpl:* **yaahun**}

**badal** بَدَلْ *conj also prep* instead of

**diik** دِيكْ *pron fs* that, far demonstrative {*ms:* **daak**, *fs:* **diik**, *pl:* **deelak**}

**marra** مَرَّة *nfs* time, occasion {*pl:* **marraat**}

## Notes

**1** 'Qur'an school' The /**xalwa**/ 'Qur'an school' of SA is known by various names in the Arabic-speaking world. Instruction stresses memorization of the Qur'an and provides basic instruction in reading, writing, and arithmetic. The teacher is usually a man of religion, often the imam of the local mosque. The /**xalwa**/ today supplements and in some cases replaces government-run schools in Sudan.

**2** The simple imperfect /**azzakkar**/ 'I remember' has as its perfect /**izzakkar**/ 'to remember'. The same verb occurs in SA as /**itzakkar**/ as well as /**idzakkar**/. In /**izzakkar**/ 'to remember', the /**t**/ (voiceless dental stop) duplicates the features of the following sound to become /**z**/ (voiced alveolar fricative) in an example of total assimilation. Partial assimilation, in contrast, is a change in a single feature of a sound. One sound becomes similar to, without becoming identical to, the sound that follows, as in /**idzakkar**/, where the voiceless dental stop /**t**/ becomes the voiced dental stop /**d**/.
Note that the sound changes like this in the derived verbs of SA are similar but not identical to sound changes that occur in MSA Form VIII verbs.

**3** The Qur'an is divided into 30 parts, each called in MSA a juzu? 'portion; part'. Each portion is named for the word or words that begin the first chapter of that portion. Children who memorize the Qur'an begin with its final portion, /**juzuu ʕamm**/. The first chapter of this portion is Sura 78, whose first words are: ʕamma yatasaaʔaluuna 'Whereof do they question one another?' Note that the chapters of the Qur'an are arranged in order of length, beginning with the longest chapter. By beginning with the final portion, children start by learning the shortest chapters of the Qur'an.

**4** The clause /attaʕliim **kaanat zamaan leehuu kiima**/ 'education in the old days had value' illustrates a feature of agreement in SA. The clause shows agreement between /**kaanat**/ 'it (fs) was' and the FS noun /**kiima**/ 'value' that serves as its grammatical subject. Speakers of SA also have the option of using /**kaan**/ invariably, with no inflection for number or gender: /attaʕliim **kaan** zamaan leehuu kiima/ 'education in the old days had value'.

**5** The word /**kiima**/ 'value' (compare MSA qiima 'value, worth') illustrates another of the ways in which SA pronounces the Arabic letter ق. It most often has the sound /g/ (voiced velar stop); the sound /ɣ/ (voiced velar fricative) tends to occur in recent borrowings from MSA. The variant /k/ (voiceless velar stop) occurs in some environments, as it does here, and /q/ (voiceless uvular stop) may occur in careful speech.

**6** The negative particle /**maa**/ in the phrase /**maa** ʕaadii/ 'extraordinary' negates the adjective /ʕaadii/ 'usual'. This negative particle was first encountered in selection 2, note 13, where it negates a verb.

**7** The phrase /muʔahhaliin taʔhiil/ lit. 'qualified (mp) a qualification' that occurs in the phrase /**muʔahhaliin taʔhiil** fiʕlan kwayyis jiddan jiddan/ 'really very, very highly qualified, lit. qualified (mp) a qualification that is really very, very good' is an example of the construction called the cognate or absolute accusative. The passive participle /muʔahhiliin/ 'qualified (mp)' here is followed by the verbal noun of the same root /taʔhiil/ 'qualification'. The construction gives greater prominence and a slightly formal feel to the entire phrase.

**8** The form /ʔisi**mm**aa/ 'its (fs) name', with a doubled or geminate /m/, also occurs as /ʔisimaa/. The doubling of the final consonant of a word preceding a suffixed pronoun is not uncommon in SA.

**9** Although the speaker talks about to the past, he uses no perfect verb in the clause /ʔisimmaa lmadrasa lʔawwaliyya zamaan/ 'its (fs) name was "primary school" in the old days'. The only indicator of the time frame of this clause is the adverbial /**zamaan**/ 'in the old days'. This use of the grammatical present to refer to the actual past or to speak of events as though they occurred at the moment of speaking is called the historical present.

**10** The speaker makes a 2MS reference here in the verb /**wa-b-taaxud**/ 'and you (ms) take' even though he addresses a female. His use of the 2MS reference here and elsewhere may be similar to the English use of "you" to mean "someone; a person."

**11** The phrase /**l?arbaʕa sniin dii**/ 'these four years' treats the counted-noun construction /**?arbaʕa sniin**/ 'four years' as a syntactic unit. It has the definite article /**al-**/ prefixed only to the first element of the construction. This is one of two possibilities that exist in SA for a definite counted-noun construction.

**12** This clause /**bi-tkuun fiʕlan ta?ahhilak bi-ṣuura kwaysa jiddan jiddan**/ 'they (fs) would really qualify you (ms) in a very, very good way' contains a pre-verb. It is the prefixed imperfect /**bi-tkuun**/ 'they (fs) are', which is followed by the simple imperfect /**ta?ahhilak**/ 'they (fs) qualify you (ms)'. The addition of /**bi-tkuun**/ 'lit. they (fs) are' in the prefixed imperfect here does not affect the time frame of the main verb /**ta?ahhal**/ 'they (fs) qualify'. Instead, it highlights the actuality of the qualification, emphasizing that, according to speaker, this qualification really did occur.

**13** The noun /**ḥifiz**/ 'memorization' (compare MSA **ḥifð̣**) illustrates a sound change of SA. The pronunciation of the Arabic letter ظ/ varies in SA. Here, it is /**z**/ (voiced alveolar fricative). In other cases, the final /**z**/ (voiced alveolar fricative) of this word would be pronounced as /**ḍ**/ (voiced pharyngealized dental stop) as in /**ḥifiḍ**/ or, less often, as /**ẓ**/ (voiced pharyngealized alveolar fricative) as in /**ḥifiẓ**/.

**14** The speaker names three aspects of education in the phrase /**min naaḥiyat ?imlaa min naaḥiyat ḥifiz min naaḥiyat ḥisaab**/ 'in dictation, in memorization, in arithmetic'. Dictation or /**?imlaa**/ is the ability to write language correctly when a text is read aloud. Memorization or /**ḥifiz**/ means learning a text by heart. Arithmetic or /**ḥisaab**/ is basic calculation. These are the basis of teaching and learning in Sudan and elsewhere.

**15** The clause /**w-almadrasa lwusṭaa** barḍuu **kaan** ?arbaʕa sniin/ 'middle school was also four years' has an unusal example of agreement. The perfect /**kaan**/ 'it (ms) was' does not show grammatical agreement with the FS noun phrase that appears to be its grammatical subject, /**almadrasa lwusṭaa**/ 'middle school'. The speaker may have omitted a noun referent that is grammatically MS, or this may be a slip of the tongue.

**16** In May of 1969, Jaafar Muhammad Nimeiri (b. 1930) led a group called the Free Officers' Movement in the coup that overthrew Sudan's civilian government in /**al?inɣilaab bitaaʕ nimeerii**/ 'Nimeiri's revolution'. He became prime minister later that year. In 1971, Nimeiri became president, a position he held until a coup in 1985 deposed him.

**17** The sound written /**q**/ (voiceless uvular stop) in /**ʕaqiim**/ 'ineffective' is, rather, a voiced uvular stop (IPA [ɢ]). This is not a sound that typically occurs in

SA.

**18** In the relative clause /almaa **b-iirjaʕuu** yʕiiduu/ 'those who didn't go back to repeat [a year of classwork]', the verb /b-iirjaʕuu/ 'they (mp) return' is a pre-verb. In verb strings like this, the action of the main verb is the reason for that of the verb of motion. In other words, the relationship between the two verbs can be translated as 'to, in order to'. Note that promotion in school in Sudan and elsewhere in the Arabic-speaking world is based entirely on final examinations. A student who fails in one subject, no matter what the year's coursework or scores in other subjects may be, must repeat the entire year. The best students, as the speaker points out, spent only four years in the old primary school system.

**19** The phrase /wa-ʔitxarrajuu/ 'when they (mp) graduate' is a ḥaal or circumstantial clause. It is embedded in a longer clause, /almaa b-iirjaʕuu yʕiiduu deel **wa-ʔitxarrajuu** leehum ʔarbaʕa sniin bass b-iikuunuu naas maa muʔahhaliin ʃadiid/ 'who don't go back to repeat [a year of classwork], when they (mp) graduate, they (mp) have only four years [of schooling] and they (mp) are people who are not well qualified'. The ḥaal clause describes a condition or circumstances at the time of the event of the main clause, here /leehum ʔarbaʕa sniin bass/ 'they (mp) have only four years'.

**20** The use of the past /kaanuu/ 'they (mp) were' in the phrase /fii ḥiin ʔannuu fiʕlan **kaanuu** mumtaaziin jiddan jiddan/ 'although, actually, they (mp) were very, very excellent' is a marked shift here. The previous utterance, which begins /laa ʔanniẓaam daa/ 'no, this system' and ends /b-iikuunuu maa muʔahhaliin ʃadiid/ 'they (mp) are actually not very well qualified', uses the present consistently. The present in that utterance suggests that it is a direct quote. The shift to the past here, combined with the use of /fii ḥiin/ 'although', indicates that the speaker has finished the quote and returned to his narrative.

**21** Following the educational reforms described here, the Sudanese /madrasa wusṭaa/ 'middle school' was known as /assaanawii lʕaam/ 'general secondary [school]'. This sets it in contrast to /assaanawii lʕaalii/ 'upper secondary [school]; high school'.

**22** The basis of the form /ʔagr**eeya**a/ 'I studied it (fs)' is /ʔagr**aaha**a/. The /h/ of the suffixed pronoun /-**ha**a/ is replaced by /y/, as seen in selection 5, note 6. That replacement would produce the sequence /-aay/, which is possible but not usual in SA. That sequence, therefore, changes from /-aay/ to /-eey/ (it is monophthongized). The end result is the form seen here, /ʔagr**eeya**a/.

**23** As the speakers states, /madrasat ḥantuub assaanawiyya/ Hantoub Secondary School' in al-Jazira Province was at that time the best and most prestigious secondary school in Sudan.

# ʕaadil wa-hudaa

*This selection is excerpted from a Sudanese musalsal or serial drama. These serials are broadcast every evening for a certain period and can be quite popular. They usually have elements of drama, suspense, comedy, romance, and social commentary. The two characters featured here, young professionals, use language that is educated but recognizably Sudanese.*

A: maalik?[1]

B: ʕaadil, fii zool min giibaalik b-iiʕạayin leek.

A: kidaa?

B: [Hoda points him out.] aywa, haadaak, ʕaayin leehuu.

A: weenuu?[2]

B: aywa haadaak wa-baayin ʕaleeh[3] naawii leek ba-niyya baṭṭaala.

A: arraajil daa?

B: aywa.

[Adil heads towards the man and is hit by a car. Later, in the hospital, he and Hoda continue their conversation.]

A: hudaa.

B: ḥaamdi llaah ʕa-ssalaama yaa ʕaadil.

A: aḷḷaa yasallimik yaa hudaa.

B: leeh taʕmal[4] fiinii kidaa yaa ʕaadil?

A: maʕliiʃ yaa hudaa, ɣaẓban ʕannii.

# عَادِلْ وَهُدَى

أ:  مَالِكْ؟[1]

ب: عَادِلْ، فِي رَاجِلْ مِنْ قِيبَالِكْ بِيعَايِنْ لَيْكْ.

أ:  كِدَا؟

ب: [Hoda points him out.] اَيْوَهْ، هَدَاكْ، عَايِنْ لَيْهُ.

أ:  وَيْنُهْ؟[2]

ب: اَيْوَهْ هَدَاكْ وَبَايِنْ عَلَيْهْ[3] نَاوِي لَيْكْ بَنِيَّهْ بَطَّالَهْ.

أ:  اَلرَّاجِلْ دَا؟

ب: اَيْوَهْ.

[Adil heads towards the man and is hit by a car. Later, in the hospital, he and Hoda continue their conversation.]

أ:  هُدَى.

ب: حَامْدِ اللَّهْ عَالسَّلَامَهْ يَا عَادِلْ.

أ:  اَللَّهْ يَسَلِّمِكْ يَا هُدَى.

ب: لَيْهْ تَعْمَلْ[4] فِينِي كِدَا يَا عَادِلْ؟

أ:  مَعْلِيشْ يَا هُدَى، غَصْبًا عَنِّي.

B: maa ʕaarfa lḥaṣal leeh ʃnuu.

A: ʃifigtii ʕaleey, miʃ kidaa?[5, 6]

B: inta[7] zzool daa mnuu? jareet ba-waraah ba-ṣuura maa ʕaadiyya.

A: kunta ʕaayiz ʔaḥaṣṣiluu yaa hudaa, kaan laazim ʔaḥaṣṣiluu.[8]

B: inta zzool daa mnuu? maa tguul leey daa ...

A: yaa hudaa, yaahuu[9] xaalii[10] lkunta b-afattiʃ fiih yaa hudaa.

B: bass inta mutʔakkid?

A: mutʔakkid aywa.

B: bass laakin daa ʃakluu maa ẓariif wa-naẓaraatuu muxiifa.

A: maskiin yaa hudaa, b-iiʕaanii min alwaḥda w-attaʃarrud.

B: laakin baayin ʕalee b-iriidak[11] yaa ʕaadil.

A: fii ʃii b-iʃiddanii leeh yaa hudaa, fii ḥasaas daayman, daayman b-iiʃiddanii leehuu, fi rtibaaṭ beenii wa-beenuu maa gaadir afhamuu laakin yaa xaṣaara maa ḥaṣṣaltuu.

ب: مَا عَارْفَه الْحَصَلْ لَيْه شْنُو.

أ: شِفِقْتِي عَلَيّ، مِشْ كِدَا؟[5, 6]

ب: اِنْتَ[7] الزَّوْلْ دَا مْنُو؟ جَرَيْتْ بَوَرَاهْ بَصُورَهْ مَا عَادِيَّهْ.

أ: كُنْتَ عَايِزْ أَحَصِّلْهُ يَا هُدَى، كَانْ لاَزِمْ أَحَصِّلْهُ.[8]

ب: اِنْتَ الزَّوْلْ دَا مْنُو؟ مَا تْقُولْ لَيّ دَا...

أ: يَا هُدَى، يَاهُ[9] خَالِي[10] الْكُنْتَ بَافَتِّشْ فِيهْ يَا هُدَى.

ب: بَسّ اِنْتَ مُتْأَكِّدْ؟

أ: مُتْأَكِّدْ اَيْوَهْ.

ب: بَسّ لَكِنْ دَا شَكْلُهُ مَا ظَرِيفْ وَنَظَرَاتْهُ مُخِيفَهْ.

أ: مَسْكِينْ يَا هُدَى، بِيعَانِي مِنْ اَلْوَحْدَهْ وَالتَّشَرُّدْ.

ب: لَكِنْ بَايِنْ عَلَيْهْ بِرِيدَكْ[11] يَا عَادِلْ.

أ: فِي شِي بِشِدَّنِي لَيْهْ يَا هُدَى، فِي حَسَاسْ دَايْمًا، دَايْمًا بِيشِدَّنِي لَيْهُ، فَارْتِبَاطْ بَيْنِي وَبَيْنْهُ مَا قَادِرْ اَفْهَمْهُ لَكِنْ يَا خَصَارَهْ مَا حَصَّلْتْهُ.

## Vocabulary

**maal-** مَال *interrog takes pronoun suffix* what about s.o., what's wrong with s.o.

**giibaalik** قيبَالك *adv* for a while

**ʕaayan li-** عَايَن ل *vi* to look at; to stare at {*imperf:* **yaʕaayin,** *vn:* **muʕaayana**}

**kidaa** كدَا *interrog* is that so, really

**aywa** أيْوه **[iywa; ay; ayya]** *interj* yes

**haadaak** هَدَاك *pron ms* that, far demonstrative {*fs:* **haadiik,** *mpl:* **haadoolak,** *fpl:* **haadeelak**}

**ween** وَيْن *interrog may take suffixed pronoun* where

**baayin ʕalaa** بَايِن عَلَى *invariable* it seems that, it appears that

**baṭṭaal** بَطَّال *adj* bad; evil; spoiled (of food) {*fs:* **baṭṭaala,** *mpl:* **baṭṭaaliin,** *fpl:* **baṭṭaalaat**}

**raajil** رَاجِل *nms* man {*pl:* **rujaal**}

**ʕa-** عَ **[ʕalaa; ʕalee]** *prep* for, about (object of reference or concern)

**ʕalaa** عَلَى **[ʕa; ʕalee]** *prep* for, about (object of reference or concern); of duty, obligation; according to; on

**ḥamdi ḷḷaah ʕa-ssalaama** حَمْد لله عَالسّلَامَة **[(al)ḥamdi (li-)ḷḷaa(h) ʕa(laa) ssalaama]** thank God for s.o.'s safety (used when s.o. recovers from an illness or returns after an absence)

**aḷḷaa yasallim-** اللّه يَسَلِّم may God keep s.o. safe (possible response to /ḥamdi llaa ʕa ssalaama/ 'thank God for s.o.'s safety')

**maʕliiʃ** مَعْلِيش **[maʕleeʃ]** *interj* never mind, I'm sorry, don't worry

**ɣaṣbaan ʕan** غَصْبَان عَن **[ɣaẓbaan ʕan]** against s.o.'s will

**ʃin-** شِن **[ʃin]** *interrog takes suffixed pronoun* what {*ms:* **ʃinuu,** *fs:* **ʃinaa,** *pl:* **ʃinum**}

**ʃnuu** شْنُو *interrog invariable* what

**miʃ** مِش **[muʃ]** *particle* not

**miʃ kidaa** مِش كدَا isn't that so, right

**inta** انْتَ *disc marker invariable* you (device to get listener's attention and underscore urgency of question or request)

**min-** مِن *interrog takes suffixed pronoun* who {*ms:* **minuu,** *fs:* **minaa,** *pl:* **minum**}

**minuu** مِنُو **[mnuu]** *interrog invariable* who

**ʕaayiz** عَايِز **[ʕaawiz]** *adj pre-verb* wanting, desiring {*fs:* **ʕaayza,** *mpl:* **ʕaayziin,** *fpl:* **ʕaayzaat**}

**ḥaṣṣal** حَصَّل *vt* to catch up to, reach {*imperf:* **yaḥaṣṣil,** *vn:* **taḥṣiil**}

**fattaʃ fi-** فَتَّش في *vt* to search for {*imperf:* **yafattiʃ fii-,** *vn:* **taftiiʃ fii-**}

**ẓariif** ظَرِيف *adj* nice; elegant {*fs:* **ẓariifa,** *mpl:* **ẓurafa,** *fpl:* **ẓariifaat**}

**naẓra** نَظْرَة *nfs* look in s.o.'s eyes {*pl:* **naẓraat, naẓaraat**}

**raad (ridta)** رَاد (رِدْت) *vt* to like, love {*imperf:* **yariid,** *vn:* **reed**}

**daayman** دَايْماً *adv* always, constantly

**gaadir** قَادِر *adj pre-verb* able to {*fs:* **gaadra,** *mpl:* **gaadriin,** *fpl:* **gaadraat**}

**yaa xaṣaara** يا خَصَارَة what a pity, too bad *(lit. o loss!)*

## Notes

**1** The interrogative /**maalik**?/ 'what's wrong with you (fs)?' differs from certain other interrogatives of SA that take suffixed pronouns. The interrogative /maal-/ does not occur in isolation as, for example, /ween/ 'where' can (see selection 7, note 2). It always has a suffixed pronoun, even where the referent of the interrogative is named, as in /**maaluu xaalid**?/ 'what's wrong with Khalid?'

**2** The interrogative /ween/ 'where?' may take a suffixed pronoun, as it does here in the form /weenuu/ 'where is he?' It may also stand alone.

**3** The word /baayin/ 'seeming' in the phrase /**baayin** ʕaleeh/ 'it (ms) seems that he' is the active participle of the verb /baan/ - /yabiin/ 'to be visible, apparent'. It occurs invariably (with no change for gender or number) in this phrase. The suffixed pronoun that occurs with the preposition /ʕalaa/, however, must agree in gender and number with the logical subject of the clause: /baayin ʕalee**haa** taʕbaana/ 'it seems she is tired'.

**4** The simple imperfect of /taʕmal/ 'you (ms) would do' occurs in more limited contexts than does the prefixed imperfect of /**bi**-taʕmal/ 'you (ms) do'. The simple imperfect is most often seen in verb strings such as /ʕaawziin **iimʃuu**/ 'they (mp) want to go'. When it occurs independently, the simple imperfect usually indicates that the action of the verb is potential rather than actual. For example Hoda expresses her distress over Adil's accident here with the simple imperfect /leeh **taʕmal** fiinii kidaa?/ 'why would you (ms) do this to me?' She does not use the prefixed imperfect

/leeh **bi-taʕmal** fiinii kidaa?/ 'why do you (ms) do this to me?' Note, however, that in rapid or casual speech, the simple imperfect sometimes occurs where the prefixed imperfect would be expected.

**5** The exchange, /B: **maa ʕaarfa lḥaṣal lee ʃnuu.** A: **ʃifigtii ʕaleey miʃ kidaa**?/ 'B: I don't know what happened to him. A: You (fs) were worried about me, isn't that so?', seems to make no sense. The two speakers are trying to take the conversation in different directions. Hoda is preoccupied with the mysterious stranger, while Adil wants to take advantage of Hoda's sympathy for his injury. In Sudan and elsewhere in the Arabic-speaking world, opportunities for private conversation between the two sexes can be limited, so a Sudanese audience might sympathize with Adil's situation or even find it amusing.

**6** The use of the negative particle /**miʃ**/ in the phrase /**miʃ kidaa**?/ 'isn't that so?' is somewhat unusual in SA. The most-used negative particle of SA is /**maa**/, as discussed in selection 2, note 13. Both /**miʃ**/ and the more frequent /**muʃ**/ occur in SA. Some speakers of SA, however, consider the use of /**muʃ**/ and /**miʃ**/ to be non-Sudanese.

**7** The pronoun /**inta**/ 'you (ms)' does not indicate the listener in the question /**inta zzool daa mnuu**?/ 'who's that man?' It is, rather, a marker of attitude that gets the listener's attention and underscores the urgency of the speaker's question.

**8** There are two verb strings in the utterance /**kunta ʕaayiz ʔaḥaṣṣiluu yaa hudaa kaan laazim ʔaḥaṣṣiluu**/ 'I wanted to catch up with him, Hoda. I had to catch up with him.' The two verb strings, /**kunta ʕaayiz ʔaḥaṣṣiluu**/ 'I wanted to catch up with him' and /**kaan laazim ʔaḥaṣṣiluu**/ 'I had to catch up with him', differ in terms of agreement. The pre-verb /**laazim**/ 'necessary' is invariable. When /**kaan**/ 'to be' sets /**laazim**/ in the past, /**kaan**/ does not inflect for gender or number. In contrast, /**ʕaayiz**/ 'wanting (ms)' has gender and number agreement, as does /**kaan**/ 'to be' when it defines the time frame of /**ʕaayiz**/ (as in /**kunta ʕaayza ʕmaluu suudaanii**/ 'I wanted to make it (ms) Sudanese').

**9** The particle /**yaa**-/ (also /**aa**-/) occurs only with a suffixed pronoun, as in the form /**yaahuu**/ 'he is'. It identifies someone or something whose identity was previously unknown, as it does here.

**10** Adil's concern about the person he calls /**xaalii**/ 'my [maternal] uncle' evokes stereotypes of family life in Sudan and elsewhere in the Arabic-speaking world. These portray the relationship between a person and her or his /**xaal**/ 'maternal uncle, mother's brother' as close and affectionate. This may explain why Adil injures himself trying to catch up with the mysterious stranger and then describes his reaction to him in emotional terms.

**11** The full form **/bi-yariidak/** retains the short /i/ of the imperfect /bi-/ prefix and the short /a/ of the simple imperfect /**yariid**/ 'he loves'. The form **/b-iiriidak/** deletes the unstressed short vowel /a/ in an open syllable, then merges the /i/ and /y/ of **/bi-yriid/** to produce **/b-iiriidak/**. The example cited here further shortens the long vowel /ii/ to produce **/b-iriidak/**.

# albaḥas ʕan waẓiifa

*This selection comes from a longer conversation between two friends living in the Washington, DC area. The male speaker is understandably concerned about not having a job. He describes his job hunt in some detail and in language that shows some features of MSA.*

A: haloo?

B: aloo, zayy alḥaal?

A: ahlan wa-sahlan, ʔazzeeyik?

B: keef ʔaḥwaalak?

A: w-aḷḷaahii[1] xeer ḥamdi llaah.

B: ʕamalta ʃnuu ʕa-ʃʃuɣul?

A: w-aḷḷaahii yaa ḥanaan, aʃʃuɣul daa ʕaamil lii muʃkila kabiira jiddan, ʔawwal ḥaaja zeey maa ʃaayfa lbalad dii[2] yaʕnii ẓuruuf alʕamal fiihaa ṣaʕba ʃwayya.

B: aa.

A: fa ... muhimm yaʕnii ʕan ṭariig almunaẓẓama, ʕan ṭa ..., ṭariigtii lxaaṣṣa b-iiḥaawil[3] ɣaaytuu ʔalgaa ṭariiga.

B: yaʕnii ligiit ʔa ... ʔa ... furaṣ fii ḥittaat muʕayyana wallaa lissa?

A: w-aḷḷaahii ʔa ... ṭabʕan fii jariida b-ṭiṭlaʕ yoom allaḥad.

B: aha ...

# اَلْبَحَسْ عَنْ وَظِيفَه

أ: هَلَوْ؟

ب: اَلَوْ، زَيّ اَلْحَالْ؟

أ: اَهْلاً وَسَهْلاً، أَزَّيِّكْ؟

ب: كَيْفْ أَحْوَالَكْ؟

أ: وَاللَّهِ[1] خَيْرْ حَمْدِ اللَّهْ.

ب: عَمَلْتَ شْنُو مَعَ الشُّغُلْ؟

أ: وَاللَّهِ يَا حَنَانْ، اَلشُّغُلْ دَا عَامِلْ لِي مُشْكِلَهْ كَبِيرَهْ جِداً، أَوَّلْ حَاجَهْ زَيّ مَا شَايْفَه الْبَلَدْ دِي[2] يَعْنِي ظُرُوفْ اَلْعَمَلْ فِيهَا صَعْبَهْ شْوَيَّهْ.

ب: آ.

أ: فَ... مُهِمّ يَعْنِي عَنْ طَرِيقْ اَلْمُنَظَّمَهْ، عَنْ طَ... ، طَرِيقْتِي الْخَاصَّهْ بِيحَاوِلْ[3] غَايْتُهْ أَلْقَى طَرِيقَهْ.

ب: يَعْنِي لِقِيتْ أَ... أَ... فُرَصْ فِي حِتَّاتْ مُعَيَّنَهْ وَلاَّ لِسَّهْ؟

أ: وَاللَّهِ أَ... طَبْعًا فِي جَرِيدَهْ بْطِطْلَعْ يَوْمْ اَلاَّحَدْ.

ب: اَهَهْ...

A: kull yoom ʔaḥad takuun fiihaa ʕlaanaat katiira jiddan[4, 5] ʕan alwaẓaayif w-aʃʃuɣul hinaa.

B: gaddamta minnaa?

A: w-aḷḷaahii yaʕnii ɣaddamta -mkin[6] gariib ʕaʃara[7] ṭalab.[8]

B: gaddamta ween u-ween?

A: w-aḷḷaahii gaddamt awwal ḥaaja[9] kaan lii-ʃarika fii farjiinyaa.

B: aha …

A: wa-taanii gaddamta lii-maʕhad kidaa ʕaayziin waaḥid yakuun bitaaʕ musa … naayib musajjil.

B: aha …

A: u-saaʕii, ṭabʕan intii ʕaarfa ʔanaa, ṭabʕan ʔahuu ʃuɣlii majaal alluɣaat wa-majaal ʕamal almunaẓẓamaat daa[10] ba-ṣifa xaaṣṣa …

B: a …

A: ʕaʃaan kidaa yaʕnii marakkiz innii ʔalgaa ḥaaja fi lmajaal illii[11] ʔanaa ʕaarfaa[12] ṭabʕan baxa … majaal ʕamal almunaẓẓamaat daa.

B: ay akiid liyanna daa b-iifiidak[13] katiir lee-giddaam yaʕnii fii lmustaɣbal waa … ʕamalta maʕaahum muʕaayanaat wallaa lissa?

أ: كُلّ يَوْمْ أَحَدْ تَكُونْ فِيهَا اعْلانَاتْ كَتِيرَهْ جِدّاً[4, 5] عَنْ اَلْوَظَايِفْ وَالشُّغُلْ هِنَا.

ب: قَدَّمْتَ مِنَّها؟

أ: وَاللَّهِ يَعْنِي غَدَّمْتَ -امْكِنْ[6] قَرِيبْ عَشَرَهْ[7] طَلَبْ.[8]

ب: قَدَّمْتَ وَيْنْ أُوَيْنْ؟

أ: وَاللَّهِ قَدَّمْتْ اَوَّلْ حَاجَهْ[9] كَانْ لِيشَرِكَهْ فِي فَرْجِينْيَا.

ب: اَهَهْ...

أ: وَتَانِي قَدَّمْتَ لِيمَعْهَدْ كِدَا عَايْزِينْ وَاحِدْ يَكُونْ بِتَاعْ مُسَـ... نَايِبْ مُسَجِّلْ.

ب: اَهَهْ...

أ: أُسَاعِي، طَبْعًا انْتِي عَارْفَهْ أَنَا، طَبْعًا أَهْمُ شُغْلِي مَجَالْ اَللُّغَاتْ وَمَجَالْ عَمَلْ اَلْمُنَظَّمَاتْ دَا[10] بَصِفَهْ خَاصَّهْ...

ب: اَ...

أ: عَشَانْ كِدَا يَعْنِي مَرَكِّزْ انِّى أَلْقَى حَاجَهْ فَالْمَجَالْ اِللِّي[11] أَنَا عَارْفْهَا[12] طَبْعًا بَخَـ... مَجَالْ عَمَلْ اَلْمُنَظَّمَاتْ دَا.

ب: اَي اَكِيدْ لِينَّ دَا بِيفِيدَكْ[13] كَتِيرْ لَيْقدَّامْ يَعْنِي فِي الْمُسْتَغْبَلْ وَا... عَمَلْتَ مَعَاهُمْ مُعَايَنَاتْ وَلاَّ لِسَّهْ؟

A: w-aḷḷaa ʔintii ʕaarfa ʔa ... ʕamalta muʕaayana, ah, muʕaayanteen ḥagiiga,[14] waḥda ʕamaltaa fii farjiinyaa fii munaḍ̣ḍama naas ismum joon asnoo, ʕaarfa ʃuɣulum zeey ʃuɣul naas alaay aar sii fi ssuudaan.

B: aha.

A: yaʕnii munaẓẓama kidaa zeey maa -dguulii ʃaɣɣaala fii majaal alam ... ʔal ... ʔal ... ʔal ... xadamaat aṣṣaḥḥa b-taʕmal daa, ʕuguudaat maʕ alḥukuuma fil ... ʔifriiɣyaa fi lʕaalam alʕarabii wa-hnaay, fa ... ʔalmuhim yaʕnii hiya waẓiifa ẓariifa ʃwiyya laakin alwaaḥid kaan ligaahaa yakuun xaamma ʃadiid[15, 16] yaʕnii.

أ: وَاللَّهْ إِنْتِي عَارْفَهْ أَ... عَمَلْتَ مُعَايَنَهْ، اَهْ، مُعَايَنْتَيْنْ حَقِيقَهْ،[14] وَحْدَهْ عَمَلْتْهَا فِي فَرْجِينْيَا فِي مُنَظَّمَهْ نَاسْ اِسْمْهُمْ جَوْنْ اَسْنَوْ، عَارْفَهْ شُغْلُهُمْ زَيّ شُغْلْ نَاسْ اَلاَي اَرْ سِي فِالسُّودَانْ.

ب: اَهَهْ.

أ: يَعْنِي مُنَظَّمَهْ كِدَا زَيّ مَا -دْقُولِي شَغَّالَهْ فِي مَجَالْ اَلْمَـ... أَلْـ... أَلْـ... خَدَمَاتْ اَلصَّحَّهْ بْتَعْمَلْ دَا، عُقُودَاتْ مَعَ الْحُكُومَهْ فِالْـ... إِفْرِيغْيَا فِالْعَالَمْ اَلْعَرَبِي وَهْنَايْ، فَـ... أَلْمُهِمْ يَعْنِي هِيَ وَظِيفَهْ ظَرِيفَهْ شْوِيَّهْ لَكِنْ اَلْوَاحِدْ كَانْ لِقَاهَا يَكُونْ خَامّ شَدِيدْ[15, 16] يَعْنِي.

## Vocabulary

**zayy alḥaal** زَيّ اَلْحَالْ how are you

**azzeey** اَزَّيّ **[azzayy]** *interrog* how is, how are

**keef aḥwaal** كَيْفْ اَحْوَالْ how is, how are

**w-al̤l̤aahii** وَاللَّه **[w-al̤l̤aah]** really and truly, by God (oath or exclamation)

**ẓuruuf** ظُرُوفْ *nmpl* unfortunate circumstances

**ɣaaytuu** غَايْتُه *adv* to the utmost; very much

**lissa** لِسَّه *adv* not yet; still

**hinaa** هِنَا *adv* here

**gaddam** قَدَّمْ *vt* to submit, present, turn in {*imperf:* **yagaddim**, *vn:* **tagdiim**}

**gariib** قَرِيبْ *prep* about, approximately; *adj* near, close

**ween u-ween** وِيْنْ اُوِيْنْ where exactly *(lit. where and where)*

**taanii** تَانِي *adv* also, as well; again, another time

**waaḥid** وَاحِدْ *nms* someone, a person

**saʕaa** سَعَى *vi* to try, attempt {*imperf:* **yasʕaa**, *vn:* **saʕii**}

**intii** اِنْتِي **[ittii]** *pron fs* you

**aa-** آ **[yaa-]** *particle takes suffixed pronoun* he/she/it is, they are {*ms:* **aahuu**, *fs:* **aahaa**, *mpl:* **aahum**, *fpl:* **aahin**}

**akiid** اَكِيدْ *adj* certain; *adv* for sure, certainly {*fs:* **akiida**, *mpl:* **akiidiin**, *fpl:* **akiidaat**}

**katiir** كَتِيرْ *adv* a lot; very much; *adj* much, many

**giddaam** قِدَّامْ *prep* in the future, the time to come; ahead, forward

**muʕaayana** مُعَايَنَة *nfs* interview; inspection {*pl:* **muʕaayanaat**}

**ḥagiiga** حَقِيقَة **[alḥagiiga]** *disc marker* truly, the fact is that (softens opinion or correction)

**ʃwiyya** شْوِيَّه **[ʃiwayya]** *adv* somewhat, a bit

**kaan** كَانْ *particle invariable conditional* if

**xaamma** خَامّْ *adj invariable* great, terrific

## Notes

**1** The male speaker begins his answer to every question the female speaker asks with the oath /**w-aḷḷaahii**/ 'by God', as he does here. Oaths such as this or the milder /**wa-ḥaatak**/ 'by your (ms) life' (discussed in selection 4, note 3) add force or emphasis to a statement. For this speaker, however, the oath may be a verbal routine that has lost much of its meaning, not unlike the American "you know" or "I mean."

**2** The phrase /**lbalad dii**/ 'this country' contains the FS demonstrative pronoun /**dii**/. The noun /**balad**/ is grammatically F or M in SA, in other varieties of spoken Arabic, and in MSA.

**3** The speaker uses the 3MS referent in the form /**b-iiḥaawil**/ 'he is trying' although the context indicates that he is talking about himself. This is apparently a slip of the tongue.

**4** In the clause /**kull yoom ʔaḥad takuun fiihaa ʕlaanaat katiira jiddan**/ 'every Sunday it (fs) has a lot of advertisements', the simple imperfect /**takuun**/ 'it (fs) is' agrees with its non-human P subject /**ʕlaanaat**/ 'advertisements'. Agreement of /**kaan**/ in clauses with /**fii**/ 'there is, there are', with /**ʕind**/ 'to have' is common in SA. It is less common in certain other varieties of spoken Arabic, in which /**kaan**/ is usually invariable, as in /**kaan ʕindii muʃkila**/ 'I had a problem'.

**5** The speaker uses the simple imperfect /**takuun**/ 'they (fs) are' to describe a regular occurrence in the clause /**kull yoom ʔaḥad takuun fiihaa ʕlaanaat katiira jiddan**/ 'every Sunday it (fs) has a lot of advertisements'. The event is a regular occurrence and, therefore, is actual rather than potential (as discussed in selection 7, note 4). Thus, the prefixed imperfect would usually occur. In this case, however, the imperfect /**bi-**/ prefix can be omitted because it occurs in the speaker's previous utterance, /**fii jariida b-ṭiṭlaʕ yoom allaḥad**/ 'there is a newspaper that comes out on Sunday'. That use of the prefixed imperfect carries over into this one. The imperfect /**bi-**/ prefix could recur here, but does not have to.

**6** In the phrase /**ɣaddamta -mkin**/ 'I submitted, maybe', the verb /**-mkin**/ 'maybe; it is possible' occurs as a reduced form of the imperfect /**yimkin**/ or of another variant /**imkin**/.

**7** SA, like certain other varieties of spoken Arabic, uses a single, invariable form of the number in the counted-noun construction. SA, however, uses the invariable form of the number that ends in /**a**/, as here, /**ʕaʃara**/ 'ten'.

**8** The speaker uses the S form of the noun in the phrase /**ʕaʃara ṭalab**/ 'ten applications'. More usually, the P form of the noun occurs in counted-noun constructions where the number is between three and ten, as in /ʕaʃara ṭalaba**at**/ 'ten applications'.

**9** The phrase /**awwal** ḥaaja/ 'the first thing' is an indefinite construct phrase that resembles a superlative, such as /**aḥsan** ḥaaja/ 'the best thing'. In both the ordinal number construct phrase and the superlative structure, an adjective stands as the first term of the construct phrase. Both phrases are translated as definite, although neither contains a grammatical marker for definiteness.

**10** In the phrase /**majaal** ʕamal almunaẓẓamaat **daa**/ 'this field of organization work', the demonstrative /daa/ follows the noun it modifies, as it usually does. The noun it modifies, however, is /majaal/ 'field', the first noun of a three-noun construct phrase. The demonstrative cannot immediately follow the noun (as in /almajaal **daa**/ 'this field') because that noun is in a construct phrase and, under most circumstances, nothing stands between the elements of a construct phrase. Therefore, the demonstrative appears at the end of the construct phrase.

**11** The speaker here uses the relative pronoun /illii/ (also /allii/), associated with Cairene and pan-Arabic (the variety used by educated Arabic speakers in the eastern Arabic-speaking world), rather than the SA relative pronoun /al-/. Where speakers have options, they may use them to shift up and down the scale from formal to casual speech, or simply for the sake of variety. As mentioned in selection 7, note 6, however, some view these usages as non-Sudanese.

**12** The resumptive pronoun /-aa/ (for /-haa/) 'it (fs)' in the relative clause /**lmajaal** illii ʔanaa ʕaarf**aa**/ 'something in the field I know' is FS. It does not agree with its apparent grammatical subject /lmajaal/ 'the field'. Instead, this pronoun appears to refer to the preceding noun /ḥaaja/ in /**ḥaaja** fi lmajaal illii ʔanaa ʕaarf**aa**/ 'something in the field I know'. This is an apparent slip of the tongue.

**13** The prefixed imperfect, as in /b-iifiidak/ 'it (ms) will benefit you (ms)', occurs in the region of the capital and other Arabic-speaking regions of Sudan to refer to the future as well as to the present. In addition, in the region of the capital the prefix /ḥa-/ can be added to the simple imperfect (as in /**ha**-yfiidak/ 'it (ms) will benefit you (ms)') to refer to the future.

**14** The word /ḥagiiga/ in the phrase /ah, muʕaayanteen **ḥagiiga**/ 'ah, actually two interviews' functions as a marker of attitude. It indicates (and perhaps softens) the speaker's self-correction. In other contexts, /ḥagiiga/ (more usually /alḥagiiga/) mitigates a speaker's statement, as in /**alḥagiiga** maa ʃuftum/ 'really, I haven't seen them (mp)'.

**15** The form /kaan/ is a conditional particle in the sentence /alwaaḥid **kaan** ligaahaa yakuun xaamma ʃadiid/ 'if a person got it (fs), it (ms) would be really great'. It does not refer to past time. Note that the conditional particle /**kaan**/ and the verb /**kaan**/ are homophonous. Only context indicates the way in which this item should be translated.

**16** The adjective /**xaamma**/ 'great, wonderful' is invariable. It does not inflect for gender or number. In this, it resembles the invariable MSA adjective xaam 'raw, unprocessed'.

# alḥayaa f -ʔamriikaa

*In this selection, speakers heard in previous selections talk about some of the possibilities and problems of life in the US. Their language still shows some formal features, such as the use of /taɣriiban/ 'approximately'. In general, however, their speech here is relaxed and informal.*

A: gutta leek ʔintii ya ... jaaya[1] min ween?

B: anaa jaaya min assuudaan wa-min ajjiziira.

A: aha ... min ajjiziira wam ... ḥillatkum isimaa ʃnuu?

B: isimhaa ʔum jiriis laakin mawluuda fii ṭayyib aʃʃeex ʕabd albaagii.

A: wa-ṭayyib um jiriis dii ʔa ... ʔa ... ʔismuu ʃnuu huu ... ʔabahaanik[2] ʃaɣɣaaliin ʃnuu ʔintii?[3]

B: anaa ʔabuuy muzaariʕ u-raajil aʕmaal, wa-ʔummii ha ... ʔa ... yaʕnii maa ʃaɣɣaala bass fi lbeet ʔaa ... ʔitta[4] jiit miteen assuudaan?[5] ʔinta jiit miteen amriikaa?[6]

A: wa-laa ... -mriikaa ʔanaa jiit zeey aa ... leey, leey talaata sniin[7] taqriiban yaʕnii.

B: taɣriiban talaata sniin.

A: aa.

B: aha ... ʔanaa jaaya min taɣriiban ʔa ... taɣriiban xamsa sanawaat.[8]

A: aha ...

B: garrabt akammal xamsa sanawaat.

# اَلْحَيَاهْ فَأَمْرِيكَا

أ: قُتَّ لَيْكْ إِنْتِي يَـ... جَايَهْ[1] مِنْ وَيْنْ؟

ب: اَنَا جَايَهْ مِنْ اَلسُّودَانْ وَمِنْ اَلْجِّزِيرَهْ.

أ: اَهَهْ... مِنْ اَلْجِّزِيرَهْ وَمْـ... حِلَّتْكُمْ اِسِمْهَا شْنُو؟

ب: اِسِمْهَا أُمْ جِرِيسْ لَكِنْ مَوْلُودَهْ فِي طَيِّبْ اَلشَّيْخْ عَبْدْ اَلْبَاقِي.

أ: وَطَيِّبْ أُمْ جِـرِيسْ دِي أ... أ... إِسْـمُـهُ شْنُو هُو... أَبَهَانِكْ[2] شَغَّالِينْ شْنُو إِنْتِي؟[3]

ب: اَنَا أَبُوي مُزَارِعْ أُرَاجِلْ اَعْمَالْ، وَأُمِّي هَـ... أ... يَعْنِي مَا شَغَّالَهْ بَسّ فَالْبَيْتْ آ... إِتَّ[4] جِيتْ مِتَيْنْ اَلسُّودَانْ؟[5] إِنْتَ جِيتْ مِتَيْنْ اَمْرِيكَا؟[6]

أ: وَلاَ... امْـرِيكَا أَنَا جِـيتْ زَيّ آ... لَيّ، لَيّ تَلاَتَهْ سْنِينْ[7] تَقْرِيبًا يَعْنِي.

ب: تَغْرِيبًا تَلاَتَهْ سْنِينْ.

أ: آ.

ب: اَهَهْ... أَنَا جَايَهْ مِنْ تَغْرِيبًا أ... تَغْرِيبًا خَمْسَهْ سَنَوَاتْ.[8]

أ: اَهَهْ...

ب: قَرَّبْتْ اَكَمِّلْ خَمْسَهْ سَنَوَاتْ.

A: aha.

B: aha … wabiṭar … naawii tarjaʕ miteen?

A: w-aḷḷaahii b-irjaʕ yaʕnii baʕad xamsa sniin[8] ta … ḥaaja zeey dii, ʔay baʕd sanateen, talaata sniin.[9]

B: kunta bi-ttwoogaʕ[10] ʔin talgaa jinsiyyaat katiira bi-lmustawaa daa?

A: ṭabʕan ʔay, ʔay, ʔah, b-aguul lik ay, b-atwakkaʕ laʔannuu kullu zool fi lʕaalam wa-b-iḥlam ʕinduu lḥilm alʔameerikii.

B: ṣaḥḥ.

A: annuu yaʕnii yḥlam bi-ʔinnuu b-jii[11] ʔamriikaa ʕaʃaan iḥaggig iḥlaamuu.

B: ṣaḥḥ.

A: laakin hum alal … annaẓra btaaʕtum muftakriin alʕamaliyya -nnaa sahla saakit.

B: haa …

A: annuu mimmaa jaa[12] -mriikaa hinaa bigaa milyuuneer wa-ḥaggag addaayir yaʕmaluu wa-rikib leehuu -f ʕarabiyya kabiira[13] …

B: wa-ʕaaʃ murtaaḥ.

A: w-kidaa, laakin hinaa laa, ʔinta bi-tjii tabdaahaa[14] fiʕlan minn az-*zero*.

B: haa …

A: min xamsa doolaar fi ssaaʕa …

أ: اَهَهْ.

ب: اَهَهْ... وَبِطَرْ... نَاوِي تَرْجَعْ مِتَيْنْ؟

أ: وَاللَّهِ بِارْجَعْ يَعْنِي بَعَدْ خَمْسَهْ سْنِينْ[8] تَـ... حَاجَهْ زَيّ دِي، أَي بَعْدْ سَنَتَيْنْ، تَلاَتَهْ سْنِينْ.[9]

ب: كُنْتَ بِتَّوْقَعْ[10] إِنْ تَلْقَى جِنْسِيَّاتْ كَتِيرَهْ بِالْمُسْتَوَى دَا ؟

أ: طَبْعًا أَيْ، أَيْ، أَهْ، بَاقُولْ لِكْ اَيْ، بَاتْوَكَّعْ لأَنّهُ كُلُّ زَوْلْ فِالْعَالَمْ وَبِحْلَمْ عِنْدُهُ الْحِلْمْ اَلأَمَيْرِكِي.

ب: صَحّ.

أ: اَنّهُ يَعْنِي يَحْلَمْ بِإِنّهُ بْجِي[11] أَمْرِيكَا عَشَانْ اِحَقِّقْ اِحْلاَمْهْ.

ب: صَحّ.

أ: لَكِنْ هُمْ اَلْلْـ... اَلنَّظْرَهْ بْتَاعْتْهُمْ مُفْتَكْرِينْ اَلْعَمَلِيَّهْ انّهَا سَهْلَهْ سَاكِتْ.

ب: هَا...

أ: اَنّهُ مِمَّا جَا[12] امْرِيكَا هِنَا بِقَى مِلْيُونَيْرْ وَحَقَّقْ اَلدَّايِرْ يَعْمَلُهْ وَرِكِبْ لَيْهُ فْعَرَبِيَّهْ كَبِيرَهْ...[13]

ب: وَعَاشْ مُرْتَاحْ.

أ: وْكِدَا ، لَكِنْ هِنَا لاَ، إِنْتَ بِتْجِي تَبْدَاهَا[14] فِعْلاً مِنّ اَلـ*zero*.

ب: هَا...

أ: مِنْ خَمْسَهْ دَوْلاَرْ فِالسَّاعَهْ...

B: haa ...

A: ... w-bi-jahjaha ʃadiida w-maa taʕrif feen u-kidaa, w-yaa ʔaḷḷaa yaamiin.[15]

B: ha ...

A: fa-maa fii, maa yaʕnii, maa bi-ssuhuula dii wallaa ʔay ḥaaja ma ... hinaa ʔamriikaa fiʕlan ʔinta kaan da ... bii-taḥlam wallaa ḥaaja zeey dii liʔannuu ṭṭallab[16] minnak taʃtaɣal ʃuɣul ʃadiid jiddan jiddan.

ب: هَا...

أ: ... وْبِجَهْجَهَهْ شَدِيدَهْ وْمَا تَعْرِفْ فَيْنْ أُكِدَا، وْيَا أَللَّهْ يَامِينْ.[15]

ب: هَا...

أ: فَمَا فِي، مَا يَعْنِي، مَا بِالسُّهُولَهْ دِي وَلاَّ أَي حَاجَهْ مَـ... هِنَا أَمْرِيكَا فِعْلاً إِنْتَ كَانْ دَ... بِيِتْحَلَّمْ وَلاَّ حَاجَهْ زَيّ دِي لأَنّهُ طَلَّبْ[16] مِنَّكْ تَشْتَغَلْ شُغُلْ شَدِيدْ جِدّاً جِداً.

## Vocabulary

**ḥilla** حلّة *nfs* village; neighborhood {*pl:* **ḥallaal, ḥilal**}

**um jiriis** أمّ جريس **[umm jirees]** *prop* Umm Jurays (village east of Khartoum)

**ṭayyib aʃʃeex ʕabd albaagii** طَيِّب اَلشَّيْخ عَبْد اَلْبَاقِي *prop* Tayyib al-Shaykh Abd al-Bagi (place in al-Jazira)

**abahaan** اَبَهَان **[abahaat]** *nmpl not conventional* parents {*nms:* **ab**, *nms:* **abuu**}

**itta** اِتّ **[inta; itt]** *pron ms* you

**miteen** مِتَيْن **[biteen]** *interrog* when

**li-** لِ **[li-; lee-; lii-]** *prep* to have been for (amount of time); to, for

**garrab** قَرَّب *vi pre-verb* to be at the point of (doing s.th.) {*imperf:* **yagarrib**, *vn:* **tagriib**}

**ʕamaliyya** عَمَلِيَّة *nfs* matter, affair, business; process; operation {*pl:* **ʕamaliyyaat**}

**saakit** سَاكِت **[saay]** *adv* just, only

**mimmaa** مِمَّا *conj* from the time that; as soon as

**bigaa** بِقَى *vt also pre-verb* to become; to be; to begin; to get to the point that (inchoative action) {*imperf:* **yabgaa**, *vn:* **bagayaan**}

**daayir** دَايِر *adj pre-verb* wanting, desiring; needing; intending to, going to {*fs:* **daayra**, *mpl:* **daayriin**, *fpl:* **daayraat**}

**ʕarabiyya** عَرَبِيَّة *nfs* automobile {*pl:* **ʕarabaat, ʕarabiyyaat**}

**murtaaḥ** مُرْتَاح *adj* prosperous, well-off; relaxed, at ease {*fs:* **murtaaḥa**, *mpl:* **murtaaḥiin**, *fpl:* **murtaaḥaat**}

**jahjaha** جَهْجَهَة *nfs* aggravation; worry; confusion

**feen** فَيْن *interrog* where

**yaa ... yaa** يَا ...يَا *conj* either ... or

**yaa ʔaḷḷaa yaamiin** يَا أَللَّهْ يَا مِين barely; by the skin of one's teeth *(lit. either God or amen)*

## Notes

**1** The use of the active participle /**jaaya**/ 'coming; having come' here does not mean that the speaker is still in the process of arriving. As she says later in this selection, she came to the US five years ago. The active participle here indicates that her arrival is still relevant: she will always be /**jaaya**/ 'having come' from Sudan. As mentioned in selection 5, note 10, the exact meaning of an active participle depends on usage as much as grammar. In general, however, in SA and other varieties of spoken Arabic, the active participle indicates the result of an action or describes a condition that still holds true as well as action that is ongoing at the moment of speaking.

**2** The P /**ʔabahaan**/ 'parents' is not conventional in Sudanese Arabic as spoken in the region of the capital. The more usual form is /**abahaat**/ 'parents'.

**3** The sentence /**ʔabahaanik ʃaɣɣaaliin ʃnuu ʔintii**?/ 'what do your (fs) parents do?' is a topic-comment sentence (discussed in selection 4, note 1). Here, however, the topic /**ʔintii**/ 'you (fs)' follows the comment /**ʔabahaanik ʃaɣɣaaliin ʃnuu**?/ 'what do your (fs) parents do?' More usually, the topic precedes the comment, as in /**ʔintii ʔabahaanik ʃaɣɣaaliin ʃnuu**?/ 'what do your (fs) parents do?' The unusual position of the topic here draws our attention and presumably that of the other speaker to it. Note that this clause is the speaker's third (and finally successful) attempt to change the topic.

**4** The pronoun /**ʔitta**/ 'you (ms)' is one of several variants of the 2MS pronoun. Others are /**ʔinta**/, more usual in cities, and /**ʔitt**/, heard in cities but more often from rural speakers.

**5** The perfect verb /**jiit**/ 'you (ms) came' in the question /**jiit miteen assuudaan**?/ 'when did you (ms) come to Sudan?' is the 3MS perfect of the verb /**jaa**/ - /**yajii**/ 'to come'. This verb, whose imperative is /**taʕaal**/, is one of the few verbs of SA that can be called irregular.

In addition, the question comes when the female speaker mistakenly asks /**jiit miteen assuudaan**?/ 'when did you (ms) come to Sudan?' rather than /**jiit miteen amriikaa**?/ 'when did you (ms) come to America?' Note that the speaker corrects herself with no indication of her error. In general, a speaker's last version is likely to be the correct one, an assumption confirmed here by the context.

**6** The perfect /**jiit**/ 'you (ms) came' here stands in contrast to the active participle /**jaaya**/ 'having come (fs)' discussed in selection 9, note 1. The act of arriving in both cases took place in the past. The arrival described with the perfect in this question, /**jiit miteen amriikaa**?/ 'when did you (ms) come to America?' is finished.

The active participle of /**jaaya min ween?**/ 'where do you (fs) come from?' however, refers to an act that is still relevant or a condition that still holds.

7 The preposition /li-/ 'to; for', as in /**leey** talaata sniin/ 'I've been here three years', occurs with expressions of time with the meaning 'to have been (for that amount of time)'. The subject is expressed by a suffixed pronoun following /li-/, here, the 1S /-y/.

8 As the contrasting uses of /xamsa **sanawaat** ... xamsa **sniin**/ 'five years ... five years' demonstrate, the S noun /**sana**/ 'year' has two P forms. They differ in style rather than meaning. Because SA shares the P /**sanawaat**/ with MSA, this form sounds more educated or more formal. The P /**sniin**/, in contrast, is not necessarily uneducated but is less formal and more colloquial.

9 The phrase /**sanateen, talaata** sniin/ 'two or three years' does not contain a word meaning 'or', such as /ʔaw/ or /wallaa/. In SA and other varieties of Arabic, however, consecutive numbers may occur without an intervening word or particle (conjunction) to join them. When they do, the meaning 'or' is implied.

10 The form /bi-ttwoogaʕ/ 'you (ms) expect' derives from the verb /itwaggaʕ/ - /yitwaggaʕ/ 'to expect'. The form used here is not conventional in SA.

11 The form /b-jii/ in the phrase /bi-ʔannuu **b-jii**/ 'that he comes' occurs in rapid or casual speech. It is reduced from /**bi-ya**jii/ (or /b-**ii**jii/ ) 'he comes'.

12 The referent of the 3MS pronoun is not clear in the utterance that begins with the clause /**ʔannuu mimmaa** jaa -mriikaa/ 'that as soon as he came to America'. The referent may be the general /**kullu** zool/ 'everybody' who entered the conversation six utterances previously. It is more likely, however, to be /**huwa**/ 'he' for /**alwaaḥid**/ 'a person, someone'. As discussed in selection 3, note 13, this may be a way for the speaker either to describe experience in general terms or to refer to himself.

13 The prepositional phrase /leehuu/ 'himself, lit. for him' makes no clear contribution to the clause /rikib **leehuu** -f ʕarabiyya kabiira/ 'he rode himself around in a big car'. Instead, it gives greater prominence to the referent of the 3MS suffixed pronoun, who is also the subject of the verb. It thus highlights the entire clause. This use of the preposition /li-/ with a suffixed pronoun is called the benefactive.

14 The apparent referent of the 3FS suffixed pronoun /-haa/ in /tabdaa**haa**/ 'you (ms) start it (fs)' is /alʕamaliyya/ 'the process'. This noun occurs in the clause /annaẓra btaaʕtum muftakriin **alʕamaliyya** -naa sahla saakit/ 'lit. their (mp) view is, they (mp) think the process, that it's (fs) just easy', which occurs four utterances earlier.

**15** The phrase /**yaa ʔaḷḷaa yaamiin**/ 'by the skin of one's teeth, lit. either God or amen' describes a narrow escape or a close call. The implication is that only the word "God" or the word "amen," the words that begin and end a prayer, stood between the speaker and disaster.

**16** The subject of the verb /**ṭṭallab**/ 'it (fs) demands' is not clear. It may be /**alʕamaliyya**/ 'the process', mentioned in selection 9, note 14. Another possible candidate is /**ʔamriikaa**/ 'America', occurring in the same utterance.

# amriikaa

*In this selection, two speakers discuss their impressions of life in the US and their advice to other newcomers to the country. Their opinions on life here are somewhat abstract, but their advice is very practical.*

A: aha yaa ḥanaan, ʔintii hassaʕ waṣaltii ʔamriikaa, ʔaktar ḥaaja ʕajabatik fii ʔamriikaa ʃinuu?[1]

B: w-aḷḷaahii ḥagiiga yaʕnii bi-jjadd[2] aktar ḥaaja ʕajabatnii fi lbalad dii, ʔawwal ḥaaja ṭabʕan muxtalfa ʕan kulla duwal alʕaalam ʔaw kull albilaad azzurnaahaa. ʔaʃʃii ttaanii, kimmiyyat alḥurriyya w-addiimuɣraaṭiyya ʔalfiihaa.

A: aa ...

B: aaʔ baʕdeen ṭabaʕan balad munaẓẓama jiddan jiddan, yaʕnii, ʔaṣluu txayyal leey maa fii masiil leehaa fii ... fii ... fii nniḍ̣aam. ṭabʕan dii ḥaaja kwaysa ʃadiid.

A: aa ...

B: aa ... yaʕnii ʃʃii lanaa ʔak ... yaʕnii b-aftagadtuu[3] ...

A: aa ...

B: ṭabʕan azzool yaʕnii ʃii ṭabiiʕii ʔinnuu yiftagid naasuu w-ʔahaluu.[4]

A: aha ...

B: al ... ʔaʃʃii lb-anṣaḥ beehuu lii- masalan ʔayyi naas jaayiin hinaa daa[5] fi lbalad dii yaʕnii ygawwii lluɣa btaaḥtuu.

A: w-aḷḷaahii maʕaaki ḥagg[6] yaʕnii.

# اَمْرِيكَا

أ: اَهَـهْ يَـا حَنَـانْ، إِنْتِـي هَسَّعْ وَصَلْتِـي أَمْرِيكَا، أَكْتَـرْ حَاجَهْ عَجَبَتِكْ فِـي أَمْرِيكَا شِنُـو؟[1]

ب: وَاللَّهِ حَقِيقَـهْ يَعْنِي بِالجَدّ[2] اَكْتَـرْ حَاجَـهْ عَجَبَتْنِي فَـالْبَلَدْ دِي، أَوَّلْ حَاجَـهْ طَبْعًا مُخْتَلْفَـهْ عَنْ كُلّ دُوَلْ اَلْعَالَمْ أَوْ كُلّ اَلْبِلاَدْ اَلزُّرْنَاهَا. أَلشِّي التَّانِي، كِمِّيَّةْ اَلْحُرِّيَّهْ وَالدِّيمُغْرَاطِيَّهْ أَلْفِيهَا.

أ: اَ...

ب: اَ؟ بَعْدَيْنْ طَبَعًا بَلَدْ مُنَظَّمَهْ جِداً جِداً، يَعْنِي، أَصْلُهُ تْخَيَّلْ لَيّ مَا فِي مَسِيلْ لَيْهَا[3] فِي... فِي... فِي النِّظَامْ. طَبْعًا دِي حَاجَهْ كْوَيْسَهْ شَدِيدْ.

أ: اَ...

ب: اَ... يَعْنِي الشِّي الاَنَا أَكْ... يَعْنِي بَافْتَقَدْتُهُ[3]...

أ: اَ...

ب: طَبْعًا اَلزَّوْلْ يَعْنِي شِي طَبِيعِي إِنّهُ يِفْتَقِدْ نَاسْهُ وْأَهَلْهُ.[4]

أ: اَهَهْ...

ب: اَلْـ ... أَلشِّي الْبَانْصَحْ بَيْهُ لِي مَسَلاً أَيِّ نَاسْ جَايِنْ هِنَا دَا[5] فِالْبَلَدْ دِي يَعْنِي يْقَوِّي اللُّغَهْ بْتَاحْتَهُ.

أ: وَاللَّهِ مَعَاكِ حَقّ[6] يَعْنِي.

B: liiʔannaa luɣat ttawaaṣul wa-kidaa dayya. ʔaha bi-nnizba leek ʔitta, ʔaktar ḥaaja ʕajabatak?

A: w-aḷḷaahii yaa ḥanaan, [laughing] maa xalleetii leey ḥaaja. laakin aktar ḥaaja ṭabaʕan ʕajabatnii zayy maa zakartii -ntii gabli ʃwayy allii hiya ʔa ... ʔannaẓaam ʔawwal ḥaaja. w-baʕdeen yaʕnii ʔinnahaa balad fiʕlan yaʕnii tastaḥigg innaa masalan tusammaa maθalan[7] ʔumm addunyaa yaʕnii. llinsaan bi-ra ... bi ... raɣmi ʃaṭaartuu w-b-raɣmi lhinaay laakin annaẓaam gaadir yaẓbuṭ[8] ʔeeyi ʃaxṣ wa-ʔeey zool maaxud[9] ḥurriituu[10] bi-lkaamil fi ḥuduud alɣaanuun w-iḥtiraam alɣaanuun w-annaas. yaʕnii ʔa ... ʔal ... yaʕnii zzool lammaa yaḥiss bi ... b-ismaʕ bi-kilmat ḥuguug allinsaan w-allinsaan dii, [laughing] fiʕlan lammaa b-iijii hinaa b-ilgaahaa fiʕlan mawjuuda. ʔa ... w-fii nafs alwakit barḍuu waṣiitii lil ... lil ... lil ... lil ... li-ʔaṣdiɣaa ʔaw annaas ʔallii jaayiin masalan ʔahuu ʔal ... yaʕnii ʔahamma ʃii waaḥid yiḥaawil yatɣin alluɣa min baladuu ʔizaa fii ayyi ṭariiga. wa-loo maa tɣannaa hinaak masalan yiijii hinaa wa-yḥaawil awwal ḥaaja yḥaawil yirakkiz innuu yi ... yi ... yi ... yidris lluɣa yaʕnii. bi-lliḍaafa li-kidaa yaʕnii annaas maa taʕgid ʔaamaal kabiir innaa mujarrad waṣalat amriikaa maʕnaataa[11] ʔumuuraa[12] kullaa tḥallat wallaa maʃaakilaa tḥallat. laa ʔitxayyal leey almasʔala b-tuṭlub, bi-ṭṭallab ʃwayyat majhuud. yaʕnii zzool yooxud[13] ʕalaa nafsuu[14] ʃwayya w-laakin allumuur fi nnihaaya titḥalla lannuu lfuraṣ mutwaffira li-kulli ʃaxṣ yaʕnii. ʔayyi zool b-iibzil majhuud[15] ʔitxayyal leey b-iilgaa al ... al ... al ... ʔaʃʃii lʕaayizuu yaʕnii.

ب: لِيأَنّهَا لُغَةْ التَّوَاصُلْ وكِدَا دِيَّا. أَهَهْ بِالنِّزْبَهْ لِيكْ إِتّ، أَكْتَرْ حَاجَهْ عَجَبْتَكْ؟

أ: وَاللَّه يَا حَنَانْ [laughing] مَا خَلَّيْتِي لَيّ حَاجَهْ. لَكِنْ اَكْتَرْ حَاجَهْ طَبَعًا عَجَبَتْنِي زَيّ مَا زَكَرْتِي انْتِي قَبْلِ شْوَيّ اَللِّي هِيَ أَ... أَلنِّظَامْ أَوَّلْ حَاجَهْ. وْبَعْدَيْنْ يَعْنِي إِنَّهَا بَلَدْ فِعْلاً يَعْنِي تَسْتَحِقّ انّهَا مَسَلاً تُسَمَّى مَثَلاً[7] أُمّ اَلدُّنْيَا يَعْنِي. الاِنْسَانْ بِرَ ... بِ... رَغْمِ شَطَارْتْهُ وْبَرغَمِ الْهِنَاي لَكِنْ اَلنِّظَامْ قَادِرْ يَظْبُطْ[8] أَيِّ شَخْصْ وَأَيّ زَوْلْ مَاخُدْ[9] حُرِّيتْهُ[10] بِالْكَامِلْ فِحُدُودْ اَلْقَانُونْ وِاحْتِرَامْ اَلْقَانُونْ وَالنَّاسْ. يَعْنِي أَ... أَلْ... يَعْنِي الزَّوْلْ لَمَّا يَحِسّ بِ... بِسْمَعْ بِكِلْمَةْ حُقُوقْ اَلاِنْسَانْ وَالاِنْسَانْ دِي، [laughing] فِعْلاً لَمَّا بِيجِي هِنَا بِلْقَاهَا فِعْلاً مَوْجُودَهْ. أَ... وْفِي نَفْسْ اَلْوَكتْ بَرْضُهْ وَصِيتِي لِلْ... لِلْ ... لِلْ... لِلْ... لأَصْدِغَا أَوْ اَلنَّاسْ أَللِّي جَايِينْ مَسَلاً أَهَهْ أَلْ.. يَعْنِي أَهَمّ شِي وَاحِدْ يِحَاوِلْ يَتْغِنْ اَللُّغَهْ مِنْ بَلَدْهُ إِزَا فِي اَيِّ طَرِيقَهْ. وَلَوْ مَا اتْغَنّهَا هِنَاكْ مَسَلاً يِيجِي هِنَا وَيْحَاوِلْ اَوَّلْ حَاجَهْ يْحَاوِلْ يِركِّزْ انّهُ يِ... يِ... يِ... يِدْرِسْ اللُّغَهْ يَعْنِي. بِالاِضَافَهْ لِكِدَا يَعْنِي اَلنَّاسْ مَا تَعْقِدْ اَمَالْ كَبِيرْ انّهَا مُجَرَّدْ وَصِلَتْ اَمْرِيكَا مَعْنَاتْهَا[11] أُمُورْهَا[12] كُلّهَا تْحَلَّتْ وَلاَّ مَشَاكِلْهَا تْحَلَّتْ. لاَ إِتْخَيَّلْ لَيّ اَلْمَسْأَلَهْ بْتُطْلُبْ، بِطَّلَّبْ شْوَيَّةْ مَجْهُودْ. يَعْنِي الزَّوْلْ يَوْخُدْ[13] عَلَى نَفْسْهُ[14] شْوَيَّهْ وْلَكِنْ اَللاُمُورْ فَالنِّهَايَهْ تِتْحَلّ لاَنّهُ الْفُرَصْ مُتْوَفِّرَهْ لِكُلِّ شَخْصْ يَعْنِي. أَيِّ زَوْلْ بِيبْزِلْ مَجْهُودْ[15] إِتْخَيَّلْ لَيّ بِيلْقَى اَلْ ... اَلْ... اَلْ... أَلشِّي الْعَايِزْهُ يَعْنِي.

## Vocabulary

**hassaʕ** هَسَّعْ **[hassii; hassaa]** *adv* now; just now

**ʕajab** عَجَبْ *vt impersonal construction* to please s.o. {*imperf:* **yaʕjib**, *vn:* **ʕajab**}

**baʕdeen** بَعْدَيْنْ *adv* afterwards, then, next; too, also

**aṣluu** أصْلُو *adv* the fact is

**itxayyal li-** اتْخَيَّلْ لِ *vi impersonal construction* to imagine (where the logical subject is the object of the preposition) *(lit. to be or become the object of imagination for s.o.)* {*imperf:* **yitxayyal li-**, *vn:* **taxayyul**}

**naas** نَاسْ *nmpl* a person's social circle (non-familial friends, neighbors, colleagues, and acquaintances); people

**ayy** أيّ **[eey]** *adj invariable, precedes noun* every; any

**maʕa- ḥagg** مَعَ حَقّ s.o. is right, what s.o. says is right *(lit. with s.o. is right)*

**tawaaṣul** تَوَاصُلْ *nms* social interaction

**xallaa** خَلّى *vt* to leave (behind); to let, allow; to cause to be; to leave alone, let be {*imperf:* **yaxallii**, *vn:* **xilleey**}

**ʃwayya** شْوَيَّهْ *nfs* a short period of time; *adv* for a little while {*pl:* **ʃwayyaat**}

**umm addunyaa** أُمّ اَلدُّنْيَا the greatest place *(lit. mother of the world)*

**ʃaṭaara** شَطَارَهْ *nfs* cleverness

**axad** أخَدْ *vt* to take up to use; to take, receive; to take, spend (time) {*imperf:* **yaaxud**, *vn:* **axid**}

**maaxud** مَاخُدْ **[maaxid]** *adj* taking, getting, obtaining; taking up to use {*fs:* **maaxda**, *mpl:* **maaxdiin**, *fpl:* **maaxdaat**}

**bi-lkaamil** بِالْكَامِلْ completely, entirely

**lammaa** لَمَّا **[lamman]** *conj* when

**waṣiyya** وَصِيَّهْ *nfs* advice {*pl:* **waṣaayaa**}

**ʕagad aamaal** عَقَدْ آمَالْ to set one's hopes on {*imperf:* **yaʕgid aamaal**, *vn:* **ʕagda aamaal**}

**mujarrad** مُجَرَّدْ *adv* merely, solely

**masʔala** مَسْأَلَهْ *nfs* matter, affair {*pl:* **masaaʔil**}

## Notes

**1** The verb /**ʕajab**/ 'to please' occurs in an impersonal construction, as here in /**ʔaktar ḥaaja ʕajabatik** fii ʔamriikaa ʃinuu?/ 'what is the thing you (fs) like most about America?, lit. the biggest thing that pleased you (fs) about America is what?' The grammatical subject of this verb is the noun phrase /**ʔaktar ḥaaja**/ 'the biggest thing'. Note also that this verb typically occurs in the perfect, referring to a liking that began in the past and continues in the present. SA, like certain other varieties of spoken Arabic, uses this variant of the MSA verb ʔaʕjaba'to please'.

**2** The series of words and phrases that precede the female speaker's statement about America, /**w-aḷḷaahii ḥagiiga yaʕnii bi-jjadd**/ 'by God, the truth is, you know, seriously', can be understood in two ways. She is, of course, assuring the male speaker of her frankness. At the same time, this string of intensifiers and qualifiers lets her hold her place in the conversation while she decides what to say next. These words and phrases are a kind of conversational filler. The forms /**yaʕnii**/ 'you know, lit. it (ms) means' and /**fiʕlan**/ 'really' occur in this way throughout this selection, as their equivalents do in American English.

**3** The form /**b-aftagadtuu**/ 'I miss it (ms)' is an unusual combination. It has the imperfect /**bi-**/ prefix and the imperfect 1S prefix /**a**/. At the same time, it has the perfect 1S suffix /**t**/. This combination of prefix and suffix, not typical of SA, is probably a slip of the tongue. The slip is not, however, serious enough for comment or correction, as context makes meaning clear here.

**4** The phrase /**naasuu w-ʔahaluu**/ 'his friends and family' names a person's entire social network. The /**ahal**/ are family, a group that includes distant as well as close kin. Everyone else is /**naas**/, a group that includes friends, neighbors, colleagues, and even acquaintances.
Note also that the epenthetic vowel /**a**/ of /**ahal**/ 'family' is retained. Even the addition of a vowel-initial suffixed pronoun, as in /**ahaluu**/ 'his family', does not affect the appearance of this vowel.

**5** The phrase /**hinaa daa**/ 'here' contains the demonstrative /**daa**/ 'this (ms)' as a modifier of /**hinaa**/ 'here'. This use is an exception to the general rule that demonstratives modify only nouns and noun phrases. Here it is an acceptable way to underline the "hereness" also described by the following phrase, /**fi lbalad dii**/ 'to this country'. In other contexts, /**hinaa daa**/ could be translated as 'right here' or 'on this very spot'.

**6** The idiomatic expression /**maʕaaki ḥagg**/ 'lit. with you (fs) is truth' is conventional in SA and other varieties of spoken Arabic for 'you're right'. The opposite, 'you're wrong', uses the preposition /ʕalaa/ 'on; at' in the phrase /ʕaleeki ḥagg/ 'you're (fs) wrong, lit. against you is truth'.

**7** The sequence /**masalan tusammaa maθalan**/ 'for example, it (fs) is called, for example' is noteworthy for two reasons. First, it contains an example of the passive voice, the verb /**tusammaa**/ 'it (fs) is called'. This is an MSA passive, although SA has a true passive for a limited number of verbs. Second, the first occurrence of /**masalan**/ 'for example' contrasts with the second, which is pronounced formally as /**maθalan**/ 'for example'.

**8** Another example of the pre-verb in SA is the verb string /**gaadir yaẓbuṭ**/ 'it (ms) can control'. Pre-verbs vary in the kinds of structures in which they occur. The pre-verb /**gaadir**/ 'able (ms)', for example, agrees in gender and number with its subject. A contrating example is the pre-verb /**laazim**/ 'necessary', which is impersonal and shows no agreement.

**9** The participle /**maaxud**/ 'taking (ms)' has the short vowel /**u**/. More often, this participle is pronounced /**maaxid**/ with the short vowel /**i**/, as would be usual in a Form I active participle.

**10** The form /**ḥurriituu**/ 'his freedom' demonstrates a regular sound change in SA. It occurs where the sequence /**ya**/ occurs before the FS ending /-t/ followed by a vowel, as in /**ḥurriyyatuu**/. The sequence /**ya**/ elides to produce /**ḥurriytuu**/, and the resulting sequence /**iy**/ becomes /**ii**/, as in /**ḥurriituu**/.

**11** The word /**maʕnaa**/ in SA and certain other varieties of spoken Arabic is often treated as grammatically F, as it is in the form /**maʕnaataa**/ 'its (fs) meaning'. In SA, the word retains the long vowel /**aa**/ and takes a word-final /-t/ when it precedes a suffixed pronoun, as here.
Note that the suffixed pronoun occuring here has no apparent referent. In SA and other varieties of spoken Arabic, a pronoun whose referent is vague or unspecified is often grammatically FS, as here, /**maʕnaataa**/.

**12** The referent of the suffixed pronoun in the form /**ʔumuuraa**/ 'their (fs) personal circumstances' is /**annaas**/ 'people'. The noun phrase /**annaas**/ 'people' serves as the referent for most of the sentence that begins /**yaʕnii annaas**/ 'you know, people' and ends /**maʃaakilaa tḥallat**/ 'their (fs) problems have been solved'. The sole exception to this consistent reference is the noun phrase /**maʕnaataa**/ 'its (fs) meaning', discussed in selection 10, note 11.

**13** The form /**yooxud**/ 'you (ms) take' is, in other instances, pronounced /**yaaxud**/.

**14** The idiomatic expression /**yooxud ʕalaa nafsuu**/ 'he takes on responsibility, lit. he takes on himself' has as its opposite /**yooxud ʕan nafsuu**/ 'he lets up on himself, lit. he takes off of himself'.

**15** Based on sound, the verb /-iibzil/ in the clause /**b-iibzil majhuud**/ 'he makes an effort, lit. he expends an effort' could derive from two MSA verbs. One possibility is bazala 'to split; make a hole in', which it mostly closely resembles. The other possibility is baðala 'to expend', which fits the context better. Actually, the verb /iibzil/ derives from baðala 'to expend' as a result of sound changes that eliminate most interdental fricatives (/ð/, /θ/, and /ð̣/) in SA. Either /z/, as here, or /d/ (as in /**dahab**/ 'gold', compare MSA ðahab 'gold') are the most usual replacements for /ð/.

# lamma tisaafir assuudaan

*The two speakers in this selection discuss plans to visit Sudan. Earlier in this conversation, they are frank about missing family and friends, and about looking forward to a visit. Here, they are equally open about some of the problems a visit presents.*

B: gaaʕid taraasil ʔahalak[1] wallaa gaaʕid tarsil leehum guruuʃ[2] wallaa bi-taḍrab leehum taliifoonaat?[3]

A: ay yaʕnii ba ... b-arsil leehum yaʕnii [xxx] maa b-arsil luhum, laakin, katiir kidaa, marra marra kidaa b-arsil luhum guruuʃ.

B: aywa ʔu-ṭayyib maʕnaa kidaa ʔinta xaattii[4] fii raasak[5] yaʕnii ʔam ... ʔa ... ʔa ... kimmiyya kabiira min alguruuʃ ʕaʃaan tisaafir assuudaan, ʕaʃaan tiwaddii[6] lii-nnaas guruuʃ wa-hadaayaa w-kidaa? ʔinta ʕindakum naas kaθiiriin yaʕnii?

A: keef? niḥnaa hnaak fi ssuudaan al ... al ... al ... ʔinta miʃ bii-tkuun ʕalaa ʔummak w-abuuk bass. yaʕnii biti ... biti ... lammaa bi-tiʃiil min hinaa bi-ʃʃiil li-xaaltak wa-bi-ʃʃiil li-ʕammatak wa-l-oolaad ʔa ... xaalak wa-l-oolaad ʕammatak wa-kullaa wa-li-ɣaryitkum kullaa bi-tirsil leehum bita ... bi-taddiihum.[6] w-annaas b-iijuu wa-b-iiguuluuk,[7] 'yaa xii, ʔitta jiit.' wa-ʔalmuhim, fa-ʔinta bi-tḥaawil ʔada ... tabsuṭ annaas kullum, tabsuṭum basuṭ ʃadiid jiddan jiddan. ʔa ... w-awwal maa yajii ʔahuu bassi ṭawwaalii lwaaḥid b-iilim fiik, 'ʔaa zool, jiit miiteen? ʔaha wa-keef ʔaxbaar albalad daak?' wa-yitaḥaddisum w-algoom daa b-isʔaluu fiik ṭabʕan fa ... ḥitta zayy dii laazim inta tkuun masalan mustaʕidd min hinaa taʃiil maʕaak kimmiyya bitaaʕat guruuʃ kwaysa[8, 9]

# لَمَّا تِسَافِرْ اَلسُّودَانْ

ب: قَاعِدْ تَرَاسِلْ أَهَلَكْ[1] وَلاَّ قَاعِدْ تَرْسِلْ لَيْهُمْ قُرُوشْ[2] وَلاَّ بِتَضْرَبْ لَيْهُمْ تَلِيفُونَاتْ؟[3]

أ: اَي يَعْنِي بَـ... بَارْسِلْ لَيْهُمْ يَعْنِي [xxx] مَا بَارْسِلْ لُهُمْ لَكِنْ كَتِيرْ كِدَا، مَرَّهْ مَرَّهْ كِدَا بَارْسِلْ لُهُمْ قُرُوشْ.

ب: اَيْوَهْ أُ... طَيِّبْ مَعْنَى كِدَا إِنْتَ خَاتِّي[4] فِي رَاسَكْ[5] يَعْنِي أَمْ ... أَ... أَ... كِمِّيَّهْ كَبِيرَهْ مِنْ اَلْقُرُوشْ عَشَانْ تِسَافِرْ اَلسُّودَانْ عَشَانْ تِوَدِّي[6] لِيالنَّاسْ قُرُوشْ وَهَدَايَا وْكِدَا؟ إِنْتَ عِنْدَكُمْ نَاسْ كَتِيرِينْ يَعْنِي؟

أ: كَيْفْ؟ نِحْنَا هِنَاكْ فَالسُّودَانْ اَلْـ... اَلْـ... اَلْـ... إِنْتَ مِشْ بِيتْكُونْ عَلَى أُمَّكْ وَابُوكْ بَسّ. يَعْنِي بِتِـ... بِتِـ... لَمَّا بِتِشِيلْ مِنْ هِنَا بِشِّيلْ لِخَالْتَكْ وَبِشِّيلْ لِعَمَّتَكْ وْلاَوْلاَدْ أَ... خَالَكْ وْلاَوْلاَدْ عَمَّتَكْ وَكُلِّهَا وَلِغَرْيَتْكُمْ كُلّهَا بِتِرْسِلْ لَيْهُمْ بِتـ... بِتَـ... بِتَدِّيهُمْ.[6] وَالنَّاسْ بِيجُوا وَبِيقُولُوك،[7] «يَا خِي، إِتَّ جِيتْ.» وَأَلْمُهِمْ، فَإِنْتَ بِتْحَاوِلْ أَدَ... تَبْسُطْ اَلنَّاسْ كُلّهُمْ، تَبْسُطْهُمْ بَسُطْ شَدِيدْ جِدّاً جِدّاً. أَ... وَاوَّلْ مَا يِجِي أَهَهْ بَسِّ طَوَّالِي اَلْوَاحِدْ بِيلِمْ فِيكْ، «أَ زَوْلْ، جِيتْ مِيتَيْنْ؟ أَهَهْ ... وَكَيْفْ أَخْبَارْ اَلْبَلَدْ دَاكْ؟» وَيِتْحَدِّسْهُمْ وَالْقَوْمْ دَا بِسْأَلُوا فِيكْ طَبْعًا فَـ... حَتَّهْ زَيّ دِي لاَزِمْ إِنْتَ تْكُونْ مَسَلاً مُسْتَعِدّ مِنْ هِنَا تَشِيلْ مَعَاكْ كِمِّيَّهْ بِتَاعَةْ قُرُوشْ كْوَيْسَهْ[8,9]

wa-ḥaajaat zayy dii kidaa. wa-lamman jaay jaay[10] ʔayyi zool yasʔal ah … yaguul, 'laa yaa zool, laa. ʔinta tamʃii ʔamriikaa hinaak wa-fiʕlan hiya zaataa[11] leehaa, maa dii, dii, dii maa ḥaaja kidaa, maa b-tiʃbah,[12] dii zaataa ʕaalam taanii daa.'[13] liyannuu fiʕlan hiyya mutgaddima ʔamriikaa tagaddum ʃadiid jiddan jiddan. laakin nnaas barḍuu maa hum naas wa-daa barḍuu ba … lbalad hinaa fii … fii naas wa-fii ʕalaaɣaat ʔinsaaniyya b-talgaa been annaas w-ayyi zool ʃaɣɣaal u-fii ʔa … ʔusir wa-hinaa lʔusir. barḍuu bi-tilgaa ʔinnuu fiʕlan fi ʔusir fii ʔabb u-ʔumm w-uxut zayy maa ʕindanaa hnaak fi ssuudaan. fa-hum fiʕlan b-ikuunuu muʃtaagiin jiddan jiddan, lamman ʔajii raajiʕ min hinaa ʔaḥkii luhum kulla ḥaaja ʕan amriikaa.

وَحَاجَاتْ زَيّ دِي كِدَا. وَلَمَّنْ جَاي جَاي[10] أَيِّ زَوْلْ يَسْأَلْ اَهْ...
يَقُولْ، «لاَ يَا زَوْلْ، لاَ. إِنْتَ تَمْشِي أَمْرِيكَا هِنَاكْ وَفِعْلاً هِيَ
زَاتْهَا[11] لَيْهَا، مَا دِي، دِي، دِي مَا حَاجَهْ كِدَا، مَا بْتِشْبَهْ، [12]دِي
زَاتْهَا عَالَمْ تَانِي دَا.»[13] لاَنّهُ فِعْلاً هِيَّ مُتْقَدِّمَهْ أَمْرِيكَا تَقَدُّمْ
شَدِيدْ جِدّاً جِدّاً. لَكِنْ النَّاسْ بَرْضُهْ مَا هُم نَاسْ وَدَا بَرْضُهْ بَ
... الْبَلَدْ هِنَا فِي... فِي نَاسْ وَفِي عِلاَغَاتْ إِنْسَانِيَّهْ بِتِلْقَاهَا
بَيْنْ اَلنَّاسْ وَايِّ زَوْلْ شَغَّالْ اُفِي أَ... أُسِرْ وَهِنَا الأُسْرَهْ.
بَرْضُهْ بِتِلْقَى إِنّهُ فِعْلاً فأُسِرْ فِي أَبّ أُمّ وُاخُتْ زَيّ مَا عِنْدَنَا
هْنَاكْ فَالسُّودَانْ. فَهُمْ فِعْلاً بِكُونُوا مُشْتَاقِينْ جِدّاً جِدّاً، لَمَّنْ
أَجِي رَاجِعْ مِنْ هِنَا أَحْكِي لُهُمْ كُلَّ حَاجَهْ عَنْ اَمْرِيكَا.

## Vocabulary

**gaaʕid** قَاعِدْ *adj pre-verb* keeping on, continuing (continuous action); sitting, sitting down; staying, remaining {*fs:* **gaaʕda,** *mpl:* **gaaʕdiin,** *fpl:* **gaaʕdaat**}

**guruuʃ** قُرُوشْ *nfpl* money (in general) {*nms:* **giriʃ**}

**ḍarab li- taliifuun** ضَرَبْ لِ تَلِيفُونْ *vt* to phone, call s.o. on the telephone {*imperf:* **yaḍrub li- taliifuun,** *vn:* **ḍarib li- taliifuun**}

**xatta** خَتّ *vt* to put, place; to set down; to set up, implement {*imperf:* **yaxutt,** *vn:* **xatta,** *vn:* **xatataan**}

**xaattii** خَاتِّي *adj* putting; having put {*fs:* **xaatta,** *mpl:* **xaattiin,** *fpl:* **xaattaat**}

**waddaa** وَدَّى *vt* to take (s.o. or s.t. to a place), convey; to send; to put, place {*imperf:* **yawaddii,** *vn:* **widdeey**}

**keef** كَيْفْ *interrog* what, I'm sorry, what did you say (indicates mishearing or misunderstanding)

**ʕalaa** عَلَى **[ʕalee]** *prep* of duty, obligation; for, about (object of reference or concern); according to; on

**yaa xii** يَا خِي my brother (informal term of adddress to male of same status)

**lamma fii** لَمَّ فِي *vi* to get together with; to find, encounter, meet; to put s.o. in touch with s.o. {*imperf:* **yalimm fii**, *vn:* **lamm fii**, *vn:* **limm fii**}

**ḥitta** حِتّة *nfs* situation, condition; place, locale; portion, piece {*pl:* **ḥitat, ḥittaat**}

**jaay** جَاي *adv* here; this side, this end

**zaat** زَات *disc marker takes suffixed pronoun* oneself (adds emphasis or prominence to preceding noun phrase)

**ʃabah** شَبَه *vt* to resemble {*imperf:* **yaʃbah**, *vn:* **ʃabah**}

**daa... daa** دَا ... دَا *disc marker with indef. noun or noun phrase* indicates positive or negative emotion toward noun phrase {*fs:* **dii... dii**, *mpl:* **dool ... dool**, *fpl:* **deelaa ... deelaa**}

**barḍuu** بَرْضُو **[barduu; barðuu]** *adv* nevertheless, even so; also, too

**maa** مَا *disc marker* come on, but (adds emphasis or prominence to following phrase)

**ḥakaa** حَكَى *vt* to tell, narrate (a story, joke, etc.) {*imperf:* **yaḥkii**, *vn:* **ḥakii**}

## Notes

**1** The clause /**gaaʕid taraasil ʔahalak**/ 'are you (ms) writing to your (ms) family?' contains the participle /**gaaʕid**/ 'lit. sitting' that functions as a pre-verb. Followed by a simple imperfect, here /**taraasil**/ 'you (ms) correspond', /**gaaʕid**/ indicates ongoing or continuing action. Note that /**gaaʕid**/ has the form of a participle and inflects for gender and number.
Note also that /**gaaʕid**/ may have another sense, that of 'to start to', in other parts of Sudan.

**2** The general term for 'money' in Sudan is /**guruuʃ**/. This noun is treated as F because it is a non-human P noun. Its S form is /**giriʃ**/ 'one-hundredth of a pound, piaster'.

**3** The question /**gaaʕid tarsil leehum guruuʃ walla bi-taḍrab leehum taliifoonaat**/ 'are you (ms) sending them (mp) money or do you (ms) call them (mp)?' expresses the ongoing present in two ways. One is the verb string of /**gaaʕid tarsil leehum guruuʃ**/ 'are you (ms) sending them (mp) money?'; the other is the prefixed imperfect of /**bi-taḍrab leehum taliifoonaat**/ 'do you (ms) call them (mp)?' The two forms, the ongoing present with /**gaaʕid**/ and the prefixed imperfect, are near synonyms. The shift here from /**gaaʕid**/ to the prefixed imperfect may occur for the sake of variety, so that /**gaaʕid**/ does not occur three times in the utterance.

**4** The form /**xaattii**/ 'putting; having put (ms)' is the participle of the verb /**xatta**/

'to put' - /**yaxutt**/. The MS active participle of the doubled or geminate Form I verb regularly has a word-final /**ii**/, as in /**xaattii**/. It appears that — only for the derivation of the MS active participle — doubled or geminate Form I verbs are seen as similar to finally-weak verbs. The active participle of finally-weak Form I verbs also has a word-final /**ii**/, as in /**maashii**/ 'going (ms)'. That /**ii**/, however, is the third root consonant of /**maaʃii**/. The FS, MP, and FP active particles of the doubled or geminate Form I verbs, however, lack this /**ii**/: /**xaatta**/ 'putting (fs)'; /**xaattiin**/ 'putting (mp)'; and /**xaattaat**/ 'putting (fp)'.

**5** The phrase /**xaattii fii raasak**/ 'having (ms) in your mind (2ms), lit. having put (ms) into your (ms) mind'. The verb /**xatta**/ - /**yaxutt**/ 'to put' plays a role in a number of idiomatic expressions. These include /**xatta baal-**/ 'to pay attention, lit. to put attention'. See selection 11, note 4 on the derivation of /**xaattii**/ 'putting (ms)'.

**6** The verb /**addaa**/ - /**yaddii**/ means 'to give'. In contrast, the verb /**waddaa**/ - /**yawaddii**/ means 'to take (s.o. or s.t.), convey'. In rapid or informal speech, especially, these verbs may sound alike. Context, however, is an aid to comprehension.

**7** The form /**b-iiguuluuk**/ 'they (mp) tell you (ms)' occurs here in rapid speech. The preposition /**li-**/ 'to' that would normally govern the indirect object of the verb is omitted. In slow or careful speech, this form would occcur as /b-iiguuluu **lee**-k/ (or /b-iiguuluu **la**-k/).

**8** Note the placement of the adjective /**kwaysa**/ 'good (fs)' in the phrase /**kimmiyya bitaaʕat guruuʃ kwaysa**/ 'a good amount of money'. This adjective would be expected to directly follow the noun it modifies, /**kimmiyya**/ 'amount', as the adjective does in a similar phrase, /kimmiya **kabiira** min al-guruuʃ/ 'a large amount of money'. In this case, however, the adjective /**kwaysa**/ 'good (fs)' follows the entire possessive adjective phrase /**kimmiyya bitaaʕat guruuʃ**/ 'an amount of money'. That is, the possessive adjective phrase is modified as if it were a construct phrase.

**9** The adjective /**kwaysa**/ 'good (fs)' derives from /**kwayyisa**/ as the result of a regular sound change. The combination /**-yi-**/, when it occurs in the sequence /v**yyi**Cv/, often elides. This produces the form that occurs here, as well as /**ṭayba**/ 'good (fs)' (from /ṭa**yyi**ba/).

**10** The two instances of /**jaay**/ in the clause /**lamman jaay jaay**/ 'when I was coming here' are homophones. The first /**jaay**/ 'coming' is the MS active participle of the verb /**jaa**/. The second is an adverbial meaning 'here; this side, this end'; its opposite is /**ɣaadii**/ 'there; that side, that end'.

**11** The form /**zaataa**/ 'its (fs) self' in the phrase /**hiya zaataa**/ 'it (fs) itself' does not affect the meaning of the utterance in which it occurs. Instead, it adds prominence or emphasis to the word it follows. The preceding word and /**zaat**/ are linked by a suffixed pronoun whose referent is that word (here, /**ʔamriikaa**/ 'America'). In the phrase /**hiya zaataa**/, the suffixed pronoun is /**-haa**/.
Translation of /**zaat**/ depends on context. Note, for examples, the two uses of /**zaat**/ in the following: /**maa ʕaarif alwaddaanii ʃnuu zaatuu** w-maa ʕaarif anaa **zaatii** lwaddaanii leehuu ʃnuu/ 'I don't know *exactly what* led me here. *I myself* don't know what brought me to him'.

**12** The two instances of /**maa**/ have different meanings in the segment /dii **maa** ḥaaja kidaa, **maa** b-tiʃbah.../ 'this (fs) is really something, it's (fs) not like ....' The first, in /dii **maa** ḥaaja kidaa/ 'this (fs) is really something', is a marker that adds emphasis or prominence to the phrase it precedes. The second, in /**maa** b-tiʃbah.../ 'it's (fs) not like ...' is the negative particle of SA.
Context helps differentiate the two uses of /**maa**/. In the flow of speech, the two are clearly unlike. The first, in /dii **maa** ḥaaja kidaa/ 'this is really something', is pronounced as if it were a part of the following word (cliticized), with a lower pitch and volume than the following word. The second, in /**maa** b-tiʃbah.../ 'it's not like ...', is pronounced as an independent word with pitch and volume similar to that of the word that follows.

**13** The demonstratives /**dii**/ 'this (fs)' and /**daa**/ 'this (ms)' function as a pair in the clause /**dii** zaataa ʕaalam taanii **daa**/ 'this (fs) itself (fs) is a whole other world'. Together, they add an exclamatory quality to the clause that can indicate either positive or negative emotion. In this case, the quality is positive.
In most cases, the paired demonstratives are identical, as in /**daa** ʕaalam taanii **daa**/ 'this (ms) is a whole other world'. Here, however, /**dii**/ refers not to the predicate of the clause, /**ʕaalam taanii**/ 'another world', but to /**amriikaa**/ 'America', the topic of that stretch of talk.

# Selection 11

# warriinii bass alḥaaṣil ʃinuu

*This selection comes from the television serial first heard in Selection 7. Here, the mysterious stranger is revealed to be Adil's uncle Khalid. Khalid expresses his concern about Adil's accident to his friend the Hajj. The Hajj, worried about Khalid's secretive behavior, is not reassured by what he hears. The language used by both speakers is quite colloquial, although the Hajj's pronunciation tends to be more precise.*

A: [approaching] xaalid, xaalid, xaalid, ʔin ʃaa ḷḷaa maa fii ʕawaja?

B: w-aḷḷaah yaa ḥaajj, ʔaguul leek ʃnuu, maa ʕaarif alwaddaanii ʃinuu zaatuu wa-maa ʕaarif ʔanaa zaatii lwaddaanii leehuu ʃinuu.[1]

A: fii ʃinuu bi-ḍḍabṭ?

B: tsabbabta fii ʔazaa ʔinsaan ʕaziiz yaa ḥaaj.

A: min weenuu, gariibak?

B: a ... ʔa ... laaʔ laaʔ laaʔ huwa maa, maa ay ...

A: xaalid, ʔanaa gabli kidaa saʔaltak, ʕindak ʔahal hinaa? gutta[2] leey laaʔa, nakarta. guul alḥagiiga yaa xaalid, ʕindak ʔahal fi lbalad dii?

B: laa laa laa laa yaa ḥaaj, ʔanaa hinaa maa ʕindii ʔahal.

A: ahalak ween?

B: ahalii min aʃʃimaaliyya.

A: yaʕnii barḍak[3] maa daayir taguul leey alḥagiiga, ʔinta lissa bi-tdiss ʕaleey yaa xaalid.

# وَرِّينِي بَسّ اَلْحَاصِلْ شِنُو

أ: [approaching] خَالِدْ، خَالِدْ، خَالِدْ، إِنْشَا اللَّهْ مَا فِي عَوَجَهْ؟

ب: وَاللَّهْ يَا حَاجّ، أَقُولْ لَيْكْ شْنُو، مَا عَارِفْ اَلْوَدَّانِي شِنُو زَاتْهُ وَمَا عَارِفْ أَنَا زَاتِي الْوَدَّانِي لَيْهُ شِنُو.[1]

أ: فِي شِنُو بِالظَّبْطْ؟

ب: تْسَبَّبْتَ فِي أَزَى إِنْسَانْ عَزِيزْ يَا حَاجْ.

أ: مِنْ وَيْنْهُ، قَرِيبَكْ؟

ب: اَ... أَ... لاَءْ لاَءْ لاَءْ هُوَ مَا، مَا اَيْ...

أ: خَالِدْ، أَنَا قَبْلِ كِدَا سَأَلْتَكْ، عِنْدَكْ أَهَلْ هِنَا؟ قُتَّ[2] لَيّ لاَءَ، نَكَرْتَ. قُولْ اَلْحَقِيقَهْ يَا خَالِدْ، عِنْدَكْ أَهَلْ فِالْبَلَدْ دِي؟

ب: لاَ لاَ لاَ لاَ يَا حَاجْ، أَنَا هِنَا مَا عِنْدِي أَهَلْ.

أ: اَهَلَكْ وَيْنْ؟

ب: اَهَلِي مِنْ اَلشِّمَالِيَّهْ.

أ: يَعْنِي بَرْضَكْ[3] مَا دَايِرْ تَقُولْ لَيّ اَلْحَقِيقَهْ، إِنْتَ لِسَّهْ بِتْدِسّ عَلَيّ يَا خَالِدْ.

B: laa yaa ḥaajj.

A: maa leehuu daaʕii, maa waktuu, maa waktuu. zoolak daa hassa ḥaaltuu keef?

B: maa ʕaarif, xaayif yikuun taʕawwag ʃadiid.

A: lamman itʕaṭṭalta w-maa jiit almaɣlag, gutt ajii ʔaʃuuf alhaaṣil ʃinuu.

B: anaa min umbaariḥ fii ḥaala ṣaʕba jiddan.

A: guʕaadak daa zaatuu b-iiziid min ḥaaltak wa-b-iitʕibak ziyaada, guum yaḷḷaa lmaɣlag, guum-araḥ maʕaay[4] ʕalaa lʔagall tafarriɣ ʃwayya, guum yaa xii. yaa bnii, maa tirfaʕ alkulfa lbeenaatnaa[5] wa-ʔamrug alfii galbak.

B: yaa ḥaaj, maa, maa, maa fii ʃii[6] laakin …

A: laa fiih, fiih, ʔanaa leey yoomeen mulaaḥðak mahmuum wu-saariḥ ṭawwaalii, ʔakiid fii ḥaaja, warriinii[7] bass alḥaaṣil ʃinuu. kallimnii, ʔiʕtabirnii zayy ʔaxuuk alkabiir, warriinii bi-ẓẓabṭ alḥaaṣil ʕaleek ʃinuu.

B: maa fii ḥaaja yaa ḥaajj, maa fii ḥaaja ʔanaa b-adissaa minnak kulluu kulluu yaa ḥaaj.

A: laaʔ yaʕnii maa daayir titkallam. maa daayir taguul leey.

B: yaa ḥaaj, aguul ʃinuu, loo fii ḥaaja ʔanaa b-aguulaa leek ṭawwaalii.[8]

A: anaa saʔaltak, ʔinta ʕindak ʔahal hinaa fi lʕaaṣima?

B: yaa ḥaaj, anaa maa gutta leek maa ʕindii ʔahal hinaa, ʔahalii fi lʔaɣaaliim.

ب: لاَ يَا حَاجّ.

أ: مَا لَيْهُ دَاعِي، مَا وَكْتْه، مَا وَكْتْه. زَوْلَكْ دَا هَسَّهْ حَالْتْه كَيْفْ؟

ب: مَا عَارِفْ، خَايِفْ يِكُونْ تَعَوَّقْ شَدِيدْ.

أ: لَمَّنْ اِتْعَطَّلْتَ وْمَا جِيتْ اَلْمَغْلَقْ، قُتّ اَجِي أَشُوفْ اَلْحَاصِلْ شِنُو.

ب: اَنَا مِنْ أُمْبَارِحْ فِي حَالَهْ صَعْبَهْ جِدّاً.

أ: قُعَادَكْ دَا زَاتْهُ بِيزِيدْ مِنْ حَالْتَكْ وَبِيتْعِبَكْ زِيَادَهْ، قُومْ يَلاَّ الْمَغْلَقْ، قُومَارَحْ مَعَاي[4] عَلَى الأَقَلّ تَفَرِّغْ شْوَيَّهْ، قُومْ يَا خِي. يَا ابْنِي، مَا تِرْفَعْ اَلْكُلْفَه الْبَيْنَاتْنَا[5] وَأَمْرُقْ اَلْفِي قَلْبَكْ.

ب: يَا حَاجْ، مَا، مَا، مَا فِي شِي[6] لَكِنْ...

أ: لاَ فِيهْ، فِيهْ، أَنَا لِيّ يَوْمَيْنْ مُلاَحْظَكْ مَهْمُومْ وُسَارِحْ طَوَّالِي، أَكِيدْ فِي حَاجَهْ، وَرِّينِي[7] بَسّ اَلْحَاصِلْ شِنُو. كَلِّمْنِي إِعْتَبِرْنِي زَيّ أَخُوكْ اَلْكَبِيرْ، وَرِّينِي بِالظَّبْطْ اَلْحَاصِلْ عَلَيْكْ شِنُو؟

ب: مَا فِي حَاجَهْ يَا حَاجّ، مَا فِي حَاجَهْ أَنَا بَادِسّهَا مِنَّكْ كُلّهُ كُلّهُ يَا حَاجْ.

أ: لاَءْ، يَعْنِي مَا دَايِرْ تِتْكَلَّمْ. مَا دَايِرْ تَقُولْ لَيّ.

ب: يَا حَاجْ، اَقُولْ شِنُو، لَوْ فِي حَاجَهْ أَنَا بَاقُولْهَا لَيْكْ طَوَّالِي.[8]

أ: اَنَا سَأَلْتَكْ، إِنْتَ عِنْدَكْ أَهَلْ هِنَا فَالْعَاصِمَهْ؟

ب: يَا حَاجْ، اَنَا مَا قتَّ لَيْكْ مَا عِنْدِي أَهَلْ هِنَا، أَهَالِي فِالأَغَالِيمْ.

A: barḍuu maa daayir titkallam, ṭayyib, maʕleeʃ, xalleetak[9] yaa xaalid, ʕalee keefak, ʔanaa maa b-ajburak, ʕalee raaḥtak.

أ:    بَرْضُهُ مَا دَايِرْ تِتْكَلَّمْ، طَيِّبْ، مَعْلَيْشْ، خَلَّيْتَكْ[9] يَا خَالِدْ، عَلَي كَيْفَكْ، أَنَا مَا بَاجْبُرَكْ، عَلَي رَاحْتَكْ.

## Vocabulary

**warraa** وَرَّى *vt* to tell; to show {*imperf:* **yawarrii**, *vn:* **warraa**}

**in ʃaa llaa** انْ شَا اللّٰه God willing (conventionally used when discussing the future) *(lit. if God wills)*

**ʕawaja** عَوَجَة *nfs* harm, damage {*pl:* **ʕawajaat**}

**maa fii ʕawaja** مَا فِي عَوَجَة everything's OK; there is no problem; no harm done

**ḥaajj** حَاجّ *nms* hajj; sir (respectful form of address to an older man) *(lit. man who has made Meccan pilgrimage )* {*fs:* **ḥaajja**, *mpl:* **ḥujjaaj**, *fpl:* **ḥaajjaat**}

**itsabbab fii-** اتْسَبَّبْ فِي *vi* to be the cause of {*imperf:* **yitsabbab**, *vn:* **tasabbub**}

**azaa** أَزَى *nms* hurt; harm

**aʃʃimaaliyya** اَلشِّمَالِيَّة **[aʃʃamaaliyya]** *prop* al-Shamaliyya, Northern Province

**barḍ-** بَرْضْ *with suffixed pronoun* nevertheless, even so; also, too {*ms:* **barḍuu**, *fs:* **barḍaa**, *mpl:* **barḍum**, *fpl:* **barḍun**}

**lissa** لِسَّه *adv* still; not yet

**dassa** دَسّ *vt* to hide, conceal {*imperf:* **yadass**, *vn:* **dassa**}

**maa li- daaʕii** مَا لِ دَاعِي there's no need for s.t.

**maa wakit-** مَا وَكِتْ this is not the time for s.o.

**zool** زَوْلْ *nms* friend, pal, buddy; individual, person {*fs:* **zoola**, *pl:* **naas**}

**itʕawwag** اتْعَوَّقْ *vi* to be injured {*imperf:* **yitʕawwag**, *vn:* **ʕawaga**}

**itʕaṭṭal** اتْعَطَّلْ *vi* to be late; to not work, be idle; to break down, be out of order {*imperf:* **yitʕaṭṭal**, *vn:* **taʕṭiil**}

**maɣlag** مَغْلَقْ *nms* hardware store {*mpl:* **maɣaalig**}

**gaal (gutta)** (قُتَّ) قَالْ *vt* to think; to say {*imperf:* **yaguul**, *vn:* **gool**}

**umbaariḥ** أُمْبَارِحْ *adv* yesterday

**ziyaada** زِيَادَةْ *nfs* increase; *adv* more {*pl:* **ziyaadaat**}

**ziyaada** زِيادة *nfs* increase; *adv* more {*pl:* **ziyaadaat**}

**gaam (gumta)** (قُمْت) قام *vi pre-verb, agrees in number, gender, and tense with main verb* to get up (in order to do s.t.); to wake up, get up; to do, go ahead and do (as a consequence or result of previously described event); to up and (do s.t.), suddenly (do); to get up, stand up {*imperf:* **yaguum**, *vn:* **goom**}

**yaḷḷaa** يَلاّ *interj invariable* come on, move; let's go

**araḥ** أرَحْ *particle suffix of imperative verb* adds inclusive meaning (with me, you, etc.)

**itfarraɣ** اتفَرَّغْ **[yitfarrig; yitfarraɣ]** *vi* to have leisure; to take time, set aside time {*imperf:* **yitfarraɣ**, *vn:* **tafarruɣ**}

**kulfa** كُلْفة *nfs* formality; fuss

**beenaat-** بَيْنات **[been]** *prep with plural noun or suffixed pronoun* between, among

**marag** مَرَقْ *vt* to release, set free; to go out, exit {*imperf:* **yamrug**, *vn:* **muruug**}

**fii** في *particle invariable* to be going on; be wrong, be a problem; there is, there are (existential) *(lit. there is, there are)*

**saariḥ** سارِحْ *adj* distracted; absent-minded {*fs:* **saarḥa**, *mpl:* **saarḥiin**, *fpl:* **saarḥaat**}

**ṭawwaalii** طَوّالي *adv* always, continuously; immediately, right away

**kulluu kulluu** كُلّه كُلّه at all, completely (also negative)

**maʕleeʃ** مَعْلَيْشْ **[maʕliiʃ]** *interj* never mind, I'm sorry, don't worry

**ʕalaa** عَلَى **[ʕalee; ʕa]** *prep* according to; for, about (object of reference or concern); of duty, obligation; on

**keef** كَيْفْ *nms* wish, desire, preference; enjoyment of life's simple pleasures (especially tea, coffee, and cigarettes)

**ʕalaa keef** عَلَى كَيْفْ **[ʕalee keef-]** whatever s.o. wants, as s.o.wishes *(lit. according to s.o.'s preference)*

**ʕalaa raaḥat-** عَلَى راحَة **[ʕalee raaḥat-]** take your time; take it easy; whenever (as deadline) *(lit. at s.o.'s convenience)*

## Notes

**1** Note the two uses of /**zaat**/ in the utterance /**maa ʕaarif alwaddaanii ʃnuu zaatuu** w-maa ʕaarif anaa **zaatii** lwaddaanii leehuu ʃnuu/ 'I don't know *exactly what* led me here. *I myself* don't know what brought me to him'. As seen in selection 11, note 11, the form /**zaat**/ 'self' can function as a marker of organization. It does not affect the meaning of the utterance in which it occurs but, instead, adds prominence or emphasis to the word it follows. The preceding word and /**zaat**/ are linked by a suffixed pronoun whose referent is that word. In this case (as in selection 11, note 11), translation of /**zaat**/ depends on context.

**2** The verb /**gutta**/ 'you (ms) said' derives from the perfect /**gaal**/ - /**yaguul**/ 'to say; to think'. The third radical /l/ assimilates to the /t/ of the perfect suffix to produce /**gutta**/ 'you (ms) said'.

**3** The form /**barḍak**/ 'you (ms) still' consists of /**barḍ-**/ and the 2MS suffixed pronoun /**-ak**/. The form /**barḍ-**/ may take any of the suffixed pronouns. It is a variant of the invariable /**barḍuu**/ 'still'. The suffixed pronoun allows the speaker to give the referent of the suffixed pronoun greater prominence than is possible using /**barḍuu**/.

**4** The form /**guum-araḥ**/ 'come (ms) with me' is made up of the imperative verb /**guum**/ 'get up (ms)' and the suffix /**-araḥ**/ that indicates inclusive meaning or 'with s.o., let's'. The suffix /**-araḥ**/ occurs only with imperatives.

**5** The form /**lbeenaatnaa**/ 'that's between us' is composed of the relative pronoun /**al-**/ 'that, which', the preposition /**beenaat**/ 'between, among', and the suffixed pronoun /**-naa**/ 'us'. The preposition /**beenaat**/ derives from the preposition /**been**/ 'between, among'. This derived form occurs only with a P suffixed pronoun, as here, or a P object noun phrase, as in /**beenat albanaat**/ 'among the girls'.

**6** The phrase /**maa fii ʃii**/ literally means 'there is not a thing'. Note, however, that it occur several times in this selection with the meaning 'there is nothing wrong; there is nothing going on; there is no problem'. The positive phrase /**fii ʃii**/ (or /**fii ḥaaja**/) 'there is something wrong; there is something going on; there is a problem' also occurs.

**7** The imperative /**warriinii**/ 'tell (ms) me' has as its perfect /**warraa**/ - /**yawarrii**/. SA, like certain other varieties of spoken Arabic, uses this verb for 'to show', as in /**yiiwarriihuu yaktib alʕarabii**/ 'he shows him how to write Arabic'. Unlike certain other varieties of spoken Arabic, however, SA also uses this verb for 'to tell', as here.

**8** The conditional sentence /**loo fii ḥaaja b-aguulaa leek**/ 'if there is something wrong, I'll tell you (ms)' uses the conditional particle /**loo**/ to describe a real condition, one that predicts, promises, or threatens. As seen in Selection 8, note 15, the conditional particles of SA (/**loo**/, /**kaan**/, and /**izaa**/) are nearly synonymous. The most reliable indictor of the reality of the condition comes in the result clause. The verb of the result clause here is the prefixed imperfect /**b-aguulaa leek**/. It describes an event that does or will actually occur. This makes Khalid's protest to the Hajj a promise of frankness.

**9** The use of the perfect in the form /**xalleetak**/ 'I'm leaving you (ms) alone' is performative. That is, the action of speaking is equal to the act of the verb itself. By saying /**xalleetak**/ 'I'm leaving you (ms) alone', the Hajj indicates that his questions to Khalid are finished. The performative use of the perfect often occurs in legal or contractual contexts, such as buying, selling, and divorce.

# Selection 12

# jaziirat ʔartimiirii

*This selection is taken from a television quiz show whose contestants and audience all come from the same region in Sudan. Here, a guest speaker from Artimiry Island describes the community at the request of the program host. Note the difference in speech style between the two. The guest speaks slowly, carefully, and formally. Among the MSA features that characterize his speech is the irregular replacement of* ث, ذ *, and* ظ *(interdental fricatives) with /s/, /z/, and /ẓ/. The host, in contrast, switches smoothly between a formal, MSA-influenced style and an informal, more SA style of speaking.*

A: alʔahal w-alʔaḥbaab ʔa ... daaxil assuudaan wa-xaarij assuudaan allixwa lḥuḍuur[1] salaamu ʕaleekum wa-raḥmatu ḷḷaahi taʕaalaa wa-barakaatuu[2] wa-b-ismi llaahi rraḥmaan arraḥiim. nabdaa barnaamijnaa lii-haaðaa lyoom wa-yusʕidnaa jiddan ʔan yakuun ḍuyuufnaa fii haaðihi lḥalqa ʔa ... raabiṭat ʔabnaaʔ jaziirat ʔartimiirii lmaḥas[3] bi-xxurṭuum. wa-ʕaʃaan niḥnaa naʕrif ʔartimiirii lmaḥas yusʕidnaa ʔinnuu yataqaddam[4,5] ʔaxuunaa ʃʃeex idriis maḥammad ṣaadig yuḥaddisnaa ʕan ʔartimiirii ʔa ...

B: a... alḥagiiga jaziirat ʔartimirii hiya min ʔiḥdaa juzur ʔalmaḥas, taabiʕa lii-muḥaafaẓat waadii ḥalfaa, maḥalliyyat albirka. wa-hiya jaziira tanʕam bii ... ʔa ... kasaafa sukkaaniyya ʕaaliya wa-kull ʔalmuwaaṭiniin min sulaala waaḥida.[6] wa-tanʕam haazihi jjaziira min ʔalʔanʃiṭa ʔalkasiira minhaa ʔanniʃaaṭ azziraaʕii wa-hiya ʔalḥirfa ʔarraʔiisiyya lii-muwaaṭiniin haazihi ʔajjaziira, ḥaysu tanʕam ajjaziira bi-maʃruuʕi ziraaʕii kabiir wa-yabluɣ ʔalmisaaḥa ʔalkulliyya lee ... almaʃruuʕ fii daaxil ajjaziira ḥawaaleey tultumiyyat faddaan.[7] ʔa ... haaðaa lmaʃruuʕ ʔaẓbaḥa min almaʃaariiʕ alʕimlaaqa[8] fii ʔalwilaaya ʔaʃʃamaaliyya yuʃiiruu biihii kullu

# جَزِيرَةْ أَرْتمِيرِي

أ: اَلأَهَلْ وَالأَحْبَابْ أَ... دَاخِلْ اَلسُّودَانْ وَخَارِجْ اَلسُّودَانْ اَلإِخْوَه الْحُضُورْ[1] سَلاَمُ عَلَيْكُمْ وَرَحْمَةُ اللّه تَعَالَى وَبَرَكَاتُهُ[2] وَبِسْمِ اللّه الرَّحْمَنْ اَلرَّحِيمْ. نَبْدَا بَرْنَامِجْنَا لِيهَذَا الْيَوْمْ وَيُسْعِدْنَا جِداًّ أَنْ يَكُونْ ضُيُوفْنَا فِي هَذِه الْحَلْقَهْ أَ... رَابِطَةْ أَبْنَاءْ جَزِيرَةْ أَرْتمِيرِي الْمَحَسْ[3] بِالْخُرْطُومْ. وَعَشَانْ نِحْنَا نَعْرِفْ أَرْتِيمِيرِي الْمَحَسْ يُسْعِدْنَا إِنّه يَتَقَدَّمْ[4,5] أَخُونَا الشَّيْخْ اِدْرِيسْ مَحَمَّدْ صَادِقْ يُحَدِّسْنَا عَنْ أَرْتمِيرِي أَ...

ب: أَ... اَلْحَقِيقَهْ جَزِيرَةْ أَرْتمرِي هِيَ مِنْ إِحْدَى جُزُرْ أَلْمَحَسْ، تَابِعَهْ لِيمُحَافَظَةْ وَادِي حَلْفَا، مَحَلِّيَّةْ اَلْبِرْكَهْ. وَهِيَ جَزِيرَه تَنْعَمْ بِيـ... أَ... كَسَافَهْ سُكَّانِيَّهْ عَالِيَهْ وكُلّ أَلْمُوَاطِنِينْ مِنْ سُلاَلَهْ وَاحِدَهْ.[6] وَتَنْعَمْ هَذِه الجَّزِيرَهْ مِنْ أَلأَنْشِطَهْ أَلْكَسِيرَهْ مِنْهَا أَلنِّشَاطْ اَلزِّرَاعِي وَهِيَ أَلْحِرْفَهْ أَلرَّئِيسِيَّهْ لِيمُوَاطِنِينْ هَزِه أَلجَّزِيرَهْ، حَيسُ تَنْعَمْ اَلجَّزِيرَه بِمَشْرُوعِ زِرَاعِي كَبِيرْ وَيَبْلُغْ أَلْمِسَاحَهْ أَلْكُلِّيَّهْ لَيـ... اَلْمَشْرُوعْ فِي دَاخِلْ الْجَّزِيرَهْ حَوَالَيّ تُلْتُمِيَّةْ فَدَّانْ.[7] أَ... هَذَا الْمَشْرُوعْ أَصْبَحَ مِنْ اَلْمَشَارِيعْ اَلْعِمْلاَقَهْ[8] فِي أَلْوِلاَيَهْ أَلشَّمَالِيَّهْ يُشِيرُ بِيهِ كُلُّ

man zaarahuu. min ala … alʔanʃiṭa ssaqaafiyya ṭabaʕan b-iiqiimuu nadaawaat waa …

A: ṭabʕan maʕruufa diyyat [xxx].

B: waa … [audience chuckles] fi ʔalʔijtimaaʕiyya bi-tkuun fii ʔal … ʔa … ljalsaat alʔusariyya wa-bi-yarassiluu gawaafil min alxurṭuum ʔilaa …

A: artimiirii.

B: aljaziira ʔalʔum ʔaw ʔartimirii ʔalʕaziiza wa-qariiban qabla ʃahar ʔaw ʃahareen ʔa … suyyarat gaafila min alxurṭuum ʔilaa ʔartimrii lii-taʃyiid assadd. wa-min haaðihi nnuqṭa kuntu ʔatmannaa min kull alḥaadibiin ʕalaa maṣlaḥat assuudaan ʔan yazuuruu jaziirat ʔartimirii li-yajiduu fiihaa …

A: maa yasurhum.[9]

B: ðaalik assadd alʕimlaaq …

A: aha …

B: allaðii suyyida …

A: a …

B: duuna ʔaaliyaat wa-bi-ʔaydii ʔa …

A: abnaaʔ almanṭiga.

مَنْ زَارَهُ. مِنْ اَلَـ... اَلأَنْشِطَه السَّقَافِيَّهْ طَبَعًا بِيقِيمُوا نَدَاوَاتْ وَا...

أ: طَبْعًا مَعْرُوفَهْ دِيَّتْ [xxx].

ب: وَا • • • [audience chuckles] فَالإِجْتِمَاعِيَّهْ بِتْكُونْ فِي أَلْـ... أَ... اَلْجَلْسَاتْ اَلأُسَرِيَّهْ وَبِيَرَسِّلُوا قَوَافِلْ مِنْ اَلْخُرْطُومْ إِلَى...

أ: اَرْتِمِيرِي.

ب: اَلْجَزِيرَهْ أَلأُمْ أَوْ أَرْتِمْرِي أَلْعَزِيزَهْ وَقَرِيبًا قَبْلَ شَهَرْ أَوْ شَهَرَيْنْ أَ... سُيِّرَتْ قَافِلَهْ مِنْ اَلْخُرْطُومْ إِلَى أَرْتِمْرِي لِيَتَشْيِيدْ اَلسَّدّ. وَمِنْ هَذِهِ النُّقْطَهْ كُنْتُ أَتْمَنَّى مِنْ كُلّ اَلْحَادِبِينْ عَلَى مَصْلَحَةْ اَلسُّودَانْ أَنْ يَزُورُوا جَزِيرَةْ أَرْتِمِرِي لِيَجِدُوا فِيهَا...

أ: مَا يَسُرْهُمْ.[9]

ب: ذَلِكْ اَلسَّدّ اَلْعِمْلَاقْ...

أ: اَهَهْ...

ب: اَلَّذِي سُيِّدَ...

أ: اَ...

ب: دُونَ اَلِيَّاتْ وَبِأَيْدِي أَ...

أ: اَبْنَاءْ اَلْمَنْطِقَهْ.

B: abnaaʔ almanṭiga wa-ʔabnaaʔ ʔartimirii wa-lee-yajuu lee-yusajjiluu ʔa ... li-ttaariix.

A: a ... al ... al ... alkalaam ʔallii guttuu daa kulluu kalaam ʕaẓiim yaʕnii niḥnaa bi-nḥayyii ʔa ... ʔalʔahal fii ʔartimiirii ʔaa ... ʕalaa juhuudhum alkabiira wa-xuṣuuṣ almasʔala bitaaʕt assadd laakin anaa daayr aʕrif artimiirii yaʕnii ʃnuu?

B: artimiirii fii ʔa ... al ... llahja ʔannuubiyya ʕindanaa[10] bii-tingasim, liiyaa gismeen.

A: a ...

B: 'artii,' 'ʔartii' bi-rruṭaana ...

A: a ...

B: hiya bii-taʕnii 'jaziira.'

A: naʕam.

B: 'miirii' ʔallii hiyaa 'jadiit.'[11]

A: aha ... yibgaa 'jaziira jadiida' yaʕnii.

B: 'ajjaziiraa ʔajjadiida.'

A: jamiil jiddan.

ب: اَبْنَاءْ اَلْمَنْطِقَهْ وَأَبْنَاءْ أَرْتِمِرِي وَلَيَّجُوا لَيُّسَجِّلُوا أ...
لِلتَّارِيخْ.

أ: اَ... اَلْـ... اَلْـ... اَلْكَلاَمْ أَللِّي قُتّهُ دَا كُلّهُ كَلاَمْ عَظِيمْ يَعْنِي نِحْنَا بِنْحَيِّي أ... أَلأَهَلْ فِي أَرْتِمِيرِي اَ... عَلَى جُهُودْهُمْ اَلْكَبِيرَهْ وَخُصُوصَ الّمَسْأَلَهْ بِتَاعْةْ اَلسَّدّ لَكِنْ اَنَا دَايِرْ اَعْرِفْ ارْتِمِيرِي يَعْنِي شْنُو؟

ب: اَرْتِمِيرِي فِي أ... اَلْـ... اللَّهْجَهْ أَلنُّوبِيَّهْ عِنْدَنَا[10] بِيتِنْقِسِمْ، لِيّاَ قِسْمَيْنْ.

أ: اَ...

ب: «اَرْتِي»، «أَرْتِي» بَالرُّوطَانَهْ...

أ: اَ...

ب: هِيَ بِيتَعْنِي «جَزِيرَه.»

أ: نَعَمْ.

ب: «مِيرِي» أَللِّي هِيَ «جَدِيت».[11]

أ: اَهَهْ... يِبْقَى «جَزِيرَهْ جَدِيدَه» يَعْنِي.

ب: «أَلجَّزِيرَه أَلجَّدِيدَهْ.»

أ: جَمِيلْ جِداً.

## Vocabulary

**raabiṭa** رَابِطَهْ *nfs* association, group (in urban centers, organized on basis of village or regional origin and possessing legal identity) {*pl:* **rawaabiṭ**}

**almaḥas** اَلْمَحَس *prop* Mahas (region of northern Sudan)

**alḥagiiga** اَلْحَقِيقَة **[ḥagiiga]** *disc marker* truly, the fact is that (softens opinion or correction)

**muḥaafaẓa** مُحَافَظَة *nfs* administrative district {*pl:* **muḥaafaẓaat**}

**waadii ḥalfaa** وادي حَلْفَا *prop* Wadi Halfa (city and district in northern Sudan)

**maḥalliyya** مَحَلِّيَة *nfs* district, region; municipality {*pl:* **maḥalliyyaat**}

**albirka** اَلْبِرْكَة *prop* Birka (district in Northern Province)

**faddaan** فَدّان *nms* feddan (land measure approximately one acre or half a hectare) {*pl:* **fadaadiin, afdina**}

**wilaaya** وِلايَة *nfs* province {*pl:* **wilaayaat**}

**aʃʃamaaliyya** اَلشَّمَالِيَة **[aʃʃimaaliyya]** *prop* al-Shamaliyya, Northern Province

**maʕruuf** مَعْرُوف *adj* known; it is known that {*fs:* **maʕruufa**, *mpl:* **maʕruufiin**, *fpl:* **maʕruufaat**}

**diyyat** دِيَّت **[deeya; dii; dayya]** *pron fs* this, near demonstrative {*ms:* **daa**, *fs:* **diyyat**, *pl:* **deel**}

**sarra** سَرّ *vt* to please, make happy {*imperf:* **yasurr**, *vn:* **suruur**}

**ruṭaana** رُطانَة *nfs* rutana (any non-Arabic language variety spoken in Sudan; tribe in eastern Sudan) *(lit. dialect; jargon)* {*pl:* **ruṭaanaat**}

## Notes

**1** The use of the vocabulary of family in /**allixwa lḥuḍuur**/ 'our brothers and sisters here today' occurs in this and other selections. The English translation may seem unusual, but this is a conventional way to refer to one's fellow citizens in Sudan and elsewhere in the Arabic-speaking world.

**2** The phrase /**salaamu ʕaleekum wa-raḥmatu ḷḷaahi taʕaalaa wa-barakaatuu**/ 'may the peace, mercy, and blessing of God the Exalted be upon you (mp)' is recognizable as an expanded version of the common greeting /**(as)salaamu ʕaleekum**/ 'peace be upon you (mp)'. The expanded version tends to occur on ceremonial or formal situations. The context of this usage, the start of a quiz show on Sudanese national television, clearly qualifies as formal to those involved.

**3** Artimiry Island is also referred to as /**jaziirat ʔartimiirii lmaḥas**/ 'Artimiry Island of the Mahas'. Mahas names a place as well as a people. The Mahas region is in northern Sudan, along the Nile north of the city of Dongola. The Mahas people were originally speakers of a Nubian language, although many who call themselves Mahas today are monolingual speakers of Arabic.

**4** Note the host's shift of style. He begins in an informal, SA style with /**ʕaʃaan niḥnaa naʕrif ʔartimiirii lmaḥas**/ 'so that we get to know Artimiry of the Mahas'. His language changes to a more formal, MSA-influenced style with /**yusʕidnaa ʔinnuu yataqaddam**/ 'we are pleased to present'. These shifts in style are common among speakers of Arabic in Sudan and elsewhere.

**5** The phrase /**yusʕidnaa ʔinnuu yataqaddam**/ 'we are pleased to present' is both formal and conventional. Its literal translation is 'it (ms) gives us pleasure that he present himself'. The translation given here, however, attempts to match the conventional phrasing of the Arabic with equally conventional English usage.

**6** The speaker makes a point of saying that the inhabitants of Artimiry Island are /**min sulaala waaḥida**/ 'from a single ethnic group'. Given the history of Sudan, ethnic homogeneity may be worth noting.

**7** The /**faddaan**/ 'feddan' is a unit of land measure. Officially, a feddan is an approximately one acre or one-half of a hectare. Note, however, that the actual or perceived size of a feddan may vary from place to place.

**8** In the clause /**ʔaẓbaḥa min almaʃaariiʕ alʕimlaaqa**/ 'it (ms) is one of the largest projects', note two features. The first is the use of the verb /**ʔaẓbaḥa**/ (MSA ʔaṣbaḥa) to mean 'to be' rather than 'to become'. Both uses are acceptable, but 'to become' may be more common. The second is the use of the construction /**min al-**/ followed by a P noun phrase to mean 'one of the most'.

**9** The relative clause /**maa yasurhum**/ 'something to like, lit. that which pleases them (mp)' (MSA maa yasurruhum) is formal, conventional, and not particularly meaningful in this context. It occurs here as the host's third (unsuccessful) attempt to hurry the guest speaker to his conclusion.

**10** The phrase /**ʕindanaa**/ 'back home, lit. where we are, among us' begins a style shift by the guest speaker. At this point, he moves away from the careful formality of MSA-influenced style to casual, SA speech.

**11** The pronunciation of /**jadiit**/ for /**jadiid**/ 'new' is an unusually clear example of a feature of SA. Under certain conditions, speakers of SA (and certain other varieties of spoken Arabic) replace voiced stops like /b/, /d/, /ḍ/, and /g/ with their unvoiced counterparts /p/, /t/, /ṭ/, and /k/. This usually happens when the voiced stop occurs at the end of a word and when it is followed by silence or a pause, as here.

# ḥall siyaasii li-muʃkilt ajjanuub

*The two speakers in this selection are not optimistic about prospects for a political solution to the conflict in Sudan. Note the difference in styles employed by these speakers. The male speaker uses an MSA-influenced political vocabulary with language structures that are SA-based. The vocabulary of the female speaker is similarly MSA-influenced. In addition, she uses function words (/***munzuu***/ 'since', /***ka-***/ 'as', and the negative particle /***lam***/) that add an additional degree of MSA-influenced formality to her speech.*

A: b-ismi llaa rraḥmaan arraḥiim ʔa … al … allaxbaar assuudaanii … yaa raajaa, ssiyaasiyya ʔintii ʕaarfa lleela kaatbiin leek ʃinuu.[1] ʔannuu ʔa … naas alḥakuuma w-almutmarridiin ʔittafaguu ʕalaa ʔannuu ywaggifuu ʔiṭlaaɣ annaar fii jjanuub ʕaʃaan yaɣiisuu nnaas bitaan … ʔa … bitaaʕ baḥr alɣazaal bii-zzaat.[2] waa … yaʕnii fii muḥaadasaat jaariya wallaa fii wasaaṭaat kidaa ʕal aasaas innuu masalan ḥa-ykuun fii[3] ḥall dibluumaasii lii … wallaa ḥall siyaasii li-muʃkilt ajjanuub. yaʕnii annaas hinaak fiʕlan ḥarb daamat siṭṭaaʃar sana[4] wa-ḥaajaat zayy dii kidaa fa … ʔalmuʔassira taʔsiir ʃadiid jiddan jiddan. w-alḥarb fi jjanuub ʕumuuman yaʕnii hiya mimmaa lsuudaan[5] naal ʔistiɣlaaluu yaʕnii l … al … alʔixwa fii januub assuudaan ʔa … yaʕnii ṭawwaalii bii … b-iitmarraduu ʕa-lḥakuumaat assuudaaniyya, yaʕnii min ʔawwal ḥakuuma waṭaniyya la-ɣaayat hassaʕ alḥakuuma lḥaaliyya. wa-maa gidrit annaas la-hassaʕ taṣal li-ḥall yaʕnii siyaasii fiʕlan li-lmuʃkila dii ʔallii hiya maa ʔa … yaʕ … yaʕ … yaʕnii ɣaaliban assuudaan yaʕnii ffaɣra bitaaʕuu wal … al … al … al … ʕadam ʔa … ʔismuhuu, ʕadam numuu lʔiqtiṣaad w-kidaa. ʔa … assabab arraʔiisii fiihuu[6] haazihi lḥarb addaayra ʔallii hiya yaʕnii kattalat ʔalaaf ʔal

# حَلّ سِيَاسِي لِمُشْكِلْة اَلجَنُّوب

أ: بِسْمِ اللَّه الرَّحَمَنْ اَلرَّحِيمْ أَ... اَلْـ... اَلاّخْبَارْ اَلسُّودَانِيـ ... يَا رَاجَا، السِّيَاسِيَّهْ إِنْتِي عارْفَه اللَّيْلَهْ كَاتْبِينْ لَيْكْ شِنُو.[1] أَنَّهُ أَ... نَاسْ اَلْحَكُومَهْ وَالْمُتْمَرِّدِينْ إِتَّفَقُوا عَلَى أَنَّهْ يُوَقِّفُوا إِطْلاَغْ اَلنَّارْ فِي الجَنُّوبْ عَشَانْ يَغِيسُوا النَّاسْ بِتَانْـ... أَ ... بِتَاعْ بَحْرْ اَلْغَزَالْ بِيالزَّاتْ.[2] وَا... يَعْنِي فِي مُحَادَسَاتْ جَارِيَهْ وَلاَّ فِي وَسَاطَاتْ كِدَا عَلَى اَسَاسْ اِنَّهْ مَسَلاً حَيْكُونْ فِي[3] حَلّ دِبْلُومَاسِي لِيـ... وَلاَّ حَلّ سِيَاسِي لِمُشْكِلْة اَلجَنُّوبْ. يَعْنِي اَلنَّاسْ هِنَاكْ فَعْلاً حَرْبْ دَامَتْ سِطَّاشَرْ سَنَهْ[4] وَحَاجَاتْ زَيّ دِي كِدَا فَـ... أَلْمُؤَسِّرَهْ تَأْسِيرْ شَدِيدْ جِدّاً جِدّاً. وَالْحَرْبْ فِالجَنُّوبْ عُمُومًا يَعْنِي هِيَ مِمَّا اَلْسُودَانْ[5] نَالْ إِسْتِغْلاَلْهُ يَعْنِي لْـ... اَلْـ... اَلإِخْوَهْ فِي جَنُوبْ اَلسُّودَانْ أَ... يَعْنِي طَوَّالِي بِيـ... بِيتْمَرَّدُوا عَالْحَكُومَاتْ اَلسُّودَانِيَّهْ، يَعْنِي مِنْ أَوَّلْ حَكُومَهْ وَطَنِيَّهْ لَغَايَةْ هَسَّعْ اَلْحَكُومَهْ الْحَالِيَّهْ. وَمَا قَدْرِتْ اَلنَّاسْ لَهَسَّعْ تَصَلْ لِحَلّ يَعْنِي سِيَاسِي فَعْلاً لِلْمُشْكِلَهْ دِي أَلِّي هِيَ مَا أَ... يَعْـ... يَعْـ... يَعْنِي غَالِبًا اَلسُّودَانْ يَعْنِي الفَّغْرَ بِتَاعْهُ وَالْـ... اَلْـ... اَلْـ... اَلْـ... عَدَمْ أَ... إِسْمُهُ، عَدَمْ نُمُو الإِقْتِصَادْ وَكْدَا. أَ... اَلسَّبَبْ اَلرَّئِيسِي فِيهُ[6] هَزِهِ الْحَرْبْ اَلدَّايْرَهْ أَلِّي هِيَ يَعْنِي كَتَّلَتْ أَلآفْ أَلْـ...

... wallaa malaayiin almuwaaṭaniin wa-fii nafs alwakit yaʕnii l ... ʔa ... halk alʔiqtiṣaad assuudaanii bi-ʃakli maa ʕaadii. fa ... ʔin ʃaa llaa yaʕnii tmannaa minn aḷḷaa[7] ʔinnuu masalan fiʕlan annaas deel yaṣaluu li-ḥalla siyaasii kidaa w-ʕaʃaan albalad ʃwiyya kidaa tamʃii bi-ṣuura kwayyisa wa-ḥaaja zayy dii. waa ... ʃaayif barḍuu lḥakuuma llamriikiyya raḥḥabat bila ... bila ... waqf ʔitlaaɣ annaar daa kidaa waa ... maa ... maa ... gaaluu naas alʔiigaad[8] ḥa-yijtamiʕuu ʃʃahr ajjaay ʔa ... ɣaaliban ʕaʃaan barḍuu ywaaṣluu lḥiwaar fi lḥitta dii ʕalaa ʔasaas ʔann yaṣaluu lii-ḥall ʔa ... siyaasii.

B: alḥagiiga ʔan ... ḥarb ajjanuub ṭabaʕan niḥnaa kullinaa yaʕnii min, munzuu wilaadatnaa ʔa ... muʕaayʃiin ḥarb ajjanuub wa-fiʕlan ʔiɣtiṣaadiyyan mu ... muhaddida ssuudaan ʃadiid, alḥarb ʔa ... fii jjanuub maa ʔaʕtaɣid ʔinnahaa bii-tantahii yaa lmaaḥii, bi ... bi-ssaahil maa lam assuudaan taku ... ykuun fiihuu ḥukim diimuuɣraaṭii.[9] ʔa ... la ... attadmiir alḥaaṣil wa ... wa-ʕaʃaan assuudaan ya ... yarajjiʕ ʔiɣtiṣaaduu ʔaw yirjaʕ bii-waḍʕihaa lmumtaaz. al ... al ... alḥukuuma lmawjuuda la-ṭaalmaa ʔinnahaa ʔislaamiyya mutaṭarrifa maa mumkin taddii ḥagg kabiir ʔa ... lila ... li-jjanuub ka ... ka-juzuʔ min assuudaan masiiḥii.[10] fa-lanaa b-aʕtaɣid ʔinnuu al ... al ... alwaḍaʕ assiyaasii ʕumuuman maa b-iikuun yaʕnii ʔimʃii[11] bi-ṭṭariig aṣṣaḥḥ ʔaw ʃii ykuun murḍii li-kull alaṭraaf maa lam yikuun fii niẓaam diimuɣraaṭii fi ssuudaan.

وَلاَّ مَـلاَيِـينْ اَلْمُـوَاطْنِـينْ وَفِـي نَفْسْ اَلْوَكِتْ يَعْنِـي لْـ...   أ... هَلْك اَلإِقْـتْـصَـادْ اَلسَّـودَانِـي بِشَكْلِ مَـا عَـادِي. فَـ...   إِنْ شَـا اللَّهْ يَعْنِـي اتْمَنَّى مِنّ اَللَّهْ[7] إِنَّـهُ مَـسَلاً فِـعْلاً اَلنَّاسْ دَيْلْ يَصَلُوا لِحَلّ سِيَاسِـي كِدَا وْعَشَانْ اَلْبَلَدْ شْوِيَّهْ كِدَا تَمْشِي بِصُورَهْ كْوَيِّسَهْ وَحَـاجَـهْ زَيّ دِي. وَا...   شَـايِفْ بَـرْضْـهْ اَلْحُكُومَـهْ اَلأَمْـرِيكِيَّـهْ رَحَّبَتْ بِلَـ...   بِلَـ...   وَقْفْ إِطْلاَغْ اَلنَّارْ دَا كِدَا وَا...   مَـا... مَـا...   قَـالُوا نَـاسْ اَلإِيـگَادْ[8] حَـيِجْـتَـمِـعُوا الشَّـهْـرْ اَلجَّـاي أ... غَـالِبًـا عَشَانْ بَرْضْهُ يْوَاصْلُوا الْحِـوَارْ فَـالْحِتَّـهْ دِي عَلَى أَسَـاسْ أَنّ يَصَلُوا لِيحَلّ أ...   سِيَاسِي.

ب: اَلْحَـقِـيقَـهْ أَنْـ...   حَـرْبْ اَلجَّنُوبْ طَبَـعًـا نِحْنَـا كُلِّنَـا يَعْنِـي مِنْ، مُنْزُو وِلاَدَتْنَـا أ...   مْـعَايْشِينْ حَرْبْ اَلجَّنُوبْ وَفِـعْلاً إِغْـتِـصَـادِيًّا مُـ...   مْـهَدِّدَه السُّودَانْ شَدِيدْ، اَلْحَـرْبْ أ...   فِي الجَّنُوبْ مَـا أَعْـتَـغِدْ إِنَّـهَا بِيـتَـنْتَـهِي يَا الْمَـاحِي، بِـ...   بِالسَّاهِلْ مَـا لَمْ اَلسُّودَانْ تَكُـ...   يْكُونْ فِيـهُ حُكُمْ دِيمُوغْـرَاطِي.[9] أ...   لَـ... اَلتَّـدْمِـيـرْ اَلْحَـاصِلْ وَ...   وَعَـشَـانْ اَلسُّـودَانْ يَـ...   يَرَجِّعْ إِغْـتِـصَـادْهُ أَوْ يِرْجَعْ بِيـوَضْـعِـهَـا الْمُـمْـتَـازْ. اَلْـ...   اَلْـ... اَلْحُكُومَـه الْمَوْجُودَهْ لَطَالْمَـا إِنَّـهَا إِسْلاَمِـيَّهْ مُتَطَرِّفَهْ مَـا مُمْكِنْ تَدِّي حَقّ كَـبِـيـرْ أ...   لِيـ...   لِلجَّنُوبْ كَـ...   كَـجُـزْءْ مِنْ اَلسُّودَانْ مَسِيحِي.[10] فَلاَنَـا بَـاعْتَـغِدْ إِنَّـهُ اَلْـ...   اَلْـ...   اَلْوَضعْ اَلسِّـيَـاسِـي عُـمُـومًا مَـا بِيكُونْ يَعْنِي إِمْشِي [11] بِالطَّرِيقْ اَلصَّحّ أَوْ شِي يْكُونْ مُـرْضِي لِكُلّ اَلاَطْرَافْ مَـا لَمْ يِكُونْ فِي نِظَامْ دِيمُغْرَاطِي فَالسُّودَانْ.

## Vocabulary

**alleela** اَللَّيْلَة *adv* today; now

**ɣaas (ɣista)** غَاسْ (غِسْتَ) *vt* to help {*imperf:* **yaɣiis,** *vn:* **ɣaws**}

**baḥar** بَحَرْ *nms* river; ocean {*pl:* **buḥuur**}

**baḥr alɣazaal** بَحْرْ اَلْغَزَال *prop* Bahr al-Ghazal (region and river of southwestern Sudan)

**bi-zzaat** بِالزَّاتْ **[bii-zaat]** especially, in particular

**ḥa-** حَ *particle* will (future marker)

**kattal** كَتَّلْ *vt* to massacre, slaughter {*imperf:* **yakattil,** *vn:* **katteel**}

**amriikii** أَمْرِيكِي *adj* American {*fs:* **amriikiyya,** *mpl:* **amriikaan,** *fpl:* **amriikiyyaat**}

**munzuu-** مُنْذُ *prep* since

**bi-ssaahil** بِالسَّاهِلْ easily

**ḥagg** حَقّ *nms* share, right, legal claim; right, truth {*pl:* **ḥuguug**}

## Notes

**1** The translation of the phrase /**kaatbiin leek** ʃ**inuu**/ 'what they (mp) wrote?' omits the form /**leek**/ 'for you (fs)', as it is unlikely that the media would write especially for the female speaker. This use of the preposition /**li-**/ with a suffixed pronoun is another example of the benefactive, seen in selection 9, note 13. Here, however, the benefactive does not serve to give greater prominence to the suffixed pronoun. Instead, direct address to the listener through the use of /**leek**/ 'for you (fs)' attempts to increase the listener's involvement in the speaker's utterance.

**2** The phrase /**nnaas bitaan … ʔa … biitaaʕ baḥr alɣazaal bii-zzaat**/ 'the people of … ah … of Bahr al-Ghazal especially' names a region particularly hard hit by famine in 1998. The humanitarian situation there led to the cease-fire noted by the male speaker.

**3** The use of the prefix /**ḥa-**/ in the phrase /**ḥa-ykuun fii**/ 'there will be' is one way of expressing future action in SA. Another way to express future action is through the prefixed imperfect, as in /**b-iifiidak**/ 'it (ms) will benefit you (ms)' (see selection 8, note 13). The use of the prefix /**ḥa-**/ occurs mostly in the region of the capital. Speakers in other parts of Sudan use the prefixed imperfect to express future action.

**4** The war referred to in the phrase /**ḥarb daamat siṭṭaaʃar sana**/ 'a war that's lasted sixteen years' is the Sudanese civil war. The beginning of that conflict is usually dated to 1983.

**5** The male speaker says /**lsuudaan**/ 'Sudan', without assimilation of the definite article, rather than /**ssuudan**/. This kind of slip of the tongue is not uncommon and does not interfere with communication in otherwise fluent speech.

**6** The form /**fiihuu**/ 'for it (ms)' is conventional in SA. The combination of the preposition /**fii**/ and suffixed pronoun is completely regular, with no changes to vowels (compare with MSA fiihii 'for it (ms)').

**7** The doubled /**n**/ of the preposition in the phrase /**minn aḷḷaa**/ 'to God, lit. from God' often occurs when the word that follows /**min**/ begins with a vowel. The doubling (gemination) of /**n**/ in this environment resembles what occurs when /**min**/ takes a suffixed pronoun that begins with a vowel, as in /**minnuu**/ 'from him'.

**8** The group called here /**naas alʔiigaad**/ 'people from IGAD' is the Inter-Governmental Authority on Development (formerly the Inter-Governmental Authority on Drought and Desertification, IGADD), made up of Ethiopia, Eritrea, Djibouti, Somalia, Sudan, Kenya, and Uganda. In 1998, drought and famine threatened Sudan, particularly in the Bahr al-Ghazal region. IGAD was among those attempting to negotiate a cease-fire between the Sudanese government and the Sudan People's Liberation Army (SPLA).
Note this English-language acronym occurs here with no indication of its meaning or of the fact that it is not Arabic. Similar borrowings tend to occur especially in political and technological contexts.

**9** In the phrase /**maa lam** assuudaan taku ... **ykuun** fiihuu ḥukim diimuuɣraaṭii/ 'as long as there's ... there's no democratic rule there', the female speaker works toward a MSA-influenced sentence. The influence of MSA appears in the phrase /**maa lam**/ 'so long as, as long as'. It is also indicated by the use of /**ykuun**/ 'it is', which is not the simple imperfect of SA but the jussive of MSA. Although the speaker makes a false start in this sentence, she is completely fluent in a later, similar sentence: /**maa lam yikuun fii niẓaam diimuɣraaṭii fi ssuudaan**/ 'so long as there is no democratic regime in Sudan'.

**10** The phrase /**ka-juzuʔ min assuudaan masiiḥii**/ 'as a part of Sudan that is Christian' contains an indefinite relative clause rather than a noun-adjective phrase. The indefinite adjective /**masiiḥii**/ 'Christian' agrees in number, gender, and definiteness with the noun /**juzuʔ**/ 'part' but is separated from it. Note that if the adjective modified the noun in a noun-adjective phrase, it would read /**ka-juzuʔ masiiḥii min assuddaan**/ 'as a Christian part of Sudan'.

**11** The form /**ʔimʃii**/ 'it (ms) goes' is the simple imperfect of the verb /**maʃaa**/ 'to walk; to go'. The prefix /**ʔi-**/ is one of several variants of the imperfect prefix usually heard as /**ya-**/ (/**yamʃii**/) or /**yi-**/ (/**yimʃii**/).

# addastuur alʔintixaabii w-ajjabha lʔislaamiyya

*The female speaker dominates this selection, in which the speakers attempt to trace the origins of the Islamicist influence in Sudanese politics. The combination of emotional engagement and intellectual content in this discussion makes for a language style that falls somewhere between a formal, MSA influence and an informal, SA influence.*

A: alḥagiiga al … al … al … addimooɣraaṭiyya ʔanaa b-aftikir ʔinnuu ʔal … ar-*regime*[1] ʔaw waḍaʕ ʔala … ʔala … ʔalḥukuuma ʔalmawjuuda fi ssuudaan ḥaaliyaan ʔa … maa ʕindahaa ʔayyi nuuʕ min addimooɣraaṭiyya. w-addimooɣraaṭiyya lammaa jaat, jaat fii wakit basiiṭ jiddan xamsa wa-θamaaniin, sitta wa-tamaaniin.[2] laakin ʔanaa yaʕnii ʔa … zawaal alḥukuuma ddimooɣraaṭiyya b-aḥammiluu lii-ʔaʕḍaaʔ alḥukuuma nafsahum liyannum hummaa lxattuu ddastuur al … al … alʔintixaabii ʔallii jaab ajjabha lʔislaamiyya marra taaniyya.[3] fa-dii masʔuuliyyitum bi-lliḍaafa liʔinnuu yaʕnii ssuudaan biduun diimuuɣraaṭiyya maa mumkin itgaddam li-giddaam liʔannuu ttadahwur kulluu lḥaaṣil, ḥaaṣil min alwaḍʕ alsiyaasii lil … li-lḥukuuma lḥaaliyya ʔa … ʔizaa kaan waḍaʕ ajjanuub wa-ʔizaa kaan ḥattaa waḍaʕ aʃʃamaal.[4] yaʕnii hassii lleela fi ʃʃamaal barḍuu ʔannaas min al … min alwaḍʕ assiyaasii maa, ʔanaa maa, maa, maa ʃaayfa ʔayyi tagaddum bal tadahwur liʔannuu ʔanaa ʃahri ʔiḥdaaʃar alfaat kunta fi ssuudaan. wa-kunta laaḥaẓt attadahwur alkaan ḥaaṣil yaʕnii fii kull almajaalaat wa-daa kulluu …

B: ay.

A: naatij min al …

# اَلدَّسْتُورْ اَلإِنْتِخَابِي واَلجَبْهَه الإِسْلَامِيَّه

أ: اَلْحَقِيقَهْ اَلْـ... اَلْـ... اَلدِّمَوغْرَاطِيَّهْ أَنَا بَافْتِكِرْ إِنَّهُ أَلْـ... اَلregime[1] أَوْ وَضَعْ اَلَـ... اَلَـ... اَلْحُكُومَهْ أَلْمَوْجُودَه فَالسُّودَانْ حَالِيّاً أَ... مَا عِنْدَهَا أَيِّ نُوعْ مِنْ اَلدِّمَوغْرَاطِيَّهْ. وَالدِّمَوغْرَاطِيَّهْ لَمَّا جَاتْ، جَاتْ فِي وَكِتْ بَسِيطْ جِدّاً خَمْسَهْ وَتَمَانِينْ، سِتَّهْ وَتَمَانِينْ.[2] لَكِنْ أَنَا يَعْنِي أَ... زَوَالْ اَلْحُكُومَه الدِّمَوغْرَاطِيَّهْ بَاحَمِّلْهُ لِيأَعْضَاءْ اَلْحُكُومَهْ نَفْسَهُمْ لِينّهُمْ هُمَّا الْخَتُّوا الدَّسْتُورْ اَلْـ... اَلْـ... اَلإِنْتِخَابِي أَلْلِّي جَابْ اَلجَبْهَه الإِسْلَامِيَّهْ مَرَّهْ تَانِيَّهْ.[3] فَدِي مَسْئُولِيِّتْهُمْ بِالاِّضَافَهْ لإِنَّهُ يَعْنِي السُّودَانْ بِدُونْ دِيمُوغْرَاطِيَّهْ مَا مُمْكِنْ اِتْقَدَّمْ لِقِدَّامْ لأَنَّهُ التَّدَهْوُرْ كُلّهُ الْحَاصِلْ، حَاصِلْ مِنْ اَلْوَضْعْ اَلْسِيَاسِي لِلْـ... لِلْحُكُومَه الْحَالِيَّهْ أَ... إِزَا كَانْ وَضَعْ اَلجَنُوبْ وَإِزَا كَانْ حَتَّى وَضَعْ اَلشَّمَالْ.[4] يَعْنِي هَسِّي اللَّيْلَهْ فَالشَّمَالْ بَرْضَهُ أَلنَّاسْ مِنْ اَلْـ... مِنْ اَلْوَضْعْ اَلسِّيَاسِي مَا، أَنَا مَا، مَا، مَا شَايْفَهْ أَيِّ تَقَدُّمْ بَلْ تَدَهْوُرْ لأَنّهُ أَنَا شَهْرِ إِحْدَاشَرْ اَلْفَاتْ كُنْتَ فَالسُّودَانْ. وَكُنْتَ لَاحَظْت اَلتَّدَهْوُرْ اَلْكَانْ حَاصِلْ يَعْنِي فِي كُلّ اَلْمَجَالَاتْ وَدَا كُلّهُ...

ب: اَيْ.

أ: نَاتِجْ مِنْ اَلْـ...

B: ay …

A: min al … min al … alwaḍʕ alʔiɣtiṣaadii yaʕnii rraahin.

B: ṣaḥḥ, ʔittii yaʕnii fiʕlan …

A: haa …

B: intii lammaa taguulii daa …

A: w-izaa maṣnaʕ aʃʃifaa, bi-titkallam ʕan maṣnaʕ aʃʃifaa[5] masalan ʔanaa laa ʔasiɣ ʔiṭlaaɣan fii ʔinnuu lḥukuuma dii maa yikuun ʕindahaa ʔa … maa ykuun ʕindahaa ʃii bi … xalf taṣniiʕ alʔadwiyya.

B: haa …

A: anaa, ʔimkin maa tittafig maʕaay fi lḥitta dii laakin ʔaʕtaɣid ʔinnuu, ʔannuu, ʔinnuu maa ʔanaa laa ʔasiɣ fil … fil … fi lwaḍiʕ dii …

B: ay …

A: liʔannuu yaʕnii fi nnihaaya waḍiʕ zayy dii kidaa lamman iikuun huwwa yaʕnii ʔa … maa mutjaawib maʕa kull adduwal attaaniya ʔaw, ʔaw maa faatiḥ ssuudaan ʕalee, ʕalee kull masalan alʕaalam b-atwaɣɣaʕ ʔinnuu mumkin yikuun ʕaʃaan yiḥmii nafsuu yaʕmil ʔaʃyaa ʔa … ta … taʔammin leehuu lii-giddaam law ḥaṣalat ʔayyi muʃkila yaʕnii.

B: ay, laa …

A: anaa b-atkallim bi-wuḍuuḥ maa ʕaarfa …

ب: اَيْ ...

أ: مِنْ اَلْـ ... مِنْ اَلْـ ... اَلْوَضْعْ اَلإِغْتِصَادِي يَعْنِي الرَّاهِنْ.

ب: صَحّ، إِتِّي يَعْنِي فِعْلاً ...

أ: هَا ...

ب: اِنْتِي لَمَّا تَقُولِي دَا ...

أ: وِازَا مَصْنَعْ اَلشِّفَا، بِتِتْكَلَّمْ عَنْ مَصْنَعْ اَلشِّفَا[5] مَسَلاً أَنَا لاَ أَسِغْ إِطْلاَغًا فِي إِنّهُ الْحُكُومَهْ دِي مَا يْكُونْ عِنْدَهَا أَ... مَا يْكُونْ عِنْدَهَا شِي بِـ... خَلْفْ تَصْنِيعَ اَلأَدْوِيَّهْ.

ب: هَا ...

أ: اَنَا، إِمْكِنْ مَا تِتَّفِقْ مَعَاي فِالْحِتَّهْ دِي لَكِنْ أَعْتَغِدْ إِنّهْ، أَنّهُ، إِنّهُ مَا أَنَا لاَ أَسِغْ فِالْـ... فِالْـ... فِالْوَضِعْ دِي...

ب: اَيْ ...

أ: لأَنّهُ يَعْنِي فِالنِّهَايَهْ وَضِعْ زَيّ دِي كِدَا لَمَّنْ يْكُونْ هُوَّ يَعْنِي أَ ... مَا مُتْجَاوِبْ مَعَ كُلّ اَلدُّوَلْ اَلتَّانِيَهْ أَوْ، أَوْ مَا فَاتِحِ السُّودَانْ عَلَيْ، عَلَي كُلّ مَسَلاً اَلْعَالَمْ بَاتْوَغَّعْ إِنّهُ مُمْكِنْ يكُون عَشَانْ يِحْمِي نَفْسُهْ يَعْمِلْ أَشْيَا أَ... تَـ... تَأَمِّنْ لَيْهْ لِيقِدَّامْ لَوْ حَصَلَتْ أَيِّ مُشْكِلَهْ يَعْنِي...

ب: اَيْ، لاَ...

أ: اَنَا بَاتْكَلِّمْ بِوُضُوحْ مَا عَارْفَهْ...

B: ay, laa, laa, ṣaḥḥ ay, maa yaʕnii laakin ittii maa guttii deek ʔa … bi-tḥammileeyaa li … li … li … lee-naas alḥukuuma ʔaddumuuɣraaṭiyya liʔannuu jaabat naas ajjabha w-kidaa. ajjabha dii ʔalḥukuuma ddumuuɣraaṭiyya wa-ṭabʕan maa jabhajii[6] wallaa ayyi ḥaaja laakin maa jaabuuhum, hun ʔasaasan alʔislaamiyya deel maa baduu min ʕahdi nimeerii.[7]

A: al … al … al … al … al … alʃii llii nnaa gaṣattuu …

B: haa …

A: innuu lḥukuuma lʔintiɣaaliyya[8] …

B: haa …

A: allii kaanat bi-ɣaadat suwaar aððahab w-ajjuzuulii dafaʕ aḷḷaa[9] hiya lwaḍaʕat addustuur bitaaʕ alʔintixaabaat. kwayyis? addistuur bitaaʕ alʔintixaabaat daa tafaaṣiiluu, tafaaṣiiluu hiya lɣaadat liʔinnuu tadaxxil ajjabha lʔislaamiyya laʔannuu jjuzuulii dafaʕ aḷḷaa waa … waa … waa … waa … wa-suwaar aððahab allitneen ʔasaasan jabha ʔislaamiyya. ʔanaa maa ḍadd alʔislaam …

B: haa …

A: anaa zoola ʔitrabbeet ʔa … tarbiyya ʔislaamiyya wa-b-aḥibb alʔislaam jiddan laakin maa b-aḥibb alʔislaam yadxul fi ssiyaasa yaʕnii lʔislaam ka-ʕaɣiida w-ʃii ʃaxṣii ʔa … yaʕnii kulli waaḥid b-iimaaris alʔislaam ka-ʕilaaɣa beenuu wa-been rabbanaa[10] wa-dii ʕilaaɣa xaaṣṣa jiddan jiddan. laakin al …

ب: اَيْ، لاَ، لاَ، صَحّ اَيْ، مَـا يَعْنِي لَكِنْ اِتِّي مَـا قُـتِّي دَيْكْ أ... بِتْحَمِّلِيَّا لِـ... لِـ... لِـ... لِيْنَاسْ اَلْحُكُومَـهْ أَلدُّمُوغْرَاطِيَّهْ لأَنَّـهُ جَـابَتْ نَـاسْ اَلجَّـبْـهَـهْ وكِدَا. اَلجَّـبْـهَـهْ دِي أَلْحُكُومَـه الدُّمُوغْرَاطِيَّهْ وَطَبْعًا مَا جَبْهَجِي[6] وَلاَّ اَيِّ حَاجَهْ لَكِنْ مَـا جَابُوهُمْ، هُنْ أَسَاسًا اَلإِسْلاَمِيَّهْ دَيْلْ مَا بَدُوا مِنْ عَهْدِ نِمَيْرِي.[7]

أ: اَلْـ... اَلْـ... اَلْـ... اَلْـ... اَلْـ... اَلْشِي اللِّي انَّا قَصَتَّهُ ...

ب: هَا...

أ: اِنَّهُ الْحُكُومَه الإِنْتِقَالِيَّهْ[8]...

ب: هَا...

أ: اَللِّي كَانَتْ بِغَادَةْ سُوَارْ اَلذَّهَبْ وَالجُّزُولِي دَفَعْ اَللَّهْ[9] هِيَ الْوَضَعَتْ اَلدُّسْتُورْ بِتَاعْ اَلإِنْتِخَابَاتْ. كْوَيِّسْ؟ اَلدِّسْتُورْ بِتَاعْ اَلإِنْتِخَابَاتْ دَا تَفَاصِيلْهُ، تَفَاصِيلْهُ هِيَ الْغَادَتْ لإِنَّهُ تَدَخِّلْ اَلجَّبْهَه الإِسْلاَمِيَّهْ لأَنَّهُ الجُّزُولِي دَفَعْ اَللّهْ وَا... وَا... وَا ... وَا... وَسُوَارْ اَلذَّهَبْ اَلاِتْنَيْنْ أَسَاسًا جَبْهَهْ إِسْلاَمِيَّهْ. أَنَا مَا ضَدّ اَلإِسْلاَمْ...

ب: هَا...

أ: اَنَا زَوْلَهْ إِتْرَبَّيْتْ أ... تَرْبِيَّهْ إِسْلاَمِيَّهْ وَبَاحِبّ اَلإِسْلاَمْ جِدّاً لَكِنْ مَا بَاحِبّ اَلإِسْلاَمْ يَدْخُلْ فَالسِّيَاسَهْ يَعْنِي الإِسْلاَمْ كَعَقِيدَهْ وْشِي شَخْصِي أ... يَعْنِي كُلِّ وَاحِدْ بِيمَارِسْ اَلإِسْلاَمْ كَعِلاَقَهْ بَيْنْهُ وَبَيْنْ رَبَّنَا[10] وَدِي عِلاَقَهْ خَاصَّهْ جِداً جِداً. لَكِنْ اَلْـ...

aʃʃariiḥa lʔislaamiyya[11] lmaaska lḥukum al ... ḥaaliyyan m ... taṭbiigaa lil ... lil ... li ... li-lsiyaasa maa maɣruun bi-lʔislaam bass alʔislaam daa maxtuut ʕaʃaan nnaas albusaṭaa b-iikuunuu malmuumiin fii l ... fii, fii tiḥit ʃariiḥa tabaʕa li-lʔislaam.

اَلشَّرِيحَه الإِسْلاَمِيَّهْ[11] الْمَاسْكَه الْحُكُمْ اَلـ...   حَالِيّاً مـْ...
تَطْبِيقْهَا لِلـْ...   لِلْـ...   لـِ...   لِلْسِيَاسَهْ مَا مَغْرُونْ بِالإِسْلاَمْ
بَسّ اَلإِسْلاَمْ دَا مَخْتُوتْ عَشَانْ النَّاسْ اَلبُسَطَا بِيكُونُوا
مَلْمُومِينْ فِي لـْ...   فِي، فِي تِحِتْ شَرِيحَهْ تَبَعَ لِلإِسْلاَمْ.

## Vocabulary

**fii-** فِي *prep* for (amount of time); of (partitive relationship); at; on

**basiiṭ** بَسِيطْ *adj* small (in amount); of humble origin, of modest social position; simple {*fs:* **basiiṭa**, *mpl:* **busaṭa**, *mpl:* **basiiṭiin**, *fpl:* **basiiṭaat**}

**ḥammal** حَمَّلْ *vt* to blame {*imperf:* **yaḥammil**, *vn:* **taḥmiil**}

**xatta** خَتّ *vt* to set up, implement; to set down; to put, place {*imperf:* **yaxutt**, *vn:* **xatt**, *vn:* **xatataan**}

**jaab (jibta)** جَابْ (جِبْتَ) *vt* to bring {*imperf:* **yajiib**, *vn:* **jayabaan**}

**ajjabha l?islaamiyya** الجَّبْهَه الإِسْلاَمِيَّهْ *prop* the National Islamic Front (NIF)

**li?innuu** لأَنَّهْ **[la?annuu; li?annuu]** *conj invariable* because, on account of; so that

**izaa kaan** اِزَا كَانْ *conj invariable or conjugated* whether s.t. be … or …, be s.t … or …

**raahin** رَاهِنْ *adj* current; present {*fs:* **raahna**, *mpl:* **raahniin**, *fpl:* **raahnaat**}

**wasaɣ** وَسَغْ *vi* to have confidence, trust {*imperf:* **yasiɣ**, *vn:* **siɣa**}

**xalaf-** خَلَفْ **[xalfa]** *prep* besides, over and above, in addition to

**mutjaawib maʕa** مُتْجَاوِبْ مَعَ *adj* to be in harmony with, be in agreement with {*fs:* **mutjaawba maʕa**, *mpl:* **mutjaawbiin maʕa**, *fpl:* **mutjaawibaat maʕa**}

**ittii** اِتِّي **[intii]** *pron fs* you

**jabhajii** جَبْهَجِي *nms stress on second (penultimate) syllable* supporter of /ajjabha l?islaamiyya/ 'the National Islamic Front (NIF)' {*fs:* **jabhajiyya**, *mpl:* **jabhajiyya**, *fpl:* **jabhajiyyaat**}

**asaasan** أَسَاساً *adv* basically, fundamentally

**intiɣaalii** اِنْتِغَالِي *adj* transitional {*fs:* **intiɣaaliyya**, *mpl:* **intiɣaaliyyiin**, *fpl:* **intiɣaaliyyaat**}

**ḥabba** حَبّ *vt* to want, like, love {*imperf:* **yaḥibb**, *vn:* **ḥubb**}

## Notes

**1** The form /**ar-regime**/ 'the regime' consists of the SA definite article followed by the non-Arabic word "regime". The female speakers treats the non-Arabic word as if it were Arabic, with assimilation of the /l/ of the definite article (/**ar-*regime***/ 'the regime'). The use of non-Arabic words frequently occurs among speakers of Arabic who use other languages. It does not indicate that they cannot express themselves in Arabic but that they can draw on a variety of linguistic resources. Speakers often follow a non-Arabic word or phrase with its Arabic equivalent, as the female speaker does here, with /**ʔalḥukuuma ʔalmawjuuda fi ssuudaan ḥaaliyyan**/ 'the government that is in Sudan currently'.

**2** The democracy referred to as covering the period /**xamsa wa-θamaaniin, sitta wa-tamaaniin**/ ''85, '86' marked a major change for Sudan. Beginning in 1985, after the overthrow of Nimeiri and the formation of the Transitional Military Council (TMC), a civilian cabinet led by Dr. Gazuli Dafalla prepared for a general election. That election in 1986 resulted in a coalition government. It was led by Sadiq al-Mahdi with the Umma Party, the Democratic Unionist Party (DUP), the National Islamic Front (NIF), and four southern parties. That government was brought down in 1987.

**3** The relative clause /**ddastuur al … al … alʔintixaabii ʔallii jaab ajjabha lʔislaamiyya marra taaniyya**/ 'the consitution, the … the … the electoral one that brought back the Islamic Front again' describes two different events. The phrase /**ddastuur al … al … alʔintixaabii**/ 'the electoral constitution' refers to the laws that set up the 1986 general election as open to a variety of political parties. The female speaker then says that the electoral constitution /**jaab ajjabha lʔislaamiyya marra taaniyya**/ '[it (ms)] brought the Islamic Front again'. She alludes to the role played by National Islamic Front (NIF) leader Dr. Hassan al-Turabi in the policies of the newly-elected government.

**4** The utterance /**ʔizaa kaan** waḍaʕ ajjanuub wa-**ʔizaa kaan** ḥattaa waḍaʕ aʃʃamaal/ 'whether it's the situation in the south or even the situation in the north' contains the coordinating conjunction /**izaa kaan … izaa kaan**/ 'whether it be … or ….' Like other conjunctions such as /**wa-**/ 'and', /**izaa kaan**/ precedes each of the items in the list.

**5** The phrase /**maṣnaʕ aʃʃifaa**/ 'al-Shifa Factory' alludes to the destruction of the al-Shifa Pharmaceuticals Factory in Khartoum by American missiles in 1998. The US administration claimed that the factory was linked to terrorist activities; the

Sudanese government protested that the factory produced only pharmaceuticals.

**6** The form /**jabhajii**/ 'a supporter of the Front' is unusual because it is a compound word. The compound consists of the noun /**jabha**/ 'Front' and the suffix /-**jii**/, 'supporter of; producer of'. This suffix also occurs in certain nouns of profession, such as /**jazmajii**/ 'shoemaker, cobbler' (from /**jazma**/ 'pair of shoes') and /**kabaabjii**/ 'kebab maker, kebab vendor' (from /**kabaab**/ 'kebab').

**7** The male speaker states here that /**alʔislaamiyya deel maa baduu min ʕahdi nimeerii**/ 'these Islamicists started in Nimeiri's time'. This may refer to the formation of the National Front in 1974. It included members of a number of conservative Islamicist groups and led opposition to the Nimeiri government in the mid-70s. The reference may also allude to the role played by conservative Islamicist groups in the controversial decision to implement a form of <u>sharia</u> or Islamic law in 1983.

**8** What the female speaker calls /**lḥukuuma lʔintiɣaaliyya**/ 'the transitional government' is usually known in English as the Transitional Military Council (TMC). Abd al-Rahman Siwar al-Dhahab, leader of the group that overthrew Nimeiri in 1985, formed the TMC. The TMC legalized political parties, scheduled elections, and handed over power to the elected civilian government in 1986.

**9** The government described here as /**bi-ɣaadat suwaar aððahab w-ajjuzuulii dafaʕ al̤l̤aa**/ 'under the leadership of Siwar al-Dhahab and Gazuli Dafalla' occurred following the overthrow of Jaafar Nimeiri in 1985. The Transitional Military Council (TMC) ruled Sudan under the leadership of Abd al-Rahman Siwar al-Dhahab, while Dr. Gazuli Dafalla led the civilian cabinet.

**10** The phrase /**beenuu wa-been rabbanaa**/ 'between him and our Lord' contains two instances of the preposition /**been**/ 'between'. This is required when /**been**/ has more than one object, and one of those objects is a suffixed pronoun, here /**-uu**/ 'him, himself'. Repetition of /**been**/ is not required when the objects are noun phrases, as in /**been alxarṭuum wa-kassalaa**/ 'between Khartoum and Kassala'.

**11** The female speaker says here /**aʃʃariiḥa lʔislaamiyya**/ 'Islamic law; <u>sharia</u>', with /**ḥ**/ (voiceless pharyngeal fricative) as the third consonant rather than the more usual /**aʃʃariiʕa lʔislaamiyya**/ with /**ʕ**/ (voiced pharyngeal fricative).

# anʃaṭ ḥiẓib kaan ajjabha lʔislaamiyya

*This selection continues the discussion of selection 16. Here, the male speaker dominates as he explains the rise to prominence of the National Islamic Front (NIF) in Sudan. As he describes it, this began with the 1986 elections, although its roots go further back. Note that the demonstrative /deel/ here almost always refers to members of the NIF.*

A: mimmaa tadaxxal atturaabii[1] kam wa ... kam wa-sab ... kam wa-sabaʕiin dii w-iʃtaɣal wa-ʔinnuu yadaxxal, u-fii nimeerii daxxaluu wa-yaʕnii lmihimm a ... ʔala ... daxxal aʃʃariiʕa lʔislaamiyya talaata wa-tamaaniin u-kidaa. fa-kaan ʃaɣɣaaliin[2] yaʕnii w-intii tazakkarii -yyaam ajjaamaʕa wa-keef ʔan kaan ʔanʃaṭ ḥizib yaahum naas ajjabha lʔislaamiyya deel.[3, 4] f-annaas deel ʔiʃtaɣaluu wa-ʕamaluu yaʕnii ʕamal luuhum[5] ʔa ... ɣaaʕida ʕariiḍa jiddan jiddan wasaṭ bi-zzaat annaas almusaɣɣafiin. fa-lamman inʃaal nimeerii[6] yaʕnii wa-fiʕlan jaat al ... jaa ɣaanuun ʔalʔintixaabaat, huum maa ... huum maa ʕamaluu, nnaas addimuuɣraaṭiin,[7] jaat dii [finger snap] maa wa-dii xalaaṣ. gaamat intifaaḍa wa-jaa ɣaanuun bitaaʕ intixaabaat. annaas deel faazuu fiihuu,[8] faazuu yaʕnii fiʕlan bil ... ʔannuu huum ʔasaasan kaanuu ʕaamliin alɣaaʕida bitaaʕtun. fa-maa minnaa deel miʃ adduuhum furṣa, maa b-idduuhum furṣa dii, joo, joo yaʕnii xaʃʃuu lma ... xaʃʃuu ʔa ... ʔal ... al ... al ... la ... ajjamʕiyya ttaʔsiisiyya,[9] xaʃʃuuhaa bi ... ʕan ṭariig alintixaabaat. wa-fiʕlan yaʕnii k ... ik ... iktasaḥuu fiʕlan baʕḍ addawaayar bitaaʕat alaḥzaab al ... alkabiiriin deel llii humma llittaḥad addimuuɣraaṭii[10] w-allumma.[11] walla ... ʔal ... almuʃkila btaaʕat ḥizb alʔumma w-littaḥad addimuuɣraaṭii ʔannuu ʔaḥzaab fiʕlan yaʕnii ʔaḥzaab

# اَنْشَطْ حِزِبْ كَانْ اَلْجَبْهَه الإِسْلَامِيَّهْ

أ: مِمَّا تَدَخَّلْ اَلتُّرَابِي[1] كَمْ وَ... كَمْ وَسَبْ... كَمْ وَسَبَعِينْ دِي وِاشْتَغَلْ وَإِنّهُ يَدخَّلْ، أُفِي نِمَيْرِي دَخَّلْهُ وَيَعْنِي الْمهِمّ اَ... أَلَ... دَخَّلْ اَلشَّرِيعَه الإِسْلَامِيَّهْ تَلَاتَهْ وتَمَانِينْ أُكدَا. فَكَانْ شَغَّالِينْ[2] يَعْنِي وِانْتِي تَزكَّرِي ايَّامْ اَلجَّامَعَهْ وكَيْفْ أَنْ كَانْ أَنْشَطْ حِزِبْ يَاهُمْ نَاسْ اَلجَّبْهَه الإِسْلَامِيَّهْ دَيْلْ.[3,4] فَالنَّاسْ دَيْلْ إِشْتَغَلُوا وَعَمَلُوا يَعْنِي عَمَلْ لُوهُمْ[5] أَ... غَاعِدَهْ عَرِيضَهْ جِدّاً جِدّاً وَسَطْ بِالزَّاتْ اَلنَّاسْ اَلْمُسَغَّفِينْ. فَلَمَّنْ اِنْشَالْ نِمَيْرِي[6] يَعْنِي وَفِعْلاً جَاتْ اَلْ... جَا غَانُونْ اَلإِنْتِخَابَاتْ، هُومْ مَا... هُومْ مَا عَمَلُوا النَّاسْ اَلدِّمُوغْرَاطِينْ[7] جَاتْ دِي [finger snap] مَا وَدِي خَلَاصْ. قَامَتْ اِنْتِفَاضَهْ وَجَا غَانُونْ بِتَاعْ اِنْتِخَابَاتْ. اَلنَّاسْ دَيْلْ فَازُوا فِيهُ،[8] فَازُوا يَعْنِي فِعْلاً بِالْ... اَنّهُ هُومْ أَسَاسًا كَانُوا عَامْلِينْ اَلْغَاعِدَهْ بِتَاعْتُهُنْ. فَمَا مِنّهَا دَيْلْ مِش اَدُّوهُمْ فُرْصَهْ، مَا بِدُّوهُمْ فُرْصَهْ دِي، جَوا، جَوا يَعْنِي خَشُّوا لْمَ... خَشُّوا أَ... أَلْ... اَلْ... اَلْ... لَ... اَلْجَمْعِيَّه اَلتَّأْسِيسِيَّهْ،[9] خَشُّوهَا بِ... عَنْ طَرِيقْ اَلانْتِخَابَاتْ. وَفِعْلاً يَعْنِي كْ... اكْ ... اكْتَسَحُوا فِعْلاً بَعْضْ اَلدَّوَايِرْ بِتَاعَة اَلاحْزَابْ اَلْ... اَلْكَبِيرِينْ دَيْلْ اللِّي هُمَّ الاِتِّحَدْ اَلدِّمُوغْرَاطِي[10] وَالأُمَّهْ.[11] وَلَّ... أَلْ... اَلْمُشْكِلَهْ بْتَاعَة حِزْبْ اَلأُمَّهْ وْالاِتَّحَدْ اَلدِّمُوغْرَاطِي أَنّهُ أَحْزَابْ فِعْلاً يَعْنِي أَحْزَابْ

mooruusa,[12] kwayyis? mooruusa wa-baʕdeen maa fii ḥaaja kidaa yaʕnii ḥaaja kidaa zayy maa gutta leek deel munaẓẓamiin ʔaydeeyooloojiyyan wa-bi … b-iiʃtaɣaluu bii … yaʕnii lwaaḥid bi-kull ɣuwwatuu w-ḥaajaat zayy dii kidaa ʕal aasaas innuu masalan daa waa … annaʃiiṭiin jiddan jiddan. ʕaks alʔaḥzaab …

B: munaẓẓamiin …

A: ay, ʕaks alʔaḥẓaab attaanya deel,[13] ḥazb allumma w-allittaḥad addimuuɣraaṭii. yaʕnii dii ʔaḥzaab fiʕlan bass muḥtamda ʕalaa lʔurs al … ʔa … zayy b-iguuluu ʕalee ttaariixii. wa-annaas deel xaʃʃuu wa-fiʕlan da … da … xaʃʃuu, daxaluu waa … waa … xad … yaʕnii ktasaḥuu dawaayir katiira jiddan jiddan w-bi-zzaat dawaayir alxiriijiin[14] yaʕnii w-naas al … dawaayir alxiriijiin liʔannahaa kullaa naas mutaʕallimiin u-kidaa liʔannuu huum asaasan ʃuɣulum[15] kaan b-iʕtamid ʕalaa lmadaaris ssaanawiyya w-ajjaamiʕaat. kwayyis? fa-joo maa, maa joo maa, maa yaʕnii maa mi … maa ɣalṭa diik walaa ḥaaja. annaas deel joo fiʕlan [xxx] laakin hum fiʕlan taʕdaadum muɣaaranatan yaʕnii wallaa llaṣwaat ʔannaaluuhaa muɣaaranatan bi-lḥizb alkabiir wallaa kidaa ṭabʕan ʔagalla min diik. daa yaʕnii ʔa … zakaa min a … ʔallii huwa dduktuur atturaabii. ʔannuu masalan fiʕlan lamman jaat alʔintixaabaat ʔa … yaʕnii badal yastamirr fii ʔannuu ʔuxwaan muslimiin galabaa li-jjabha lʔislaamiyya alɣoomiyya.[16] yaʕnii galabaa, baggaahaa kidaa ʕal asaas ʔan taʃmil majmuuʕa ʕariiḍa jiddan jiddan. wa-ʔanaa bi-zzaat yaʕnii min tajrubatnaa niḥnaa fii yaʕnii fi lmanaaṭiq ḥattaa lxaarij alxarṭuum u-kidaa

مَوْرُوسَهْ،[12] كُوَيِّسْ؟ مَوْرُوسَهْ وَبَعْدَيْنْ مَا فِي حَاجَهْ كِدَا يَعْنِي حَاجَهْ كِدَا زَيّ مَا قُتَّ لَيْكْ دَيْلْ مُنَظَّمِينْ أَيْدَيُّوْلُوْجِيّاً وَبـ... بِيشْتَغَلُوا بِيـ... يَعْنِي الْوَاحِدْ بِكُلّ غُوَّتْهُ وْحَاجَاتْ زَيّ دِي كِدَا عَلَى اَسَاسْ اِنّهُ مَسَلاً دَا وَا... اَلنَّشِيطِينْ جِدّاً جِداً. عَكْسْ اَلأَحْزَابْ...

ب: مُنَظَّمِينْ...

أ: اَيْ، عَكْسْ اَلأَحْزَابْ اَلتَّانْيَهْ دَيْلْ،[13] حَزْبْ اَلأُمَّهْ وَالاِتِّحَدْ اَلدِّمُوغْرَاطِي. يَعْنِي دِي أَحْزَابْ فِعْلاً بَسّ مُحْتَمْدَهْ عَلَى الأَرْسْ اَلْـ... أَ... زَيّ بِقُولُوا عَلَيْه التَّارِيخِي. وَاَلنَّاسْ دَيْل خَشُّوا وَفِعْلاً دَ... دَ... خَشُّوا، دَخَلُوا وَا... وَا... خَدْ... يَعْنِي اِكْتَسَحُوا دَوَايِرْ كَتِيرَهْ جِدّاً جِدّاً وْبِالزَّاتْ دَوَايِرْ اَلْخِرِيجِينْ[14] يَعْنِي وْنَاسْ اَلْـ... دَوَايِرْ اَلْخِرِيجِينْ لأَنّهَا كُلّهَا نَاسْ مُتَعَلِّمِينْ اُكِدَا لأَنّهُ هُومْ اَسَاسًا شُغُلْهُمْ[15] كَانْ بِعْتَمِدْ عَلَى الْمَدَارِسْ السَّانَوِيَّهْ وَالجَّامِعَاتْ. كْوَيِّسْ؟ فَجَوا مَا، مَا جَوا مَا، مَا يَعْنِي مَا مـ... مَا غَلْطَهْ دِيكْ وَلاَ حَاجَهْ. اَلنَّاسْ دَيْلْ جَوا فِعْلاً [xxx] لَكِنْ هُمْ فِعْلاً تَعْدَادْهُمْ مُغَارَنَةً يَعْنِي وَلاَّ الأَصْوَاتْ أَلنَّالُوهَا مُغَارَنَةً بِالْحِزْبْ اَلْكَبِيرْ وَلاَّ كِدَا طَبْعًا أَقَلّ مِنْ دِيكْ. دَا يَعْنِي أَ... زَكَا مِنْ اَ... أَللِّي هُوَ الدُّكْتُورْ اَلتُّرَابِي. أَنّهُ مَسَلاً فِعْلاً لَمَّنْ جَاتْ اَلإِنْتِخَابَاتْ أَ... يَعْنِي بَدَلْ يَسْتَمِرّ فِي أَنّهُ أُخْوَانْ مُسْلِمِينْ قَلَبْهَا لِلجَّبْهَه الإِسْلَامِيَّه الْغَوْمِيَّهْ.[16] يَعْنِي قَلَبْهَا، بَقَّاهَا كِدَا عَلَى اَسَاسْ أَنْ تَشْمِلْ مَجْمُوعَهْ عَرِيضَهْ جِدّاً جِدّاً. وَأَنَا بِالزَّاتْ يَعْنِي مِنْ تَجْرُبْتْنَا نِحْنَا فِي يَعْنِي فِالْمَنَاطِقْ حَتَّى الْخَارِجْ اَلْخَرْطُومْ اُكِدَا

ʔa … al … al … aʃʃaʕb assuudaanii ʃaʕb ṭayyib jiddan jiddan wa-yaḥibb fiʕlan yanṣur alʔislaam. fa-lamman ḥassuu bi-ʔannuu deel naas ʔa … yaahum daayriin iiṭabbiguu ʃʃariiʕa lʔislaamiyya wa-joo li-lʔislaam wallaa kidaa. fa-bi-tilgii nnaas albusaṭaa kidaa ʔalwaaḥid b-iixaaf loo maa ddaa ṣootuu lii-naas zayy deel wallaa kidaa yaʕnii zayy huwa ḍidda lʔislaam.

أَ... اَلْـ... اَلْـ... اَلشَّعْبْ اَلسُّودَانِي شَعْبْ طَيِّب جِدّاً جِدّاً
وَيَحِبّ فِعْلاً يَنْصُرُ اَلإِسْلَامْ. فَلَمَّنْ حَسُّوا بِأَنّهُ دَيْلْ نَاسْ أَ...
يَاهُمْ دَايْرِينْ يْطَبِّقُوا الشَّرِيعَه الإِسْلَامِيَّهْ وَجَوا لِلإِسْلَامْ وَلَاَّ
كِدَا. فَبِتِلْقِي النَّاسْ اَلبُسَطَا كِدَا أَلْوَاحِدْ بِيخَافْ لَوْ مَا ادَّى
صَوْتْهُ لِينَاسْ زَيّ دَيْلْ وَلَاَّ كِدَا يَعْنِي زَيّ هُوَ ضِدَّ الإِسْلَامْ.

## Vocabulary

**kam** كَمْ *particle* so many (unspecified number) *(lit. how much, how many)*

**almihimma** اَلْمِهِمَّ **[almuhim(ma); almihim(m); almuhim]** *disc marker* the important thing is; the fact is (indicates return to topic after digression; precedes and indicates evaluative comment)

**musaɣɣaf** مُسَغَّفْ *adj* educated; cultured; intellectual {*fs:* **musaɣɣafa**, *mpl:* **musaɣɣafiin**, *fpl:* **musaɣɣafaat**}

**inʃaal** انْشَالْ *vi* to be removed, taken {*imperf:* **yinʃaal**, *vn:* **ʃeel**, *vn:* **ʃeyalaan**}

**xalaaṣ** خَلَاصْ *interj* that's it, that's the end of it; *adv* finally, once and for all

**ajjamʕiyya ttaʔsiisiyya** اَلجَّامْعِيَّه التَّأْسِيسِيَّه constituent assembly (governmental group charged with drafting a constitution)

**mooruus** مُوْرُوْس *adj* traditional, inherited {*fs:* **mooruusa**, *mpl:* **mooruusiin**, *fpl:* **mooruusaat**}

**galab** قَلَبْ *vt* to change, convert s.t. {*imperf:* **yaglib**, *vn:* **galab**}

**baggaa** بَقَّى *vt* to cause s.t. to happen {*imperf:* **yabaggii**, *vn:* **tabgiyya**}

**tajruba** تَجْرُبَهْ **[tajriba]** *nfs* experience, background {*pl:* **tajrubaat**, **tajaarib**}

**naṣar** نَصَرْ *vt* to side with, take sides with {*imperf:* **yanṣur**, *vn:* **naṣar**}

## Notes

**1** The time frame referred to here began /**mimmaa tadaxxal atturaabii**/ 'the time that al-Turabi intervened' or in the mid-1970s. By 1977 al-Turabi had become chair of a commission charged with revising Sudanese law and making it conform to sharia or Islamic law. As of al-Turabi's appointment to the post of attorney-general in 1981, changes to the law began. These changes culminated in 1983 when

Nimeiri issued the controversial September Laws that made a form of sharia the law of the land.

**2** The lack of agreement of the element /**kaan**/ with the following adjective /**ʃaɣɣaaliin**/ 'working (mp)' in the phrase /**kaan ʃaɣɣaaliin**/ 'at that time, they (mp) were working' is not a slip of the tongue. This element is not the verb /**kaan**/ 'to be' nor the conditional particle /**kaan**/ 'if' (see selection 8, note 15). It is, instead, a time marker. Lack of agreement between /**kaan**/ and its predicate focuses on the fact that the event took place at a particular time in the past.

**3** The element /**yaa-**/ in the clause /**yaahum naas ajjabha lʔislaamiyya deel**/ 'it was these people in the Islamic Front, lit. they (mp) are these people in the Islamic Front' has the variant /**aa-**/. It takes a suffixed pronoun whose referent is the predicate. This element occurs in statements of identity where that identity was previously unknown.

**4** The organization identified in the clause /**yaahum naas ajjabha lʔislaamiyya deel**/ 'it was these people in the Islamic Front, lit. they (mp) are these people in the Islamic Front' has played a key role in Sudanese politics since its founding. The Islamic Front is also known as the National Islamic Front (NIF). It was founded by Hassan Abd Allah al-Turabi in 1986 following the overthrow of Nimeiri. Its membership was dominated by members of the Muslim Brotherhood (**al-ʔixwaan al-muslimiin**) and included members of smaller Islamicist parties.

**5** The phrase /**ʕamal luhum**/ 'they (mp) made themselves (mp), lit. he made for them (mp)' derives from /**ʕamaluu leehum**/ 'they (mp) made for themselves (mp)'. The long vowel /**uu**/ that indicates the 3MP of the perfect has either dropped out entirely or shifted to the following syllable as a variant of the vowel of the preposition /**li-**/.

**6** In 1985, /**lamman inʃaal nimeerii**/ 'when Nimeiri was removed', General Abd al-Rahmaan Siwar al-Dhahab led a group of military officers in the bloodless coup that overthrew Nimeiri.

**7** The group described here as /**nnaas addimuuɣraaṭiin**/ 'the democratic people' are those who supported and participated in the democratic process that led to elections in 1986.

**8** The statement /**annaas deel faazuu fiihuu**/ 'these people won it (ms)' is slightly exaggerated. No political party won a majority of seats in the 1986 elections. The National Islamic Front (NIF), at that time a new organization, came in third in the elections behind the Umma Party and the Democratic Unionist Party (DUP).

**9** Sudan has had more than one example of the institution called /**ajjamʕiyya**

**tta?siisiyya/** 'the Constituent Assembly'. Context suggests that this is the institution that drafted the transitional constitution of 1985. That constitution was abolished in 1989 by Colonel Umar Hassan Ahmad al-Bashir and the Revolutionary Command Council.

**10** The party referred to here as /**llittaḥad addimuuɣraaṭii**/ is also known as /**alḥizb allittaḥaadii addimuuɣraaṭii**/ 'the Democratic Unionist Party (DUP)'. The speaker uses an unusually short form here, /**llittaḥad**/ for /**llittaḥaadii**/ 'unionist'. Like several other Sudanese political parties, the DUP draws its membership from a religious organization. The DUP is led by a member of the Mirghani family. This family also provides hereditary leaders of the Khatmiyya, a tariiqa or Sufi brotherhood.

**11** The best-known leader of the political party known as /**allumma**/ 'the Umma Party' is Sadiq al-Mahdi. The Umma Party was founded in 1945 as the political organization of the Ansar, which follows the teaching of the Mahdi. It has continued to promote an Islamicist political agenda for Sudan.

**12** The male speaker describes the Umma Party and DUP here as /**ʔaḥzaab mooruusa**/ 'hereditary parties' because of their leadership. The leader of each party is the direct descendent of the religious figure and founder of the organization on which the party is based. The Umma Party grew out of the Ansar, who follow the teachings of the Mahdi. The best-known leader of the Umma Party is Sadiq al-Mahdi. The leader of the DUP from 1968 was Muhammad Uthman al-Mirghani, also the hereditary head of the Khatmiyya, a tariiqa or Sufi brotherhood.

**13** The phrase /**alʔaḥẓaab attaanya deel**/ 'these other parties' contains two kinds of agreement with the P noun /**alʔaḥzaab**/ 'the parties'. The adjective /**attaanya**/ 'the others (fs)' has FS agreement with non-human P forms, as occurs in SA and MSA. The demonstrative /**deel**/ 'these (mp)' has MP agreement for the non-human P, as occurs in certain other varieties of spoken Arabic.

**14** The groups described here as /**dawaayir alxiriijiin**/ 'constituencies of high school and university graduates' are the traditional base of support for the Muslim Brotherhood and, by extension, the National Islamic Front (NIF).

**15** The tasks described here as /**ʃuɣulum**/ 'their (mp) work' is, of course, the recruiting of new members and the gathering of voting support.

**16** Dr. al-Turabi is a leading figure in the process the speaker describes as /**ʔuxwaan muslimiin galabaa li-jjabha lʔislaamiyya alɣoomiyya**/ 'the Muslim Brotherhood, he turned it (fs) into the National Islamic Front'. When the National Islamic Front (NIF) was formed, members of the Muslim Brotherhood dominated the organization, which also included other, smaller Islamicist parties.

# alḥiṣaar alʔiɣtiṣaadii ʕalaa ssuudaan

*This selection is similar in language and style to the two previous selections. One marker of slightly formal speech is the use of /laa/ as a negative particle (rather than the usual SA /maa/). The topic here is the effect on income and family life of the economic sanctions imposed on Sudan beginng in 1997.*

A: a ... daxil alʕaamil assuudaanii yaʕnii daxil alʕaamil yaʕnii ʔal ... al ... ʔagalla zool fii ʔalhaykal alwaẓiifii fii lḥakuuma zayy sittiin ʔalf jineeh suudaanii.[1] ʔal ... ʔa ... sittiin ʔalf jineeh suudaanii ḥagiigatan b-iisaawii, dii fii ʃahar, sittiin ʔalf ḥagiigatan b-iisaawii, lahaa zayy aa ... ṭalaṭṭaaʃar doolaar wallaa rbaʕṭaaʃar doolaar ʔa ...

B: aktar, ʔaktar.

A: a ... niḥnaa [background noise] talaatiin doolar, *see*, talaatiin doolar yaʕnii w-huwa ddoolaar b-itneen ʔalf wa-nuṣṣ.[2] zeey maa gutta ʔa ... murattab alʕaamil albasiiṭ ʔallii huwa zeey sittiin ʔalf, alḥaaja dii laa taɣaṭṭii[3] maṣruufat yoomeen, talaata yoom. ʔizan fii farig kabiira[4] jiddan jiddan ʕaʃaa ... wa-yḥillaa min ween? ʔa ... fa-maguul[5] nasʔal annaas niḥnaa, 'yaa jamaaʕa, ʔintuu samiḥ annaas, deel b-iijiibuu keef yaʕnii yḥaawill -aɣaṭṭii[6] ʔalmablaɣ daa, b-iijiibuu min ween?' yaʕnii yguuluu luk, fii naas taanyiin b-iiʃuufuu ʔa ... ʃaɣalaaniyya taaniya baʕad ʃuɣulum rrasmii.[7] ʔa ... fii naas b-iiguuluu luk, 'yaax, w-aḷḷaahii muʕðam aʃʃaʕb assuudaanii muʕtamid ʕa-lmuɣtaribiin bitaaʕinnuu.'[8] annaas yaʕnii llii huu gaaʕdiin fi ʔameeriikaa zayyinaa kidaaʃ fi lxaliij ʔalfi lbitaaʕ yaʕnii. ʔayyi ʔusra ʔa ... laazim iikuun ʕindaa maẓdar bitaaʕ daxli taanii ɣeer addaxli bitaaʕun liyannuu hinaak fiʕlan

# اَلْحِصَارْ اَلإِغْتِصَادِي عَلَى السُّودَانْ

أ: اَ... دَخْلْ اَلْعَامِلْ اَلسُّودَانِي يَعْنِي دَخِلْ اَلْعَامِلْ يَعْنِي أَلْـ... اَلْـ... أَقَلَّ زَوْلْ فِي أَلْهَـيْكَلْ اَلْوَظِيـفِي فِي اَلْحَكُومَـهْ زَيّ سِتِّينْ أَلْفْ جِنَيْـهْ سُودَانِي.[1] أَلْـ... أَ... سِتِّينْ أَلْفْ جِنَيْـهْ سُودَانِي حَقِيقَةً بِيسَاوِي، دِي فِي شَهَرْ، سِتِّينْ أَلْفْ حَقِيقَةً بِيسَاوِي، لَهَا زَيّ اَ... طَلَطَّاشَرْ دَوْلاَرْ وَلاَّ ارْبَعْطَاشَرْ دَوْلاَرْ أَ...

ب: اَكْتَرْ، أَكْتَرْ.

أ: اَ... نِحْنَا [background noise] تَلاَتِينْ دَوْلاَرْ، *see*، تَلاَتِينْ دَوْلاَرْ يَعْنِي وْهُوَ الدَّوْلاَرْ بِاتْنَيْنْ أَلْفْ وَنُصّ.[2] زَيّ مَـا قُتَّ أَ... مُرَتَّبْ اَلْعَامِلْ اَلْبَسِيطْ أَلْلِّي هُوَ زَيّ سِتِّينْ أَلْفْ، اَلْحَاجَهْ دِي لاَ تَغَطِّي[3] مَصْرُوفَةْ يَوْمَيْنْ تَلاَتَهْ يَوْمْ. إِزًا فِي فَرِقْ كَبِيرَهْ[4] جِدّاً جِدّاً عَشَا... وَيْحِلّهَا مِنْ وَيْنْ؟ أَ... فَمَقُول[5] نَسْأَلْ اَلنَّاسْ نِحْنَا، «يَا جَمَاعَهْ، إِنْتُو سَمِحْ اَلنَّاسْ، دَيْلْ بِيجِيبُوا كَيْفْ يَعْنِي يِحَاوِلّ -اغَطِّي[6] أَلْمَبْلَغْ دَا، بِيجِيبُوهْ مِنْ وَيْنْ؟» يَعْنِي يْقُولُوا لُكْ فِي نَاسْ تَانْيِينْ بِيشُوفُوا أَ... شَغَلاَنِيَّهْ تَانِيَهْ بَعَدْ شُغُلْهُمْ اَلرَّسْمِي.[7] أَ... فِي نَاسْ بِيقُولُوا لُكْ، «يَاخْ، وَاللَّهِ مُعْظَمْ اَلشَّعْبْ اَلسُّودَانِي مُعْتَمِدْ عَالْمُغْتَرِبِين بِتَاعِنّهْ.»[8] اَلنَّاسْ يَعْنِي اللِّي هُو قَاعْدِينْ فِأَمَيْرِيكَا زَيِّنَا كِدَا فَالْخَلِيجْ أَلْفَالْبِتَـاعْ يَعْنِي. أَيِّ أُسْرَهْ أَ... لاَزِمْ يْكُونْ عِنْدْهَا مَصْدَرْ بِتَاعْ دَخِلْ تَانِي غَيْرْ اَلدَّخْلِ بِتَاعْهُنْ لِيَنّهْ هِنَاكْ فِعْلاً

daa. waa … ʔam … li … li … almihim badat alḥaajaat zeey dii w-hassaʕ daa lwaḍaʕ bi-zzaat alʕaayʃiinuu fa-fii, b-iiḥkuu ḥakaawii kidaa. fiʕlan azzool yitʔassar leehaa wa-yitʔallam leehaa liʔannuu fiʕlan fii ḥiṣaar ʔiɣtiṣaadii ʃadiid jiddan jiddan ʕalaa ssuudaan. wa-maʕruuf yaʕnii ʔinna ḥattaa naas alḥakuuma laa tankur albitaaʕ daa wa-laa naas almuʕaaraḍa yankur albitaaʕ daa,[9] yankur ʔannuu masalan fiʕlan fii ḥiṣaar wa-yankur ʔannuu fii tadahwur wa-yankur ʔannuu fii yaʕnii fiʕlan ʔa … ʔal … ʔal … almuwaaṭniin mutḥammiliin ʕib kabiir jiddan jiddan. wal … ʔala … natiija li … li-lḥaajaat dii bi-tilgii kull aʃʃaʕb assuudaanii muʕẓamuu min gabil gaaluu ʃʃaʕb assuudaanii daa laa yaʕrif alɣurba, maa fii suudaanii b-iisaafir barraa min baladuu ʔillaa fi lʕuhuud lʔaxiira dii. ʔannuu gannab fiʕlan ʔayyi beet laazim yirassil zool barraa ssuudaan ʕalaa lʔagall yaʕnii yʔammin leehum baʕḍ ʔiḥtiyaajaatum ʔa … min almaṣruufaat wa-ɣeeruu.[10] fa … yaʕnii lmihim yaʕnii fiʕlan ma … mooɣif yaʕnii la … la … ya … yaʕnii ma … ṣaʕb ʃadiid jiddan jiddan w-atmannaa ʔannuu fiʕlan ʔa … taḥṣul ḥaaja kwaysa.

دَا. وَا... أَمْـ... لِـ... لِـ... اَلْمِهِمْ بَدَتْ اَلْحَاجَاتْ زَيّ دِي وْهَسَّعْ دَا الْوَضَعْ بِالزَّاتْ اَلْعَايْشِينْهُ فَفِي، بِيحْكُوا حَكَاوِي كدَا. فِعْلاً اَلزَّوْلْ يِتْأَسَّرْ لَيْهَا وَيِتْأَلَّمْ لَيْهَا لأَنّهُ فِعْلاً فِي حِصَارْ إِغْتِصَادِي شَدِيدْ جِدّاً جِدّاً عَلَى السُّودَانْ. وَمَعْرُوفْ يَعْنِي إِنَّ حَتَّى نَاسْ اَلْحَكُومَهْ لاَ تَنْكُرْ اَلْبِتَاعْ دَا وَلاَ نَاسْ اَلْمُعَارَضَهْ يَنْكُرْ اَلْبِتَاعْ دَا،[9] يَنْكُرْ أَنّهُ مَسَلاً فِعْلاً فِي حِصَارْ وَيَنْكُرْ أَنّهُ فِي تَدَهْوُرْ وَيَنْكُرْ أَنّهُ فِي يَعْنِي فِعْلاً أَ... أَلْـ... أَلْـ... اَلْمُوَاطْنِينْ مُتْحَمِّلِينْ عِبْ كَبِيرْ جِدّاً جِدّاً. وَلْـ... أَلَـ... نَتِيجَهْ لِـ... لِلْحَاجَاتْ دِي بِتِلْقِي كُلّ اَلشَّعْبْ اَلسُّودَانِي مُعْظَمْهُ مِنْ قَبِلْ قَالُوا الشَّعْبْ اَلسُّودَانِي دَا لاَ يَعْرِفْ اَلْغُرْبَهْ، مَا فِي سُودَانِي بِيسَافِرْ بَرَّا مِنْ بَلَدْهُ إِلاَّ فَالْعُهُودْ الأَخِيرَهْ دِي. أَنّهُ قَنَّبْ فِعْلاً أَيِّ بَيْتْ لاَزِمْ يِرَسِّلْ زَوْلْ بَرَّا السُّودَانْ عَلَى الأَقَلّ يَعْنِي يْأَمِّنْ لَيْهُمْ بَعْضْ إِحْتِيَاجَاتْهُمْ أَ... مِنْ اَلْمَصْرُوفَاتْ وَغَيْرُهْ.[10] فَـ... يَعْنِي الْمِهِمْ يَعْنِي فِعْلاً مَـ... مَوْغِفْ يَعْنِي لَـ... لَـ... يَـ... يَعْنِي مَـ... صَعْبْ شَدِيدْ جِدّاً جِدّاً وَاتْمَنَّى أَنّهُ فِعْلاً أَ... تَحْصُلْ حَاجَهْ كْوَيْسَهْ.

## Vocabulary

**jineeh** جِنَيْهْ *nms in number-counted noun structures, singular may be used for numbers 2-10* Sudanese pound, unit of Sudanese currency {*pl:* **jineehaat**}

**basiiṭ** بَسِيطْ *adj* of humble origin, of modest social position; small (in amount); simple {*fs:* **basiiṭa**, *mpl:* **busaṭa**, *mpl:* **basiiṭiin**, *fpl:* **basiiṭaat**}

**izan** إِزًا *conj* so, therefore

**jamaaʕa** جَمَاعَهْ *nfs may take MP agreement* group, people {*pl:* **jamaaʕaat**}

**yaa jamaaʕa** يَا جَمَاعَهْ hey everyone *(lit. o group)*

**intuu** انْتُو **[ittuu]** *pron mp* you

**ʃaaf (ʃufta)** (شُفْتَ) شَاف *vt* to find; to understand, get, see; to see {*imperf:* **yaʃuuf**, *vn:* **ʃoof**}

**ʃaɣalaaniyya** شَغَلانِيَّة *nfs* job; task; headache {*pl:* **ʃaɣalaaniyyaat**}

**yaax** يَاخ brother, friend, buddy (polite term of address to male of same or lesser status)

**gaaʕid** قَاعِد *adj pre-verb* staying, remaining; keeping on, continuing (continuous action); sitting, sitting down {*fs:* **gaaʕda**, *mpl:* **gaaʕdiin**, *fpl:* **gaaʕdaat**}

**bitaaʕ** بِتَاع *nms* thing, what's-its-name {*fs:* **bitaaʕa**, *mpl:* **bitaaʕiin**, *fpl:* **bitaaʕaat**}

**ḥikaaya** حِكَايَة *nfs* story, tale; affair, matter {*pl:* **ḥakaawii**}

**itʔassar** اتْأَسَّر *vi* to be emotionally moved; to be affected, be touched {*imperf:* **yitʔassar**, *vn:* **taʔassur**}

**muʕaaraḍa** مُعَارَضَة *nfs* opposition {*pl:* **muʕaaraḍaat**}

**barraa** بَرَّا *prep* outside of

**gannab** قَنَّب *vt* to begin to; to sit down {*imperf:* **yagannib**, *vn:* **ginneeb**}

## Notes

**1** The word /**jineeh**/ in the phrase /**jineeh suudaanii**/ 'Sudanese pound' ultimately derives from the English word "guinea." This and other foreign borrowings frequently pronounce as /j/ the sound that is /g/ in the original language of the borrowing. Such borrowings include, for example, the word /**jaaluun**/ 'gallon'.

**2** The number /**itneen ʔalf**/ 'two thousand' in the phrase /**b-itneen ʔalf** wa-nuṣṣ/ 'at two-and-a-half thousand' does not make use of the morphological dual familiar in MSA (ʔalfayn 'two thousand'). SA, like certain other varieties of spoken Arabic, uses the dual most frequently for expressions of time and for body parts. Other uses, such as the /**muʕaayanteen**/ 'two interviews' of selection 8, are possible but less common.

**3** Note the use of /**laa**/ as the negative particle in the phrase /**laa** taɣaṭṭii/ 'it (fs) will not cover'. SA typically uses /**maa**/ rather than /**laa**/, so the use of /**laa**/ here gives the speaker's language a slightly formal feel.

**4** The phrase /**farig kabiira**/ 'a big difference' has the MS noun /**farig**/ 'difference' modified by the FS adjective /**kabiira**/ 'big'. This appears to be a slip of the tongue.

**5** The speaker here says /**fa-maguul**/ 'so let's say' rather than the expected /**fa-naguul**/ 'so let's say', in what is apparently a slip of the tongue.

**6** The unusual sequence of sounds in the phrase /yḥaa**will -a**ɣaṭṭii/ 'he tries to cover' is due to assimilation. This phrase in slow or careful speech is pronounced /yḥaa**wil ya**ɣaṭṭii/. In this case, the initial /y/ (voiced palatal semi-vowel) of the simple imperfect verb /yaɣaṭṭii/ 'he covers' becomes like the preceding sound, the /l/ (voiced lateral dental). The result is the phrase heard here, /yḥaa**will -a**ɣaṭṭii/.

**7** Sudanese who find /**ʃaɣalaaniyya taaniya baʕad ʃuɣulum rrasmii** / 'a second job after their (mp) official job' begin this second job in the mid- to late afternoon. Regular office hours in government and many private companies in Sudan, as in other parts of the Arabic-speaking world, begin around 8:00 a.m. and end around 2:30 p.m. Other kinds of business, like retail or service firms, keep different hours.

**8** The form taken by the MP suffix /-iin/ when followed by the 3MS suffixed pronoun /-uu/ in the phrase /lmuɣtaribiin **bitaaʕinnuu**/ 'its (ms) expatriates' is a regular change — for participles and adjectives only. The MP suffix /-**iin**/ becomes /-**inn**-/ when followed by a suffixed pronoun (with the exception of the 1P suffixed pronoun). A similar change occurs in the FP suffix /-**aat**/, as in /ʃaayfaatannuu/ 'seeing (fp) him'.

**9** The negation of /laa/ 'not' and /wa-laa/ 'nor, lit. and not' continues beyond the sentence /ḥattaa naas alḥakuuma **laa** tankur albitaaʕ daa **wa-laa** naas almuʕaaraḍa yankur albitaaʕ daa/ 'even people in the government don't deny this thing, nor do people in the opposition deny this thing'. It applies to each repetition of the verb /yankur/ 'he denies' in the rest of the utterance: /**yankur** ʔannuu masalan fiʕlan fii ḥiṣaar wa-**yankur** ʔannuu fii tadahwur wa-**yankur** ʔannuu fii yaʕnii fiʕlan ʔa ... ʔal ... ʔal ... almuwaaṭniin mutḥammiliin ʕib kabiir jiddan jiddan/ 'deny that, for example, there is really an embargo, deny that there is deterioration, deny that there is, you know, really ah ... the ... the ... the citizens are holding up under a very, very heavy burden'. Note also that the verb /yankur/ 'he denies' is used consistently. It does not agree with its subject, /naas almuʕaaraḍa/ 'people in the opposition'. The noun /naas/ takes MP agreement, and FS agreement also occurs.

**10** The phrase /wa-ɣeeruu/ 'and other things, lit. and other than it (ms)' is used invariably in /almaṣruufaat **wa-ɣeeruu**/ 'expenses and other things'. That is, the suffixed pronoun /-**huu**/ does not agree in gender and number with the P noun /almaṣruufaat/ 'expenses' as might be expected (/almaṣruufaat wa-ɣeeri**haa**/). Both usages, invariable and agreeing, occur in SA.

# li?annakum maa dafaʕtuu lfaatuura

*This selection, taken from a radio broadcast, presents another style of talk about politics. Using humor and colloquial language, it aims to educate the Sudanese population about civic duties, here, the problem of water outages. As with other texts in a colloquial style, this selection poses a challenge of vocabulary rather than grammatical structure.*

A: aḷḷaa ʔaḷḷaa ʔaḷḷaa ʔaḷḷaa ʔaḷḷaa. ʔalleela yaʕnii lḥaajja jaat badrii.

[all respond]

B: maa ʃaa ʔaḷḷah.

C: w-aḷḷaahii kamaan ʃaayifaa mabsuuṭa.

D: ayya, ʔaḷḷaa yadoowim allinbisaaṭ yaa ʔaxwaannaa, rabnaa yadoowim allinbisaaṭ.

E: w-aḷḷaahii huu fi lḥagiiga -naa mabsuuṭa yaʕnii maa mabsuuṭa ʃadiid laakin kamaan maa zaʕlaana.

A: barḍuu yaa ḥaajja, xeer. laakin maaleek? ḥaaṣil ʕaleek ʃinuu?

E: jaanii jawaab min ṣaaḥibtii wa-ḥabiibtii …

F: haa …

E: bitt ḥaaj alfaḍul.[1]

F: haa …

G: yaa ḥaajja, min ʔum durmaan? min ʔum baddaa?

E: ayyaa, heey, ʔillaa gaalat fiihuu kalaam ʕajiib kadii.

H: kadee bagaa, warriinaa lkalaam alʕajiib daa yiṭlaʕ ʃinuu yaʕnii.

# لأَنَّكُمْ مَا دَفَعْتُوا الْفَاتُورَهْ

أ: اَللَّهْ أَللَّهْ أَللَّهْ أَللَّهْ. أَللَّيْلَهْ يَعْنِي الْحَاجَّهْ جَات بَدْرِي.

[all respond]

ب: مَا شَا أَللَّهْ.

ت: وَاللَّهِ كَمَانْ شَايِفْهَا مَبْسُوطَهْ.

ث: اَيّ، أَللَّهْ يَدَوِّمْ اَلاِنْبِسَاطْ يَا أَخْوَانَّا، رَبْنَا يَدَوِّمْ اَلاِنْبِسَاطْ.

ج: وَاللَّهِ هُو فَالْحَقِيقَه انَا مَبْسُوطَهْ يَعْنِي مَا مَبْسُوطَهْ شَدِيدْ لَكِنْ كَمَانْ مَا زَعْلاَنَهْ.

أ: بَرْضَهْ يَا حَاجَّهْ، خَيْرْ. لَكِنْ مَالَيْكْ؟ حَاصِلْ عَلَيْكْ شْنُو؟

ج: جَانِي جَوَابْ مِنْ صَاحِبْتِي وَحَبِيبْتِي...

ح: هَا...

ج: بِتّ حَاجْ اَلْفَضُلْ.[1]

ح: هَا...

خ: يَا حَاجَّهْ، مِنْ أُمْ دُرْمَانْ؟ مِنْ أُمْ بَدَّا؟

ج: اَيَّا، هَيّ، إِلاَّ قَالَتْ فِيهُ كَلاَمْ عَجِيبْ كَدِي.

د: كَدَي بَقَى، وَرِّينَا اَلْكَلاَمْ اَلْعَجِيبْ دَا يِطْلَعْ شِنُو يَعْنِي.

I: aha … guulii, guulii.

E: ayya, gaalat joohaa naas almooya.

J: aha …

E: wa-gaaluu leehaa, 'ʔasmaʕii yaa ḥaajja, niḥnaa daayriin nagṭaʕ almooya dii.'

D: wa-gaalat lahum, 'assabab ʃinuu?' wa-gaaluu leehaa …

A: 'liʔannakum maa dafaʕtuu lfaatuura.'

D: [all respond] ayya.

B: 'wa-ʔayyi zool maa dafaʕ alfaatuura niḥnaa nagṭaʕ minnuu lmooya ṭagg.'

G: liʔannuu yaa ḥaajja, ʔalʔiɣtiṣaad alwaṭanii b-itwakkaf ʕalaa musaahamat almuwaaṭaniin fii dafʕi maa ʕaleehim.

D: w-almafruuḍ almuwaaṭniin yidfaʕuu.

E: ay laakin yaa waladii, ʔalmaasuura dee leeyaa yaʕnii ʃahar u-ʃahreen wa-talaata maa naggaṭat nugṭa waaḥda ḥaggat mooya.

A: maahuu, yaa ḥaajja, law ʔintuu bi-tadfaʕuu maa kaan yaʕnii …

E: haay, laakin niḥnaa nadfaʕ leekuu ʔittuu wallaa nadfaʕ lee-siid albaraamiil[2] alb-iijiib leenaa lmooya bi-lḥuumaar?

G: aha … yaa ḥaajja, ʔawʕii yakuun baʕd daa gaṭaʕuuhaa.[3]

J: ʕalaa kulla ḥaal, ʔaaxir alaxbaar …

ذ: اَهَـهْ... قُـولِي، قُـولِي.

ج: اَيَّ، قَـالَتْ جَوْهَا نَـاسْ اَلْمَـوْيَـهْ.

ر: اَهَـهْ...

ج: وَقَـالُـوا لَـيْـهَا، «أَسْـمَـعِي يَـا حَـاجَّـهْ، نِـحْـنَـا دَايْـرِيـنْ نَـقْـطَـعْ اَلْـمَـوْيَـهْ دِي.»

ث: وَقَـالَـتْ لَـهُـمْ، «اَلسَّـبَـبْ شِـنُـو؟» وَقَـالُـوا لَـيْـهَا...

أ: «لأَنَّـكُـمْ مَـا دَفَـعْـتُـوا الْـفَـاتُـورَهْ.»

ث: [all respond] اَيَّ.

ب: «وَأَيِّ زَوْلْ مَـا دَفَـعْ اَلْـفَـاتُـورَهْ نِـحْـنَـا نَـقْـطَـعْ مِـنّـهُ الْـمَـوْيَـهْ طَـقّ.»

خ: لأَنّـهُ يَـا حَـاجَّـهْ، أَلإِغْـتِـصَـادْ اَلْـوَطَـنِـي بِـتْـوَكَّـفْ عَـلَـى مُـسَـاهَـمَـةْ اَلْـمُـوَاطَـنِـينْ فِـي دَفْـعِ مَـا عَـلَـيْـهِـمْ.

ث: وَالْـمَـفْـرُوضْ اَلْـمُـوَاطْـنِـينْ يِـدْفَـعُـوا.

ج: اَي لَـكِـنْ يَـا وَلَـدِي، أَلْـمَـاسُـورَهْ دَي لَـيَّـا يَـعْـنِـي شَـهَـرْ أُشَـهْـرَيْـنْ وَتَـلاتَـهْ مَـا نَـقَّـطَـتْ نُـقْـطَـهْ وَاحْـدَهْ حَـقَّـةْ مَـوْيَـهْ.

أ: مَـاهْ، يَـا حَـاجَّـهْ، لَـوْ إِنْـتُـو بِـتَـدْفَـعُـوْا مَـا كَـانْ يَـعْـنِـي...

ج: هَـايْ، لَـكِـنْ نِـحْـنَـا نَـدْفَـعْ لَـيْـكُـوْ إِتُّـو وَلاَّ نَـدْفَـعْ لَـيْـسِـيـدْ اَلْـبَـرَامِـيـل[2] اَلْـبِـيـجِـيـبْ لَـيْـنَـا الْـمَـوْيَـهْ بِـالْـحُـومَـارْ؟

خ: اَهَـهْ... يَـا حَـاجَّـهْ، أَوْعِـي يَـكُـونْ بَـعْـدْ دَا قَـطَـعُـوهَـا.[3]

ر: عَـلَـى كُـلَّ حَـالْ، آخِـرْ اَلاَخْـبَـارْ...

D: aha ...

J: bi-tguul ʔinnuu mawgif almooya fi lxarṭuum badaa yitḥassin.

E: huu kaan maa saakit,[4] almooya takṭaʕ fi lxarṭuum?

A: ayya w-aḷḷaahii, gaaluu bi-ʃʃuhuur.

G: ʕuu yaa zool, haa ... w-aḷḷaahii laakin ḥikaayatun annaas deel yaʕnii bi-lḥeel tamraḍ.

E: ahaa ... yaa xwaanii, waddaḥtakun aḷḷaa.

I: laa maa badrii yaa ḥaajja.

G: aha ... yaa ḥaajja, maa guttii leey, keef ḥaal tallaajat ṣaaḥbatik bitt ḥaajj alfaḍul?

A: aha ... wa-guul leenaa, ʕaamla keef maʕa lkahrabaa?

E: ahaa ... dii baraahaa daayra leehaa kalaam.[5]

H: yaa ḥaajja, yaa ḥaajja, waddaʕnaak aḷḷaa, maʕa ssalaama.

ث: اَهَـهْ...

ر: بِتْقُولْ إِنّـهُ مَوْقِفْ اَلْمَوْيَهْ فِالْخَرْطُومْ بَدَا يِتْحَسِّنْ.

ج: هُو كَانْ مَا سَاكِتْ،[4] اَلْمَوْيَـهْ تَكْطَعْ فِالْخَرْطُومْ؟

أ: اَيَّ وَاللَّهِ، قَالُوا بِالشُّهُورْ.

خ: عُـو يَا زَوْلْ، هَـا... وَاللَّهِ لَكِنْ حِكَايَتْـهُنْ اَلنَّاسْ دَيْلْ يَعْنِي بِالْحَيْلْ تَمْرَضْ.

ج: اَهَـا... يَا خْوَانِي، وَدَّحْتَكُنْ اَللَّهْ.

ذ: لاَ مَـا بَدْرِي يَا حَاجَّهْ.

خ: اَهَـهْ... يَا حَاجَّهْ، مَا قُتِّي لَيَّ، كَيْـفْ حَالْ تَلاَّجَةْ صَاحْبَتِكْ بِتّ حَاجّ اَلْفَضْلْ؟

أ: اَهَـهْ... وَقُـولْ لَيْنَـا، عَامْلَهْ كَيْفْ مَعَ الْكَهْرَبَا؟

ج: اَهَـا... دِي بَرَاهَا دَايْرَهْ لَيْهَا كَلاَمْ.[4]

د: يَا حَاجَّهْ، يَا حَاجَّهْ، وَدَّعْنَاكْ اَللَّهْ، مَعَ السَّلاَمَهْ.

## Vocabulary

**faatuura** فَاتُورَهْ *nfs* bill, receipt {*pl:* **fawaatiir**}

**badrii** بَدْرِي *adv* early

**maa ʃaa ʔaḷḷah** مَا شَا أَللَّهْ my goodness (used alone as an expression of admiration or with another such expression) *(lit. what God wills)*

**kamaan** كَمَانْ *adv* also, as well

**mabsuuṭ** مَبْسُوطْ *adj* happy, glad {*fs:* **mabsuuṭa,** *mpl:* **mabsuuṭiin,** *fpl:* **mabsuuṭaat**}

**ayya** أيّ **[ay; aywa; iywa]** *interj* yes

**doowam** دَوَّمْ **[dawwam]** *vt* to prolong s.th. {*imperf:* **yadoowim**, *vn:* **tadwiim**}

**aḷḷaa yadoowim allinbisaaṭ** ألّلهْ يدَوِّمْ ألاِنْبِساطْ God keep s.o. happy *(lit. may God make the happiness continue)*

**rabnaa** رَبْنَا **[rabbanaa]** God, our Lord

**zaʕlaan** زَعْلانْ *adj* upset, angry {*fs:* **zaʕlaana**, *mpl:* **zaʕlaaniin**, *fpl:* **zaʕlaanaat**}

**ṣaaḥib** صَاحِبْ *nms* friend {*fs:* **ṣaaḥba**, *mpl:* **aṣḥaab**, *fpl:* **ṣaaḥbaat**}

**bitt** بِتّ **[bint]** *nfs* daughter; girl; unmarried woman {*pl:* **banaat**}

**um baddaa** أُمْ بَدّاً **[umm badda]** *prop* Ombadda (town in Omdurman region)

**illaa** إلاّ *conj* but, however; *prep* except, unless

**ʕajiib** عَجِيبْ *adj* strange, odd {*fs:* **ʕajiiba**, *mpl:* **ʕajaayiib**, *fpl:* **ʕajiibaat**}

**bagaa** بَقَى *adv invariable* so, then, now

**ṭalaʕ** طَلَعْ *vt* to turn out to be; to exit, leave; to get up, stand up; to go up, ascend {*imperf:* **yaṭlaʕ**, *vn:* **ṭuluuʕ**}

**mooya** مَوْيَهْ *nfs* water

**ṭagg** طَقّ *adv* completely, absolutely

**maasuura** مَاسُورَهْ *nfs* pipe; faucet; water hydrant {*pl:* **mawaasiir**, **maasuuraat**}

**ḥagg** حَقّ *adj possessive* of, belonging to {*fs:* **ḥaggat**, *mpl:* **ḥaggiin**, *fpl:* **ḥaggaat**}

**maahuu** مَاهُ *adv* but, the fact is

**ittuu** إتّو **[intuu]** *pron mp* you

**barmiil** بَرْمِيلْ *nms* barrel, cask {*pl:* **baraamiil**}

**awʕaa** أوْعَى **[ooʕaa]** *vi used in imperative* let it not be that (preceding imperfect of /kaan/); do not do s.t. (preceding simple imperfect); watch out (without following verb) {*fs:* **awʕii**, *mpl:* **awʕuu**, *fpl:* **awʕan**}

**ʕalaa kulla ḥaal** عَلَى كُلّ حَالْ in any case

**huu kaan maa saakit** هُو كَانْ مَا سَاكِتْ who would believe it (ironic question) *(lit. but if it isn't nonsense)*

**ʕuu** عُو *interj* hey (used mainly by older persons)

**bi-lḥeel** بِالْحَيْلْ indeed, certainly

**waddaʕ aḷḷaa** وَدَّع اَللَّهْ *used in perfect* to say goodbye, bid farewell *(lit. I entrust s.o. to God)*

**tallaaja** تَلاَّجَةْ *nfs* refrigerator {*pl:* **tallaajaat**}

**kahrabaa** كَهْرَبَا *nfs* electricity; lamp {*pl:* **kahaarib**}

**baraa-** بَرَا *prep* alone, by oneself; oneself

**daayir** دَايِرْ *adj pre-verb* needing; intending to, going to; wanting, desiring {*fs:* **daayra**, *mpl:* **daayriin**, *fpl:* **daayraat**}

## Notes

**1** The form /**bitt ḥaaj alfaḍul**/ 'Bitt Hajj al-Fadul' reflects one way to talk about and to adult women in SA. Rather than using her personal name, it calls her 'the daughter of Hajj al-Fadul'.
Note that the word /**bitt**/ 'daughter; girl' derives from /**bint**/ or /**binit**/ through assimilation. The P /**banaat**/ indicates that the word /**bitt**/ derives from /**binit**/.

**2** Note the difference between /**siid albaraamiil**/ 'the man with the barrels, lit. the owner of the barrels' and /**arraajil bitaaʕ albaraamiil**/ 'the man with the barrels'. The first phrase describes the owner of the barrels. The second indicates that, although he has the barrels, the man is not their owner.

**3** The form /**ʔawʕaa**/ 'let (fs) not' is a pre-verb in the sentence /**ʔawʕaa yakuun baʕd daa gaṭaʕuuhaa**/ 'they'd (mp) better not have cut it (fs) off after that, lit. let (ms) it (ms) not be that after that they (mp) cut it (fs) off'. It has the form of an imperative and precedes the simple imperfect of /**kaan**/, as here, or the simple imperfect of another verb to state a warning (/**ʔawʕii tansii**/ 'you (fs) had better not forget').

**4** The sentence /**huu kaan maa saakit**/ 'who would believe such a thing?, lit. but if it isn't nonsense' is idiomatically SA. It typically occurs, as it does here, as an ironic response to a statement or question.

**5** The preposition /**baraa**/ is one way to say 'by oneself, alone' in SA. An example occurs in the utterance /**dii baraahaa daayra leehaa kalaam**/ 'that's (fs) a whole other story, lit. this (fs) by itself (fs) wants for itself (fs) talk'. This preposition takes a suffixed pronoun.

# naguul li-nnaas ʃinuu?

*This selection continues the story of Adil's mysterious uncle Khalid (see selection 7). Shortly after his conversation with Khalid (see selection 12), the Hajj is murdered during an attempted robbery, and Khalid is accused of the crime. Here Khalid's family hears the bad news. Following popular ideas of family behavior, Khalid's sisters worry about him while his male kin focus on family reputation and status.*
*Note that this selection contains colloquial and idiomatic language. The effect of strong emotion on pronunciation and intonation may also present a challenge.*

A: muṣiiba wa-ḥallat ʕaleenaa, ʔalkaan naagiṣ ḥaṣal.

B: fii ʃinuu?

A: nawaddii wiʃʃanaa ween min annaas?

B: fii ʃnuu, fii ʃnuu yaa ʕawaḍ, yaa xuuy, fii ʃnuu?

A: xaalid.

B: maaluu xaalid?

A: xaalid katal leehuu zool. tṣoowarii, tṣoowarii yiktul minuu?

B: ah, minuu?

A: yiktul taajir fi ssuug.

B: [gasps]

A: annaas kullaa bi-tʃakkir fiihuu.

B: laa ʔilaaha ʔillaa ḷḷaah [xxx].

A: anaa ʔagabbil ween? ʔanaa, ʔanaa, ʔanaa, ʔanaa -ṭiir ween anaa? ʔagaabil annaas keef, ʔagaabil annaas keef anaa? ʔaʔ daa, daa, daa, daa banii ʔaadam daa?[1]

# نَقُولْ لِلنَّاسْ شِنُو؟

أ: مُصِيبَهْ وَحَلَّتْ عَلَيْنَا، أَلْكَانْ نَاقِصْ حَصَلْ.

ب: فِي شِنُو؟

أ: نَوَدِّي وِشَّنَا وَيْنْ مِنْ اَلنَّاسْ؟

ب: فِي شْنُو، فِي شْنُو يَا عَوَضْ، يَا خُويْ، فِي شْنُو؟

أ: خَالِدْ.

ب: مَالْهُ خَالِدْ؟

أ: خَالِدْ كَتَلْ لَيْهُ زَوْلْ. تْصَوَّرِي، تْصَوَّرِي يِكْتُلْ مِنُو؟

ب: اَهْ، مِنُو؟

أ: يِكْتُلْ تَاجِرْ فِالسُّوقْ.

ب: [gasps]

أ: اَلنَّاسْ كُلّهَا بِتْشَكِّرْ فِيهُ.

ب: لاَ إِلَهَ إِلاَّ اللَّهْ [xxx].

أ: اَنَا أَقَبِّلْ وَيْنْ؟ أَنَا، أَنَا، أَنَا اطِيرْ وَيْنْ اَنَا؟ أَقَابِلْ اَلنَّاسْ كَيْفْ، أَقَابِلْ اَلنَّاسْ كَيْفْ اَنَا؟ أَ؟ دَا، دَا، دَا، دَا بَنِي اَدَمْ دَا؟[1]

[in another room]

C: kur ʕaleek yaa wad ʔummii [crying], kur ʕaleeya, kullu muṣiiba biguu ysawwuuwaa[2] ʕaleek iiguuluu ʔinta ssawweetaa.

D: bi-tabkii ʕalee ʃnuu? ʕalee faḍaayiḥ ʔaxuuk? dii ʕamla yaʕmilaa? yiktul leeh waaḥid lammaahuu[3] min aʃʃaariʕ wa-fataḥ leehuu beetuu.

C: axuuy maa katal yaa ʕabbaas, yaa ʕabbaas, ʕaleek aḷḷaa ʕtaraḍtak b-annabii xalliinii fii balwatii w-xalliinii fii naṣiibtii.[4]

D: balwatik?

C: ay, xalliinii yaa ʕabbaas, ʕaleek ʔaḷḷaa.

D: daa mujrim, ḥaagid, waḥʃi baʃarii, ʔaʕuuzuu bi-llaah. daa, daa, daa, daa, hassaʕ anguul li-nnaas ʃinuu?

C: yaa xuuy, ʕaleek ʔaḷḷaa balaa nnaas, annaas taṭiir fii ssamaa, ʔinta maa ʕindak ʃaɣala ɣeer annaas, kulli ʃii nnaas, annaas, daa ʔaxuuy wa-deek annaas.

D: kafaa! ʔaḷḷaa yilʕan ʔabuu dii ʕiiʃa dii. [woman crying]

[back to first room]

A: axuuk ʃinuu? bi-llaahii siibiinaa, ntuu b-tabkuu ʕalee ʃnuu?[5] waaḥid kaatil.

C: [xxx] kur ʕaleey yaa wad ʔummii.[6] [crying continues]

[in another room]

ت: كُـرْ عَلَيْكْ يَا وَدْ أُمِّي [crying]، كُـرْ عَلَيَّ، كُلُّ مُـصِـيـبَـهْ بِقُـوا يْسَوُّوهْ[2] عَلَيْكْ يْقُولُوا إِنْتَ السَّوَّيْتَها.

ث: بِتَبْكِي عَلَى شِنُو؟ عَلَى فَضَايِحْ أَخُوكْ؟ دِي عَامْلَهْ يَعْمِلْها؟ يِكْتُلْ لَيْهْ وَاحِدْ لَمّاه[3] مِنْ اَلشَّارِعْ وَفَتَحْ لَيْهُ بَيْتْهُ.

ت: اَخُوي مَـا كَتَلْ يَا عَبَّاسْ، يَـا عَبَّاسْ، عَلَيْكْ اَللَّهْ اعْتَرَضْتَكْ بَالنَّبِي خَلِّينِي فِي بَلْوَتِي وْخَلِّينِي فِي نَصِيبْتِي.[4]

ث: بَلْوَتِكْ؟

ت: اَيْ، خَلِّينِي يَا عَبَّاسْ، عَلَيْكْ أَللَّهْ.

ث: دَا مُـجْـرِمْ، حَـاقِـدْ، وَحْشِ بَشَـرِي، أَعُـوزْ بِـاللَّهْ. دَا، دَا، دَا، دَا، هَسَّعْ اَنْقُولْ لِلنَّاسْ شِنُو؟

ت: يَا خُوِيْ، عَلَيْكْ أَللَّهْ بَلاَ النَّاسْ، اَلنَّاسْ تَطِيرْ فِي السَّمَا، إِنْتَ مَـا عِنْدَكْ شَـغَلَهْ غَـيْـرْ اَلنَّاسْ، كُلِّ شِي النَّاسْ، اَلنَّاسْ، دَا أَخُوي وَدَيْكْ اَلنَّاسْ.

ث: كَفَى! أَللَّهْ يِلْعَنْ أَبُو دِي عِيشَهْ دِي. [woman crying]

[back to first room]

أ: اَخُوكْ شِنُو؟ بِاللَّهِ سِيبِينَا، انْتُو بْتَبْكُوا عَلَى شْنُو؟[5] وَاحِدْ كَاتِلْ.

ت: [xxx] كُرْ عَلَيّ يَا وَدْ أُمِّي.[6] [crying continues]

A: yuktul. laa wa-yuktul minuu? yuktul arraajil alʔakramuu, arraajil alfataḥ leehuu beetuu. wa-ʕaʃaan ʃinuu? ʕaʃaan yisriguu.

B: [crying] wa-ligoowuu, masakooh[7] yaa ʕawaḍ? kur ʕaleey yaa xuuy, kur ʕaleey yaa wad ummii.

A: maa masakuu laakin ḥa-yamsikuu, ḥa-yamsikuuhuu,[8] ay, ḥa-yruuḥ ween yaʕnii? buuliis albalad dii kullahaa yiifattiʃ ʕaleehuu, kullahaa.

C: kur ʕaleey yaa xuuy. [crying continues]

A: alfaḍiiḥa ʔinnuu naaʃiriin ṣuurtuu fi jjaraayid. xalaaṣ ...

C: kur ʕaleeya ...

A: sumaʕatnaa ntahat.

C: kur ʕaleey yaa ʕawaḍ, ʔinta bi-tfakkir fii ragibtak,[9] maa bi-tfakkir fii ʔaxuuk yaa xuuya.

A: axuuk, bi-llaahii siibiinaa balaa xuuk balaa kalaam faariɣ. gaayil nafsuu ḥa-yahrub, yahrub ween? yahrub yamʃii ween? ḥa-yitgibiḍ w-ḥa-yitḥaakam wa-ḥa-yitʃinig, ʔaywa, ḥa-yitʃinig, yadfaʕ taman jariimtuu.

C: laa yaa xuuy.

A: laazim yadfaʕ taman jariimtuu.

أ: يُكْتُلْ. لاَ وَيُكْتُلْ منُو؟ يُكْتُلْ اَلرَّاجِلْ اَلأكْرَمْهُ، اَلرَّاجِلْ اَلْفَتَحْ لَيْهُ بَيْتْهُ. وَعَشَانْ شِنُو؟ عَشَانْ يِسْرِقْهُ.

ب: [crying] وَلِقَوُّوهْ، مَسَكَوْهْ[7] يَا عَوَضْ؟ كُرْ عَلَيّ يَا خُويْ، كُر عَلَيّ يَا وَدْ أُمِّي.

أ: مَا مَسَكُوا لَكِنْ حَيَمْسِكُوهْ، حَيَمْسِكُوا،[8] اَيْ، حَيْرُوحْ وَيْنْ يَعْنِي؟ بُولِيسْ اَلْبَلَدْ دِي كُلَّهَا بِيفَتِّشْ عَلَيْهُ، كُلَّهَا.

ت: كُرْ عَلَيّ يَا خُوي. [crying continues]

أ: اَلْفَضِيحَهْ إِنَّهُ نَاشِرِينْ صُورْتْهُ فَالجَّرَايِدْ. خَلاَصْ...

ت: كُرْ عَلَيَّ...

أ: سُمَعْتْنَا انْتَهَتْ.

ت: كُرْ عَلَيّ يَا عَوَضْ، إِنْتَ بِتْفَكِّرْ فِي رَقَبْتَكْ،[9] مَا بِتْفَكِّرْ فِي أَخُوكْ يَا خُويَ.

أ: اَخُوكْ، بِاللَّه سِيبِينَا بَلاَ خُوكْ بَلاَ كَلاَمْ فَارِغْ. قَايِلْ نَفْسُهُ حَيَهْرُبْ، يَهْرُبْ وَيْنْ؟ يَهْرُبْ يَمْشِي وَيْنْ؟ حَيِتْقِبِضْ وْحَيِتْحَاكَمْ وَحَيِتْشِنِقْ، أَيْوَهْ، حَيِتْشِنِقْ، يَدْفَعْ تَمَنْ جَرِيمْتْهُ.

ت: لاَ يَا خُويْ.

أ: لاَزِمْ يَدْفَعْ تَمَنْ جَرِيمْتْهُ.

## Vocabulary

**ḥalla ʕalaa** حَلّ عَلَى *vi* to befall {*imperf:* **yaḥill**}

**waddaa** وَدَّى *vt* to put, place; to take (s.o. or s.t. to a place), convey; to send {*imperf:* **yawaddii,** *vn:* **widdeey**}

**wiʃʃ** وِشّ **[waʃʃ]** *nms* face {*pl:* **wuʃuuʃ, awʃaaʃ**}

**waddaa wiʃʃ- min- feen** وَدَّى وِشّ مِنْ فَيْنْ to be able to face s.o. (used in embarrassing situations) *(lit. to put one's face with respect to s.o. else)* {*imperf:* **yawaddii,** *vn:* **widdeey**}

**fii ʃnuu** فِي شْنُو what's going on, what's up, what's wrong *(lit. there is what)*

**ʃakkar** شَكَّرْ *vt* to speak highly of {*imperf:* **yaʃakkir,** *vn:* **taʃkiir**}

**laa ʔilaaha ʔillaa ḷḷaah** لاَ إِلاَهْ إِلاَّ اللَّهْ God rest s.o.'s soul (first response upon hearing of a death); Muslim profession of faith *(lit. there is no god but God)*

**gabbal** قَبَّلْ *vi* to turn toward *(lit. to turn or go south)* {*imperf:* **yagabbil,** *vn:* **tagbiil**}

**banii ʔaadam** بَنِي آدَمْ *nms* human being *(lit. son of Adam)* {*fs:* **banii ʔaadma,** *mpl:* **banii ʔaadmiin,** *fpl:* **banaat ḥawwaa**}

**kur ʕalaa-** كُرْ عَلَى poor dear s.o. (used by women in response to unpleasantness or pain)

**wad** وَدْ **[walad]** *nms* boy; child {*pl:* **oolaad**}

**wad ʔummii** وَدْ أُمِّي **[wid ummii]** my brother *(lit. son of my mother)*

**sawwaa** سَوَّى *vt* to do, make {*imperf:* **yasawwii,** *vn:* **suwaa**}

**sawwaa ʕalaa** سَوَّى عَلَى *vt* to set s.o. up, entrap s.o. *(lit. to do against s.o.)* {*imperf:* **yasawwii ʕalaa,** *vn:* **suwaa ʕalaa**}

**ʕamla** عَمْلَهْ *nfs* deed, act (usually bad) {*pl:* **ʕamaayil**}

**lamma** لَمّ *vt* to gather up, gather in {*imperf:* **yalimm,** *vn:* **lamm,** *vn:* **limm**}

**ʕalaa- aḷḷaa** عَلَى اَللَّهْ for God's sake, for the love of God (adds emphasis to requests and questions) *(lit. by s.o.'s oath to God; on s.o. is the oath "by God")*

**iʕtaraḍ** اِعْتَرَضْ *vt* to protest, object {*imperf:* **yiʕtariḍ,** *vn:* **iʕtiraaḍ**}

**b-annabii** بَالنَّبِي by the Prophet (oath or exclamation)

**xallaa** خَلَّى *vt* to leave alone, let be; to cause to be; to leave (behind); to let, allow {*imperf:* **yaxallii,** *vn:* **xilleey**}

**balwa** بَلْوَهْ *nfs* calamity, misfortune {*pl:* **balaawii**}

**naṣiiba** نَصِيبَهْ **[maṣiiba]** *nfs* calamity, disaster (used by women; euphemism for /maṣiiba/ 'calamity, disaster') {*pl:* **naṣaayib**}

**ḥaagid** حَاقِدْ *adj* vicious {*fs:* **ḥaagda**, *mpl:* **ḥaagdiin**, *fpl:* **ḥaagdaat**}

**aʕuuzuu bi-llaah** أَعُوزُ بِاللّهْ God help me (pious response to sin or occasion of sin) *(lit. I seek refuge in God)*

**balaa** بَلَا *disc marker* enough of, forget about (indicates disapproval or disagreement)

**ṭaar fii ssamaa** طَارْ فِي السَّمَا to get lost *(lit. to fly in the sky)* {*imperf:* **yaṭiir fii ssamaa**, *vn:* **ṭayaraan fii ssamaa**}

**ʃaɣala** شَغَلَهْ *nfs* concern, interest; task, work {*pl:* **ʃaɣalaat**}

**kafaa** كَفَى *interj invariable* enough; stop that

**abuu** أَبُو **[ab]** *nms* souce, origin; elderly person; ancestor; father, parent {*pl:* **abahaat**}

**aḷḷaa yilʕan abuu dii ʕiiʃa dii** اَللّهْ يِلْعَنْ اَبُو دي عيشَهْ دي **[aḷḷaa yalʕan abuu dii ʕiiʃa dii]** God curse this life *(lit. God curse the source of this life)*

**bi-llaahii** بِاللّه by God (oath or exclamation)

**buuliis** بُولِيسْ *nms singular and plural* police

**sumʕa** سُمْعَهْ *nfs* good name, reputation {*pl:* **sumʕaat**}

**ragiba** رَقَبَهْ *nfs* person, self; neck {*pl:* **ragibaat**, **rigaab**}

**kalaam faariɣ** كَلَامْ فَارِغْ nonsense *(lit. empty talk)*

**gaayil** قَايِلْ *adj* thinking; saying {*fs:* **gaayla**, *mpl:* **gaayliin**, *fpl:* **gaaylaat**}

**itgabaḍ** اتْقَبَضْ *vi* be arrested, seized {*imperf:* **yitgabiḍ**, *vn:* **gabiḍ**}

**itḥaakam** اتْحَاكَمْ *vi* to be prosecuted, put on trial {*imperf:* **yitḥaakam**, *vn:* **maḥaakama**}

**itʃanag** اتْشَنَقْ *vi* to be hanged, be executed by hanging {*imperf:* **yitʃanig**, *vn:* **ʃanig**}

## Notes

**1** The use of /daa/ 'this (ms)' in the sentence **/daa** banii ʔaadam **daa/** 'is this (ms) a human being?' differs from the use of /daa/ as a demonstrative. Here, /daa/ modifies the indefinite noun phrase /banii ʔaadam/ and it both precedes and follows that noun phrase. These facts as well as the context in which /**daa**/ occurs indicate that it does not function here as a demonstrative. It is rather a marker that conveys a positive or, in this case, negative reaction. See selection 11, note 13 for another example of this structure.

**2** The form /**ysawwuuwaa**/ 'they (mp) do it (fs)' derives from (/**ysawwuuhaa**/ or /**ysawwoohaa**/ 'they (mp) do it (fs)'). It results from assimilation of the /**h**/ of the suffixed pronoun /**-huu**/ to the preceding long vowel /**uu**/.

**3** The form /**lammaahuu**/ 'he took him in' derives from the verb /**lamma**/ 'to gather in, gather up'. The final /**a**/ of /**lamma**/ is added to the perfect stem /**lamm-**/ to prevent a word-final consonant cluster. That final short vowel is then lengthened before a suffixed pronoun.

**4** The word /**naṣiiba**/ in the form /**naṣiibtii**/ 'my disaster' derives from /**maṣiiba**/ 'disaster, calamity', with an apparently unmotivated change of /**m**/ to /**n**/. This is an euphemism, a pleasant or unthreatening expression that is substituted for another that is unpleasant or threatening.

**5** The utterance /**bi-llaahii siibiinaa, ntuu b-tabkuu ʕalee ʃnuu?**/ 'by God, leave (fs) us alone! What are you (fp) crying about?' has 2FS as well as a 2FP address. The 2FS address, /**bi-llaahii siibiinaa**/ 'by God, leave (fs) us alone!', is from a male speaker to a young female relative. He orders her to leave the room before discussing Khalid's scandalous behavior. The 2FP address, /**ntuu b-tabkuu ʕalee ʃnuu?**/ what are you (fp) crying about?', is the brusque question with which he opens discussion with two other female relatives.

**6** The phrase /**wad ʔummii**/ 'my brother, lit. son of my mother' sounds flowery in English. In Arabic, it sounds affectionate, as it evokes the closeness of siblings and the comfort of a mother's love.

**7** The combination of verb and suffixed pronoun in the question /**ligoowuu, masakooh?**/ 'did they (mp) find him, did they (mp) catch him?' has two different results. The 3MP perfect suffix /**-uu**/ becomes /**-oo-**/ before the suffixed pronoun in the form /**ligoowuu**/ 'they (mp) found him'. At the same time, the /**h**/ of the 3MS suffixed pronoun /**-huu**/ becomes /**w**/ through assimilation to the preceding long vowel /**uu**/ (/**ligoowuu**/).
In contrast, the form /**masakooh**/ has the change of the 3MP perfect suffix from /**-uu**/ to /**-oo-**/, but the 3MS suffixed pronoun is audible only as a final /**h**/. Note, however, that there is no shift of stress to the final syllable, as occurs in certain other varieties of Arabic, to indicate the presence of the 3MS suffixed pronoun.

**8** The two forms /**ḥa-yamsikuu**/ and /**ḥa-yamsikuuhuu**/ in the statement /**ḥa-yamsikuu, ḥa-yamsikuuhuu**/ 'they (mp) will catch him, they (mp) will catch him' mean the same thing. In the first of the two forms, /**ḥa-yamsikuu**/, the 3MS suffixed pronoun /-**huu**/ is not pronounced (is realized as Ø). The second of the two forms, /**ḥa-yamsikuuhuu**/, has the 3MS suffixed pronoun /-**huu**/ in its full form. This second form, longer and more carefully pronounced, adds prominence to the statement.

**9** In the form /**ragibtak**/ 'yourself (ms)', the word /**ragiba**/ literally means 'neck'. Through an extension in meaning, however, it also occurs with the meaning of 'person, self', as it is used here and as the word "neck" does in English in expressions like "to save one's neck."

# ʕaadaat azzawaaj

*This selection begins with a general discussion of marriage in language heavily influenced by MSA. It soon shifts, however, to a detailed description of the process that ends in a formal engagement. A shift in language style accompanies the shift in topic, with the language becoming more colloquial but still educated. Note that, in Sudan as in other parts of the Arabic-speaking world, members of both families participate in the wedding negotiations.*

A: azzawaaj fii ssuudaan ɣad yakuun masalan alʔixtiyaar ʔa … alʔitneen yixtaaruu baʕaḍ ʔizaa kaanuu min ʔusar basiiṭa w-min ʔusar ʔa … raaɣiya wu … ʔaw alʔahal mumkin yixtaaruu lila … lila … lil … li-lwilid albint alʔitizawwajaa. laakin fii baʕḍ alʔusar ʔinnuu laazim yiikuun fii ḥubb wa-laazim yiikuun fii ʔirtibaaṭ wa-laazim yiikuun fii ʔa … ʔa …

B: tafaahum …

A: attafaahum …

B: haa …

A: gabli zzawaaj.

B: haa …

A: w-dii ʔimkin ʔaktar ʔal … ʔaktar ʔal … alḥaalaat albi-tkuun ʔa … ma … fil … fi lʔusar ʔimkin arraaɣiya ʔaw a … a ʃwayya mu … mutḥaḍḍara muʃ basiiṭa fi lmujtamaʕ.

B: mutʕallima ay [xxx].

A: liʔannuu lmujtamaʕ assuudaanii …

B: ay.

# عَادَاتْ اَلزَّوَاجْ

أ: اَلزَّوَاجْ فِي السُّودَانْ غَدْ يَكُونْ مَسَلاً اَلإِخْتِيَارْ أ... اَلإِتْنَيْنْ يِخْتَارُوا بَعَضْ إِزَا كَانُوا مِنْ أُسَرْ بَسِيطَهْ وْمِنْ أُسَرْ أ... رَاغِيَهْ وُ... أَوْ اَلأَهَلْ مُمْكِنْ يِخْتَارُوا لِلَ... لِلَ... لِلْ... لِلْوِلِدْ اَلْبِنْتْ اَلإِتِزَوَّجْهَا. لَكِنْ فِي بَعْضْ اَلأُسَرْ إِنَّهُ لاَزِمْ يِيكُونْ فِي حُبّ وَلاَزِمْ يِيكُونْ فِي إِرْتِبَاطْ وَلاَزِمْ يِيكُونْ فِي أ... أ ...

ب: تَفَاهُمْ...

أ: اَلتَّفَاهُمْ...

ب: هَا...

أ: قَبْلِ الزَّوَاجْ.

ب: هَا...

أ: وْدِي إِمْكِنْ أَكْتَرْ أَلْ... أَكْتَرْ أَلْ... اَلْحَالاَتْ اَلْبِتْكُونْ أ... مَ... فِلْ... فَالأُسَرْ إِمْكِنْ اَلرَّاغِيَهْ أَو اَ... شْوَيَّهْ مُ... مُتْحَضَّرَهْ مُشْ بَسِيطَهْ فِالْمُجْتَمَعْ.

ب: مُتْعَلِّمَهْ اي [xxx].

أ: لأَنّهُ الْمُجْتَمَعْ اَلسُّودَانِي...

ب: اَيْ.

A: fiihuu ṭabaɣaat katiira, fiihuu ṭabaɣaat ...

B: huwa, huwa, huwa ttaɣliid alʔasaasii yaa rajaaʔ, attaɣliid yaʕnii biʔan ... ʔan ... ʔan ... ʔan ... annaas mujarrad masalan maa lʔusra[1] ʔa ... waladum iiguul ʔa ... ḥaddad aʃʃaxṣi mmuʕayyan.

A: 'anaa daayir fulaana.'[2]

B: ay, bitt muʕayyana ʔala ... ʔala ... b-iiguumuu ʔalʔaxawaat, alʔaxawaat ɣaalibam -muʃ alʔumm b-iimʃuu li-hal albitt yaʕnii ymʃuu yitkallamuu maʕ ummahaa ...

A: maʕ albitt nafsahaa ...

B: ay, maʕ albitt u-maʕ ummahaa ...

A: [xxx]

B: almihim b-iimʃuu beetun hinaak wa-b-iiḥaddisuuhum iiguuluuhum, 'yaax w-aḷḷaahii daayir, daayir bittakun.'

A: wa-dii b-iiguul leehaa fatḥat alxaʃam.[3]

B: ay, fa ... fa ... fa-dii lxaṭwa lʔuulaa ʔalʕaadtan bi-titʕamil yaʕnii. b-iimʃuu nniswaan wa-baʕd anniswaan imʃuu rrujaal.

A: haa ...

أ: فِيهُ طَبَقَاتْ كَتِيرَهْ، فِيهُ طَبَقَاتْ...

ب: هُوَ، هُوَ، هُوَ التَّقْلِيدْ اَلأَسَاسِي يَا رَجَاءْ، اَلتَّقْلِيدْ يَعْنِي بِأَنْ ... أَنْ... أَنْ... أَنْ... اَلنَّاسْ مُجَرَّدْ مَسَلاً مَا الأُسْرَهْ[1] أَ ... وَلَدْهُمْ يْقُولْ أَ... حَدَّدْ اَلشَّخْصِ الْمُعَيَّنْ.

أ: «أَنَا دَايِرْ فُلاَنَهْ.»[2]

ب: اَيْ، بِتّ مُعَيَّنَهْ أَلَـ... أَلَـ... بِيقُومُوا أَلأَخَوَاتْ، اَلأَخَوَاتْ غَالِبَنْ -مُشْ اَلأُمّ بِيمْشُوا لاِهَلْ اَلْبِتّ يَعْنِي يْمْشُوا يِتْكَلَّمُوا مَعْ أُمَّهَا...

أ: مَع اَلْبِتّ نَفْسَهَا...

ب: اَيْ، مَع اَلْبِتّ أُمَعْ أُمَّهَا...

أ: [xxx].

ب: اَلْمِهِمْ بِيمْشُوا بَيْتْهُنْ هِنَاكْ وَبِيحَدِّسُوهُمْ يْقُولُوهُمْ، «يَاخْ وَاللَّهِ دَايِرْ، دَايِرْ بِتَّكُنْ.»

أ: وَدِي بِيقُولْ لَيْهَا فَتْحَةْ اَلْخَشَمْ.[3]

ب: اَيْ، فَـ... فَـ... فَدِي الْخَطْوَه الأُولَى أَلْعَادَةً بِتِتْعَمِلْ يَعْنِي. بِيمْشُوا النِّسْوَانْ وَبَعْدْ اَلنِّسْوَانْ اِمْشُوا الرُّجَالْ.

أ: هَا...

B: wa-baʕad maa haṣlat muwaafaga arrujaal yimʃuu xalaaṣ tammat albitaaʕa dii[4] nnaas b-iibduu yizaɣriduu. ʔaha … ʔa … ṭawwaalii baʕad daa xalaaṣ ḥaṣal albitaaʕ wallaa kidaa nnaas b-iibduu yiḥaḍḍruu li-lʕamaliyya bitaaʕt azzawaaj fa-fii …

A: guulat xeer …

B: guulat xeer, yaʕnii ʕaʃaan gaaluu, 'xeer,'[5] yaʕnii nnaas deel gaaluu, gaaluu, 'xeer.' b-iimʃuu ydduuhun juzuʔ yaʕnii maa mablaɣ kabiir yaʕnii maa zeey almuhar[6] …

A: haa …

B: gaaluu, 'xeer,' xalaaṣ. iiguuluu, 'xalaaṣ yaa flaan, daa maa ʔistalmuu dii ɣuruuʃkun, dii guulat xeer bitaaʕatkum. ʔi … niḥnaa ka … ʔalyoom alfulaanii kidaa kidaa, b-najii nsidd almahar.' wa-ʕaadatan …

A: sidd almarr …

B: sidd almaal, wa-sadd almaal bi-ykuum -maʕaahuu barḍuu ʃʃanṭa bitaaḥat alʕaruus. aʃʃeela.[7]

A: ay.

B: ay, bi-nguul leehaa ʃʃeela ṭabʕan. fa … xalaaṣ itḥaddad alyoom bitaaʕ aʃʃeela wa-sadd almaal …

A: allii hii ʃʃeela fiihaa ʃnuu w-ʃnuu w-ʃnuu?

ب: وَبَعَدْ مَا حَصَلْتْ مُوافَقَه اَلرُّجَالْ يِمْشُوا خَلاَص تَمَّتْ اَلْبِتَاعَهْ دِي[4] النَّاسْ بِيِبْدُوا يِزَغْرِدُوا. أَهَهْ... أ... طَوَّالِي بَعَدْ دَا خَلاَصْ حَصَلْ اَلْبِتَاعْ وَلاَّ كِدَا النَّاسْ بِيِبْدُوا يِحَضّرُوا لِلْعَمَلِيَّهْ بِتَاعَةْ اَلزَّوَاجْ فَفِي...

أ: قُولَةْ خَيْرْ.

ب: قُولَةْ خَيْرْ، يَعْنِي عَشَانْ قَالُوا، «خَيْرْ،»[5] يَعْنِي النَّاسْ دَيْلْ قَالُوْا، قَالُوا، «خَيْرْ.» بِيِمْشُوا يْدُّوهُنْ جُزْء يَعْنِي مَا مَبْلَغْ كَبِيرْ يَعْنِي مَا زَيّ اَلْمُهْر[6]...

أ: هَا...

ب: قَالُوا، «خَيْرْ،» خَلاَصْ. يْقُولُوا، «خَلاَصْ يَا فْلاَنْ، دَا مَا إِسْتَلْمُوا دِي غُرُوشْكُنْ، دِي قُولَةْ خَيْرْ بِتَاعَتْكُمْ. إِ... نِحْنَاكَ ... أَلْيَوْمْ اَلْفُلاَنِي كِدَا كِدَا، بْنَجِي نْسِدّ اَلْمَهْرْ.» وَعَادَةً...

أ: سِدّ اَلْمَرّ ...

ب: سِدّ اَلْمَالْ، وَسَدّ اَلْمَالْ بِيْكُومْ -مَعَاهُ بَرْضُهُ الشَّنْطَهْ بِتَاحَةْ اَلْعَرُوسْ. اَلشَّيْلَهْ.[7]

أ: اَيْ.

ب: اَيْ، بِنْقُولْ لَيهَا الشَّيْلَهْ طَبْعًا. فَ ... خَلاَصْ اِتْحَدَّدْ اَلْيَوْمْ بِتَاعْ اَلشَّيْلَهْ وَسَدّ اَلْمَالْ...

أ: اَللِّي هِي الشَّيْلَهْ فِيهَا شْنُو وْشْنُو وْشْنُو؟

B: aʃʃeela maa b-ikuunuu fiihaa l … yaʕnii l … niḥnaa ṭabʕan ʔala … fii, fii ssuudaan hinaak ala … ʔanniswaan ʕaadatan b-yilbasan attiyaab,[8] yaʕnii ma …

A: attoob assuudaanii[9] lmaʕruuf …

B: attoob assuudaanii, ay. alḥaaja lʔasaasiyya wu … wa-ɣaaliya ʃadiid jiddan jiddan wa-b-iijiibuuhuu yaʕnii ʔintii b-tilgii fii, fi ʃʃanṭa yaʕnii b-iikuun fiihaa ʔagalla ḥaaja ʕalaa ḥasaba gudrat annaas, yaʕnii fii naas b-iijiibuu talaata tiyaab fii ʃʃanṭa, fii naas b-iijiibuu sitta …

A: wu-maʕaahuu fasaatiin wu-ʔaryaaḥ[10] …

B: ay.

A: wu-jizam wu …

B: ṣaḥḥ, ṣaḥḥ. maahuu ʔalḥaaja rrayiisiyya fiihaa huwwa muʃ al … al … al … attiyaab bass attiyaab w-addahab.

A: kull allibis ʔa … al …

B: dii alḥa …

A: al … alɣaaliya.

B: alɣaaliya.

ب: اَلشَّيْلَهْ مَا بِكُونُوا فِيهَا لْـ ... يَعْنِي لْـ ... نحْنَا طَبْعًا أَلَـ ... فِي، فِي السُّودَانْ هِنَاكْ اَلَـ ... أَلنِّسْوَانْ عَادَةً بْيِلْبَسَنْ اَلتِّيَابْ،[8] يَعْنِي، مَـ ...

أ: اَلتَّوْبْ اَلسُّودَانِي[9] اَلْمَعْرُوفْ ...

ب: اَلتَّوْبْ اَلسُّودَانِي، اَيْ. اَلْحَاجَه الأَسَاسِيَّهْ وُ ... وَغَالِيَهْ شَدِيدْ جِداً جِداً وَبِيجِيبُوهُ يَعْنِي إِنْتِي بْتِلْقِي فِي، فَالشَّنْطَهْ يَعْنِي بِيكُونْ فِيهَا أَقَلَّ حَاجَهْ عَلَى حَسَبَ قُدْرَةْ اَلنَّاسْ، يَعْنِي فِي نَاسْ بِيجِيبُوا تَلاَتَهْ تِيَابْ فِي الشَّنْطَهْ، فِي نَاسْ بِيجِيبُوا سِتَّهْ...

أ: وُمَعَاهُ فَسَاتِينْ وُأَرْيَاحْ[10] ...

ب: اَيْ.

أ: وُجِزَمْ وُ...

ب: صَحّ، صَحّ. مَاهُ أَلْحَاجَه الرَّيِيسِيَّهْ فِيهَا هُوَّ مُشْ اَلْـ... اَلْـ ... اَلْـ... اَلتِّيَابْ بَسّ اَلتِّيَابْ وَالدَّهَبْ.

أ: كُلّ اَللِّبِسْ أ... اَلْـ ...

ب: دِي اَلْحَـ ...

أ: اَلْـ ... اَلْغَالِيَهْ.

ب: اَلْغَالِيَهْ.

A: aktar ḥaaja mukallifa.[11]

B: ay.

A: ṣaḥḥ, aywa.

B: fa-ʕalaa lʕumuum annaas ala … b-iijiiban aʃʃeela[12] wa-sadd almaal daa, barḍuu b-iiguuman beeh niswaan zeey maa gaamam -bee-guulat xeer barḍuu lḥaajaat dii b-iijiibuuhaa niswaan.

A: niswaan.

B: yaʕnii rrujaal baʕad maa rraajil xaṭab albitt min ala … min abuuhaa, taanii maa ʕanduu door ɣeer innuu yaʕgid maʕ, yaʕgid leeh ʕal … ʕalaa lbitt.

A: ṣaḥḥ.

أ: اَكْتَرْ حَاجَهْ مُكَلِّفَهْ.[11]

ب: اَيْ.

أ: صَحّ، اَيْوَهْ.

ب: فَعَلَى الْعُمُومْ اَلنَّاسْ اَلَـ ... بِيجِيبَنْ اَلشَّيْلَهْ[12] وَسَدّ اَلْمَالْ دَا، بَرْضُهْ بِيقُومَنْ بَيْهْ نِسْوَانْ زَيّ مَا قَامَمْ -بَيْقُولَةْ خَيْرْ بَرْضُهُ الْحَاجَاتْ دِي بِيجِيبُوهَا نِسْوَانْ.

أ: نِسْوَانْ.

ب: يَعْنِي الرُّجَالْ بَعَدْ مَا الرَّاجِلْ خَطَبْ اَلْبِتّ مِن اَلَـ... مِنْ اَبُوهَا، تَانِي مَا عِنْدُهْ دَوْرْ غَيْرْ اِنُّهُ يَعْقِدْ مَعْ، يَعْقِدْ لَيْهْ عَلْـ... عَلَى الْبِتّ.

أ: صَحّ.

## Vocabulary

**baʕaḍ** بَعَضْ *nms invariable* each other, one another (indicates reciprocity)

**mujarrad maa** مُجَرَّدْ مَا *conj* as soon as, no sooner than

**ḥaddad** حَدَّدْ *vt* to determine, set {*imperf:* **yaḥaddid,** *vn:* **taḥdiid**}

**fulaan** فُلاَنْ *nms* so and so, what's-his-name {*fs:* **fulaana**}

**gaam (gumta)** قَامْ (قُمْت) *vi pre-verb, agrees in number, gender, and tense with main verb* to do, go ahead and do (as a consequence or result of previously described event); to get up (in order to do s.t.); to wake up, get up; to up and (do s.t.), suddenly (do); to get up, stand up {*imperf:* **yaguum,** *vn:* **goom**}

**xaʃam** خَشَمْ **[xaʃum]** *nms* mouth; entrance {*pl:* **xuʃuum**}

**fatḥat alxaʃam** فَتْحَةْ اَلْخَشَمْ **[fatḥat alxaʃum]** opening of negotiations for marriage *(lit. opening the mouth)*

**niswaan** نِسْوَانْ *nfpl* married women; women (in general) {*fs:* **mara**}

**tamma** تَمّ *vt* to complete, finish {*imperf:* **yatimm,** *vn:* **tamaam**}

**zaɣrad** زَغْرَدْ *vi* to produce a high trilling sound (by women on happy occasions) {*imperf:* **yazaɣrid,** *vn:* **zaɣrada**}

**guulat xeer** قُولَةْ خَيْرْ guulat xeer (good-faith offering, small gift from man's family to woman's family that begins negotiations for marriage) *(lit. a speaking of goodness)*

**muhar** مُهَرْ **[mahar]** *nms* mahar (gift from groom to bride consisting of money or property; dowry) {*pl:* **muhuur**}

**fulaanii** فُلاَنِي *adj* so-and-so, what's his name (family name) {*fs:* **fulaaniyya,** *mpl:* **fulaaniyyiin,** *fpl:* **fulaaniyyaat**}

**kidaa kidaa** كِدَا كِدَا so-and-so; so-so, not so great; either ...or ...

**sadda** سَدّ *vt* to pay (debt, bill, etc.); to close, shut {*imperf:* **yasidd,** *vn:* **sadd**}

**mahar** مَهَرْ **[muhar]** *nms* mahar (gift from groom to bride consisting of money or property; dowry) {*pl:* **muhuur**}

**sidd almaal** سِدّ اَلْمَالْ **[sadd almaal]** sadd al-maal (payment or delivery of the entire mahar)

**ʃanṭa** شَنْطَة *nfs* suitcase; handbag {*pl:* **ʃunaṭ**}

**ʕaruus** عَرُوس *nfs* bride {*nfpl:* **ʕaruusaat**}

**ʃeela** شَيْلَة *nfs* sheela (bride's clothing, cosmetics, and basic foodstuffs for wedding celebrations, given to the bride's family by the bridegroom's family before the wedding) {*pl:* **ʃeelaat**}

**toob** تَوْب *nms* traditional Sudanese wrap worn by women and men {*pl:* **tiyaab, teebaan**}

**fustaan** فُسْتَان *nms* woman's dress, frock {*pl:* **fasaatiin**}

**riiḥa** رِيحَة *nfs* perfume, cologne {*pl:* **aryaaḥ**}

**jazma** جَزْمَة *nfs* pair of shoes {*pl:* **jizam**}

**xaṭab** خَطَب *vt* to ask for a girl's hand in marriage {*imperf:* **yaxṭub**, *vn:* **xuṭuuba**}

**ʕagad ʕalaa** عَقَد عَلَى to sign a contract of marriage for (the woman one marries) {*imperf:* **yaʕgid ʕalaa**, *vn:* **ʕagad ʕalaa**}

## Notes

1 The form /**maa**/ in the phrase /annaas **mujarrad** masalan **maa** lʔusra/ 'people as soon, for example, as the family' is not the negative but another particle. In the phrase /**mujarrad maa**/ 'as soon as, no sooner than', it combines with the participle /**mujarrad**/ 'pure, mere, nothing more than' to form a conjunction. Such phrases, like the construct phrase described in selection 2, note 12, typically occur in unbroken units. Here, however, the filler /**masalan**/ intrudes on this phrase.

2 As the speaker notes earlier, people at either end of the social scale have a relationship with their spouse before deciding to marry. For those in the middle, however, the stereotype has the man saying something like /**anaa daayir fulaana**/ 'I want so-and-so' to his female relatives. His request sets the families in motion to negotiate the marriage.

3 The phrase /**fatḥat alxaʃam**/ appears in the English translation of this selection with no translation. This was done deliberately, because the literal translation of /**fatḥat alxaʃam**/, 'an opening of the mouth', adds nothing to the translation.

4 The referent of /**albitaaʕa**/ 'this thing, lit. this what-do-you-call-it (fs)' in the sentence /**tammat albitaaʕa dii**/ 'this thing is finished, lit. this what-do-you-call-it (fs) is finished' is the noun phrase /**fatḥat alxaʃam**/ 'the fatḥat alxaʃam'. The speaker does not use the term here, but retains its grammatical gender (FS) when referring to it.

**5** The speaker describes the guulat xeer by saying /**guulat xeer, yaʕnii ʕaʃaan gaaluu 'xeer'**/ 'the guulat xeer, you know, because they (mp) said "may it be good"'. The guulat xeer occurs when members of the man's family visit the woman's family with a small gift. Once that happens, the families begin to negotiate the details of the wedding preparations, the festivities, and the mahar.

**6** The speaker describes the guulat xeer as /**maa mablaɣ kabiir yaʕnii maa zeey almuhar**/ 'not a large sum, you know, it's not like the dowry'. The /**guulat xeer**/ is the small gift from the man's family to the woman's family that begins negotiations about the wedding. The /**mahar**/, on the other hand, is given by the groom to the bride. It may take the form of money or property. Its value depends on family circumstance as well as social expectations. The /**mahar**/, like the American engagement ring, is seen as the visible sign of the bride's value to the groom

**7** The /**sadd almaal**/ 'the sadd almaal' is when the payment of the /**mahar**/ 'dowry' takes place. This is not necessarily a large or formal party, but it may be combined with the delivery of the ʃeela in a family celebration. What the speaker describes as /**ʃʃanṭa bitaaḥat alʕaruus. aʃʃeela**/ 'the bride's suitcase: the ʃeela' may be as small as a suitcase or as large as a truck. The /**ʃeela**/ includes the cosmetics and perfumes used by the bride in the traditional wedding preparation process as well as her clothing. It often also includes basic foodstuffs, a contribution by the groom's family to the costs of the wedding festivities.

**8** In the phrase /**ʔanniswaan ʕaadatan b-yilbasan**/ 'women generally wear', the speaker uses the imperfect verb /**yilbasan**/ in the FP. FP forms of the verb are not often heard in the region of the capital, except when women speak with each other. This is an exception to that generalization.

**9** Traditional dress for Sudanese women is /**attoob assuudaanii**/ 'the Sudanese toob'. Worn over a long dress, it consists of a length of fabric wrapped around the body and draped over the head. An everyday toob may be of inexpensive fabric, but for formal occasions like weddings the fabric of the toob is elaborately and expensively decorated.

**10** The referent of the 3S suffixed pronoun /**-huu**/ in the phrase /**maʕaahuu fasaatiin wu-ʔaryaaḥ**/ 'with it (ms) are dresses and perfumes' is the word /**toob**/.

**11** The phrase /**aktar ḥaaja mukallifa**/ 'the most costly thing' would translate literally as 'the greatest thing that is costly'. This is the only way to make a superlative phrase with the adjective /**mukallifa**/ 'costly'. Because this adjective is itself a derived form, it cannot form an elative. The speaker therefore builds on an elative phrase with a general meaning, /**aktar ḥaaja**/ 'the greatest thing'. The adjective modifies the indefinite noun /**ḥaaja**/ to become /**aktar ḥaaja mukallifa**/ 'the most costly thing'.

**12** The speaker uses the FP form of the imperfect verb in the sentence /b-iijjii**ban** aʃʃeela/ 'they (fp) bring the ʃeela'. This form occurs twice more as the speaker emphasizes the role played by women in the wedding preparations. The final sentence of this utterance, however, casts prominence on the objects and events themselves, **/barḍuu lḥaajaat dii** b-iijiibuuhaa **niswaan/** 'these things, too, women bring'. At this point, the more usual MP form of the imperfect verb occurs /b-iijii**buu**ha**a**/ 'they (mp) bring them (fs)'.

# ajarrib ḥaaja zayy dii

*The female speaker in this selection talks about her background. She starts with her education and moves on to the medical problems that influenced her decision to emigrate from Sudan. She admits that she would at least consider one traditional Sudanese approach to her problems. Some people might call her superstitious, but others would see her as respectful of tradition.*

A: waa ... ʔismuu ʃinuu huu, wa-guttii, w-intii, w-intii gareetii ʃnuu, guttii leey?

B: anaa gareet ʔa ... fii ʔa ... fi alxarṭuum, gareet kulliyyat azziraaʕa, ʔiɣtiṣaad ziraaʕii[1] waa ... b-aḥaawil taanii ʔad ... gareet, ʕamalta diblooma fi ssuudaan fii, fii ttanmiyya w-ttaxṭiiṭ alʔiɣtiṣaadii. laakin alba ... ba ... b-aḥibb jiddan almajaal bitaaʕ alkumbyuutar fa-hassii badeet leey maastar bitaaḥ kumbyuutar. laakin bass maa gaadira mʃii fiihuu sariiʕ ʕaʃaan aʃʃuɣul wa-marraat b-akuun ʔa ... ḥaamil[2] wallaa ḥaaja zayy dih,[3] bi-taaxud min zamaanii katiir.

A: haa ... waa ... wajii ..., jiitii jii ... jiitii ntii ssabab ajjaabik ʃnuu lbalad dii?

B: anaa ʔaṣlan jiit ʔa ... fii ʃuɣul u-kunta ḥaamil u-fii nafs alwakit kaan ʕindii muʃkila yaʕnii fi lḥimil u-lwilaada w-kidaa ʕindii muʃkila fi lʔaṭfaal, ʕindii muʃkila bitaaʕat wiraaθa. fam ... ʔa ... ʔiṭṭarratnii ẓẓuruuf innii ʔatʔaxxar hinaa liʔannii jiit ḥaamil ḥasab ɣaraaraat adduktoor wa-baʕd daak almuʃkila ʔiṭṭawwarat wa-ḥaawalta ʔa ... ʔakammil lʕilaaj w-istaɣarreet.

A: haa ...

# أَجَرِّبْ حَاجَهْ زَيّ دِي

أ: وَا... إِسْمَهُ شِنُو هُو، وَقُتِّي لَيّ وِانْتِي، وِانْتِي قَرَيْتِي شْنُو، قُتِّي لَيّ؟

ب: اَنَا قَرَيْتْ أَ... فِي أَ... فَالْخَرْطُومْ، قَرَيتْ كُلِّيَّةْ اَلزِّرَاعَهْ، إِغْتِصَادْ زِرَاعِي[1] وَا... بَاحَاوِلْ تَانِي أَدْ... قَرَيْتْ، عَمَلْتَ دِبْلَومَهْ فَالسُّودَانْ فِي، فِي التَّنْمِيَّهْ وْالتَّخْطِيطْ اَلإِغْتِصَادِي. لَكِنْ اَلبَـ... بَـ... بَاحِبّ جِدّاً اَلْمَجَالْ بِتَاعْ اَلكُمْبْيُوتَرْ فَهَسِّي بَدَيْتْ لَيّ مَاسْتَرْ بِتَاحْ كُمْبْيُوتَرْ. لَكِنْ بَسّ مَا قَادْرَه اَمْشِي فِيهُ سَرِيعْ عَشَانْ اَلشُّغُلْ وَمَرَّاتْ بَاكُونْ أَ... حَامِلْ[2] وَلاَّ حَاجَهْ زَيّ دِهْ،[3] بِتَاخُدْ مِنْ زَمَانِي كَتِيرْ.

أ: هَا... وَا... وَجِيـ... ، جِيتِي جِيـ... جِيتِي انْتِي السَّبَبْ اَلجَّابِكْ شِنُو الْبَلَدْ دِي؟

ب: اَنَا أَصْلاً جِيتْ أَ... فِي شُغُلْ أُكُنْتَ حَامِلْ أُفِي نَفْسْ اَلْوَكتْ كَانْ عِنْدِي مُشْكِلَهْ يَعْنِي فَالْحِمِلْ اُلْوِلاَدَهْ وْكِدَا عِنْدِي مُشْكِلَهْ فَالأَطْفَالْ، عِنْدِي مُشْكِلَهْ بِتَاعَةْ وِرَاثَهْ. فَمْ... أَ... إِطَّرَّتْنِي الظُّرُوفْ اِنِّي أَتْأَخَّرْ هِنَا لأَنِّي جِيتْ حَامِلْ حَسَبْ غَرَارَاتْ اَلدُّكْتَورْ وَبَعْدْ دَاكْ اَلْمُشْكِلَهْ إِطَّوَّرَتْ وَحَاوَلْتَ أَ... أَكَمِّلْ الْعِلاَجْ وِاسْتَغَرَّيْتْ.

أ: هَا...

B: wa-baʕad daaka nizbatan liʔannuu zoojii ʔaxad al … al … al … ala … ala … al*green card* al … alʔamriikii bi-lgurʕa ʔalʕaʃwaaʔiyya fa-ʔistaɣarreenaa baʕad daaka.

A: wu-fii ssuudaan hinaak maa al … al … al … ḥaajaat al … al … alzayy dii kidaa al … al … alwilaada walal … w-almara janaahaa b-muut wa-b-yimʃuu leehaa li-ʃʃuyuux[4] u-kidaa.

B: anaa barḍuu lamman maʃeet assuuddaan gabli sana ḥaawalta ʔamʃii li-ʃʃuyuux ʕaʃaan ʔa … almuʃkila ṭṭawwarat yaʕnii kaanuu talaata ʔitfagaduu. wa-yaʕnii ḥasseet ʔinnuu kadaa ʔajarrib liʔannii jarrabta ʔayyi ḥaaja fi lʕilaaj. fa-ḥaawalta ʔajarrib ḥaaja zayy dii, ʕasaa wa-laʕalla ʔinnahaa tanfaʕ fa-maa muʕtariḍa ʕalee lfikra yaʕnii.

ب: وَبَعَدْ دَاكَ نزْبَةً لأَنّهُ زَوْجِي أَخَدْ اَلْـ...   اَلْـ...   اَلْـ...   اَلَـ... اَلَـ...   الgreen card اَلْـ...   اَلأَمْـرِيكِي بِـالْقُـرْعَـهْ أَلْعَـشْـوَائِيَّـهْ فَإِسْـتَـغْرَيّْـنَا بَعَدْ دَاكَ.

أ: وُفِي السُّودَانْ هِنَاكْ مَا اَلْـ...   اَلْـ...   اَلْـ...   حَاجَاتْ اَلْـ... اَلْـ...   اَلْزَيّ دِي كِدَا اَلْـ...   اَلْـ...   اَلْوِلاَدَهْ وَلَلْـ...   وَالْمَـرَاهْ جَنَاهَا بْمُوتْ وَبْيِمْشُوا لَيْهَا لِلشُّيُوخْ[4] أُكِدَا.

ب: اَنَا بَـرْضُـهُ لَمَّنْ مَـشَـيْتْ اَلسُّودَانْ قَـبْلِ سَنَـهْ حَـاوَلْتَ أَمْـشِي لِلشُّـيُوخْ عَـشَـانْ أَ...   اَلْمُـشْكِلَهْ اطَّوَّرَتْ يَعْنِي كَـانُوا تَلاَتَـهْ إِتْفَقَدُوا. وَيَعْنِي حَسَّيْتْ إِنّهُ كَدَا أَجَرِّبْ لأَنِّي جَرَّبْتَ أَيِّ حَاجَهْ فَالْعِلاَجْ. فَحَاوَلْتَ أَجَرِّبْ حَاجَهْ زَيّ دِي، عَسَى وَلَعَلَّ إِنَّهَا تَنْفَعْ فَمَا مُعْتَرِضَهْ عَلَي الْفِكْرَهْ يَعْنِي.

## Vocabulary

**sariiʕ** سَرِيعْ *adj* quick; *adv* quickly {*fs:* **sariiʕa,** *mpl:* **suraaʕ,** *fpl:* **sariiʕaat**}

**marraat** مَرَّاتْ *adv* at times, sometimes

**mara** مَرَاهْ *nfs* married woman; woman (in general) {*nfpl:* **niswaan**}

**janaa** جَنَى *nms* child (term of endearment); embryo {*pl:* **jiniyaat**}

**maʃaa li-** مَشَى لِ *vi* to take s.o. or s.t. {*imperf:* **yamʃii,** *vn:* **maʃii**}

**ʃeex** شَيْخْ *nms* religious authority {*pl:* **ʃuyuux**}

**itfagad** اِتْفَقَدْ *vi* to be, have been lost {*imperf:* **yitfagid,** *vn:* **fugdaan**}

**kadaa** كَدَا *adv* thus, in such a way

**ʕasaa wa-laʕalla** عَسَى وَلَعَلّ perhaps, maybe

## Notes

**1** The fact that the name of the institution precedes the subject studied in the sentence /gareet **kulliyyat azziraaʕa,** ʔiɣtiṣaad ziraaʕii/ 'I studied at the College of Agriculture, agricultural economics' is not unusual in SA. The verb /garaa/ 'to study' in SA may take a location as a direct object.

**2** The adjective /ḥaamil/ 'pregnant' in the clause /b-akuun ʔa ... **ḥaamil**/ 'I'm, ah, pregnant' correctly lacks the FS /-a/ ending. This adjective is one of a small group of adjectives that describe women's biologial and social roles. These adjectives therefore do not need the FS /-a/ ending to differentiate between F and M referents. The adjective /ḥaamil/ is the best-known of this group.

**3** The form /dih/ 'this' in the phrase /zayy dih/ 'like that, lit. like this (fs)' is a common variant of /dii/. A word-final long vowel in SA may be pronounced as a short vowel followed by /h/, as it is here. This pronunciation is most noticeable when it occurs at the end of a phrase or sentence.

**4** The speaker does not describe what happens when /b-yimʃuu leehaa li-ʃʃuyuux/ 'they (mp) take her to religious men'. Such practices vary a great deal, from simple prayer to more elaborate rituals.

# ʃin guulik fiihaa?

*This selection continues the budding romance of Huda and Adil (selection 7). Here, three of Adil's female relatives talk about Huda. Note that the voices of these women, high-pitched and with extremes of intonation, are not unusual when women talk to each other in an informal setting. Note also the use of the feminine plural, which is unusual in the Sudanese capital except when women speak together.*

A: [speaking on the telephone] ʔaywa, maʕaak[1] ay. daa kwayyis xaaliṣ. ʔasmaʕii ʔintii maa djiinaa fi lbeet? ʔaḷḷaah! fiihaa ʃnuu[2] yaa mʕaggada? yaa zoola, maa zamiiltuu, ʕaadii. ay, xalaaṣ yaa sittii, niʃuufik. huu lfi lguluub daa fii zool b-iiʕarfuu[3] yaʕnii? ṭayyib, yaa maamaa, maʕ assalaama. [hangs up the telephone] baalaɣtii, yaa xaaltii, yaʕnii ʔillaa ʕaadil yitṣadim ḥattaa nʃuufik kulli yoom?

B: ittii yaa bitt, ʔittii gaayla nnaas deel kullahum faaḍyiin kadii maa ʕindahun ʔayy ʃaɣala, kulla maa marra yajuukum yasʔaluu minnakum, ʔaa? kadaa guul lee, ʔittii kuttii[4] bi-tanḍumii maʕa mnuu? maʕa lbitt assamḥa diik ajjaat zaarat ʕaadil fi lʔistibaaliya?[5]

A: yaahaa zaataa yaa xaaltii, muʃ ḥilwa ʕaleek ʔaḷḷaa?

B: areetaa yaa yammaa, samaaḥt albannuut li-ḥaddihin, ẓariifa wa-dammaa xafiif, yeh! wa-leehaa nuura.

A: haay, laakin ʃakkartiihaa maa xalleetii laa ḥaaja. kaan maa ʕaajabatik maa kaan guttii fiihaa kidaa.

B: alḥagg li-llaahii, ʕaad yaa bittii, gaaṭʕa lkalaam, maa fiihaa gool, ʔanaa ʕaayanta leehaa min foog lii-tiḥit.

# شِنْ قُولِكْ فِيهَا؟

أ: [speaking on the telephone] أَيْوَهْ، مَـعَـاك[1] اَيْ. داَ كْـوَيِّـس خَالِص. أَسْمَعِي إِنْتِي مَا دْجِينَا فَالْبَيْتْ؟ أَللَّهْ! فِيهَا شْنُو[2] يَا مْـعَـقَّدَهْ؟ يَـا زَوْلَهْ، مَـا زَمِـيلْتَـهُ، عَـادِي. اَيْ، خَـلاَصْ يَـا سِـتِّـي، نِشُوفِكْ. هُو الْفَالْقُلُوبْ دَا فِي زَوْلْ بِيعَرْفَهْ[3] يَعْنِي؟ طَيِّبْ، يَا مَـامَـا، مَعْ اَلـسَّـلاَمَـهْ. [hangs up the telephone] بَـالَـغْـتِـي، يَا خَالْتِي، يَعْنِي إِلاَّ عَادِلْ يِتْصَدِمْ حَتَّى نْشُوفِكْ كُلِّ يَوْمْ؟

ب: اِتِّي يَا بِتّ، إِتِّي قَـايْلَه النَّـاسْ دَيْلْ كُلَّهُمْ فَـاضْـيِـينْ كَـدِي مَـا عِنْدَهُنْ أَيّ شَغَلَهْ، كُلَّ مَا مَرَّهْ يَجُوكُمْ يَسْأَلُوا مِنَّكُمْ، اَ؟ كَدَا قُـولْ لَيْ، إِتِّي كُتِّي[4] بِتَنْضُمِي مَعَ مْنُو؟ مَعَ الْبِتّ اَلـسَّـمْـحَـه دِيكْ اَلجَّاتْ زَارَتْ عَادِلْ فَالإِسْتِبَالِيَهْ؟[5]

أ: يَاهَا زَاتْهَا يَا خَالْتِي، مُشْ حِلْوَهْ عَلَيْكْ أَللَّهْ؟

ب: اَرَيْتْـهَـا يَـا يَمَّـا، سَـمَـاحْـةْ اَلْبَنُّوتْ لِحَدِّهِنْ، ظَرِيفَـهْ وَدَمّـهَـا خَفِيـفْ، يَهْ! وَلَـيْهَا نُورَهْ.

أ: هَايْ، لَكِنْ شَكَّرْتِيهَا مَا خَلَّيْتِي لْهَا حَاجَهْ. كَانْ مَا عَاجَبْتِكْ مَا كَانْ قُتِّي فِيهَا كِدَا.

ب: اَلْحَقّ لِلَّه، عَـادْ يَـا بِتِّي، قَـاطْعَـه الْكَلاَمْ، مَـا فِـيـهَـا قَـوْلْ، أَنَـا عَايَنْتَ لَيْهَا مِنْ فَوْقْ لِيتِحِتْ.

A: min ʃaʕaraa lii-ḍufurhaa.[6]

B: ay, w-aḷḷaahii yammaa tabbaara.

A: aywa.

B: ʕaad ḥaaja tamaam attamaam.

A: ʕaajabitik?

B: ay, w-aḷḷaahii ʕaajabatnii, maa fiihaa gool kulluu kulluu. ʔillaa guulii leey, ʕaadil ʔaxuuk xaattii baaluu ʕaleehaa, maa kadii?

A: w-aḷḷaahii yaʕnii ḥaaja zayy dii kidaa.

B: laa naa ʕaarfa.

C: titwaswasan wa-titnasnasan bi-tguulan fii ʃnuu ʔittan allitneen, ʔah ...?[7]

B: maa gulnaa ʃii, laakin b-aduur ʔasʔalik.

C: ay?

B: albiiniyya[8] jjaat ʃaafat ʕaadil fi lʔisbitaaliya, ʕaad ʃin guulik fiihaa?

C: w-aḷḷaahii, ʕaad gaaṭʕa lgool, bitt tamaam. hii maa zamiilat ʕaadil, ʔittii gaayla ʃnuu?

B: ah.

C: maḥaamiyya maʕuu fii lmaktab.

أ: مِنْ شَعَرْهَا لِيضُفُرْهَا.[6]

ب: اَيْ، وَاللّٰهِ يمَّا تبَّرَهْ.

أ: اَيْوَهْ.

ب: عَادْ حَاجَهْ تمَامْ اَلتَّمَامْ.

أ: عَاجَبتِك؟

ب: اَيْ، وَاللّٰهِ عَاجَبَتْنِي، مَا فِيهَا قَوْلْ كُلّهُ كُلّهُ. إلاَّ قُولِي لَيّ، عَادِلْ أَخُوكْ خَاتِّي بَالْهُ عَلَيْهَا، مَا كَدِي؟

أ: وَاللّٰهِ يَعْنِي حَاجَهْ زَيّ دِي كِدَا.

ب: لاَ انَا عَارْفَهْ.

ت: تِتْوَسْوَسَنْ وَتِتْنَسْنَسَنْ بِتْقُولَنْ فِي شْنُو إِتَّنْ اَلاِتّْنَيْنْ، أَهْ ...؟[7]

ب: مَا قُلْنَا شِي، لَكِنْ بَادُورْ أَسْأَلِكْ.

ت: اَيْ؟

ب: اَلْبِينِيَّه[8] الجَّاتْ شَافَتْ عَادِلْ فَالإِسْبِتَالِيَهْ، عَادْ شِنْ قُولِكْ فِيهَا؟

ت: وَاللّٰه، عَادْ قَاطْعَه الْقَوْلْ، بِتّ تَمَامْ. هِي مَا زَمِيلَةْ عَادِلْ، إِتِّي قَايْلَهْ شْنُو؟

ب: اَهْ.

ت: مَحَامِيَّهْ مَعْهُ فِي الْمَكْتَبْ.

B: ʕaarfa.

C: muʃ ʔisimmaa hudaa yaa raʃaa?

A: hiya zaataa.

C: baʕdeen bi-lmunaasab alkalaam daa maa mumkin yikuun saakit, laazim yikuun alkalaam daa waraahuu kalaam, guulii yaa miryam, yaa xtii.

B: yaa xtii, b-nisʔal saakit, maa nisʔal?

ب: عَارْفَهْ.

ت: مُشْ إِسِمّهَا هُدَى يَا رَشَا؟

أ: هِيَ زَاتْهَا.

ت: بَعْدَيْنْ بِالْمُنَاسَبْ اَلْكَلَامْ دَا مَا مُمْكِنْ يِكُونْ سَاكِتْ، لَازِمْ يِكُونْ الْكَلَامْ دَا وَرَاهُ كَلَامْ، قُولِي يَا مِرْيَمْ، يَا خْتِي.

ب: يَا خْتِي، بْنِسْأَلْ سَاكِتْ، مَا نِسْأَلْ؟

## Vocabulary

**guul** قَول **[gool]** *nms* opinion; act of speaking {*pl:* **agwaal**}

**sitt** سِتّ *nfs* lady; married woman {*pl:* **sittaat**}

**maamaa** مَاما *nfs* mamma; affectionate form of address to a young woman

**baalaɣ** بَالَغ *vi* to be absent for too long (used jokingly); to go overboard *(lit. to do s.t. too much or too long; to exaggerate)* {*imperf:* **yabaaliɣ**, *vn:* **mubaalaɣa**}

**illaa** إلاّ *particle* of all things, imagine (of a sudden or unexpected development); come on, you can't be serious (introduces skeptical question)

**itṣadam** اِتْصَدَم *vi* to be hit, be in a collision; to be deeply shocked {*imperf:* **yitṣadim**, *vn:* **ṣadim**}

**faaḍii** فَاضِي *adj* unoccupied, having free time; empty {*fs:* **faaḍya**, *mpl:* **faaḍyiin**, *fpl:* **faaḍyaat**}

**kulla maa marra** كُلّ مَا مَرَّة each time, every time, each and every time

**sa?al min-** سَأَل مِن *vi* to check on, ask after s.o. {*imperf:* **yas?al min-**, *vn:* **su?aal min-**}

**samiḥ** سَمِح *adj* pretty, beautiful; pleasant; good {*fs:* **samḥa**, *mpl:* **samḥiin**, *fpl:* **samḥaat**}

**istibaaliya** اَسْتِبَالِيَة **[istibaaliya]** *nfs* hospital {*pl:* **istibaalyaat**}

**areet** اَرَيْت **[yaa reet]** *disc marker* would that, if only (indicates contrary-to-fact wish)

**yammaa** يَمَّا *interj* o mamma (exclamation used by women)

**samaaḥa** سَمَاحَة *nfs* beauty

**areet- samaaḥt albannuut li-ḥaddihin** اَرَيْت سَمَاحْة اَلْبَنُّوت لِحَدِّهِن if only the other girls were so pretty (used proverbially by women) *(lit. if only the beauty of the little girls [was] to their limit)*

**damm xafiif** دَم خَفِيف nice, easy to get along with

**yeh** يَه *interj* my goodness (with exaggerated intonation, an expression of admiration)

**nuura** نُورَة *nfs* beautiful glow

**alḥagg li-llaahi** اَلْحَقّ لِلّه as God is my witness (in self-validation); to tell the truth, to be fair (in support of a statement with which one does not agree) *(lit. truth belongs to God)*

**ʕaad** عَادْ *adv* actually; if you ask me; as a matter of fact

**gaaṭiʕ alkalaam** قَاطِعْ اَلْكَلاَمْ the last word, the living end, the ultimate (high praise) *(lit. cutting off speech)* {*fs:* **gaaṭʕa lkalaam,** *mpl:* **gaaṭʕiin alkalaam,** *fpl:* **gaaṭʕaat alkalaam**}

**gool** قَوْلْ **[guul]** *nms* opinion; act of speaking {*pl:* **agwaal**}

**maa fii- gool** مَا فِي قَوْلْ there is nothing bad to say about s.o., there is nothing to say against s.o.

**ḍufur** ضُفُرْ *nms* toenail; fingernail {*pl:* **ḍufuur**}

**tabbaara** تَبَّارَهْ *nfs* admirable woman; (a kind of) flower

**tamaam** تَمَامْ *adj invariable* complete, perfect; *adj* completely

**tamaam attamaam** تَمَامْ اَلتَّمَامْ absolutely perfect

**baal** بَالْ *nms* intention; mind

**xatta baal- ʕalaa** خَتَّ بَالْ عَلَى to have an eye on; to be preoccupied by; to care about {*imperf:* **yaxutt baal- ʕalaa,** *vn:* **xatt baal- ʕalaa,** *vn:* **xatataan baal- ʕalaa**}

**maa kadii** مَا كَدِي **[miʃ kidaa]** right, isn't that so

**itwaswas** اِتْوَسْوَسْ *vi* to whisper; to gossip, talk about s.o. behind s.o.'s back {*imperf:* **yitwaswas,** *vn:* **tawaswus**}

**itnasnas fii** اِتْنَسْنَسْ فِي *vi* to poke into, snoop {*imperf:* **yitnasnas,** *vn:* **nasnas**}

**ittan** اِتَّنْ *pron fp* you

**daar (durta)** دَارْ (دُرْتَ) *vt* to want {*imperf:* **yaduur,** *vn:* **door**}

**biniyya** بِنِيَّهْ **[biiniyya]** *nfs diminutive* little girl {*pl:* **biniyyaat, bannuut**}

**isbitaaliya** اِسْبِتَالِيَهْ **[istibaaliya]** *nfs* hospital {*pl:* **isbitaalyaat**}

## Notes

**1** In the phrase /**maʕaak ay**/ 'I'm still on the line, yes, lit. with you (fs), yes', the final /i/ of the 2FS suffixed pronoun /**-aki**/ is elided. In slower or more careful speech, this phrase is pronounced /**maʕaaki ʔay**/.

**2** The question /**fiihaa ʃnuu**/ 'what's wrong with that (fs)?, lit. what is in it (fs)?' has the 3FS suffixed pronoun /**-haa**/ but no clear reference for that pronoun. In cases like this, where a pronoun referent is vague, unclear, or unknown, SA and certain other varieties of spoken Arabic use the 3FS form.

3 The question /**huu lfi lguluub daa fii zool b-iiʕarfuu?**/ 'does any mere human know what's in another person's heart?, lit. it (ms) that is in hearts, that (ms), is there a person who knows it (ms)?' is rhetorical. It is a reference to the Muslim belief that only God knows what is hidden from human sight, including human thoughts and intentions.

4 The form /**kuttii**/ 'you (fs) were' derives from the verb /**kaan**/ 'to be'. The root consonant /n/ of /**kaan**/ is assimilated to the /t/ of the perfect suffix to produce /**kuttii**/ rather than /**kuntii**/. A similar assimilation is described in selection 12, note 2.

5 The form /**l?istibaaliyya**/ 'the hospital' looks familiar because it derives from a word related to the English "hospital." This form has a variant, /**isbitaaliyya**/, that occurs later in this selection. There is a single difference between the form cited here, /**istibaaliyya**/, and the form that occurs later, /**isbitaaliyya**/. The /t/ and /b/ have changed places, a process known as metathesis.

6 The speaker here says /**ḍufurhaa**/ 'her toenail', pronouncing the /**h**/ of the suffixed pronoun that would normally be elided, as in /**ḍufuraa**/. Whether this pronunciation is intentional or not, it casts greater prominence on an already emphatic statement.

7 The speaker uses 2FP inflections and pronouns in the utterance /**titwaswasan wa-titnasnasan bi-tguulan fii ʃnuu ?ittan allitneen, ?ah ?**/ 'you (fp) are whispering and gossiping, what are you (fp) two talking about, eh?' FP forms occur in other contexts (see selections 20 and 25), but more often in contexts like this one, where women speak to other women.

8 The form /**albiiniyya**/ 'sweet girl; girlie, lit. little girl' is a diminutive or noun form indicating small size. It derives from the noun /**bitt**/ 'girl'. Diminutives in SA, as in English, often indicate affection. They are used by most speakers but are especially frequent in the speech of women.

# alxalaawii fi ssuudaan

*This selection describes Qur'an schools in Sudan. Before the founding of a government school system, Qur'an schools gave boys the fundamentals of education. Today, as the speakers discuss, Qur'an schools have become an important part of the government school system.*

A: ḥa-nitkallam ʕan al ... ʕan al ... alḥaajaat ʔala ... al ... addiiniyya fi ssuudaan. ʔanaa kunta b-asmaʕ zamaan ʕan alxalaawii. laakin ʃuftaa hassii ʔa ... ʔala ... yaʕnii, yaʕnii zamaan niḥnaa lammaa kunnaa ṣuɣaar ʔa ... maa ku ... kaanat fii xalaawii laakin niḥnaa lbanaat maa kaanuu b-iwadduunaa ...

B: a ...

A: al ... alxalaawii dii hassaʕ dii, ḥattaa lbanaat biguu ywadduuhum.

B: a ...

A: yaʕnii dii ʔalḥaajaat addiiniyya. al ... al ... attaʕaaliim addiiniyya hassaʕ fi lwaḍaʕ alḥaalii fi lḥukuuma lmoojuuda dii bii ... bi-trakkiz katiir jiddan ʕalaa ttaʕliim bitaaʕ lxalaawii liʔannuu hassaʕ ʔanaa b-aʕrif ʔaṭfaal ...

B: [xxx] hassii ya rajaa ...

A: laa -naa b-aʕrif ʔaṭfaal hassii ḥaafiẓiin yaʕnii ṭṭifil talgaah ʕumruu ʔa ... tisʕa w-ʕaʃara sniin laakin ḥaffiẓuu ʔiṭnaaʃar wa-ṭalaaṭaaʃar w-arbaʕṭaaʃar juzuʔ min alɣurʔaan[1] ...

B: *okay*, maa ...

# اَلْخَلاَوِي فِالسُّودَانْ

أ: حَنـتْكَلَّمْ عَنْ اَلْـ... عَنْ اَلْـ... اَلْحَـاجَـاتْ أَلَـ... اَلْـ... اَلدِّينِيَّهْ فِالسُّودَانْ. أَنَا كُنْتَ بَاسْمَعْ زَمَانْ عَنْ اَلْخَلاَوِي. لَكِنْ شُفْتْهَا هَسِّي أَ... أَلَـ... يَعْنِي، يَعْنِي زَمَانْ نِحْنَا لَمَّا كُنَّا صُغَارْ اَ... مَا كُـ... كَانَتْ فِي خَلاَوِي لَكِنْ نِحْنَا اَلْبَنَاتْ مَا كَانُوا بِوَدُّونَا...

ب: اَ...

أ: اَلْـ... اَلْخَلاَوِي دِي هَسَّعْ دِي، حَتَّى اَلْبَنَاتْ بِقُوا يَوَدُّوهُمْ.

ب: اَ...

أ: يَعْنِي دِي أَلْحَاجَاتْ اَلدِّينِيَّهْ. اَلْـ... اَلْـ... اَلتَّعَالِيمْ اَلدِّينِيَّهْ هَسَّعْ فِالْوَضْعْ اَلْحَالِي فِالْحُكُومَه اَلْمَوْجُودَهْ دِي بِيـ... بِتْرَكِّزْ كَتِيرْ جِدّاً عَلَى التَّعْلِيمْ بِتَاعْ اَلْخَلاَوِي لأَنُّهْ هَسَّعْ أَنَا بَاعْرِفْ أَطْفَالْ...

ب: [xxx] هَسّي يَا رَجَا...

أ: لاَ انَا بَاعْرِفْ أَطْفَالْ هَسِّي حَافِظِينْ يَعْنِي الطِّفِلْ تَلْقَاهْ عُمْرُهْ أَ... تِسْعَهْ وْعَشَرَهْ سِنِينْ لَكِنْ حَفِّظُوهْ إِطْنَاشَرْ وَطَلاَطَاشَرْ وَارْبَعْطَاشَرْ جُزْءْ مِنْ اَلْغُرْآنْ[1]...

ب: okay، مَا ...

A: dii maa kaanat fii ...

B: maa ... maa fii ḥaaja, maa fii, maa fii ḥaaja jadiida, huum annaas deel aḍaafaahuu fiʕlan yaʕnii masalan guulii ...

A: aḥyoohaa maa ʔaḍaafoowaa, laakin ʔaḥyoohaa.

B: *okay*, ay, ʔaḥyoowaa wallaa nnaas bigat ʕandum yaʕnii ḥaaja zayy dii kidaa, ʔannuu masalan nnaas yamʃuu ytʕallamuu ddiin wa-ḥaajaat zayy dii kidaa.

A: ay, ay.

B: laakin dii moojuuda, yaʕnii lxalwa dii moojuuda. wa-ʔintii kaan badeetii ʕan nnaaḥya ddiiniyya dii maa -saasan ssuudaan huwa maa kaan fuu ttaʕliim, yaʕnii gabli ttaʕliim anniẓaamii daa ...

A: gabli ttaʕliim kaan fi lxalaawii.

B: bass kaan fii ʔalxalaawii, kwayyis? wa-baʕdeen taʕliim almara fi ssuudaan yaʕnii badaa bi ... yaʕnii ʔa ... muttaxxir min taʕliim arraajul. ʕaarfaʔ ṭabʕan bii-taʕliim rufaaʕa[2] ...

A: rufaaʕa walaa [xxx] ...

B: ay, wu-kidaa ʔannuu waaḥid ɣaatal ʕalaa ʔannuu ...

A: baabikir badrii.[3]

B: ay, baabikir badrii, ʔannuu masalan ammara laazim titʕallam w-ikuun ʕandaa naṣiib zayy alwalad.

أ: دِي مَا كَانَتْ فِي...

ب: مَا... مَا فِي حَاجَهْ، مَا فِي، مَا فِي حَاجَهْ جَدِيدَهْ، هُومْ اَلنَّاسْ دَيْلْ اَضَافَاهُ فِعْلاً يَعْنِي مَسَلاً قُولِي...

أ: اَحْيَوْهَا مَا أَضَافُوّهَا، لَكِنْ أَحْيَوْهَا.

ب: *okay*، اَيْ، أَحْيَوّهَا وَلاَّ النَّاسْ بِقَتْ عَنْدْهُمْ يَعْنِي حَاجَهْ زَيّ دِي كِدَا، أَنَّهُ مَسَلاً النَّاسْ يَمْشُوا يَتْعَلَّمُوا الدِّينْ وَحَاجَاتْ زَيّ دِي كِدَا.

أ: اَيْ، اَيْ.

ب: لَكِنْ دِي مَوْجُودَهْ، يَعْنِي الْخَلْوَهْ دِي مَوْجُودَهْ. وَإِنْتِي كَانْ بَدَيْتِي عَنْ النَّاحْيَه الدِّينِيَّهْ دِي مَا اسَاسًا السُّودَانْ هُوَ مَا كَانْ فَهُ التَّعْلِيمْ، يَعْنِي قَبْلِ التَّعْلِيمْ اَلنِّظَامِي دَا...

أ: قَبْلِ التَّعْلِيمْ كَانْ فِالْخَلاَوِي.

ب: بَسّ كَانْ فِي أَلْخَلاَوِي، كُوَيِّسْ؟ وَبَعْدَيْنْ تَعْلِيمْ اَلْمَرَاهْ فَالسُّودَانْ يَعْنِي بَدَا بِ... يَعْنِي أَ ... مُتَّاخِّرْ مِنْ تَعْلِيمْ اَلرَّجُلْ. عَارْفَهْ؟ طَبْعًا بِيتَعْلِيمْ رُفَاعَهْ[2]...

أ: رُفَاعَهْ وَلاَ [xxx] ...

ب: اَيْ، وكِدَا أَنَّهُ وَاحِدْ غَاتَلْ عَلَى أَنَّهُ ...

أ: بَابِكِرْ بَدْرِي.[3]

ب: اَيْ، بَابِكِرْ بَدْرِي، أَنَّهُ مَسَلاً اَلْمَرَّاهْ لاَزِمْ تِتْعَلَّمْ وِكُونْ عَنْدْهَا نَصِيبْ زَيّ اَلْوَلَدْ.

A: w-ibtadat fii rufaaʕa [xxx].

B: *okay*? fa-kaanuu nnaas zamaan yaʕnii lammaa badaa ttaʕliim fii ssuudaan wallaa lammaa badaa ʔalwaʕii fi ssuudaan kidaa kaanat hiya ʔal … aṭṭurug addiiniyya[4] ʔal … al … alb-iitaʕallim …

A: w-aṣṣuufiyya.

B: ay, maa ṭṭurug addiiniyya dii zaatiihaa ṣuufiyya ajjaat daxalat assuudaan.

A: a …

B: yaʕnii ʔassuu … li … ʔassuudaan daa lammaa xaʃʃaa lee llislaam, xaʃʃaa bi-ṭṭurug aṣṣuufiyya bitaaʕum dii.[5]

A: ṣaḥḥ.

B: aṭṭariiga ddardiiriyya, ṭṭariiga ʃʃaazaliyya, ṭṭariiga llaḥmadiyya,[6] deel xaʃʃuu w-ʕamaluu masaayid, fa-ʔalmasiid daa ʔallii hiyya lmaḥalla btaaʕt aʃʃeex ʔallii hiyya maḥalla …

A: b-iiʕallimuu fiihaa lɣurʔaan w-b-iiḥaffiðuu ʔayḍan lɣurʔaan.

B: aywa, maḥalla kabiira jiddan jiddan, yaʕnii nnaas maaxdiinnahaa[7] lii-ɣaraḍeen, yaʕnii zamaan aʃʃeex huwwa ʔa … huwa ʔazzool alb-iigraa mumkin yaʕnii ʕalaa ḥasab mafhuum annaas ʔannuu masalan li-gurbuu min aḷḷaa[8] wallaa kidaa mumkin yaʕaalij w-fii nafs alwakit mumkin yimsik alwalad bitaaʕak daa ʔa … ygaʕʕiduu leek w-iigarriihuu ʔalɣurʔaan, wa …

أ: وِابْتَدَتْ فِي رُفَاعَهْ [xxx].

ب: *okay*؟ فَكَانُوا النَّاسْ زَمَانْ يَعْنِي لَمَّا بَدَا التَّعْلِيمْ فِي السُّودَانْ وَلاَّ لَمَّا بَدَا أَلْوَعِي فِالسُّودَانْ كِدَا كَانَتْ هِيَ أَلْـ... اَلطُّرُقْ اَلدِّينِيَّهْ[4] أَلْـ... اَلْـ... اَلْبِيتَعَلِّمْـ...

أ: وَالصُّوفِيَّهْ.

ب: اَيْ، مَا الطُّرُقْ اَلدِّينِيَّهْ دِي زَاتِيهَا صُوفِيَّه الجَّاتْ دَخَلَتْ اَلسُّودَانْ.

أ: اَ...

ب: يَعْنِي أَلسُّو... لـ... أَلسُّودَانْ دَا لَمَّا خَشَّا لَيْهْ الاِّسْلاَمْ، خَشَّا بِالطُّرُقْ اَلصُّوفِيَّهْ بِتَاعْهُمْ دِي.[5]

أ: صَحّ.

ب: اَلطَّرِيقَه الدَّرْدِيرِيَّهْ، الطَّرِيقَه الشَّازْلِيَّهْ، الطَّرِيقَه الأَحْمَدِيَّهْ،[6] دَيْلْ خَشُّوا وْعَمَلُوا مَسَايِدْ، فَأَلْمَسِيدْ دَا أَلِّي هِيَّ الْمَحَلَّهْ بْتَاعْةْ اَلشَّيْخْ أَلِّي هِيَّ مَحَلَّهْ...

أ: بِيعَلِّمُوا فِيهَا الْغُرْآنْ وْبِيحَفِّظُوا أَيْضًا الْغُرْآنْ.

ب: اَيْوَهْ، مَحَلَّهْ كَبِيرَهْ جِدّاً جِدّاً، يَعْنِي النَّاسْ مَاخْدِينَّهَا[7] لِيغَرَضَيْنْ، يَعْنِي زَمَانْ اَلشَّيْخْ هُوَّ أَ... هُوَ أَلزَّوْلْ اَلْبِيقْرَا مُمْكِنْ يَعْنِي عَلَى حَسَبْ مَفْهُومْ اَلنَّاسْ أَنَّهُ مَسَلاً لِقُرْبَهُ مِنْ اَللَّهْ[8] وَلاَّ كِدَا مُمْكِنْ يَعَالِجْ وْفِي نَفْسْ اَلْوَكِتْ مُمْكِنْ يِمْسِكْ اَلْوَلَدْ بِتَاعَكْ دَا أَ... يْقَعِّدْهُ لَيْكْ وِيقَرِّيهْ أَلْغُرْآنْ، وَ...

A: yiiḥaffiẓuu.

B: wa … wa-yiiwarriihuu yaktib alʕarabii fi lluuḥ.

A: aywa.

أ: يِحَفِّظْهُ.

ب: وَ... وَيِيوَرِّيهُ يَكْتِبْ اَلْعَرَبِي فِاللُّوحْ.

أ: اَيْوَهْ.

## Vocabulary

**ḥaffaẓ** حَفَّظْ *vt* to cause s.o. to memorize; to teach s.o. (through memorization) {*imperf:* **yaḥaffiẓ**, *vn:* **taḥfiiẓ**}

**alɣurʔaan** اَلْغُرْآنْ *prop* the Qur'an (scripture of Islam)

**diin** دِينْ *nms* religion (specifically Islam) {*pl:* **adyaan**}

**rufaaʕa** رُفَاعَة *prop* Rufaa (town southeast of Khartoum on the Blue Nile)

**ɣaatal** غَاتَلْ *vt* to carry on a fight with, carry on a struggle with {*imperf:* **yaɣaatil**, *vn:* **muɣaatala**}

**naṣiib** نَصِيبْ *nms* fate, destiny; share, portion {*pl:* **naṣaayib**}

**waʕii** وَعِي *nms* consciousness; attention

**ṭariiga** طَرِيقَة *nfs* Sufi brotherhood, Sufi order; way, method {*pl:* **ṭurug**}

**ṣuufii** صُوفِي *adj* of Sufism, Islamic mysticism {*fs:* **ṣuufiyya**, *mpl:* **ṣuufiyyiin**, *fpl:* **ʃuufiyyaat**}

**masiid** مَسِيدْ *nms* mosque {*pl:* **masaayid**}

**axad** اَخَدْ *vt* to take up to use; to take, spend (time); to take, receive {*imperf:* **yaaxud**, *vn:* **axid**}

**maaxid** مَاخِدْ **[maaxud]** *adj* taking up to use; taking, getting, obtaining {*fs:* **maaxda**, *mpl:* **maaxdiin**, *fpl:* **maaxdaat**}

**mafhuum** مَفْهُومْ *nms* conception, notion, what is understood {*pl:* **mafaahiim**}

**gaʕʕad** قَعَّدْ *vt* to cause s.o. to sit, cause s.o. to stay {*imperf:* **yagaʕʕid**, *vn:* **gaʕʕeed**}

**luuḥ** لُوحْ *nms* tablet (piece of wood for reading and writing practice in a xalwa); wooden board, panel {*pl:* **alwaaḥ**}

## Notes

**1** The speaker's statement, /**ḥaffiẓuu ʔiṭnaaʃar wa-ṭalaaṭaaʃar w-arbaʕṭaaʃar juzuʔ min alɣurʔaan**/ 'they (mp) have made him memorize twelve, thirteen, fourteen juzuʔ of the Qur'an', is somewhat surprising. The Qur'an is divided into 30 juzuʔ or parts. Therefore, a child of nine or ten who has memorized somewhere between 12 and 14 of these has learned nearly half of the Muslim holy book by heart.

**2** The phrase /**taʕliim rufaaʕa**/ 'education in Rufaa' refers to the fact that Sheikh Babikir Badri (see selection 23, note 3) came from Rufaa, a town south-east of Khartoum, and began his career of educational reform there.

**3** The sheikh /**baabikir badrii**/ 'Babikr Badri' was an influential Muslim scholar who played a pioneering role in promoting the education of women in Sudan.

**4** The institutions known as /**aṭṭurug addiiniyya**/ 'the religious brotherhoods' are also referred to in English as 'Sufi orders'. Sufism is a movement in Islam that seeks a closer or more personal relationship with the deity. The brotherhoods or orders are institutions that guide the seeker and may prescribe special prayers, meditations, and other forms of spiritual discipline. Sufi brotherhoods first came to Sudan in the sixteenth century and by the eighteenth century had begun to play an important role there.

**5** Gender and number agreement is unusual in the phrase /**bi-ṭṭurug aṣṣuufiyya bitaaʕum dii**/ 'the Sufi brotherhoods belonging to them (mp)'. This phrase would more typically occur as /**bi-ṭṭurug aṣṣuufiyya bitaaʕtum dii**/ **'the Sufi brotherhoods belonging to them (mp)'**. This is because the possessive adjective /**bitaaʕ**/ usually agrees in number and gender with the noun phrase it modifies, /**ṭṭurug aṣṣuufiyya**/ 'the Sufi brotherhoods'.

**6** The speaker give the names /**aṭṭariiga ddardiiriyya, ṭṭariiga ʃʃaazaliyya, ṭṭariiga llaḥmadiyya**/ 'the Dardiriya brotherhood, the Shadhaliya brotherhod, the Ahmadiya brotherhood' as examples of Sufi brotherhoods in Sudan. These three brotherhoods continue to exist in Sudan and elsewhere.

**7** The speaker here says /**maaxdiinnahaa**/ 'people take it (fs) on' with a long /ii/ in the P suffix rather than a short /i/, as in /**bitaaʕinnuu**/ 'belonging (mp) to him (ms)'. Under certain circumstances, the long vowel is the preferred choice for some speakers of SA.

**8** According to this speaker, the sheikh is known for /**gurbuu min aḷḷaa**/ 'his closeness to God'. This closeness comes in part, as the speaker says, from the fact that the sheikh can read and has direct access to the scriptures. This gives him skills and knowledge that he can pass on to children in the Qur'an school and, perhaps, gifts that treat physical as well as spiritual disorders.

# laakin yoom alʕiid ...

*This selection begins by comparing the daily morning routine to the special events of a feast day. It finishes by describing the importance of the family slaughter of an animal on Eid al-Adha, the Feast of Sacrifice. For Sudanese living abroad, where animal slaughter is regulated, these memories are deeply nostalgic.*

A: a ... ṭṭabiiʕa bitaaʕt annaas ʔa ... fi lʕiid hinaak yaʕnii yoom alʕiid daa kulla, yaʕnii ʔizaa kaan fii ɣarya wallaa fi lmadiina kidaa, ʔaguul leek ʕan alɣarya -naa, yaʕnii niḥnaa min aṣṣabaaḥ bi-nguum b-iikuun fii ʃakil a ... faṭuur kidaa. b-ixtalif yaʕnii niḥnaa ʕaadatan bi-niʃrab fii ṣṣabaaḥ ʔawwal ḥaaja b-tabdaa beehaa bi-tiʃrab ʃaahii.

B: daa yoom alʕiid?

A: ma ... fi llayyaamaat alʕaadiyya ʔinta b-tuguum ...

B: haa ...

A: tiʃrab ʃaahii ʔala .... mawaaʕiid ala ... wa-la-ɣaayat assaaʕa ʕaʃara wallaa tizʕa kidaa b-tufṭur. yaʕnii maa, niḥnaa liʔanna ʔiḥtimaal naxtalif barḍuu ʃwayya kidaa min aʃʃuʕuub attaanya, maa b-naakul faṭuur awwal ḥaaja.

B: fi lbidaaya.

A: ay, bi-niʃrab ʃaahii fi ṣṣabaaḥ la-ɣaayat ala ... ssaaʕa tisʕa wallaa ʕaʃara kidaa ḥattaa baʕad daak nufṭur, nufṭur ...

B: aʃʃaahii ḥawaaleey sitta ...

A: ay, min badrii, annaas awwal maa gaamuu, ʔay.

# لَكِنْ يَوْمْ اَلعِيدْ ...

أ: اَ... الطَّبِيعَهْ بِتَاعْةْ اَلنَّاسْ أَ... فِالْعِيدْ هِنَاكْ يَعْنِي يَوْمْ اَلْعِيدْ دَا كُلَّهْ، يَعْنِي إِزَا كَانْ فِي غَرْيَهْ وَلاَّ فِالْمَدِينَهْ كِدَا، أَقُولْ لَيْكْ عَنْ اَلْغَرْيَه انَا، يَعْنِي نِحْنَا مِنْ اَلصَّبَاحْ بِنْقُومْ بِيكُونْ فِي شَكِلْ اَ... فَطُورْ كِدَا. بِخْتَلِفْ يَعْنِي نِحْنَا عَادَةً بِنِشْرَبْ فِي الصَّبَاحْ أَوَّلْ حَاجَهْ بْتَبْدَا بِيْهَا بْتِشْرَبْ شَاهِي.

ب: دَا يَوْمْ اَلْعِيدْ؟

أ: مَـ... فِالأَيَّامَاتْ اَلْعَادِيَّهْ إِنْتَ بْتُقُومْ...

ب: هَا...

أ: تِشْرَبْ شَاهِي أَلَـ... مَوَاعِيدْ اَلَـ... وَلَغَايَةْ اَلسَّاعَهْ عَشَرَهْ وَلاَّ تِزْعَهْ كِدَا بْتُفْطُرْ. يَعْنِي مَا، نِحْنَا لأَنَّ إِحْتِمَالْ نَخْتَلِفْ بَرْضُهْ شْوَيَّهْ كِدَا مِنْ اَلشُّعُوبْ اَلتَّانْيَهْ، مَا بْنَاكُلْ فَطُورْ اَوَّلْ حَاجَهْ.

ب: فِالْبِدَايَهْ.

أ: اَيْ، بِنِشْرَبْ شَاهِي فِالصَّبَاحْ لَغَايَةْ اَلَـ... السَّاعَهْ تِسْعَهْ وَلاَّ عَشَرَهْ كِدَا حَتَّى بَعَدْ دَاكْ نُفْطُرْ، نُفْطُرْ...

ب: اَلشَّاهِي حَوَالَيّ سِتَّهْ...

أ: اَيْ، مِنْ بَدْرِي، اَلنَّاسْ اَوَّلْ مَا قَامُوا، أَيْ.

B: sitta wa-nuṣṣ, sabʕa ṣabaaḥan liʔannuu bi-nuṣḥaa badrii ṣṣabaaḥ.

A: ay, laakin yoom alʕiid yoom b-ikuun muxtalif jiddan jiddan b-iikuun maʕ aʃʃaahii, fii faṭuur laakin faṭuur fuuh[1] sukkariyyaat yaʕnii. nnaas yaʕmaluu zalaabiya wa ... marraat ʃiʕiriyya yiguul leehaa ʃiʕiriyya yaʕnii ḥaaja zayy makaroona kidaa.

B: aw albiskaawiit.

A: fa-b-tilgaa, tilgaa ʔummak wallaa ʔuxtak wallaa kidaa ʕamaluu lḥaajaat dii badrii wa-ʃiribt aʃʃaahii. wa-ʔayyi zool b-ikuun ʕinduu ḥaaja jadiida li-lʕiid, ʕanduu libis jadiid yaʕnii ʔizaa kaan jallaabiyya ʔizaa kaan banṭaloon wa-gamiiṣ li-laṭfaal ʔizaa kaan ʃinuu ʔizaa kaan ʃinuu. w-annaas kullahaa yaʕnii zayy assaaʕa sabʕa, sabʕa wa-nuṣṣ kadaa bi-tabgaa *ready* kull albeet b-ikuun ṣaaḥii. ʔala ... yaʕnii ʔal ... anniswaan yijahhizuu ʔala ... ʔala ... ʔal ... albeet yifarriʃuu bi-ṣuura kwayyisa ya ... ḥaajaat zayy dii kidaa. ʔal ... arrujaal ya ... almihimm yaḥalguu, yjahhizuu ʔanfusum li-ṣṣalaa, fa-b-imruguu kulla naas alɣarya yimʃuu yṣalluu fii maydaan kabiir jiddan jiddan. ʕaadatan albanaat aṣṣuɣaar w-anniswaan maa b-imruguu li-ṣṣalaa dii,[2] b-imʃuu bagaa nniswaan alkubaar wa-kull ar ... rrujaal, yaʕnii ḥattaa lʔaṭfaal aṣṣuɣaar b-imʃuu, yaʕnii lʔaṭfaal deel ʔizaa kaanuu min ajjinseen b-imruguu. fa-b-tilgii barraa fiʕlan fii mahrajaan bitaaʕ ʔalwaan bitaaʕat malaabis jadiida ṭaalʕa lleela w-annaas yihalliluu w-ikabbiruu yaʕnii fil ... fii ssaaḥa lʔamaam alɣarya dii. fa-yaʕnii ʔal ... ʔal ...

ب: سِتَّهْ وَنُص، سَبْعَهْ صَبَاحًا لأنَّهُ بِنُصْحَى بَدْرِي الصَّبَاحْ.

أ: اَيْ، لَكِنْ يَوْمْ اَلعِيدْ يَوْمْ بِكُونْ مُخْتَلِفْ جِدّاً جِدّاً بِيكُونْ مَعَاهْ الشَّاهِي، فِي فَطُورْ لَكِنْ فَطُورْ فْيهُ[1] سُكَّرِيَّاتْ يَعْنِي. النَّاسْ يَعْمَلُوا زَلَابِيَهْ وَ... مَرَّاتْ شِعِرِيَّهْ يِقُولْ لَيْهَا شِعِرِيَّهْ يَعْنِي حَاجَهْ زَيّ مَكَرُونَهْ كِدَا.

ب: اَوْ اَلْبِسْكَاوِيتْ.

أ: فَبْتِلْقَى، تِلْقَى أُمَّكْ وَلاَّ أُخْتَكْ وَلاَّ كِدَا عَمَلُوا الْحَاجَاتْ دِي بَدْرِي وَشَرِبْتْ اَلشَّاهِي. وَأَيِّ زَوْلْ بِكُونْ عِنْدُهْ حَاجَهْ جَدِيدَهْ لِلْعِيدْ، عِنْدُهْ لِبِس جَدِيدْ يَعْنِي إِزَا كَانْ جَلاَّبِيَّهْ إِزَا كَانْ بَنْطَلَوْنْ وَقَمِيصْ لِلأَطْفَالْ إِزَا كَانْ شِنُو إِزَا كَانْ شِنُو. وَالنَّاسْ كُلَّهَا يَعْنِي زَيّ اَلسَّاعَهْ سَبْعَهْ، سَبْعَهْ وَنُص كِدَا بِتَبْقَى *ready* كُلَّ الْبَيْتْ بِكُونْ صَاحِي. أَلَـ... يَعْنِي أَلْـ... اَلنِّسْوَانْ يِجَهِّزُوا أَلَـ... أَلَـ... أَلْـ... اَلْبَيْتْ يِفَرِّشُوا بِصُورَهْ كُوَيِّسَهْ يَـ... حَاجَاتْ زَيّ دِي كِدَا. أَلْـ... اَلرُّجَالْ يَـ ... اَلْمِهِمّ يَحَلْقُوا، يْجَهِّزُوا أَنْفُسْهُمْ لِلصَّلاَهْ، فَبِمْرُقُوا كُلَّ نَاسْ اَلْغَرْيَهْ يِمْشُوا يْصَلُّوا فِي مَيْدَانْ كَبِيرْ جِدّاً جِدّاً. عَادَةً اَلْبَنَاتْ اَلصُّغَارْ وَالنِّسْوَانْ مَا بِمْرُقُوا لِلصَّلاَهْ دِي،[2] بِمْشُوا بَقَى النِّسْوَانْ اَلْكُبَارْ وَكُلَّ رْ... الرُّجَالْ، يَعْنِي حَتَّى الأَطْفَالْ اَلصُّغَارْ بِمْشُوا، يَعْنِي الأَطْفَالْ دَيْلْ إِزَا كَانُوا مِنْ اَلْجِنْسَيْنْ بِمْرُقُوا. فَبْتِلْقِي بَرَّا فِعْلاً فِي مَهْرَجَانْ بِتَاعْ أَلْوَانْ بِتَاعَةْ مَلاَبِسْ جَدِيدَهْ طَالْعَه اللَّيْلَهْ وَالنَّاسْ يِهَلِّلُوا وِكَبِّرُوا يَعْنِي فَالْـ... فِي السَّاحَه الأَمَامْ اَلْغَرْيَهْ دِي. فَيَعْنِي أَلْـ... أَلْـ...

ʔal … ʔal … daa, daa, daa fi lʔiid daa, ʕiid, ʕiid, daa fii ʕiid ramaḍaan yaʕnii. liʔannuu maa fuuhuu dabiiḥa, daak alʕiid daak annaas bi-yiḍbaḥuu baʕad maa …

B: ʕiid alʔaḍḥaa.

A: yimʃuu ṣṣalaa barḍuu wa-yiijuu xaaʃʃiin, ʔiḥtimaal fiʕlan fi lʕiid bitaaʕ aḍḍaḥiyya[3] ʔayyi zool iiḥaawil yijrii beetuu, maa yimʃii ṭawwaalii li-nnaas attaaniyiin. leeh? ʕaʃaan yimʃii yaḍbaḥ.[4]

B: yiḍbaḥ alxaruuf liʔannuu ʔalxaruuf law ḍabaḥtuu ṣṣabaaḥ badrii …

A: ay.

B: ʕinduu ʔajri muḥaddad ʔaw almaksab minnuu ʕind rabbanaa[5] …

A: akbar.

B: akbar.

A: w-inta daayir annaas yaakluu zaatuu.

B: aḍḍiḥaa baʕd aṣṣalaa ʕinduu, ʕinduu ʔakbar. li … ʔaw aḍḍuhur b-iikuun ʔagilla ʔa … hinaay, ʔagilla …

A: almuhimm yaʕnii dii, dii, dii ḥaajaat zayyi diiniyya kidaa nnaas b-iisawwaa, laakin …

B: b-asmaʕ kidaa.

أَلْـ... أَلْـ... دَا، دَا، دَا فَـالْعِيـدْ دَا، عِـيـدْ، عِـيـدْ، دَا فِي عِـيـدْ رَمَـضَـانْ يَـعْنِـي. لأَنّـهُ مَـا فُـوهُ دَبِيـحَـهْ، دَاكْ اَلْعِيـدْ دَاكْ اَلنَّاس بِيِضْبَحُوا بَعَدْ مَا...

ب: عِيدْ اَلأَضْحَى.

أ: يِمْشُوا الصَّلاَهْ بَرْضُهْ وَيِيجُوا خَاشِّينْ، إِحْتِمَالْ فِعْلاً فَالْعِيدْ بِتَـاعْ اَلضَّحِيَّـهْ[3] أَيِّ زَوْلْ يْحَـاوِلْ يِجْرِي بَيْتُـهْ، مَـا يِمْـشِي طَوَّالِي لِلنَّاسْ اَلتَّانِيِينْ. لَيْهْ؟ عَشَانْ يِمْشِي يَضْبَحْ.[4]

ب: يِضْبَحْ اَلْخَرُوفْ لأَنّهُ أَلْخَرُوفْ لَوْ ضَبَحْتُهْ الصَّبَاحْ بَدْرِي...

أ: اَيْ.

ب: عِنْدُهْ أَجْرِ مُحَدَّدْ أَوْ اَلْمَكْسَبْ مِنّهُ عِنْدْ رَبَّنَا[5]...

أ: اَكْبَرْ.

ب: اَكْبَرْ.

أ: وِانْتَ دَايِرْ اَلنَّاسْ يَاكْلُوا زَاتُهْ.

ب: اَلضِّحَى بَعْدْ اَلصَّلاَهْ عِنْدُهْ، عِنْدُهْ أَكْبَرْ. لِـ... أَوْ اَلضُّهُرْ بِيكُونْ أَقَلَّ أَ... هِنَايْ، أَقَلَّ...

أ: اَلْمُهِمّ يَعْنِي دِي، دِي، دِي حَاجَاتْ زَيِّ دِينِيَّهْ كِدَا النَّاسْ بِيسَوَّى، لَكِنْ...

ب: بَاسْمَعْ كِدَا.

A: alwaaḥid b-iimʃii yaḍbaḥ ʕal aasaas innuu masalan fiʕlan yiḥassis annaas bi-ʔannuu huwwa ʔala … annaas fii ʕiid wa-ʕani … ʕalaa lʔagall yaḍman ʔannuu xaruufuu nnaas akaluuhuu. wa … ʔa … yaʕnii li … li … fiʕlan albalad ʔa … fiihaa ḥaajaat yaʕnii niḥ … fagadnaa ʃadiid jiddan jiddan hassaʕ alyoomeen deel fii … fi lʕiid hinaa w-ḥaajaat zayy dii.

أَ: اَلْوَاحِدْ بِيِمْشِي يَضْبَحْ عَلَى اَسَاسْ اِنّهُ مَسَلاً فِعْلاً يِحَسِّسْ اَلنَّاسْ بِأَنّهُ هُوَّ أَلَ... اَلنَّاسْ فِي عِيدْ وَعَنِ... عَلَى الأَقَلّ يَضْمَنْ أَنّهُ خَرُوفْهُ النَّاسْ اَكَلُوهُ. وَ... أَ... يَعْنِي لِ... لِ ... فِعْلاً اَلْبَلَدْ أَ... فِيهَا حَاجَاتْ يَعْنِي نِحْ... فَقَدْنَا شَدِيدْ جِدّاً جِداً هَسَّعْ اَلْيَوْمَيْنْ دَيْلْ فِي... فَالْعِيدْ هِنَا وْحَاجَاتْ زَيّ دِي.

## Vocabulary

**gaam (gumta)** (قُمْتَ) قَامْ *vi also pre-verb* to wake up, get up; to get up (in order to do s.t.); to do, go ahead and do (as a consequence or result of a previously described event); to up and (do s.t.), suddenly (do); to get up, stand up {*imperf:* **yaguum**, *vn:* **giyaam**, *vn:* **gooma**}

**faṭuur** فَطُورْ *nms* breakfast

**ʃaahii** شَاهِي *nms* tea {*pl:* **ʃawaahii**}

**iḥtimaal** اِحْتِمَالْ *nms* possibility; *adv* probably {*pl:* **iḥtimaalaat**}

**ṣiḥaa** صِحَى *vi* to awaken {*imperf:* **yaṣḥaa**, *vn:* **ṣaḥayaan**}

**sukkariyyaat** سُكَّرِيَّاتْ *nfpl* sweets, candies

**zalaabiya** زَلاَبِيَهْ *nfs* zalabiya (a kind of pastry fried and soaked in syrup)

**ʃiʕiriyya** شِعِرِيَّهْ *nfs* shiʕiriya (a kind of sweet made of fine spaghetti)

**makaroona** مَكَرُونَهْ *nfs* pasta

**biskawiit** بِسكَوِيتْ *nms collective* cookies {*fs:* **biskawiita**, *pl:* **biskawiitaat**}

**banṭaloon** بَنْطَلُونْ *nms* pair of pants, pair of trousers {*pl:* **banaaṭliin**}

**gamiiṣ** قَمِيصْ *nms* shirt {*pl:* **gumṣaan**}

**ṣaaḥii** صَاحِي *adj* awake {*fs:* **ṣaaḥya**, *mpl:* **ṣaaḥyiin**, *fpl:* **ṣaahyaat**}

**farraʃ** فَرَّشْ *vt* to put fresh covers on cushions and beds; to furnish; to set up, set out s.t. {*imperf:* **yafarriʃ**, *vn:* **faraʃ**}

**ṣalaa** صَلاَهْ *nfs* prayer {*pl:* **ṣalawaat**}

**marag** مَرَقْ *vt* to go out, exit; to release, set free {*imperf:* **yamrug**, *vn:* **muruug**}

**maydaan** مَيْدَان **[meedaan]** *nms* city square; playing field {*pl:* **mayaadiin**}

**mahrajaan** مَهْرَجَان *nms* festival, fair {*pl:* **mahrajaanaat**}

**ṭaaliʕ** طَالِع *adj* appearing; going out; going up {*fs:* **ṭaalʕa**, *mpl:* **ṭaalʕiin**, *fpl:* **ṭaalʕaat**}

**hallal** هَلَّل *vi* to praise God by saying /laa ʔilaaha ʔillaa ḷḷaah/ 'there is no god but God' {*imperf:* **yahallil**, *vn:* **tahliil**}

**kabbar** كَبَّر *vi* to praise God by saying /aḷḷaahu ʔakbar/ (i.e, 'God is great') {*imperf:* **yakabbir**, *vn:* **takbiir**}

**saaḥa** سَاحَة *nfs* city square; open space in or near village, town, or city {*pl:* **saaḥaat**}

**ajur** أَجُر *nms* recompense; wages

**ḍiḥaa** ضِحَى **[ḍaḥaa]** *nms* morning; late morning

**almuhimm** اَلْمُهِمّ **[(al)muhim; (al)mihim(ma)]** *disc marker* the important thing is; the fact is (indicates return to topic after digression; precedes and indicates evaluative comment)

**ḥassas** حَسَّس *vt* to make s.o. feel {*imperf:* **yaḥassis**, *vn:* **taḥsiis**}

## Notes

**1** The form /**fuuh**/ 'it (ms) has, lit. in it (ms)' is a variant of /**fiihuu**/ or /**fiih**/.

**2** The speaker states that /**ʕaadatan albanaat aṣṣuɣaar w-anniswaan maa b-imruguu li-ṣṣalaa dii**/ 'usually young girls and married women do not go out for this prayer'. This is not limited to holidays. Girls and married women, for a variety of reasons, rarely take part in public prayer. When they pray, they usually pray at home.

**3** The feast this speaker calls /**lʕiid bitaaʕ aḍḍaḥiyya**/ 'the feast of the slaughter' is also known as 'Eid al-Adha' or /**ʕiid alʔaḍḥaa**/. It falls at the end of the hajj or Muslim pilgrimage to Mecca. The slaughter is carried out by every family who is able to, whether the animal be as small as a pigeon or as large as a cow. It commemorates the prophet Abraham's willingness to sacrifice his son.

**4** Note the sound change in the form /**yaḍbaḥ**/ 'he slaughters' (compare with MSA <u>ðabaḥ</u> 'to slaughter'). The Arabic letter ذ also becomes /**d**/ in SA or, in words borrowed more recently from MSA, /**z**/.

**5** What the speaker describes as /**ʔajri muḥaddad ʔaw almaksab minnuu ʕind rabbanaa** …/ 'a specific recompense, or the return for it (ms) from our Lord …'

would be less if the slaughter were made later in the day. Muslims follow the example of the prophet Abraham and the prophet Muhammad, both of whom made their slaughter early in the day.

# karaamaat alʔawliyaa

*This selection comes from an interview conducted with a teenager from al-Shamaliyya Province. The interviewer is openly skeptical about the young man's stories of miracles performed by holy men. The young man, however, insists that these things actually happen. Note that his speech differs from that of the region of the capital, especially in his use of the feminine plural.*

A: fii ḥitta ʔisimaa ʔumm ʃiinaʃiin fi waaḥid ismuu lfakii ʕalii.

B: naʕam.

A: baʕdeen ʔa …

B: taʕrif …

A: kaan b-ibnuu luuh fii jaamiʕ.[1]

B: … ismuu? lfakii ʕalii wad minuu?[2] taʕrifuu?

A: afakkir muusaa w-aḷḷaahii maa b-aʕrif, alfakii ʕalii bass.

B: naʕam. fii ween? ʔumm ʃiinaʃiin?

A: fii ḥitta ʔisimaa ʔumm ʃiinaʃiin.

B: naʕam.

A: baʕdeen gaam, gaam b-yibnuu fii, ʔay, kubba[3] kidaa, baʕdeen maa tammat, xalaaṣ, aṭṭuub gaṣṣar [xxx] w-ajjamaaʕa ʔiḍḍayguu kidaa, lamman aṣbaḥuu ṣṣabaaḥ liguuhaa matmuuma.

B: yaa salaam.

A: baʕdeen barḍuu ʃʃeex ḥasan daa barḍuu jaahuu jaamaʕ naazil min assamaa.

# كَرَامَاتْ اَلأَوْلِيَا

أ: فِي حِتَّهْ إِسِمْهَا أُمّ شِينَشِينْ فِوَاحِدْ اِسْمُهُ الْفَكِي عَلِي.

ب: نَعَمْ.

أ: بَعْدَيْنْ أ...

ب: تَعْرِفْ...

أ: كَانْ بِبْنُوا لُهُ فِي جَامِعْ.[1]

ب: ... إِسْمُهُ؟ الْفَكِي عَلِي وَدْ مِنُو؟[2] تَعْرِفُه؟

أ: اَفَكِّرْ مُوسَى وَاللَّهِ مَا بَاعْرِفْ، اَلْفَكِي عَلِي بَسّ.

ب: نَعَمْ. فِي وَيْنْ؟ أُمّ شِينَشِينْ؟

أ: فِي حِتَّهْ إِسِمْهَا أُمّ شِينَشِينْ.

ب: نَعَمْ.

أ: بَعْدَيْنْ قَامْ، قَامْ بِيِبْنُوا فِي، أَيْ، كُبَّهْ[3] كِدَا، بَعْدَيْنْ مَا تَمَّتْ، خَلاَصْ، اَلطُّوبْ قَصَّرْ [xxx] وَالجَّمَاعَهْ إِضَّيْقُوا كِدَا، لَمَّا اَصْبَحُوا الصَّبَاحْ لِقُوهَا مَتْمُومَهْ.

ب: يَا سَلاَمْ.

أ: بَعْدَيْنْ بَرْضُهُ الشَّيْخْ حَسَنْ دَا بَرْضُهُ جَاهُ جَامَعْ نَازِلْ مِنْ اَلسَّمَا.

B: itta ʃuftaa, algubba[3] ʃuftaa?

A: ay, ʃuftaa.

B: algubba ʃuftahaa?

A: ay, lamman algubba[3] tammat dii kulla ʔannawaaḥii bitaaʕat alɣuraa dii kullaa ʔijtamaʕat ʃaafitaa.

B: haa, haa … naʕam. baʕdeen gutta taanii ʃʃeex ḥasan maaluu?

A: barḍuu nazal leehuu jaamiʕ kaamil min assamaa.

B: jaamiʕ kaamil nizil?

A: jaamiʕ kaamil nizil.

B: haa … ʔitta ʃuft ajjaamiʕ daa?

A: aywa ʃuftuu.

B: ahaa … ʔaa ṭayyib, taanii ʃnuu b-iiguuluu?

A: baʕdeen yaahuu taanii fi waaḥid kidaa bitaaʕ attaksii[4] …

B: aywa.

A: kaan maʕaahuu, raakbaat maʕaahuu banaat gaal leehuu, 'twaddiinaa ṭṭunḍub li-ʃʃeex alfaaḍil.'

B: naʕam.

A: baʕdeen hun maa bi-yaʕrifan aṭṭunḍub dii, bass saamʕaat beehuu maaʃaatan leehuu[5] li-ziyaara.

ب: إِتَّ شُفْتْهَا، اَلْقُبَّهْ[3] شُوفْتْهَا؟

أ: اَيْ، شُفْتْهَا.

ب: اَلْقُبَّهْ شُفْتَهَا؟

أ: اَيْ، لَمَّنْ اَلْقُبَّهْ[3] تَمَّتْ دِي كُلَّ أَلنَّوَاحِي بِتَاعَةْ اَلْغُرَى دِي كُلّهَا إِجْتَمَعَتْ شَافِتَها.

ب: هَا، هَا... نَعَمْ. بَعْدَيْنْ قُتَّ تَانِي الشَّيْخْ حَسَنْ مَالُه؟

أ: بَرْضُهُ نَزَلْ لَيْهُ جَامِعْ كَامِلْ مِنْ اَلسَّمَا.

ب: جَامِعْ كَامِلْ نَزِلْ؟

أ: جَامِعْ كَامِلْ نَزِلْ.

ب: هَا... إِتَّ شُفْتْ اَلْجَّامِعْ دَا؟

أ: اَيْوَهْ شُفْتْهُ.

ب: اَهَا... اَ طَيِّبْ، تَانِي شْنُو بِيقُولُوا؟

أ: بَعْدَيْنْ يَاهُ تَانِي فِوَاحِدْ كِدَا بِتَاعْ اَلتَّكْسِي[4] ...

ب: اَيْوَهْ.

أ: كَانْ مَعَاهُ، رَاكْبَاتْ مَعَاهُ بَنَاتْ قَالْ لَيْهُ، «تْوَدِّينَا الطُّنْضُبْ لِلشَّيْخْ اَلْفَاضِلْ.»

ب: نَعَمْ.

أ: بَعْدَيْنْ هُنْ مَا بِيَعْرِفَنْ اَلطُّنْضُبْ دِي، بَسّ سَامْعَاتْ بَيْهْ مَاشَاتَنْ لَيْهُ[5] لِلزِّيَارَهْ.

B: haa ... maaʃaat min ween?

A: w-aḷḷaahii jaayaat min xarṭuum almiinaa.

B: aywa.

A: maaʃaat leehuu[5] hinaak fii ma ... fii ... fi ṭṭunḍub.

B: naʕam.

A: baʕdeen bitaaʕ attaksii yaʕnii ḥabb innuu yatuuh beehun wallaa kidaa, gaam fakk aʃʃaariʕ miʃaa beehun ṭawiil li-giddaam, miʃaa, marag baʕiid xaaliṣ.

B: a ...

A: baʕdeen ʔa ... kaan ... jaa ṣagur li-ʕarabiituu ba-lgizaaz kidaa ḥamaahuu yimʃii.

B: haa ...

A: waggaf alʕarabiyya, lamman nazal, ligaa ʃʃeex alfaaḍil zaatuu, gaal leeh, 'ʔarjaʕ ba-darbak.' rajaʕ hinaak ṭawwaalii, rajaʕ aṭṭunḍub ligaa ʃʃeex alfaaḍil gaaʕid, ṭawwaalii waggaf ʕarabiituu wa-bigaa ḥwaar li-ʃʃeex alfaaḍil ḥattaa llaan, ḥattaa llaan gaaʕid maʕ aʃʃeex alfaaḍil, bigaa leehuu ḥiwaar.

B: la-ḥaddii llaan mawjuud?

A: la-ḥaddii llaan mawjuud.

ب: هَا... مَاشَاتْ مِنْ وَيْنْ؟

أ: وَاللَّهِ جَايَاتْ مِنْ خَرْطُومْ اَلْمِينَا.

ب: اَيْوَهْ.

أ: مَاشَاتْ لَيْهُ[5] هِنَاكْ فِي ... فِي مَـ... فَالطُّنْضُبْ.

ب: نَعَمْ.

أ: بَعْدَيْنْ بِتَاعْ اَلتَّكْسِي يَعْنِي حَبّ اِنّهُ يَتُوهْ بَيْهُنْ وَلاَّ كِدَا، قَامْ فَكَّ الشَّارِعْ مِشَى بَيهُنْ طَوِيلْ لِقِدَّامْ، مِشَى، مَرَقْ بَعِيدْ خَالِصْ .

ب: اَ...

أ: بَعْدَيْنْ أَ... كَانْ... جَا صَقُرْ لِعَرَبِيتْهُ بَالْقِزَازْ كِدَا حَمَاهُ يِمْشِي.

ب: هَا ...

أ: وَقَّفْ اَلْعَرَبِيَّهْ، لَمَّنْ نَزَلْ، لِقَى الشَّيْخْ اَلْفَاضِلْ زَاتْهُ، قَالْ لَيْهْ، «أَرْجَعْ بَدَرْبَكْ.» رَجَعْ هِنَاكْ طَوَّالِي، رَجَعْ اَلطُّنْضُبْ لِقَى الشَّيْخْ اَلْفَاضِلْ قَاعِدْ، طَوَّالِي وَقَّفْ عَرَبِيتْهُ وَبِقَى حْوَارْ لِلشَّيْخْ اَلْفَاضِلْ حَتَّى الآنْ، حَتَّى الآنْ قَاعِدْ مَعَ اَلشَّيْخْ اَلْفَاضِلْ، بِقَى لَيْهُ حِوَارْ.

ب: لَحَدِّي الآنْ مَوْجُودْ؟

أ: لَحَدِّي الآنْ مَوْجُودْ.

## Vocabulary

**karaama** كَرَامَة *nfs* extraordinary action performed by a wali, saint's miracle {*pl:* **karaamaat**}

**walii** وَلِي *nms* man known for his piety, holy man {*pl:* **awliyaa**}

**umm ʃinaaʃin** أُمّ شِنَاشِن *prop* Umm Shinashin (village east of Khartoum)

**fakii** فَكِي *nms* religious authority {*pl:* **fukayaa**}

**jaamiʕ** جَامِع *nms* mosque {*pl:* **jawaamiʕ**}

**gaam** قَام *disc marker invariable* so, anyway (resumes narrative after interruption or digression)

**kubba** كُبّة **[gubba]** *nfs* domed tomb {*pl:* **kubab**}

**ṭuub** طُوب *nms collective* bricks {*fs:* **ṭuuba**, *pl:* **ṭuubaat**}

**gaṣṣar** قَصّر *vi* to run out, fall short {*imperf:* **yagaṣṣir**, *vn:* **tagṣiir**}

**iḍḍaayag** اضّايَق *vi* to become annoyed {*imperf:* **yiḍḍaayig**, *vn:* **ḍiig**}

**matmuum** مَتْمُوم *adj* completed {*fs:* **matmuuma**, *mpl:* **matmuumiin**, *fpl:* **matmuumaat**}

**yaa salaam** يَا سَلاَم my goodness (exclamation of amazement)

**gubba** قُبّة **[kubba]** *nfs* domed tomb {*pl:* **gubab**}

**taksii** تَكْسِي *nms* taxi {*pl:* **takaasii**}

**aṭṭunḍub** اَلطُّنْضُب *prop* Tundub (village east of Khartoum)

**ziyaara** زِيَارَة *nfs* pilgrimage, visit to holy place; visit (in general) {*pl:* **ziyaaraat**}

**miinaa** مِينَا *nfs* port, harbor {*pl:* **mawaanii**}

**fakk aʃʃaariʕ** فَكّ اَلشَّارِع to leave the road, drive off the road *(lit. to let go of the road)* {*imperf:* **yafikk aʃʃariiʕ**, *vn:* **fakk aʃʃariiʕ**}

**ṭawiil** طَوِيل *adj* long; *adv* for a long time; for a long distance {*fs:* **ṭawiila**, *mpl:* **ṭuwaal**, *fpl:* **ṭawiilaat**}

**gizaaz** قِزَاز *nms collective* glass (material); window pane {*fs:* **gizaaza**, *pl:* **gizaazaat**}

**ḥamaa** حَمَى *vt* to prevent; to forbid {*imperf:* **yaḥmii**, *vn:* **ḥimaaya**}

**gaaʕid** قَاعِد *adj pre-verb* sitting, sitting down; keeping on, continuing (continuous action); staying, remaining {*fs:* **gaaʕda**, *mpl:* **gaaʕdiin**, *fpl:* **gaaʕdaat**}

**ḥiwaar** حوارْ *nms* disciple, follower {*pl:* **ḥawaariin**, **ḥeeyraan**}

## Notes

**1** The indirect object phrase /**fii jaamiʕ**/ 'lit. at a mosque' in the clause /**kaan b-ibnuu luuh fii jaamiʕ**/ 'they (mp) were building away at a mosque for him' indicates action taking place over time. A similar use of the indirect object is described in selection 3, note 4.
Note also that the speaker says /**luuh**/ 'for him' rather than the more usual /**leehuu**/.

**2** The speaker's question /**lfakii ʕalii wad minuu?**/ translates literally as 'Faki Ali, son of whom?' In the SA context, however, it means 'Faki Ali what?' or 'Faki Ali, what's his last name?' See selection 1, note 4 for a description of naming practices in SA.

**3** The younger speaker uses the pronunciation /**k**/ the first time that he uses the word /**kubba**/ 'domed tomb' in the phrase /**kubba kidaa**/ 'a kind of domed tomb'. The interviewer uses the same word several lines later, but with a /**g**/, saying /**lgubba ʃuftaa?**/ 'the tomb, you (ms) saw it (fs)?' The younger speaker's reply, the utterance that begins /**lamman algubba** .../ 'when the tomb ...', also uses the /**g**/ pronunciation. This shift from /**k**/ to /**g**/ appears to be an instance of accomodation, of the younger speaker's changing his speech so that it becomes more like that of the interviewer. Accomodation may be deliberate or may occur without the speaker noticing the change.

**4** Although the phrase /**waaḥid kidaa bitaaʕ attaksii**/ 'like, a taxi driver' contains the possessive adjective /**bitaaʕ**/, it does not imply ownership of the taxi. The owner of the taxi is /**ṣaaḥib attaksii**/.

**5** The form /**-aatan**/ in the phrase /**maaʃaatan leehuu**/ 'they (fp) were going to him, lit. going (fp) to him' is particular to active participles. It is the form of the FP suffix /**-aat**/ that occurs when the active participle is followed by an indirect object phrase with the preposition /**li-**/ or /**bi-**/. Note, however, that the speaker repeats the phrase in a later utterance without using this form, saying /**maaʃaat leehuu**/ 'they (fp) were going to him, lit. going (fp) to him'.

# maa bi-yuktil

*Continuing the story of Adil's mysterious uncle Khalid from selection 12, this selection contains some surprises. Khalid is revealed to be Dabba, formerly a member of a criminal gang led by the Boss. Fellow gang member Kurnaf is the real murderer of the Hajj. The language of this selection is not criminal slang, but is noticeably more colloquial than in previous selections.*

A: aa … rayyis, ʔin ʃaa ḷḷaa xeer?

B: maa ʃufta kurnaaf?

A: abadan.

B: walaa ʕargala?

A: walaa ʕargala. kam yoom kidaa lḥagiiga maa ʃuftum, ʔin ʃaa ḷḷaa xeer?

B: daayrum ḍaruurii. law lageet ayyi waaḥid fiihum talimmanii fiihuu. ʔasmaʕ, ʕargala ʕinduu xtuu, saakna fi lḥaaj yuusif, ʔisimaa ḥaliima. maa ʕaarif bi-ẓẓabṭi beetum ween?

A: abadan w-aḷḷaahii, ḥagiiga maa ʕaarif, laakin law, law, law gaabaltam b-akallimum b-aguul luhum arrayyis ʕaayizkum.

B: aa …

A: simiʕt alḥaṣal? ḍabba maa katal attaajir?

B: ḍabba maa katal walaa b-yiktul!

A: aywa ṣaḥḥ. ʔanaa zaatii baraay ʔistaɣrabta,[1] gutta ḍabba daa maa b-yuktil, maa b-yuktul, anaa zaatii mustaɣrib min alḥikaaya dii.

B: [xxx] ʔanaa ʕaarfuu wa-b-aʕrif b-algaahuu keef.

# مَـا بِـيُكْتِـلْ

أ:   اَ...   رَيِّسْ، إِنْ شَـا اللَّهْ خَيـرْ؟

ب:  مَـا شُفْتَ كُرْنَـافْ؟

أ:   اَبَدًا.

ب:  وَلاَ عَرْقَلَهْ؟

أ:   وَلاَ عَرْقَلَهْ. كَمْ يَوْمْ كِدَا الْحَقِيقَهْ مَـا شُفْتْهُمْ، إِنْ شَـا اللَّهْ خَيـرْ؟

ب:  دَايْرْهُمْ ضَرُورِي. لَوْ لَقَيْتْ اَيِّ وَاحِدْ فِيهُمْ تَلِمَّنِي فِيهُ. أَسْمَعْ، عَرْقَلَهْ عِنْدْهُ اخْتْهُ، سَاكْنَهْ فِالْحَاجْ يُوسِفْ، إِسِمْهَا حَلِيمَهْ. مَـا عَارِفْ بَـالظَّبْطِ بَيْتْهُمْ وَيْنْ؟

أ:   اَبَدًا وَاللَّه، حَقِيقَهْ مَـا عَارِفْ، لَكِنْ لَوْ، لَوْ، لَوْ قَابَلْتْهَمْ بَاكَلِّمْهُمْ بَاقُولْ لُهُمْ اَلرَّيِّسْ عَايِزْكُمْ.

ب:  اَ...

أ:   سِمِعْتْ اَلْحَصَلْ؟ ضَبَّهْ مَا كَتَلْ اَلتَّاجِرْ؟

ب:  ضَبَّهْ مَـا كَتَلْ وَلاَ بْيِكْتُلْ!

أ:   اَيْوَهْ صَحّ. أَنَـا زَاتِـي بَرَاي إِسْتَغْرَبْتَ،[1] قُتَّ ضَبَّهْ دَا مَـا بْيُكْتِلْ، مَـا بْيُكْتُلْ، اَنَـا زَاتِـي مُسْتَغْرِبْ مِنْ اَلْحِكَايَهْ دِي.

ب:  [xxx] أَنَـا عَارْفْهُ وَبَاعْرِفْ بَالْقَاهْ كَيْفْ.

A: huu ḍabba daa ʔaṣluu min aḷḷaa xalaguu maa ḥaṣal ʃaal leehuu slaaḥ. maa b-yuktil.

B: nnaas deel law lageet ʔayyi waaḥid fiihum talimmanii fiihum. ʔanaa fii rajaak, ʔaah?

A: ḥaaḍir.

[in another house]

C: minuu?

A: anaa muusaa.

C: jjaabak hinaa ʃnuu? ʕaawiz ʃinuu?

A: dagiiga yaa xii ...

C: [xxx] ʃnuu?

A: ma ... ma ... maa risilnii leek arrayyis yaa xii.

C: arrayyis? w-aḷḷaahii tiguul leeh lageetnii w-aḷḷaahi b-aʕawwigak, b-aaziik, b-antihii minnak.[2]

A: xalaaṣ maa b-akallimuu yaa ʔax, maa b-akallim.

[in a third house]

D: ʕargala?

C: ay, ʕargala. ʃaayif ʕamaaylak? arrayyis b-iikuus ʕaleenaa.

أ: هُو ضَبَّهْ دَا أَصْلْهُ مِنْ اَللَّهْ خَلَقْهُ مَا حَصَلْ شَالْ لَيْهُ سِلاَحْ. مَا بْيُكْتِلْ.

ب: النَّاسْ دَيْلْ لَوْ لَقَيْتْ أَيِّ وَاحِدْ فِيهُمْ تَلِمِّنِي فِيهُمْ. أَنَا فِي رَجَاكْ، آه ؟

أ: حَاضِرْ.

[in another house]

ت: مِنُو ؟

أ: اَنَا مُوسَى.

ت: الجَّابَكْ هِنَا شْنُو ؟ عَاوِزْ شِنُو ؟

أ: دَقِيقَهْ يَا خِي...

ت: [xxx] شْنُو ؟

أ: مَـ... مَـ... مَا رِسِلْنِي لَيْكْ اَلرَيِّسْ يَا اخِي.

ت: اَلرَّيِّسْ؟ وَاللَّهِ تِقُولْ لَيْهْ لَقَيْتْنِي وَاللَّهِ بَاعَوِّقَكْ، بَازِيكْ، بَانْتِهِي مِنَّكْ.[2]

أ: خَلاَصْ مَا بَاكَلِّمْهُ يَأَخْ، مَا بَاكَلِّمْ.

[in a third house]

ث: عَرْقَلَهْ؟

ت: اَيْ، عَرْقَلَهْ. شَايِفْ عَمَايْلَكْ؟ اَلرَّيِّسْ بِيكُوسْ عَلَيْنَا.

D: xalliih yikuus, maa b-ilimm fiinaa.

C: yaa rab, ʕaayiz minnanaa ʃinuu? ʔooʕaa ykuun faakir innuu ʔiḥnaa zugnaa bi-lguruuʃ.

D: huu ʕaarif alguruuʃ niḥnaa maa ʃilnaah, laakin ṣaaḥbak daayir yinajjii ṣaaḥbuu w-ixalliinaa niḥnaa nitḥaakam, ajjaraayid katabat kidaa, kull alʔadilla bi-dguul ʔinnuu ḍabba huwa lkaatil.

C: maa kutta taktuluu[3] yaa kurnaaf, hassii twarraṭnaa ziyaada.

D: asawwii leeh ʃinuu yaa xii? ʔitʃarbak fiinii yaax, gadur maa ṭawwalta leehuu ruuḥii tʃarbak fiinii yaa xii. maa kaan fii ṭariiga ɣeer innuu ʔanaa ʔaktuluu. laakin maa txaaf, kull alʔadilla bi-tguul ʔinnuu lkaatil ḍabba.

C: niḥnaa bass kaan xitiinaa rrayyis maa bi-tjiinaa ʔayya ʕawaja, laakin naʕmil ʃinuu, laaffii b-waraanaa ṭawwaalii. ʔaḷḷaa yikfiinaa ʃarruu. baagii leek arrayyis b-ixalliinaa yaa kurnaaf?

D: yafattiʃ gadru maa yfattiʃ baʕad daak ḥa-yignaʕ.

C: maa b-ignaʕ, huu b-iriid ḍabba ʃadiid w-maa b-irḍaa fiihuu ʃii.

D: anaa ʕaarif daa laakin huwa muɣtaniʕ ʔinnuu huwa lkataluu laakin anaa xaayif innuu yikuun ḍabba ʃaaf.

C: maa ʃaaf, huu mutʔakkid innuu ḍabba maa b-yuktul.

D: inta ʔinta yaa ʕargala, maa djaglib!

ث: خَلِّيهْ يِكُوس، مَا بِلِمّ فِينَا.

ت: يَا رَبْ عَايِزْ مِنَّنَا شِنُو؟ أَوْعَى يكُونْ فَاكِرْ اِنّهُ إِحْنَا زُغْنَا بِالْقُرُوشْ.

ث: هُو عَارِفْ اَلْقُرُوشْ نِحْنَا مَا شِلْنَاهْ، لَكِنْ صَاحْبَكْ دَايِرْ يِنَجِّي صَاحْبُهْ وِخَلِّينَا نِحْنَا نِتْحَاكَمْ، اَلجَّرَايِدْ كَتَبَتْ كِدَا، كُلّ اَلأَدِلَّهْ بِدْقُولْ إِنّهُ ضَبَّهْ هُوَ الْكَاتِلْ.

ت: مَا كُتَّ تَكْتُلْهُ[3] يَا كُرْنَافْ، هَسِّي تْوَرَّطْنَا زِيَادَهْ.

ث: اَسَوِّي لَيْهْ شِنُو يَا اخِي؟ إِتْشَرْبَكْ فِينِي يَا اخ، قَدُرْ مَا طَوَّلْتَ لَيْهُ رُوحِي تْشَرْبَكْ فِينِي يَا خِي. مَا كَانْ فِي طَرِيقَهْ غَيْرْ اِنّهُ أَنَا أَكْتُلْهُ. لَكِنْ مَا تْخَافْ، كُلّ اَلأَدِلَّهْ بِتْقُولْ إِنّهُ الْكَاتِلْ ضَبَّهْ.

ت: نِحْنَا بَسّ كَانْ خِتِينَا الرَّيِّسْ مَا بِتْجِينَا أَيَّ عَوَجَهْ، لَكِنْ نَعْمِلْ شِنُو، لاَفِّي بْوَرَانَا طَوَّالِي. أَللَّهْ يِكْفِينَا شَرّهُ. بَاقِي لَيْكْ اَلرَّيِّسْ بِخَلِّينَا يَا كُرْنَافْ؟

ث: يَفَتِّشْ قَدْرُ مَا يْفَتِّشْ بَعَدْ دَاكْ حَيِقْنَعْ.

ت: مَا بِقْنَعْ، هُو بِرِيدْ ضَبَّهْ شَدِيدْ وْمَا بِرْضَى فِيهُ شِي.

ث: اَنَا عَارِفْ دَا لَكِنْ هُوَ مُغْتَنِعْ إِنّهُ هُوَ الْكَتَلْهُ لَكِنْ اَنَا خَايِفْ اِنّهُ يِكُونْ ضَبَّهْ شَافْ.

ت: مَا شَافْ، هُو مُتْأَكِّدْ اِنّهُ ضَبَّهْ مَا بْيُكْتُلْ.

ث: اِنْتَ إِنْتَ يَا عَرْقَلَهْ، مَا دْجَقْلِبْ!

C: anaa maa gaaʕid ...

D: algaḍiyya dii laabsa ḍabba laabsaahuu w-inta maa ḥa-djiik ḥaaja.

C: ṭayyib, law maʃaa yballaɣ albuuliis?

D: maa yigdar. yaʕnii ḥa-yguul innuu huu lʔagnaʕnaa niḥnaa namʃii naktul attaajir? ḥa-yballiɣ ʕan nafsuu, maa mumkin.

C: bi-tʕaayin leey kidaa leeh yaa kurnaaf?

D: inta ʃʃaahid alwaḥiid ʃʃaafnii w-anaa b-aktul.

C: alḥaala maa waaḥda, ʔanaa wa-ʔinta maa, maa waaḥid.

D: anaa law xatiitak ʔinta taanii maa ḥa-tjiinii ḥaaja.

ت: اَنَا مَا قَاعِدْ...

ث: اَلْقَضِيَّهْ دي لاَبْسَهْ ضَبَّهْ لاَبْسَاهُ وِانْتَ مَا حَدْجِيكْ حَاجَهْ.

ت: طَيِّبْ، لَوْ مَشَى يَبْلِّغْ اَلْبُولِيسْ؟

ث: مَا يِقْدَرْ. يَعْنِي حَيْقُولْ اِنَّهُ هُو الأَقْنَعْنَا نِحْنَا نَمْشِي نَكْتُلْ اَلتَّاجِرْ؟ حَيْبَلِّغْ عَنْ نَفْسَهْ، مَا مُمْكِنْ.

ت: بِتْعَايِنْ لَيّ كِدَا لَيْهْ يَا كُرْنَافْ؟

ث: اِنْتَ الشَّاهِدْ اَلْوَحِيدْ الشَّافْنِي وَانَا بَاكْتُلْ.

ت: اَلْحَالَهْ مَا وَاحْدَهْ، أَنَا وَإِنْتَ مَا، مَا وَاحِدْ.

ث: اَنَا لَوْ خَتِيتَكْ إِنْتَ تَانِي مَا حَتْجِينِي حَاجَهْ.

## Vocabulary

**rayyis** رَيِّسْ *nms* boss, chief, leader {*pl:* **ruyasa**}

**in ʃaa ḷḷaa xeer** اِنْ شَا اللّٰهْ خَيْرْ I hope that everything is ok *(lit. if God will, it is [was; will be] good)*

**abadan** اَبَدًا *adv* never; not at all

**ḍaruurii** ضَرُورِي *adj* imperative, necessary; *adv* urgently {*fs:* **ḍaruuriyya**, *mpl:* **ḍaruuriyyiin**, *fpl:* **ḍaruuriyyaat**}

**fii-** فِي *prep* of (partitive relationship); for (amount of time)

**lamma fii** لَمّ فِي *vt* to put s.o. in touch with s.o.; to find, encounter, meet; to get together with {*imperf:* **yalimm fii**, *vn:* **lamm fii**, *vn:* **limm fii**}

**alḥaaj yuusif** اَلْحاجْ يُوسِفْ *prop* al-Hajj Yousif (neighborhood in North Khartoum)

**ḥikaaya** حِكَايَهْ *nfs* affair, matter; story, tale {*pl:* **ḥakaawii**}

**min** مِنْ *conj* since the time that; when, at the time of

**xalag** خَلَقْ *vt* to create {*imperf:* **yaxalig**, *vn:* **xalag**}

**fii rajaa-** فِي رَجَا begging s.o. (strong request or admission of weakness) *(lit. in urgent request of)*

**ḥaaḍir** حَاضِرْ *interj invariable* at your service, will do (used when agreeing to request or order) *(lit. present, here)*

**ʕawwag** عَوَّقْ *vt* to harm, damage {*imperf:* **yaʕawwig**, *vn:* **taʕwiig**}

**azaa** أَزَى *vt* to hurt, harm {*imperf:* **yaazii**, *vn:* **azaa**}

**intahaa min** انْتَهَى مِنْ *vi* to finish, put an end to {*imperf:* **yintahii**, *vn:* **intihaaʔ**, *vn:* **nihaaya**}

**kaas ʕalaa (kusta)** كَاسْ عَلَى (كُسْتْ) *vi* to look for, search for {*imperf:* **yakuus ʕalaa**, *vn:* **kawasaan**}

**ooʕaa** أَوْعَى **[awʕaa]** *vi used in imperative* let it not be that (preceding imperfect of /kaan/); do not do s.t. (preceding simple imperfect); watch out (without a following verb) {*fs:* **ooʕii**, *mpl:* **ooʕuu**, *fpl:* **ooʕan**}

**zaag (zugta)** زَاقْ (زُقْتْ) *vi* to get away; to escape undetected {*imperf:* **yazuug**, *vn:* **zagawaan**}

**itwarraṭ** اتْوَرَّطْ *vi* to become embroiled or entangled in difficulties or problems {*imperf:* **yitwarraṭ**, *vn:* **tawarruṭ**, *vn:* **warṭa**}

**itʃarbak fii** اتْشَرْبَكْ فِي *vi* to hold on to, stick to; to insist on *(lit. to become ensared, embroiled, tangled in)* {*imperf:* **yitʃarbak**, *vn:* **ʃarbaka**}

**gadur maa** قَدُرْ مَا **[gadru maa]** *conj* as much as, the more that

**ṭawwal ruuḥ-** طَوَّلْ رُوحْ to be patient; to put up (/li-/ 'with s.o.') {*imperf:* **yaṭawwal ruuḥuu**, **taṭwiil ruuḥ-**}

**xataa** خَتَى *vt* to avoid {*imperf:* **yaxtaa**, *vn:* **xatayaan**}

**laffa** لَفّْ *vi* to go around, go about; to turn, make a turn {*imperf:* **yaliff**, *vn:* **laff**, *vn:* **liff**}

**laaffii** لاَفِّي *adj* going around, going about; turning, making a turn {*fs:* **laaffa**, *mpl:* **laaffiin**, *fpl:* **laaffaat**}

**aḷḷaa yakfiinaa ʃarr-** اَللّٰهْ يَكْفِينَا شَرّ God help us (where s.o. is concerned) *(lit. God protect us from s.o.'s evil)*

**baagii leek** بَاقِي لَيْكْ do you think, would you say

**jaglab** جَقْلَبْ *vi* to lose one's nerve {*imperf:* **yajaglib**, *vn:* **jaglaba**}

## Notes

**1** In the clause /ʔanaa **zaatii baraay** ʔistaɣrabta/ 'I myself, personally, was surprised', the form /**baraay**/ is synonymous with /**zaatii**/. In other cases, however, /**baraa-**/ means 'alone, by oneself'.

**2** There is no conditional particle in the sentence /**tiguul leeh lageetnii w-aḷḷaahii b-aʕawwigak, b-aaziik, b-antihii minnak**/ 'you (ms) tell him you (ms) found me and, by God, I'll harm you (ms), I'll hurt you (ms), I'll finish you (ms) off'. The conditional meaning, however, is clear, as it is in the English translation. This is an example of an implicit conditional.

**3** The perfect of /**kaan**/ 'to be' may precede a simple imperfect verb, as in the clause /**maa kutta taktuluu**/ 'you (ms) shouldn't have killed him'. The combination of the perfect of /**kaan**/ and a simple imperfect verb implies obligation. It contrasts with the combination of the perfect of /**kaan**/ and a prefixed imperfect verb, as in /**kutta bi-taktuluu**/ 'you (ms) were killing him'.

# almuusiɣaa lfulklooriyya fi ssuudaan

*This selection, from a lecture on Sudanese music by the musician Abdel Gadir Salim, presents some challenges. Abdel Gadir gives his lecture in an educated, formal style heavily influenced by MSA. The examples he cites, however, are extremely colloquial and come from the regions of Kordofan and Darfur.*

ʔa ... alʔuɣniyya ʃʃaʕbiyya ḥasab ala ... ttaʕriif hiya ʔalʔuɣniyya ʔaṣṣaadira min aʃʃaʕab wa-ʔaẓunnakum taʕrifuuna kalimat foolkloor ʔallii hiya jaaya min ḥikmat aʃʃaʕb. fi ssuudaan kamaa taʕlamuuna hunaalika ʔuɣniyyat arriif ʔa ... mumkin naguul hiya ʔalʔuɣniyya ʔatturaasiyya ʔaw alʔuɣniyya lʔirsiyya[1] ʔaw ʔalʔuɣniyya ʃʃaʕbiyya wa-mumkin naʕtabir maa yuqaddam fii ʔalxurṭuum hiya ʔalʔuɣniyya ʔalmustaḥdasa. ʔa ... ṭabʕan ḥadiisnaa ḥa-yurakkaz ʔalʔaan ḥawl alʔuɣniyya ʃʃaʕbiyya wa-ʔalʔuɣniyya ʃʃaʕbiyya yaʕnii ḥa-ykuun taɣriiban juul alḥadiis bitaaʕnaa ʕan alʔuɣniyya lmawjuuda fii ʔalḥaql, almawjuuda fii manṭigat kurdufaan wa-daarfuur. fa ... bi-najid ʔinnuu lʔuɣniyya fii kurdufaan wa-daarfuur, ʔanaa fii tagdiirii ʔinnahaa ʔuɣniyya ʔistaṭaaʕat ʔan tatanaawal mawaaḍiiʕ ʕaajizat ʕan tanaawulaa ʔalʔuɣniyya lmustaḥdasa ʔaw alʔuɣniyya lḥadiisa, nuṣuuṣ ʕadiida tataḥaddas ʕan ɣaḍaayaa. ʔa ... fa-l-namsik masalan muʃkilat ʔalʕaṭaʃ fii minṭigat ɣarbi kurdufaan bi-nilgaa ʔuɣniyyaat kaθiira jiddan tanaawalat qaḍaayaa lʕaṭaʃ:

asgiinaa ʕaṭʃaaniin

am-naʃkii[2] maẓluumiin

maa gaẓdanaa ʔattamwiin

bi-llaahii yaa lfakii

# اَلْمُوسِيغَى الْفُلْكْلَوْرِيَّهْ فِالسُّودَانْ

أ... اَلأُغْنِيَّه الشَّعْبِيَّهْ حَسَبْ اَلَـ... التَّعْرِيفْ هِيَ أَلأُغْنِيَّه أَلصَّادِرَهْ مِنْ اَلشَّعَبْ وَأَظُنَّكُمْ تَعْرِفُون كَلِمَةْ فَوْلْكْلَوْرْ أَللِّي هِيَ جَايَهْ مِنْ حِكْمَةْ اَلشَّعْبْ. فِالسُّودَانْ كَمَا تَعْلَمُون هُنَالك أُغْنِيَّةْ اَلرِّيفْ أ... مُمْكِنْ نَقُولْ هِيَ أَلأُغْنِيَّهْ أَلتُّرَاسِيَّهْ أَوْ اَلأُغْنِيَّه الإِرْسِيَّهْ[1] أَوْ أَلأُغْنِيَّه الشَّعْبِيَّهْ وَمُمْكِنْ نَعْتَبِرْ مَا يُقَدَّمْ فِي أَلْخُرْطُومْ هِيَ أَلأُغْنِيَّهْ أَلْمُسْتَحْدَسَهْ. أ... طَبْعًا حَدِيسْنَا حَيُرَكِّزْ أَلآنْ حَوْلْ اَلأُغْنِيَّه الشَّعْبِيَّهْ وَأَلأُغْنِيَّه الشَّعْبِيَّهْ يَعْنِي حَيْكُون تَغْرِيبًا جُولْ اَلْحَدِيسْ بِتَاعْنَا عَنْ اَلأُغْنِيَّه الْمَوْجُودَهْ فِي أَلْحَقْل، اَلْمَوْجُودَهْ فِي مَنْطِقَةْ كُرْدُوفَانْ وَدَارْفُورْ. فَـ... بِنَجِدْ إِنّهُ الأُغْنِيَّهْ فِي كُرْدُوفَانْ وَدَارْفُورْ، أَنَا فِي تَقْدِيرِي إِنَّهَا أُغْنِيَّه إِسْتَطَاعَتْ أَنْ تَتَنَاوَلْ مَوَاضِيعْ عَاجِزَتْ عَنْ تَنَاوُلْهَا أَلأُغْنِيَّه الْمُسْتَحْدَسَهْ أَوْ اَلأُغْنِيَّه الْحَدِيسَهْ، نُصُوصْ عَدِيدَهْ تَتَحَدَّسْ عَنْ غَضَايَا. أ... فَلْنَمْسِكْ مَسَلاً مُشْكِلَةْ أَلْعَطَشْ فِي مَنْطِقَةْ غَرْبِ كُرْدُوفَانْ بِنَلْقَى أُغْنِيَّاتْ كَتِيرَهْ جِدّاً تَنَاوَلَتْ قَضَايَا الْعَطَشْ:

اَسْقِينَا عَطْشَانِينْ

اَمْنَشْكِي[2] مَظْلُومِينْ

مَا قَصَدْنَا أَلتَّمْوِينْ

بِاللَّهِ يَا الْفَكِي

aṣrif, attamwiin xalliih

mutʔassar b-naʃkii

wa-gall almawjuud ʔalfii.

fii taṣniif albaaḥisiin fii majaal atturaas yaʕtabiruuna haazihi ʔuɣniyya ḥadiisa ʔaw, ʔaw uɣniyya turaasiyya ʔaw ʔuɣniyya ʔakṣud ʃaʕbiyya ḥadiiθa ʔa ... ɣad yaguul, la-ɣad laa yuṭlaɣ ʕaleehaa ʔallafẓ[3] ʔuɣniyya fooklooriyya ʔaw ʔuɣniyya turaasiyya. wa-laakin haazihi hiya lḥagiiga, hiya ʔaẓbaḥat ʔuɣniyya turaddidaa kull almanṭiga fa-bi-ttaalii ʔaẓbaḥat hiya ʔalʔuɣniyya ʔalmuʕabbira w-allatii tuʕabbir ʕan kaaʔin bi-ʕaynih. bi-nilgii ʔinnuu fii ʔaɣaanii ma ... mawjuuda, ʔaɣaanii ʃʃuuraap ʕinda ʔa ... ʔahalnaa lhabbaaniyya, ʔaɣaanii ʃʃagalap ʕind ahalnaa lḥamar.[4] b-iikuun fiihaa ʕiibaaraat ṭayyiba bii ... bi-tkuun zaad bi-nnizba li-haazaa ṭṭifl wa-bii ... taɣris fiihuu giyam tanʃiʔa ṭayyiba wa-ʔayḍan tuzakkir haaðaa ṭṭifl ʔa ... bi-lxaalig alʕaalii wa-ʔayḍan tadʕuu fiihii ʔalaa yakuuna jabaanan wa-yataḥammal ʔa ... tilka lʔalam.[5] fa-nalgaa halnaa lhabbaaniyya yɣannuuna:

alleed yaa jaljaamuus

laa txaaf min ʃaraar almoos.

alleed yaʕnii ʔalwalat ʔa ... ṭabʕan manṭigat ʔa ... ʔalbaggaara fiihaa kaθiir min alʔidɣaam wa-kaθiir min taḥriif alḥuruuf.[6] fa-bi-nalgaa ʔinnuu ʔal ... ʔal ... ʔa ... ʔahii daʕwa haazaa ṭṭifl ʔa ... b-iidʕuuhuu ʔinnuu laa yaxaaf min ʃaraar almuus. wa-barḍuu lfataa yguul laa:

اَصْرِفْ، اَلتَّمْوِينْ خَلِّيهْ

مُتْأَسَّر بْنَشْكِي

وَقَلّ اَلْمَوْجُودْ أَلْفِي

فِي تَصْنِيفْ اَلْبَاحِسِينْ فِي مَجَالْ اَلتُّرَاس يَعْتَبِرُونَ هَزِهِ أُغْنِيَّهْ حَدِيسَهْ أَوْ، أَوْ أُغْنِيَّهْ تُرَاسِيَّهْ أَوْ أُغْنِيَّهْ أَكْصُدْ شَعْبِيَّهْ حَدِيثَهْ أَ ... غَدْ يَقُولْ، لَغَدْ لاَ يُطْلَغْ عَلَيْهَا أَللَّفْظْ[3] أُغْنِيَّهْ فَوكْلُورِيَّهْ أَوْ أُغْنِيَّهْ تُرَاسِيَّهْ. وَلَكِنْ هَزِهِ هِيَ الْحَقِيقَهْ، هِيَ أَصْبَحَتْ أُغْنِيَّهْ تُرَدِّدْهَا كُلّ اَلْمَنْطِقَهْ فَبِالتَّالِي أَصْبَحَتْ هِيَ اَلأُغْنِيَّهْ أَلْمُعَبِّرَهْ وَالَّتِي تُعَبِّرْ عَنْ كَائِنْ بِعَيْنِهْ. بِنِلْقِي إِنَّهُ فِي أَغَانِي مَ... مَوْجُودَهْ، أَغَانِي الشُّورَاپْ عِنْدَ أ... أَهَلْنَا الْهَبَّانِيَّهْ، أَغَانِي الشَّقَلَپْ عِنْدْ اَهَلْنَا الْحَمَرْ.[4] بِيكُونْ فِيهَا عِيبَارَاتْ طَيِّبَهْ بِي... بِتْكُونْ زَادْ بِالنِّزْبَهْ لِهَزَا الطِّفْلْ وَبِي... تَغْرِسْ فِيهُ قِيَمْ تَنْشَأَهْ طَيِّبَهْ وَأَيْضًا تُزَكِّرْ هَذَا الطِّفْلْ أ... بِالْخَالِقْ اَلْعَالِي وَأَيْضًا تَدْعُو فِيهِ أَلاَ يَكُونَ جِبَانًا وَيَتَحَمَّلْ أ... تِلْكَ الأَلَمْ.[5] فَنَلْقَى اهَلْنَا الْهَبَّانِيَّهْ يْغَنُّونَ:

اَللَّيْدْ يَا جَلْجَامُوسْ

لاَ تْخَافْ مِنْ شَرَارْ اَلْمَوْسْ.

اَللَّيْدْ يَعْنِي أَلْوَلَتْ أ... طَبْعًا مَنْطِقَةْ أ... أَلْبَقَّارَهْ فِيهَا كَثِيرْ مِنْ اَلإِدْغَامْ وَكَثِيرْ مِنْ تَحْرِيفْ اَلْحُرُوفْ.[6] فَبِنَلْقَى إِنَّهُ أَلْـ... أَلْـ ... أ... أَهِي دَعْوَهْ هَزَا الطِّفْلْ أ... بِيدْعُوهُ إِنَّهُ لاَ يَخَافْ مِنْ شَرَارْ اَلْمُوسْ. وَبَرْضُهْ الْفَتَاهْ يْقُولْ لْهَا:

faaṭma bitt annabii

yaa maḥammad alʕaalii

faaṭma bitt annabii

aleetuu yaa ṭahhaar

bi-lmaal w-alʕiyaal.[7]

ʔizan alʔuɣniyya bi-tkuun ʔaddat kaḍiyya muʕayyana ʕinda zaalika lḥadas wa-hiya ʔa ... tarakat ʔa ... ʃeeʔ min alfaraḥ ʕinda ðaalika ṭṭifl ʔaw ʕinda tilka ṭṭifla wa-ʔayḍan ʔa ... takuun ʔa ... ðakkaratuu bi-ʔaʃyaa ʕadiida. ʔa ... ʔayḍan ʔa ... zeey maa gulnaa ʔa ... ʔalʔuɣniyya bi-tkuun fiihaa ʔa ... ṭariḥ kaθiir min algaḍaayaa. wa-b-istaʕriḍ baʕḍ annuṣuuṣ min ala ... ʔannuṣuuṣ almawjuuda fii manṭigat ʔa ... ʔajjaraarii ʔaw fii manṭigat yaʕnii ʔa ... alb-iimaaris fiihaa jjaraarii. w-ajjaraarii yaa jamaaʕa, nuuʕ min alɣinaaʔ huwa ʃabii ... arraɣṣ ʃabiih bii-miʃyat alʔibl, wa-yuujad haazaa nnuuʕ min alɣinaaʔ fii ʔalmanṭiga, ʔal ... manṭigat aṣṣaḥraaʔ wa-manṭigat ʃibh aṣṣaḥraaʔ. min lʔuɣniyyaat bitaaʕat ajjaraarii ʔaḥaawil ʔagaddim namuuzaj:

ʔa ... gaddamta ʔanaa

lfarʕ alb-itannaa[8]

sallim ʕalaa halnaa

kaan gaaluu ṭawwalnaa

daar aṣṣaʕiid janna.

فَاطْمَهْ بِتّ اَلنَّبِي

يَا مَحَمَّدْ اَلْعَالِي

فَاطْمَهْ بِتّ اَلنَّبِي

اَلَيْتَهُ يَا طَهَّارْ

بِالْمَالْ وَالْعِيَالْ.[7]

إزًا اَلأُغْنِيَّهْ بِتْكُون أَدَّتْ كَضِيَّهْ مُعَيَّنَهْ عِنْدَ زَلِكَ الْحَدَسْ وَهِيَ أ ... تَرَكَتْ أ... شَيْ مِنْ اَلْفَرَحْ عِنْدَ ذَلِكَ الطِّفْلْ أَوْ عِنْدَ تِلْكَ الطِّفْلَهْ وَأَيْضًا أ... تَكُونْ أ... ذَكَّرَتْهُ بِأَشْيَا عَدِيدَهْ. أ... أَيْضًا أ... زَيّ مَا قُلْنَا أ... اَلأُغْنِيَّهْ بِتْكُونْ فِيهَا أ... طَرِحْ كَثِيرْ مِنْ اَلْقَضَايَا. وَبِسْتَعْرِضْ بَعْضْ اَلنُّصُوصْ مِنْ اَلَ... اَلنُّصُوصْ اَلْمَوْجُودَهْ فِي مَنْطِقَةْ أ... اَلْجَرَارِي أَوْ فِي مَنْطِقَةْ يَعْنِي أ... اَلْبِيمَارِسْ فِيهَا الْجَرَّارِي. وَالْجَرَّارِي يَا جَمَاعَهْ، نُوعْ مِنْ اَلْغِنَاءْ هُوَ شَبِيه... اَلرَّغْصْ شَبِيهْ بِيمِشْيَةْ اَلإِبْلْ، وَيُوجَدْ هَزَا النُّوعْ مِنْ اَلْغِنَاءْ فِي اَلْمَنْطِقَهْ، اَلْ... مَنْطِقَةْ اَلصَّحْرَاءْ وَمَنْطِقَةْ شِبْهْ اَلصَّحْرَاءْ. مِنْ الأُغْنِيَّاتْ بِتَاعَةْ اَلْجَرَارِي أَحَاوِلْ أَقَدِّمْ نَمُوزَجْ:

أ... قَدَّمْتَ أَنَا

الْفَرْعْ اَلبِتَنَّى[8]

سَلِّمْ عَلَى اهَلْنَا

كَانْ قَالُوا طَوَّلْنَا

دَارْ اَلصَّعِيدْ جَنَّهْ.

ʔa … ʔayḍan:

nitlaagaa, nitlaagaa
fi rramil addugaaga
yaa ruuḥii lmuʃtaaga
yaa daayra lmalaagaa
li-lfaarig maa laagaa.

yaʕnii ʔizaa taʔammilnaa ʔalɣinaaʔ aʃʃaʕbii fii wasaṭ assuudaan wa-fii ɣa … wa-fii januubuu wa-ʃamaaluu wa-ʃarguu bi-najid yaʕnii fii ʔaɣaanii lbaniina fii manṭigat ajjaʕliin. ʔanaa fii tagdiirii -nnuu l … al … al … ʔa … ʔaɣaanii lbaniina ʔa … maa ligat ʔa … yaʕnii naas talɣaa ʕaleehaa ḍḍawʔ bi-ʃʃakli l … alkaafii. la-ʔannuu ʔayyi ʔimraʔa ʔa … ʕindaa waladaa masalan ʔa … balaɣa ʔinnuu, marḥalat ʔinnuu yatazawwaj ʔaw marḥalat alxiitaan bi-talgaa jiddatuu ʔaw waalidtuu bigat ʃaaʕira ʔallafat baniina. wa-haazihi lbaniina ʔizaa taʔammalnaahaa ʔallii hiya xeeru misaal leehaa:

ʔalleela ʔalʕadiil w-azzeen.

bi-nalgaa fiihaa fii ɣiyam tanʃiʔa ṭayyiba mawjuuda fii tilka lkalimaat. ʻʕaawzaak tasʕad ajjaar, tagiif maʕa ḍḍaʕiif, wa-ʔinta ḍaww algabiila,ʼ wa, wa, ʔilaa ʔaaxirihi. fa … bi-nalgaa ʔinnuu ʔal … alʔuɣniyya ʃʃaʕbiyya zeey maa ɣulnaa ʔinnuu bita … bi-taḥmil maḍaamiin, yaʕnii laysa ʔuɣniyyat kurdufaan faɣaṭ bal kull alʔuɣniyya ʃʃaʕbiyya lmawjuuda bi-taḥmil maḍaamiin wa-bi-taḥmil ʔa … ʔaʃyaa bi-ḍḍiif alkasiir jiddan lee … ʔa …

أ...   أَيْضًا:

نِتْلاَقَى، نِتْلاَقَى

فَالرَّمِلْ اَلدُّقَاقَهْ

يَا رُوحِي الْمُشْتَاقَهْ

يَا دَايْرَهْ الْمَلاَقَى

لِلْفَارِقْ مَا لاَقَى.

يَعْنِي إِزَا تَأَمَّلْنَا أَلْغِنَاءْ اَلشَّعْبِي فِي وَسَطْ اَلسُّودَانْ وَفِي غَـ... وَفِي جَنُوبْهُ وَشَمَالْهُ وَشَرْقْهُ بِنَجِدْ يَعْنِي فِي أَغَانِي الْبَنِينَهْ فِي مَنْطِقَةْ اَلجَّعْلِينْ. أَنَا فِي تَقْدِيرِي انّهُ لْـ...   اَلْـ...   اَلْـ...   أَ...   أ... أَغَانِي الْبَنِينَهْ أ...   مَا لِقَتْ أ...   يَعْنِي نَاسْ تَلْغَى عَلَيْهَا الضَّوْءْ بِالشَّكْلِ لْـ...   اَلْكَافِي. لأَنّهُ أَيِّ إِمْرَأَهْ أ...   عِنْدْهَا وَلَدْهَا مَسَلاً أ...   بَلَغَ إِنّهُ، مَرْحَلَةْ إِنّهُ يَتَزَوَّجْ أَوْ مَرْحَلَةْ اَلْخِيتَانْ بِتَلْقَى جِدَّتْهُ أَوْ وَالِدْتْهُ بِقَتْ شَاعِرَهْ أَلَّفَتْ بَنِينَهْ. وَهَزِهِ الْبَنِينَهْ إِزَا تَأَمَّلْنَاهَا أَللِّي هِيَ خَيْرُ مِسَالْ لَيْهَا:

أَللَّيْلَهْ أَلْعَدِيلْ وَالزَّيْنْ.

بِنَلْقَى فِيهَا فِي غِيَمْ تَنْشَأَهْ طَيِّبَهْ مَوْجُودَهْ فِي تِلْكَ الْكَلِمَاتْ. «عَاوْزَاكْ تَسْعَدْ اَلجَّارْ، تَقِيفْ مَعَ الضَّعِيفْ، وَإِنْتَ ضَوّ اَلْقَبِيلَهْ،» ووَإِلَى آخِرِهِ. فَـ...   بِنَلْقَى إِنّهُ أَلْـ...   اَلأُغْنِيّه الشَّعْبِيَّهْ زَيّ مَا غُلْنَا إِنّهُ بِتَـ...   بِتَحْمِلْ مَضَامِينْ، يَعْنِي لَيْسَ أُغْنِيَّةْ كُرْدُوفَانْ فَغَطْ بَلْ كُلّ اَلأُغْنِيَّه الشَّعْبِيَّه الْمَوْجُودَهْ بِتَحْمِلْ مَضَامِينْ وَبِتَحْمِلْ أ...   أَشْيَا بِضِيِّفْ اَلْكَسِيرْ جِداً لَيْـ...   أ...

ʔalqiyam almawjuuda ʔa ... ʕinda haaðaa ʃʃaʕb. fa-bi-ttaalii yaʕnii ʔalwaaḥid b-iiguul innuu naḥnu naḥmil fii daaxilnaa kunuuz ḍaxma jiddan laa budda ʔan taẓhar ʔilaa lʕaalam. wa-min xalaal haazihi lmumaarasaat ʃʃaʕbiyya wa-min xilaal ɣinaaʔinaa wa-θagaafatinaa nastaṭiiʕ ʔan nuḥaqqiq alkaθiir ʔa ... w-alkasiir.

أَلْقِيَمْ اَلْمَوْجُودَهْ أَ...    عِنْدَ هَذَا الشَّعَبْ. فَبِالتَّالِي يَعْنِي أَلْوَاحِدْ
بِيقُولْ اِنّهُ نَحْنُ نَحْمِلْ فِي دَاخِلْنَا كُنُوزْ ضَخْمَهْ جِدّاً لاَ بُدَّ أَنْ
تَظْهَرْ إِلَى الْعَالَمْ. وَمِنْ خَلاَلْ هَزِهِ الْمُمَارَسَاتْ الشَّعْبِيَّهْ وَمِنْ
خِلاَلْ غِنَائِنَا وَثَقَافَتِنَا نَسْتَطِيعْ أَنْ نُحَقِّقْ اَلْكَثِيرْ أَ...    وَالكَسِيرْ.

## Vocabulary

**riif** رِيفْ *nms* countryside {*pl:* **aryaaf**}

**juul** جُولْ **[jull]** *nms* majority; entirety

**kurdufaan** كُرْدُفَانْ *prop* Kordofan (region of central Sudan)

**daarfuur** دَارْفُورْ *prop* Darfur (region of western Sudan)

**am-** اَمْ **[ab-]** *particle western Sudan* prefix of imperfect verb

**ʃuraap** شُرَاپْ *nms* shurab (a kind of Sudanese folksong)

**alhabbaaniyya** اَلْهَبَّانِيَّهْ *prop* Habbaniyya (ethnic group in western Sudan)

**ʃagalap** شَقَلاَپْ *nms* shagalab (a kind of Sudanese folksong)

**alḥamar** اَلْحَمَرْ *prop* Hamar (group in western Sudan)

**leed** لِيْدْ **[wileed]** *nms* little boy (diminutive of /wad/) {*pl:* **leedaat**}

**moos** مُوْسْ **[muus]** *nms* razor; blade {*pl:* **amwaas**}

**albaggaara** اَلْبَقَّارَهْ *prop* the Baggara, the Baqqara (general term for cattle-herding nomads of Sudan) *(lit. cowherders)*

**aleetuu** اَلَيْتُهْ *particle invariable; poetic or non-Khartoum usage* would that, if only (indicates contrary-to-fact wish)

**ṭahhaar** طَهَّارْ *nms* circumciser {*mpl:* **ṭahhaariin**}

**jaraarii** جَرَارِي *nms* jarari (a kind of Sudanese folksong)

**tannaa** تَنَّى *vi* to walk with swaying motion {*imperf:* **yatannaa**, *vn:* **tineey**}

**daar** دَارْ *nfs* region, area; house, home {*pl:* **diyaar**}

**aṣṣaʕiid** اَلصَّعِيدْ *prop* al-Sa'id, Upper Egypt (the region from south of Cairo to Lake Nasser)

**yaa** يَا *interj* how; oh (adds exclamatory quality to following word)

**baniina** بَنِينَة *nfs* banina (a kind of Sudanese folksong)

**jaʕalii** جَعَلي *prop* Ja'ali (member of a group of farmers and sedentary herders living along the Nile from Dongola to south of Khartoum) {*fs:* **jaʕliyya,** *mpl:* **jaʕliin,** *fpl:* **jaʕliyyaat**}

**ʕadiil** عَدِيل *adj* good; agreeable; morally upright *(lit. straight)* {*fs:* **ʕadiila,** *mpl:* **ʕadiiliin,** *fpl:* **ʕadiilaat**}

**zeen** زَين *adj* beautiful; *nms* beauty {*fs:* **zeena,** *mpl:* **zeeniin,** *fpl:* **zeenaat**}

## Notes

**1** The phrase /ʔalʔuɣniyya **ʔatturaasiyya** ʔaw alʔuɣniyya **lʔirsiyya**/ 'a song of our cultural heritage, a song of our cultural inheritance' contains two words derived from the MSA verb warіθa 'to inherit'. They are /**ʔatturaasiyya**/ 'relating to heritage' and /**lʔirsiyya**/ 'relating to inheritance'. Both words mean legal or genetic transmission. In this context, however, they refer specifically to cultural issues.

**2** The prefix /am-/ in the phrase /**am**-naʃkii maẓluumiin/ 'we raise a complaint' derives from the imperfect /**bi**-/ prefix. In SA, as in certain other varieties of spoken Arabic, the /b/ of the imperfect /**bi**-/ prefix may assimilate to the /na-/ imperfect prefix for 1S and 1P. This assimilation, however, is not as common in SA in the region of the capital as it is in other areas of the country.

**3** The clause /**la-ɣad** laa yuṭlaɣ ʕaleehaa ʔallafẓ/ 'it (fs) might not be given the term' is unusual. The form /**la-ɣad**/ (MSA la-qad) typically occurs before a perfect verb and adds strength or emphasis to the sentence in which it occurs. The form /**la-ɣad**/ does not usually occur with an imperfect verb.

**4** Two groups are named in the phrase /ʔaɣaanii ʃʃuuraap ʕinda ʔa … ʔahalnaa **lhabbaaniyya**, ʔaɣaanii ʃʃagalap ʕind ahalnaa **lḥamar**/ 'the shurab songs of, ah … our brothers, the Habbaniya, and the shagalab songs of our brothers, the Hamar'. They are /**lhabbaaniyya**/ 'the Habbaniyya' and /**lḥamar**/ 'the Hamar'. Both of these groups are considered sub-groups of the Baggara (or Baqqara), a general term for cattle-herding nomads of northern and western Sudan.

**5** The phrase /**tilka** lʔalam/ 'this pain' is an apparent slip of the tongue for /**tilka** lʔaalaam/ 'these pains'.

**6** The speaker describes the speech of the groups that make up the Baggara in this way: /ṭabʕan manṭigat ʔa … ʔalbaggaara fiihaa **kaθiir min alʔidɣaam wa-kaθiir min taḥriif alḥuruuf**/ 'of course, the region of … of the Baggara has a lot of assimilation of sounds and mispronunciation of letters'. The Baggara (or Baqqara), as mentioned in selection 27, note 4, is a general term for cattle-herding nomads of northern and western Sudan. The speaker's description of their speech is not technical, but is one of the ways in which non-standard speech in Arabic is described.

**7** The phrase /**bi-lmaal w-alʕiyaal**/ 'wealth and children, lit. with wealth and children' is a variation on the more common /**beet maal wa-ʕayaal**/ 'a house of wealth and children'. The phrase is a courtesy expression used at weddings to wish the bride and groom a happy life. It occurs here as an allusion to the girl's transition, through the process of circumcision, from girlhood to womanhood in her society.

**8** The clause /**gaddamta ʔanaa lfarʕ alb-itannaa**/ 'I have presented the branch that sways' is a metaphor. It describes the poet's beloved as /**lfarʕ**/ 'the branch' that is slim and supple. This slim and supple beauty is also /**alb-itannaa**/ 'the one that sways', that is, as she walks.

# Translations

**Let's get to know some Sudanese**

A: Please introduce yourselves.

B: In the name of God, the merciful and compassionate, Radwan Ali Kharraj.

A: Yes.

C: In the name of God, the merciful and compassionate, Lubna Muhammad Suliman, Islamic University of Omdurman, second year, communications, Artimiry Island.

A: May you live long. Yes?

D: In the name of God, the merciful and compassionate, Manal Jabir Abbas, Eastern Nile University College, third year, commerce and banking.

A: Yes?

E: In the name of God, the merciful and compassionate, Mazhar Sayyid Abd al-Qadir, University of Khartoum, Artimiry Island.

A: Artimiry Island, good.

## How I came to Washington

I came to Washington as follows: first thing, we left Sudan in August, ah ... and went ah ... to Nairobi. We stayed in Nairobi for about two months. Ah ... on the twenty-ninth of September, at exactly one o'clock in the morning. Ah ... we went to Washington on the Belgian airline. Ah ... ah ... we landed in Belgium for about, roughly two hours or so. After that we left Belgium and arrived in New York. Ah ... from New York, we reached New York around one o'clock in the afternoon. Ah ... we stayed there for a long time, a period of time, you know. After that we departed for Washington, where we arrived at about seven o'clock in the evening. This means that the trip was, approximately, from one o'clock in the morning until the next day at seven o'clock in the evening from Nairobi to Washington. It was a was very, very nice trip. Ah ... but a little tiring because, of course, the distance was long. It took around, about eighteen hours. Ah ... but generally, that is, it was a nice trip. Of course, my husband was with me, and ah ... the nicest thing about it ... ah ... you know, was that we landed in Belgium. Belgium was very nice even though we didn't leave the airport. But in general, you know, from afar, sort of, a person was, you know, Brussels, he got an idea of it, that it's a very, very nice country. In New York, we also didn't leave the airport, but ah ... we also learned something, you know, more or less, from the crowds of people and so forth. We learned something about the country in the airport. Ah ... now, ah ... we arrived in Washington at eight or seven-thirty in the evening. Ah ... the weather, you know, was a little cold. We weren't able to enjoy, you know, our arrival except, ah ... you know, after we settled down and so forth.

## Childhood memories

Ah ... I, of course ... ah ... my upbringing. I was born in ah ... Khartoum, this was 1960, when my father, of course, was working in Khartoum in ... as a medical assistant. At that time they used to transfer them a lot. Right after I was born they up and transferred my father to ... Southern Kordofan, to a place whose name is Hayban, you know, a small town. So ... in this town, of course, I experienced ... my upbringing really took place there, that is, a village whose population is about three or four thousand people or so. So ... you know, it was a very, very nice time. My father, of course, used to work in the ... in the ... in the clinic. It was, of course, the largest health center in the area, of course, and he headed this clinic. So, anyway, those were good times, you know, and in that area itself ... you know, ah ... they were born, almost all my siblings, that would be the ... Ahmad, who is older than me, was already born. Ibrahim was born there. Thuriya was born there, and Awatif, and Salah, and Balla and al-Jeeli, ah ... Anyway, you know, we were, as they say, a very closely knit family. Ah ... but, of course, according to the circumstances of ... of ... the war and the problems happening in Sudan, of course, they forced my father to move to Al-Ubayyid. Our upbringing was also ... we spent a long time in Al-Ubayyid and we returned to the area again. Currently, now, my father, of course ... and the family now resides in, between Khartoum and ... ah ... Kadugli, which is the ... where my father works now. Ah ... the area where I grew up was of course a region, as they say, you know, the area maybe that until this moment I remember most every day, you know. The biggest wish I have now, I only hope to make it come true, is to visit this area, because my memories of childhood and friends are connected to it, and of friends, of growing up, and my whole upbringing. A person, when one first became aware of this world, one was first aware of this region and saw it and knew life in it and even one's people, you know, the ... the ... the family and relatives and so on. So ... because of that, you know, I hope to visit it, you know.

### Love song: Two days' absence

You're gone for two days and don't reappear.
Our lives are counted in hours.
You leave us behind you, sleepless.
We spend the night in weeping and sighs.

By your life, we yearn for you.
We get lost in your lovely cheeks.
The flowers of love open wide.
They make us forget the agony that is past.

We get lost in your lovely eyelashes
and in your loosened locks.
We forget our people and the whole cosmos.
We vanish in the beauty of the words.

When you speak, my pulse stops.
I forget what has passed and what is to come.
I'm afraid the night will separate us.
I dissolve in torment and in sighs.

Why, o master, don't you have mercy
on eyes filled with tears?
Come, o master, don't be away for long!
Our lives are counted in hours.

### The Educational system in Sudan

A: At that time, until our time … When we went into college in '96 and that … or so, the universities in Sudan were the University of Khartoum. Barely … the … they had started to set up the University of Juba, ah … in the south, that's in Juba. Really, it was a very, very strong and successful university. And there was al-Jazira University. There was one university, the one that … this was, people with an Egyptian education used to go to it and so on. This was Cairo University, Khartoum branch.

B: That would be closed now.

A: Yes …

B: But you know that now, in the current situation, in order to go to college …

A: Haa …

B: … other than … the … the … the … the … the … the academic level that you're supposed to … to … you know, put on file. It is in the … in the … in the … your results …

A: Yes, there is military service …

B: Also, you have to be on compulsory military service for the period of a year.

A: Haa …

B: It, you would be completely far away from the academic field and … and schools and all that …

A: Haa …

B: You're just on military service and compulsory service …

A: True.

B: And … and if you don't do it …

A: You won't …

B: … you won't let you … They won't give you a certificate.

A: True.

B: The Sudanese School Certificate, after you … you study in upper secondary school, they won't give you the Sudanese School Certificate.

A: Haa …

B: And as a result, to escape the … the … the … the boys or girls, the girls don't have a problem with a thing like this, but the boys, most of the boys who take the certificate exam don't want to go on compulsory service or they don't want to go, ah … they would be untrained when they send them to a wartime situation.

A: Ah …

B: Hundreds of them die because they are not trained in … the … the … they call it the … complete or tactical training in order for them to face, for example, a place of war.

A: Haa …

B: So they up and get killed. In a case like this, they have suddenly become afraid to go on compulsory service.

A: True.

B: The … ah … This fear of theirs makes them not take the certificate exam …

A: True.

B: … because this certificate, something like this comes after it.

A: True.

B: It is … It's reached the point that in the street there is a very, very large number of boys, I know them, that their level, they are smart, but they are afraid to finish, to take the exam for the Sudanese School Certificate so they won't get into a situation like this.

A: True.

B: Or they may die.

A: True.

B: So they've started not finishing their education. They've started to take marginal jobs … ah … ah … ah … they are meaningless.

A: You know …

B: You feel that there's a lost future, that there is … there's a very large segment of boys …

A: No … Yes, true.

B: And now, because of that, you find, for example, the majority ...

A: But I ...

B: ...of boys, ah ... in universities and so on, you find the percentage of girls is higher than boys.

## Developments in education

A: I, if I've told you about, Rajaa, about the … the … story of my education, you know, ah … you know, something like that, there was something fun about it, you know. When I was five or four years old, my mother took me, she sent me to Qur'an school. I didn't learn, you know, really, I don't remember whether I finished the last portion of the Qur'an or whether I didn't finish it. And … all this was in '64 exactly. You know, really, education in the old days had value and education was really, you know, something unusually comfortable, you know, because the teachers themselves were people aah … you know, really very, very highly qualified. So, in '64, I started school. It was called "primary school" in the old days. Ah … you know, "primary." You took four years there, but there were many, many people who graduated from this primary school who could work as teachers because during those four years, you would really be, your curricula, aah … you know, or the things they taught you would really qualify you in a very, very good way in dictation, in memorization, in to arithmetic. You know, in the old days we used to call it arithmetic, not mathematics. So … from '64 until, ah … '68 or, you know, '69 or …, we finished this elementary school. Immediately, they tested us. So, praise God, I passed, and they took me in middle, ah … school. Middle school was also four years. You know, primary school was four years and middle school was four years. And … high school was four years. In '69 I was in the first year of middle school, ah … Nimeiri's revolution took place in '69. So they up and said, "No, this system is really an ineffective system and the people who leave, they grad …. The people, the people, you know, who don't go back to repeat [a year of classwork], when they graduate, they have only four years [of schooling], and they are people who are not well qualified." Although, really they were really, really excellent. But, the point is, this is all just politics. So … when I was in the first year of middle school, they up and changed it, they said no. "This 'elementary' school will be six years." Its name is, aah… it is, ah…

B: Elementary.

A: Elementary…

B: Instead of primary.

A: Yes, instead of primary and …. middle school, they call it, it is "general secondary school." So … I, you know …

B: This was in '72?

A: No, no in '69. This was in '69. So … I, instead this studying of mine being four years, in middle school instead of studying four years, ah … I studied there five years. And, again, praise God, you know, I was very, very successful with God's help. I passed the first time and entered really the best high school, ah … in Sudan, that is Hantoub Secondary School.

### Adil and Hoda

A: What's wrong with you?

B: Adil, there's a man who's been watching you for a long time.

A: Is that so?

B: Yes, that one, look at him.

A: Where is he?

B: [Hoda points him out.] Yes, that one there, and it seems he means you no good.

A: That man?

B: Yes.

[Adil heads towards the man and is hit by a car. Later, in the hospital, he and Hoda continue their conversation.]

A: Hoda.

B: Thank God you're safe, Adil.

A: May God keep you safe, too, Hoda.

B: Why would you do this to me, Adil?

A: I'm sorry, Hoda. I didn't mean to.

B: I don't know what happened to him.

A: You were worried about me, weren't you?

B: Who's that man? You ran after him in an extraordinary fashion.

A: I wanted to catch up with him, Hoda. I had to catch up with him.

B: Who's that man? Really, you tell me that …

A: Hoda, he's my uncle, the one I've been looking for, Hoda.

B: But you're certain?

A: I'm certain, yes.

B: But, but that one, his appearance isn't nice. The look in his eyes is frightening.

A: He's unfortunate, Hoda. He's suffering from loneliness and homelessness.

B: But it seems that he loves you, Adil.

A: There something which draws me to him, Hoda. There's a

feeling that always, always draws me to him. There's a link between him and me that I can't understand, but unfortunately I didn't catch up to him.

## Searching for a job

A: Hello?

B: Hello, how are you?

A: Hi, how are you doing?

B: How are you doing?

A: By God, I'm fine, thank God.

B: What have you done about a job?

A: By God, Hannan, this job thing is making a really big problem for me. First off, as you see, this country, working conditions here are a little hard.

B: Ah ...

A: So ... anyway, you know, through the organization, by a ..., on my own, I'm trying my best to find a way.

B: You mean, you've found ah ... ah ... opportunities at certain places or not yet?

A: By God, ah ... of course, there's a newspaper that comes out on Sunday.

B: Haa ...

A: Every Sunday it has a lot of advertisements for jobs and work here.

B: Have you applied to any of them?

A: By God, you know, I submitted maybe, nearly ten applications.

B: Where exactly did you apply?

A: By God, I applied first thing, it was to a company in Virginia.

B: Aha ...

A: And I also applied to a kind of institute. They need someone to be, for ... assistant registrar.

B: Aha ...

A: I'm trying, of course, you know I, of course, it is, my work is the field of languages and this field of organization work in particular.

B: Aha ...

A: Because of that, you know, I'm concentrating on finding something in the field I know, of course, I ... this field of organization work.

B: Yes, for sure, since this will benefit you a lot later on, you know, in the future. And ... did you do an interview with them or not yet?

A: By God, you know, ah ... I had an interview, ah, actually two interviews. One I did in Virginia, at an organization, people whose name is John Snow. You know, their work is like the work of people in the A[merican] R[efugee] C[ommittee] in Sudan.

B: Ah ...

A: You know, an organization like that, you can say, works in the field of ... of ... of ... of ... health services. They make this, contracts with the government in .... Africa, in the Arab world, and so on. So ..., anyway, you know, it's kind of a nice job. But if a person got it, it would be really great, you know.

## Life in America

A: Did I tell you… Where do you come from?

B: I'm from Sudan, from al-Jazira.

A: Aha … from al-Jazira. Your village, what's its name?

B: Its name is Umm Jurays, but I was born in Tayyib al-Shaykh Abd al-Bagi.

A: Okay, this Umm Jurays ah … ah. What's its name … What do your parents do?

B: I, my father is a farmer and businessman. My mother ah … you know, she doesn't work except at home. When did you come to Sudan? When did you come to America?

A: No, America, I came about ah … I've been, I've been here for approximately three years, you know.

B: Approximately three years.

A: Ah …

B: I came approximate ah … approximately five years ago.

A: Aha …

B: I've just about done five years.

A: Yes.

B: Aha … you … when do you plan to return?

A: By God, I'll go back, you know, after five years …, something like that. That is, in two or three years.

B: Were you expecting to find so many nationalities?

A: Of course, yes, yes, ah … I tell you, yes. I expected it because everybody in the world, when he dreams, has the American dream.

B: Right.

A: That, you know, he dreams that he will come to America to make his dreams come true.

B: Right.

A: But they … their point of view is, they think the process is just easy.

B: Haa …

A: That as soon as he came to America, he became a millionaire and achieved what he wanted to do and rode around in a big car ...

B: And lived well.

A: And so on. But here, no. You come and really start from zero ...

B: Haa ...

A: From five dollars an hour ...

B: Haa ...

A: ...and a lot of aggravation and you don't know where, and so on, by the grace of God ...

B: Haa ...

A: So there's not, not, you know, it's not so easy or anything ... Here, America, really, if you ... you dream or something like that it's because it demands that you work very, very hard.

### America

A: Aha ... Hanan, you've just arrived in America, what's the thing that you like most about America?

B: By God, the truth is, you know, seriously, the thing I like most about this country, first off, of course, it's different from all of the countries in the world or all of the countries that we've visited. The other thing is the amount of freedom and democracy here.

A: Ah ...

B: Ah? Then, of course, it's a very, very organized country, you know, the fact is, I imagine that there's nothing like it for ... for organization. Of course, this is a very good thing.

A: Ah ...

B: Ah ... you know, the thing that I ..., you know, I miss ...

A: Ah ...

B: Of course, a person, you know, it's natural that he misses his people and family.

A: Ah ...

B: The ... the thing I advise, for example, for any people coming here, that is to this country, you know, is that he strengthen his language.

A: By God, you're right, you know.

B: Because it's the language of communication and so on. Aha ... how about you, what's the thing you like most?

A: By God, Hanan [laughing], you didn't leave anything for me. But, of course, the thing I like most, as you mentioned a little earlier, it's ah ... the system, first of all. Then, you know, it's a country that really, you know, deserves, for example, to be called, for example, the greatest place in the world, you know. A person ... despite his cleverness and despite what do you call it ... But the system is able to control any individual, and everyone takes complete advantage of his freedom within the bounds of the law and with respect for the law and for other people. You know, the ... you know, a person, when he feels ... when he hears this term "human rights," and a person, this thing, [laughing] really, when he comes here, he finds that it really does exist. Ah ... at the same time, too, my advice to, to, to, to, to friends and to people who are coming here, for example, it is ... you know, the most important thing is that one try to learn the language in his own country, if there is any way to. If he doesn't learn it there, for example, he would come here and try, first thing, try to concentrate on ... on ... on studying the language, you know. In addition to that, you know, people should not set their hopes very much on the mere fact that they have gotten to America meaning that all of their personal circumstances have been settled or that their problems have been solved. No, I imagine the situation requires, demands a little effort. You know, a person should take on a little responsibility, but things in the end will be resolved because opportunities are plentiful for each individual, you know. Anyone who makes an effort, I imagine, will find the ... the ... the ... the thing he wants, you know.

## When you go to Sudan

B: Are you writing to your family or are you sending them money or do you call them?

A: Yes, you know, I … I send you, you know … Really, I send them, but, kind of often, from time to time, sort of, I send them money.

B: Yes, fine, this means you've got in mind, you know, ah … ah … a lot of money so you can go to Sudan, so you can take back money and gifts and so forth for people. Do you have a lot of family, I mean?

A: What? We, there in Sudan, the … the … the … You're not obligated just to your mother and father. You know … when you bring something from here, you bring something for your mother's sister and you bring something for your father's sister and for the children ah … of your mother's brother and for the children of your father's sister. All of it and for your whole village, you send them, you … you … you give them something. People come and say to you, "Brother, you've come." Anyway, so you try to … to make everybody happy, to make them very, very happy. Ah … as soon as he comes, there he is, absolutely right away someone gets together with you. "My man, when did you get in? So, what's new in that country?" He talks to them and everyone asks about you, of course, so …. A situation like this, you have to be, for example, ready starting from here to bring with you a good amount of money and things like that and so on. When I was coming here, everybody would ask, ah, would say, "No, man, no, you're going all the way to America. Really, it itself has, but this is, this, this is really something, it's not like, this itself is really a whole other world." Because really, it's very, very advanced, America. But people are still people. This is still … a country here, there's … there are people and there are human relationships that you find between people. Everybody works and there are ah … families. Here, there are families here, too. You find that there really are families. There's a father and a mother and a sister like we have back in Sudan. So, they really are very, very eager. When I came back from here, I tell them everything about America.

### Just tell me what's going on

A: [approaching] Khalid, Khalid, Khalid! I hope there's nothing wrong?

B: Really, Hajj, what can I tell you? I don't know exactly what led me here. Even I don't know what brought me to him.

A: Exactly what is going on?

B: I caused an injury to someone dear to me, Hajj.

A: Where is he from? A relative of yours?

B: Ah ... ah ... no, no, no, he's not, no, yes ...

A: Khalid, I asked before, do you have family here? You told me no. You denied it. Tell the truth, Khalid, do you have family in this city?

B: No, no, no, no, Hajj. I don't have family here.

A: Where's your family?

B: My family is from the Northern Province.

A: So, you still don't want to tell me the truth. You're still hiding things from me, Khalid.

B: No, Hajj.

A: There's no need for this. It's not the time for it, not now. This friend of yours, how is he now?

B: I don't know. I'm afraid he might be badly hurt.

A: When you were late and didn't come to the store. I decided to come see what's happening.

B: Since yesterday, I've been in a very difficult situation.

A: Your staying here is making things worse and wearing you out more. Get up, come to the store. Come with me. Take a little break at least. Come on, brother. My son, what's come between us, let it be lifted. Just let go of what's on your mind

B: Hajj, there's not, not, not anything, but ...

A: No, there is, there is. For two days, I've noticed that you're preoccupied and distracted all the time. Surely, there's something going on. Just tell me what's going on. Speak to me, think of me as your older brother, tell me exactly what's happening to you.

B: There's nothing wrong, Hajj. There's nothing that I'm hiding from you at all, Hajj.

A: No, there is. This means you don't want to talk. You don't want to tell me.

B: Hajj, what can I say? If there is something wrong, I'll tell you right away.

A: I asked you, do you have family here in the capital?

B: Hajj, but I told you I don't have family here. My family is in the provinces.

A: You still don't want to talk. Okay, that's all right. I'm leaving you alone, Khalid. Whatever you want. I'm not going to force you. Whatever you want.

## Artimiry Island

A: Family and friends ah … inside Sudan and outside Sudan, our brothers and sisters here today, may the peace, mercy, and blessings of God the Exalted be upon you. In the name of God, the merciful and compassionate, we begin our program for today and we are very pleased that our guests for this installment … are the Association of the Sons of Artimiry Island of the Mahas in Khartoum. So that we get to know Artimiry of the Mahas, we are pleased to present Sheikh Idris Muhammad Sadiq, to tell us about Artimiry. Ah …

B: Ah … the truth is that Artimiry Island is one of the islands of the Mahas, under the jurisdiction of the Wadi Halfa district in the Birka region. It is an island that enjoys … ah … a high population density and all of its citizens are from a single ethnic group. This island benefits from many enterprises, agriculture among them. That is the main profession of the citizens of this island, inasmuch as the island benefits from a large agricultural project. The total area of … the project that is located on the island is about three hundred feddans. Ah … this project is one of the largest projects in the Northern Province, one remarked on by everyone who has visited it. Among the … cultural activities, of course, they hold symposia and …

A: Of course, these are known and …

B: And … [audience chuckles] on the social side there are … ah … family councils. They send convoys from Khartoum to …

A: Artimiry…

B: Recently, a month or two ago, ah … a convoy was sent from Khartoum to Artimiry to construct a dam. Speaking of which, I wish that everyone who cares about the good of Sudan would visit Artimiry Island to find there …

A: Something to like …

B: …that gigantic dam …

A: Aha …

B: …that was constructed …

A: Ah ...

B: ...without mechanical devices and with the hands of ...

A: The sons of the region.

B: ...the sons of the region and the sons of Artimiry, and so that they come to record it, ah ... for history.

A: Ah ... the ... the ... what you said, all of it is great, I mean. We congratulate, ah ... our kin in Artimiry, ah ...for their great efforts, especially the matter of the dam. But I would like to know, what does "Artimiry" mean?

B: "Artimiry" in, ah ... the ... the Nubian dialect back home is divided, it has two parts.

A: Ah ...

B: "Arti," "arti" in the dialect ...

A: Ah ...

B: It means "island."

A: Yes.

B: "Miry," that is "new."

A: Ha ... it is the "new island," that is.

B: "The new island."

A: Very nice.

### A political solution to the problem of the south

A: In the name of God, the merciful and compassionate. Ah … the … the … the news from Sudan …, Rajaa, the political kind, do you know what they wrote today? That ah … the people in the government and the rebels have agreed to a cease-fire in the south to help the people of … ah … of Bahr al-Ghazal especially and … you know. There are ongoing discussions or there is mediation. This is so that, for example, there will be a diplomatic solution to … or a political solution to the problem of the south. I mean, the people there, really, a war that's lasted sixteen years and things like that and so on, so … which have a very, very serious impact. Generally, the war in the south, you know, it's been since Sudan got its independence, you know. The … the … our brothers in the south of Sudan ah … you know, have always been … been in revolt against the different Sudanese governments, you know, from the first national government up to now, the current government. Up to now, people have not been able to come to a solution, you know, a political one, really, to this problem, and that would not … you … you … you know. For the most part Sudan, you know, its poverty and the … the … the … the lack of ah … it's called, the lack of economic development and so forth. Ah … the main reason for that is this ongoing war which has slaughtered thousands of the … or millions of citizens and at the same time, you know, the … ah … the extraordinary destruction of the Sudanese economy. So … ah … God willing, you know, I hope to God that, for example, these people will indeed reach a political solution and so forth, so that the country a little and so on, that it can move ahead in a good way and something like that … I also see that the American government has welcomed the … the … the cease-fire and so forth … and not … not …. They said people from IGAD will meet next month, ah … most likely also to continue a dialogue on this situation so as to reach, a solution, ah … a political one.

B: I ah … the … the truth is, ah … The war in the south, of course, we all, that is, from, since birth, ah … we've lived with this war in the south. Economically, it really … threatens Sudan a lot. The war, ah … in the south, I don't think that it will come to an end easily, al-Mahi, as long as there's … there's no democratic rule there. Ah … the … the destruction that's taking place and … and for Sudan to … to restore its economy or to bring back its former excellent position. The … the … the present government, as long as it is an Islamic extremist one, cannot give a large share to … to the south as … as a part of Sudan that is Christian. So what I think is that the … the … the political situation in general will not, you know, go in the right direction or be anything satisfactory to all parties so long as there is no democratic regime in Sudan.

### The electoral constitution and the Islamic Front

A: To tell the truth, the … the … democracy, I think that the … the regime or the situation of the … the … the government that is in Sudan currently, ah … it doesn't have any type of democracy. When democracy came, it came for a very short time, '85, '86. But I, you know, ah … the end of democratic government, I blame it on members of the government themselves, because they are the ones that set up the … the … the constitution, the … the … the electoral one that brought the Islamic Front again. So … this is their responsibility. In addition, because, you know, Sudan without democracy cannot advance because all of the destruction that is taking place, it is taking place because of the political situation of the … of the current government, whether it's the situation in the south or even the situation in the north. You know, today in the north, as well people because of the … the political situation don't, I'm not, not, not, I don't see any progress, but rather decline. Because I was in Sudan last November, and I noticed the decline going on, you know, in all domains and all of this …

B: Yes

A: … results from the …

B: Yes …

A: … from the … from the … the current, you know, economic situation.

B: True, you, you know, really …

A: Haa …

B: When you say that …

A: If it's the al-Shifa Factory, you're going to talk about the Shifa factory, for example, I don't believe at all that this government doesn't have, ah … that it doesn't have anything besides the manufacturing of medicines.

B: Haa …

A: I, you may not agree with me in this matter, but I think that, that, that I really don't trust this … this … this situation …

B: Yes …

A: … because, you know, in the end a situation like all of this, this, when it, you know, is not in agreement with all of the other countries or, or doesn't open Sudan to, to all of, for example, of the world. I expect that it might be, in order to provide for itself, it would do things, ah … to … to insure itself for the future, if anything were to happen, you know.

B: Yes, no …

A: I'm speaking frankly, but I know …

B: Yes, no, no, true, yes. Not, you know, but you said that … that … you blame it on the … the … the … people of the democratic government, because it brought in the people of the Front and so on. This Front, the democratic government, and of course, I'm not a supporter of the Front or anything, but the democratic government didn't bring in the Islamicists. They, they originally, these Islamicists really started in Nimeiri's time.

A: The … the … the … the … the … the thing, the thing that I meant …

B: Haa …

A: … is that the transitional government …

B: Haa …

A: … that was under the leadership of Siwar al-Dhahab and Gazuli Dafalla is the one that implemented the electoral constitution. Right? This electoral constitution, its details, its details are what led to the introduction of the Islamic Front, because Gazuli Dafalla and … and … and … and … and Siwar al-Dhahab both were originally from the Islamic Front. I'm not against Islam …

B: Haa …

A: I'm a person who was raised ah … in the Islamic way. I love Islam very much, but I don't like Islam to get into politics, you know, Islam is a creed and a personal thing …

B: Ah …

A: That is, everybody practices Islam as a relationship between himself and our Lord. This is a very, very special relationship, but the … the … the Islamic law that currently holds power, its application to … to … to … to politics is not connected to Islam. This Islam was just put in place so that simple people can be gathered in the … in, in, under an Islamic law in accordance with Islam.

### The most active party was the Islamic Front

A: From the time that Turabi intervened sometime ... sometime ... sometime in seventy-something he worked and he brought in ... and there was Nimeiri, he brought him in, you know. Anyway, the ... he brought in Islamic law in '83 and so on. At that time, they were working, you know. You remember our university days and how it was the most active party, it was these people in the Islamic Front. So these people worked and made, you know, they made themselves ah ... a very, very broad base of support for themselves among educated people in particular. So when Nimeiri was removed, you know, and it really came, the election law came along, they didn't ... they didn't, they didn't do it, the democratic people. It came along and [finger snap] that really was the end of it. An uprising arose took place and election law came in. These people won it. They won, you know, really by means of the ... because they basically had been forming their base of support. So from that time these others didn't give them a chance. They weren't going to give them a chance. This, they came, they came, you know, they entered the ... They entered the ... the ... the ... the ... the Constituent Assembly, they entered it through ... by means of the elections. Really, you know, they did ... they really did sweep some of the constituencies belonging to the parties that ... those big ones, which would be the Democratic Unionist Party and the Umma Party. The ... the problem of the Umma Party and the Democratic Unionist Party is that they are parties that really, you know, are hereditary parties, right? Hereditary, and besides that there's really something, you know, something. As I told you, these people are organized by ideology. They ... they work with ... you know, a person with all his strength and things like that, so that, for example, this ...who are very, very active, the opposite of the parties ...

B: They're organized ...

A: Yes, in contrast to these other parties, the Umma and Democratic Unionist Party. You know, these are parties that really rely only on their inheritance, as they call it, the historical one. These people came in, really, this ... this ... they came in, they entered and ... and ... take ... you know, they swept many, many constituencies and especially the constituencies of high school and college graduates, you know, and people who ... the constituencies of high school and college graduates because they are all educated people and so on. Because they, basically their work depended on high schools and universities. Okay? So they came, no, they didn't come, not, not, you know, it wasn't, this was not a mistakee or anything. These people came in really, [xxx] but they, really, their count in comparison, you know, or the votes that they won in comparison to the big party or so, was, of course, less than the votes of that one. This, you know, was cleverness on the part of ah ... that would be Dr. Turabi, that, for example, when the elections came along ah ... You know, instead of continuing to be the Muslim Brotherhood, he turned it into the National Islamic Front. You know, he changed it and made it like that, so that it included a very, very broad composition. I particularly, you know, from our own experience in, you know, in the areas, even that are outside Khartoum and so on, ah ... The ... the ... the Sudanese people are a very, very good people and they really want to protect Islam. So when they felt that these are people, ah ... here they are, they want to apply the Islamic Law and they came for the sake of Islam or something like that. So you find that people who are more or less simple, a person gets scared that if he doesn't give his vote to ... to people like these or something, you know, it's as if he were against Islam.

## The economic blockade of Sudan

A: The income of a Sudanese worker, you know, the income of a worker, the …, the … the lowest person in the employment structure of the government is about sixty thousand Sudanese pounds. This sixty thousand Sudanese pounds equals in reality, this is per month, sixty thousand in reality equals, it is about thirteen or fourteen dollars, ah …

B: More, more.

A: Ah … we, [background noise] thirty dollars, see, thirty dollars, you know, when the dollar is at two-and-a-half thousand. As I said, ah … the salary of a simple worker, that would be something like sixty thousand. This does not cover two or three days' expenses. So there is a very, very big difference for … How is he going to resolve it? Ah … so let's say, let's ask people. "Hey everybody, you're the best. How do these people get it? I mean, he tries to cover this amount. Where does he get it from?" You know, they'll tell you, there are other people, who find ah … another job after their official job. Ah … there are people who will tell you, "Brother, by God, most of the Sudanese population depends on its expatriates. These are people, you know, that would be living in America kind of like us, in the Gulf, those who are wherever. You know, any family, ah … must have another source of income other than their own income, because really over there, it is that. And … um … the … the … anyway, things like this began and now this is exactly the situation they're living through. So … there are, they tell stories and such. A person really has to be moved by them and pained by them, because in reality there is a very, very severe economic embargo on Sudan. It is well known, you know, that even people in the government don't deny this thing nor do people in the opposition deny this thing, deny that, for example, there is really an embargo, deny that there is deterioration, deny that there is, you know, really ah … the … the … the citizens are suffering a very, very heavy burden. And … the … as a result of … of these things, you find that all of the Sudanese people, most of them, they said before that the Sudanese people had no experience of life away from home. There was no

Sudanese who traveled outside of his country until just recently. It's gotten to the point that every household has to send someone outside of Sudan to at least, you know, provide them with some of their needs, ah ... in the way of expenses and other things. So ... you know, anyway, you know, really ... it's a situation, you know, ah ... ah ... it ... it ... you know ... it's very, very, very difficult. I hope that really ah ... something good will happen.

**Because you didn't pay your bill!**

A: Oh my, oh my, oh my! Today the Hajja has come early.

[all respond]

B: My goodness!

C: Really and truly, I see she's happy, too.

D: Yes, may God keep her happy, brothers, may God keep her happy.

E: By God, it's true I'm happy. You know, I'm not a lot happy, but I'm not unhappy either.

A: Even so, Hajja, I hope everything is okay. But what's wrong with you? What's happening to you?

E: I got a letter from my very dear friend ...

F: Ah ...

E: Bitt Hajj al-Fadul.

F: Ah ...

G: Hajja, from Omdurman, from Ombadda?

E: Yes, absolutely. But she said some sort of strange things in it.

H: Then in that case, tell us what these strange things would be, I mean.

I: Ah ... tell, tell.

E: Yes, she said the water people came to her house.

J: Ah ...

E: They said to her, "Listen, Hajja, we're going to cut off the water."

D: And she said to them, "For what reason?" He said to her ...

A: "Because you didn't pay your bill."

D: [all respond] Yes.

B: "And anybody who doesn't pay his bill, we have to cut his water off for sure."

G: Because, Hajja, the national economy depends on citizens contributing to pay what they owe.

D: And the citizens are supposed to pay.

E: Yes, but, son, this water faucet, it's been, you know, one, two, three months since it dripped a single drop of water.

A: The fact is, Hajja, if you had paid, it wouldn't, you know ...

E: Yes, but are we supposed to pay you or do we pay the man with the barrels who brings us water on his donkey?

G: Aha ... Hajja, they'd better not have cut it off after that.

J: At any rate, the latest news ...

D: Aha ...

J: ... says that the water situation in Khartoum has begun to improve.

E: Who would believe such a thing? The water gets cut off in Khartoum?

A: Yes, by God, they said, for months.

G: O my friend, yes ... by God, but what a story, these people, you know, could really get sick.

E: Aha ... brothers, good-bye.

I: No, Hajja, it's still early.

G: Aha, ... Hajja, you didn't tell me. How is your friend Bitt Hajj Al-Fadul's refrigerator?

A: Ah ... and tell us, how's she doing with the electricity?

E: Ah ... that's a whole other story.

H: Hajja, Hajja, good-bye, good-bye.

**What will we say to people?**

A: A disaster and it's happened to us. This was the only thing missing.

B: What's going on?

A: How are we going to face people?

B: What's going on? What's going on? Awad, brother, what's going on?

A: It's Khalid.

B: What's wrong with Khalid?

A: Khalid killed himself a man. Imagine, imagine who he killed?

B: Who?

A: He killed a merchant in the market.

B: [gasps]

A: Everyone praises him.

B: God rest his soul [xxx].

A: I, where can I turn? I, I, I, where should I fly to? How can I face people? How can I look people in the face? I, ah, this, this, this, is this a human being?

[in another room]

C: Poor you, brother! [crying] Poor me! Every disaster, they are setting you up for it, but they say you were the one that did it.

D: What are you crying about? About your brother's scandals? Is this a thing to do? He kills someone who took him in off the street and opened his house to him.

C: Abbas, my brother didn't kill anyone. Abbas, for God's sake, I object. By the Prophet, leave me alone with my misfortune. Leave me alone with my disaster.

D: Your misfortune?

C: Yes, Abbas, leave me alone, for God's sake.

D: This is a criminal, a vicious man, an animal in human form. God help me. This, this, this, this, now what are we going to say to people?

C: Brother, for God's sake! Forget about people. People can go get lost. You don't think of anything but people. It's all people. This is my brother! Those are people!

D: Enough! God damn this life! [woman crying]

[back to first room]

A: What is your brother? By God, leave us alone! What are you all crying about? A killer!

C: [xxx] Poor me, brother! [crying continues]

A: He kills someone. No, and who does he kill? He kills the man who was good to him, the man who opened his house to him, and for what? To rob him.

B: [crying] Did they find him? Did they catch him, Awad? Poor me, my brother! Poor me, my brother!

A: No, they haven't caught him, but they'll catch him. They'll catch him. Yes, where is he going to go? All of the police in the city are searching for him, all of them.

C: Poor me, brother! [crying continues]

A: The scandal is they're publishing his picture in the papers. That's it ...

C: Poor me ...

A: ... our good name is finished.

C: Poor me! Awad, you're only thinking of yourself. You're not thinking of your brother, brother.

A: Your brother. By God, leave us alone! The hell with your brother and this nonsense! He thinks he'll run away. Where will he run to? He'll run away and where is he going to go? He'll be caught, he'll be tried, and he'll be hanged. Yes, he'll be hanged. He'll pay the price for his crime.

C: No, my brother.

A: He must pay the price for his crime.

## Marriage customs

A: Marriage in Sudan, for example the choice may be, ah … the two may choose each other, if they are from modest families and from families that are ah … upper-class. Or the family may choose for the … for the … for the boy the girl that he marries. But in some families it is the case that there must be love and there must be a relationship and there must be, ah …

B: Mutual understanding …

A: Mutual understanding …

B: Haa …

A: Before marriage

B: Haa …

A: Before marriage …

B: Haa …

A: This may be most of … most of … the cases that are, ah … not … in the … in families that are, maybe, upper-class or a little bit … urbanized, not modest, in society.

B: Educated, yes. [xxx]

A: Because Sudanese society …

B: Yes.

A: … has many social classes. It has social classes …

B: It, it, it, the main tradition, Rajaa, the tradition, you know, that … that … that … that … is that people as soon, for example, as the family, ah … their son says, ah … he has decided on a certain person.

A: "I want So-and-so."

B: Yes, a particular girl who … who … the sisters go ahead, in most cases it's the sisters, not the mother, who go to the girl's family. You know, they go to talk to her mother …

A: With the girl herself …

B: Yes, with the girl and with her mother …

A: [xxx].

B: Anyway, they go over there to their house and talk to them.

They say to them, "My friend, by God, he wants, he wants your daughter."

A: This is what we call *fatḥat alxaʃam*.

B: Yes, so … so … so this is the first step that is generally taken, you know, the women go and after the women, the men go.

A: Haa …

B: After the agreement occurs, the men go. That's it, this thing is finished. People start to make trills of joy, ah … ah … Right after that, that's it, the thing is done, or something like that. People start to prepare for the business of the wedding. So, there is …

A: The *guulat xeer* …

B: The *guulat xeer*, you know, because they said "May it be good." You know, these people said, said "may it be good." They go give them part of, you know, not a large sum, you know, it's not like the dowry.

A: Haa …

B: They said "May it be good," that's it. They say, "Okay, So-and-so, take it, this is your money. This is your *guulat xeer*. We … on such-and-such day we'll come to pay the dowry in full." Usually …

A: The *sidd almarr* …

B: The *sidd almaal*, and the *sadd almaal*, with it, too, is the bride's suitcase, the *ʃeela*.

A: Yes.

B: Yes, we call it the *ʃeela*, of course. So … that's it, the date has been set for the *ʃeela* and the *sadd almaal*.

A: That would be what, what and what is in the *ʃeela*?

B: The *ʃeela*, what is in it is the … you know, the … Of course, we … in, in Sudan there, the … women generally wear the *toob*, you know …

A: The well-known Sudanese *toob*.

B: The Sudanese *toob*, it's the main thing, and it's very, very, expensive. They bring it. You know, you find in, in the suitcase, you know, it has in it at least, according to people's ability, you know, there are people who bring three *toobs* in the suitcase; there are people who bring six ...

A: With it are dresses and perfumes ...

B: Yes.

A: ... and shoes and ...

B: True, true. But the main thing there, it's not the ... the ... the ... the *toobs*. It's the *toobs* and the gold jewelry.

A: All the clothing that's ...

B: This is the ...

A: That's ... that's expensive.

B: That is expensive.

A: The most costly thing.

B: Yes.

A: Right, yes.

B: So in general, people who ... they bring them the *ʃeela* and the *sadd almaal*. This thing women also go and do, like they also did with the *guulat xeer*. These things women bring.

A: Women.

B: You know, men, after the man asks for the girl's hand that ... from her father, he has no role except to sign the marriage contract with, sign the marriage contract for ... for the girl.

A: Correct.

### I might try something like this

A: And … what's it called? And you said, and you studied what, did you tell me?

B: I studied ah … in ah … Khartoum. I studied at the College of Agriculture, agricultural economics and … I'm trying again. I studied, I did a certificate in Sudan in, in economic development and planning, but the … I … I … I very much like the field of computers, so now I've started a master's in computers, but I can't move on in it fast because of work and sometimes I'm, ah, pregnant or something like that, it takes up a lot of my time.

A: Haa … and … and you … and you … you came, you … you came here. What's the reason that brought you to this country?

B: I originally came, ah … for work and I was pregnant. At the same time, I had a problem, you know, with pregnancy and delivery and so on. I have a problem with children, I have a hereditary problem. So … ah …. circumstances forced me to stay here longer because I was pregnant when I came, it was according to the doctor's decisions. After that the problem progressed and I tried to ah … finish the treatment. Then I settled down.

A: Haa …

B: After that, relative to, because my husband got the … the … the …the … the … the green card, the … the American one, through the lottery, so we settled down after that.

A: Over there in Sudan not the … the … the … things the … the … like this … childbirth and a woman whose baby dies, they take her to religious men and so on.

B: Ah … me, too, when I went to Sudan a year ago, I tried to go to religious men because ah … the problem that had progressed, you know. Three had been lost. You know, I felt that, in this way, I should try it because I'd tried everything as a treatment. So … I attempted to try something like this. Maybe, just maybe, it would work. So I'm not opposed to the idea, you know.

## What do you think of her?

A: [speaking on the telephone] Yes, I'm still on the line, yes. That's great. Listen, why don't you come visit us at home? What is this? What's wrong with that, Miss Complicated? Girlfriend, come on, you're his colleague, it's normal. ... Yes, that's it, my dear, we'll see you. I mean, does any mere human know what's in another person's heart? Fine, dear. Good-bye. [hangs up the telephone] Auntie, you haven't been here for too long. I mean, does Adil have to get in an accident for us to see you every day?

B: You, girl, do you think everybody has this kind of free time? They don't have anything to worry about? They can come all of the time to check on you, right? So tell me, who were you talking to? To that pretty girl who came and visited Adil in the hospital?

A: That's her, all right, auntie. Isn't she sweet? Tell the truth, by God.

B: O mamma! If only the other girlies were so pretty! She's nice, cheerful -- my goodness! -- and has a beautiful glow about her.

A: Yes, but you've praised her and left nothing of her out. If you didn't like her, you wouldn't talk about her like this.

B: As God is my witness. If you ask me, my girl, she's wonderful beyond words. There's nothing bad you can say about her. I've looked her over from top to bottom.

A: From head to foot.

B: Yes, by God. Mamma! She's really something.

A: Yes.

B: If you ask me, she's absolutely perfect.

A: You like her?

B: Yes, by God, I like her. There's nothing bad to say about her, not at all. Come on, tell me, your brother Adil has his eye on her, doesn't he?

A: By God, you know, something kind of like that.

B: No, I know.

C: You all are whispering and gossiping; what are you two talking about, eh?

B: We weren't talking about anything. But I want to ask you a question.

C: Yes?

B: That sweet girl that came to see Adil at the hospital. Really and truly, what do you think of her?

C: By God, she's wonderful beyond words. She's the real thing. But she's Adil's colleague at work. What are you thinking about?

B: Ah ...

C: A lawyer in the same office with him.

B: I know.

C: Rasha, isn't her name Huda?

A: That's her, all right.

C: Anyway, speaking of that, this talk can't be for nothing. There has to be another story behind this one. Maryam, sister, tell me!

B: Sister, I'm just asking a question. Can't I ask a question?

## Qur'an schools in Sudan

A: We'll talk about the … about the … the things that, the … that are religious in Sudan. A long time ago I used to hear about religious schools, but I've seen them now, ah … the … You know, you know, a long time ago when we were young, ah … there weren't … there were religious schools, but we girls, they didn't send us …

B: Ah …

A: Ah … Qur'an schools these days, they even send girls to them.

B: Ah …

A: I mean, these religious things, the … the … the religious curricula now, in the current situation, in the present government. They concentrate very much on education in Qur'an schools, because I know children now ….

B: [xxx] Rajaa, now …

A: No, I know children now who have memorized, that is, you find a child who is, ah … nine or ten years old, but they have made him memorize twelve, thirteen, fourteen *juzuʔ* of the Qur'an.

B: Okay, well, …

A: … this wasn't in …

B: But here is, there's something, there's something new, these people have added it. Really, you know, for example, say …

A: They revived it. They didn't add it, they revived it.

B: Okay, yes. They revived it or people started to have, you know, something like this, that, for example, people would go to study Islam and things like that.

A: Yes, yes.

B: But they existed. You know, the religious school existed. If you start from a religious point of view, basically Sudan didn't have an educational system, you know, before this governmental education …

A: Before education, there were Qur'an schools.

B: But there were Qur'an schools, right? Besides, the education of women in Sudan, you know, began with, ah ... you know, ah ... later than the education of men. You know? Of course, through education in Rufaa.

A: Rufaa or [xxx].

B: Yes, and in this way one person struggled for ...

A: Babikr Badri.

B: Yes, Babikr Badri, for example, that the woman has to be educated, and that she have a destiny like a boy.

A: ... and it started in Rufaa [xxx].

B: Okay? So, a long time ago people were, you know, when education started in Sudan, or when the national consciousness began in Sudan in this way, it was the ... religious brotherhoods, that ... that were educating ....

A: And the Sufi ones ...

B: Yes, in fact, the religious brotherhoods are themselves Sufi, that came and entered Sudan.

A: Ah ...

B: You know, for this Sudan, when Islam got there, it came through the Sufi brotherhoods belonging to them.

A: Correct.

B: The Dardiriya brotherhood, the Shadhaliya brotherhood, the Ahmadiya brotherhood. They entered and made mosques. The mosque is the place belonging to the sheikh, that would be the place ...

A: He teaches the Qur'an and also makes students memorize the Qur'an.

B: Yes, it's a very, very big place, you know, people take it on for two reasons. You know, a long time ago the sheikh was, ah ... the person who could read, maybe, you know, the way people understand it, for example, because of his closeness to God or something like that, maybe he can treat illness. At the same time he can take your son in hand, ah ... to make him sit make him and read the Qur'an and ...

A: Make him memorize it.

B: And, and show him how to write Arabic on a wooden tablet.

A: Yes.

### But on the feast day ...

A: Ah ... the character of people, ah ... on the feast there, you know, the day of the feast, all of it, you know, whether it is in a village or in the city, and so on. I'll tell you about the village, I, you know, we, beginning in the morning we wake up, and there is a kind of ah ... breakfast, and all, that's different, you know. We usually drink something in the morning first thing. You start with it, you drink tea.

B: This is the feast day?

A: Well ... on ordinary days, you get up ...

B: Haa ...

A: You drink tea that ... the times for the ... and until ten o'clock, or nine or so, you have breakfast. You know, it's not, we, probably because also we are, maybe, a little bit different from other peoples, we don't eat breakfast first.

B: At the beginning.

A: Yes, we drink tea in the morning until ah ... nine or ten o'clock or so, until after that we eat breakfast, we eat breakfast ...

B: Tea around six ...

A: Yes, beginning early, people as soon as they wake up, yes.

B: Six-thiry, seven in the morning, because we wake up early in the morning.

A: Yes, but the feast day is a day that is very, very different. There is breakfast with tea. There is breakfast, but breakfast, it has sweets. You know, people make *zalabiya* and, ah ... sometimes there is *shaʕiriya*. They call it *shaʕiriya*, you know, something like macaroni, and all that.

B: Or cookies.

A: So you find, you find your mother or sister or someone, they have made these things earlier. You drink tea. Everybody has something new for the feast. They have new clothes, whether it's a galabiya or pants or a shirt for the children, whether it's this or that. Everybody, you know, around seven, seven-thirty or so is ready. The entire house is awake. The ... you know, the ... the women prepare ... the ... the ... the ... the house. They put new covers and cushions on the furniture, looking nice. They … things like that. The … the men … anyway, they shave, they prepare themselves for prayer. Then everyone in the village goes out, they go to pray in a very, very big public square. Usually young girls and married women do not go out for this prayer. It's the older women, then, and all … the men, you know, even the little kids go. You know, these kids, whatever their sex, go out. So … you find that outside there's a real festival of colors belonging to new clothes appearing today. Everyone praises God and declares His greatness, you know, in the … in that square in front of the village. So, you know, the … the … the … the … this, this, this is on this feast, a feast, a feast, this is on the feast at the end of Ramadan, because there's no sacrifice then. On the other feast people slaughter an animal for the feast …

B: Eid al-Adha.

A: They go to pray, too, and they come on back in. It's possible, really, on the feast of the slaughter that everybody tries to run to his home. He doesn't go to anyone else's house right away. Why? So he can go slaughter his animal for the feast.

B: He slaughters the sheep, because, the sheep, if you slaughter it early in the morning …

A: Yes.

B: It has a specific recompense, or the return for it from our Lord …

A: Is greater.

B: Is greater.

A: And you want people to eat it.

B: The morning time after prayer has, has a greater, for… or in the afternoon it's less, ah … what do you call it, less than …

A: Anyway, you know, these, these, these are, yes, things that are like religious and all. People do but …

B: I hear things like this.

A: A person goes to slaughter his animal in order to, for example, really make people feel that that he, the … people are celebrating feast, and at least it guarantees that his sheep, people eat it. And … ah … you know, the … the … really, this country, ah … it has things, you know … we have lost very, very much now, these days on … on the feast here and things like that.

## Miracles of holy men

A: In a place called Umm Shinashin, there's a person called Faki Ali.

B: Yes.

A: Well ...

B: Do you know ...

A: They were building away at a mosque for him.

B: ... his name? Faki Ali what? Do you know?

A: I think Musa. Really, I don't know, just Faki Ali.

B: Yes. Where? Umm Shinashin?

A: In a place called Umm Shinashin.

B: Yes.

A: Well, they went, they went to build a, yes, a kind of domed tomb. Then it wasn't finished. That was it, the bricks ran out. [xxx] People were upset and all. When morning came, they found it completed.

B: Oh my!

A: Well, also Sheikh Hasan, he also had a mosque come to him, coming down from the sky.

B: Have you seen it? The domed tomb, you saw it?

A: Yes, I saw it.

B: The domed tomb, did you see it?

A: Yes, when this dome was finished everybody from all of the areas of these villages got together and saw it.

B: Ah, ah ... yes. Well, you also said Sheikh Hasan. What about him?

A: A mosque came down to him in one piece from heaven.

B: A mosque came down in one piece?

A: A mosque came down in one piece.

B: Ah ... ah, did you see this mosque?

A: Yes, I saw it.

B: Ah ... fine, what else do they say?

A: Well, there is also, there is, like, a taxi driver ...

B: Yes.

A: There were with him, girls were riding with him. They said to him, "Take us to Tundub to Sheikh al-Fadil."

B: Yes.

A: And they didn't know this Tundub. They'd only heard of it and they were going to him [Sheikh al-Fadil] for a pilgrimage.

B: Ah ... where were they coming from?

A: By God, they were coming from the port of Khartoum.

B: Yes.

A: They were going to him there in ... in ... in Tundub.

B: Yes.

A: Then, the taxi driver, you know, he wanted to get them lost or something. He drove off the road. He took them a long way past the place, he went, he went a very long way out.

B: Ah ....

A: Well, ah ... at that moment ... an eagle came to his car, on the windshield of the car and all and prevented him from moving ...

B: Haa ...

A: He stopped the car. When he got out, he found Sheikh al-Fadil himself. He told him, "Retrace your route." He went back there right away, he went back to Tundub. He found Sheikh al-Fadil sitting. Right away he stopped the car. He became a follower of Sheikh al-Fadil. To this day, to this day, he has stayed with Sheikh al-Fadil, he became his follower.

B: He's still there?

A: He's still there.

## He wouldn't kill anyone

A: Ah … Boss, I hope everything's ok?

B: Have you seen Kurnaf?

A: Not at all.

B: Or Argala?

A: Or Argala. The truth is, it's a couple of days or so since I saw them. I hope everything's okay?

B: I need them urgently. If you run into one of them, put me in touch with him. Listen, Argala has a sister, she lives in Hajj Yousif, her name's Halima. Don't you know exactly where their house is?

A: Not at all. By God, the truth is, I don't know. But if, if, if I run into them, I'll tell them, I'll say to them, the Boss wants you.

B: Ah …

A: Did you hear what happened? Dabba really killed the merchant?

B: Dabba hasn't killed anyone, nor would he kill anyone!

A: Yes, that's true. I myself, personally, was surprised. I said, our Dabba would never kill anyone. He wouldn't kill anyone. I, personally, am surprised by this affair.

B: [xxx] I know him and I know how to find him.

A: This Dabba, the fact is, since the day God made him Dabba has never picked up a weapon. He wouldn't kill anyone.

B: These people, if you see any of them, put me in touch with them. I beg of you, ah …

A: I'll do it.

[in another house]

C: Who's there?

A: It's Musa.

C: What brings you here? What do you want?

A: Just a minute, brother.

C: What [xxx]?

A: But … but … but … the Boss sent me to you, brother.

C: The Boss? By God, you tell him you found me and I'll harm you, I'll hurt you, I'll finish you off.

A: Okay, brother, I won't tell him. I won't tell him.

[in a third house]

D: Argala?

C: Yes, Argala. Do you see what you've done? The Boss is looking for us.

D: Let him look. He won't get his hands on us.

C: Lord, what does he want from us? He'd better not think we got away with the money.

D: He knows we didn't take it, the money, but your friend wants to save his friend and let us go to trial. The newspapers wrote that. All the clues say that Dabba is the killer.

C: You shouldn't have killed him, Kurnaf. Now we're in it even deeper.

D: Brother, what should I have done with him? He stuck to me, the more I put up with from him, the more he stuck to me. Brother, there was no other way except for me to kill him. But don't worry, all the clues say the killer is Dabba.

C: If we only avoid the Boss, no harm will come to us. But what should we do about him? He's always circling around behind us, God protect us from him. Kurnaf, do you think the Boss will leave us alone?

D: He can look as much as he wants to, after that he'll be convinced.

C: He won't be convinced. He loves Dabba a lot. He won't accept anything against him.

D: I know that, but he's sure that he's the one that killed him. But I'm afraid Dabba saw something.

C: He didn't see anything. He's sure Dabba would never kill anyone.

D: Argala, you, you, don't chicken out!

C: I'm not doing ...

D: This case, he's neck-deep in it and nothing is going to happen to you.

C: Fine, and if the Boss goes and tells the police?

D: He can't. I mean, is he going to say that it was he who convinced us to go kill the merchant? He'll be telling on himself. It's not possible.

C: Why are you looking at me like that, Kurnaf?

D: You're the only witness that saw me killing him.

C: But our situation is the same, you and me, we're the same.

D: If I get rid of you, too, nothing can happen to me.

## Folk music in Sudan

Ah ... a folksong according to the ... definition, it is a song that originates with the people. I think you know the word "folklore," i.e., coming from the wisdom of the people. In Sudan, as you know, there is the song of the countryside, ah ... We can say it is a song of our cultural heritage, a song of our cultural inheritance, or a folksong. We can consider what is presented in Khartoum to be the recently-invented song, ah .... Of course, our discussion will now focus on the folksong. The folksong, I mean, will be just about the bulk of our discussion of the songs that are present in the field, that are present in the region of Kordofan and Darfur. So ... we find that the song in Kordofan and Darfur, I, in my own personal estimation, that it is a song that has been able to treat topics that the recently-invented song or the modern song could not treat. Numerous lyrics address issues, ah ... Let's take, for example, the problem of thirst in the region of western Kordofan. We find very many songs that have treated issues of thirst.

Give us water, we are thirsty
We raise a complaint, we are oppressed
We don't mean the food ration
By God, al-Faki
Give it out, don't ration it
Affected, we raise a complaint
As what there is becomes more scarce

In the classification of researchers in the sphere of our cultural heritage, they consider this a modern song or, or a song of our cultural heritage or a song, I mean, a modern folksong, ah .... It might be said ... it might not be given the term a "folkloric song" or a "song of our cultural heritage." But the fact is, it has become a song that the entire region repeats over and over, and it has become a song that is expressive and that exactly expresses something. We find that there are songs in ... in existence, such as the ***shurab*** songs of, ah ... our brothers, the Habbaniya, and the ***shagalab*** songs of our the Hamar. These contain good expressions that ... that are nourishment for a child, ah ... they plant in him the values of a good upbringing. They also remind this child of ... of the sublime Creator. They also urge him not to be a coward and to bear this pain. Thus we find our brothers the Habbaniya singing:

O little boy, O *jaljamus*,

Don't be afraid of the gleam of the razor.

*Leed* means "boy," ah .... Of course, the region of ... of the Baggara has a lot of assimilation of sounds and mispronunciation of letters. Thus we find that the ... the ... ah ... there is a call to this child, ah ... It urges him not to fear the gleam of the razor. A girl, it also says to her:

Fatima, daughter of the prophet

O sublime Muhammad

Fatima, daughter of the Prophet

I wish you, the one to be circumcised,

wealth and children.

Thus, the song leads us to a particular issue at that event. It, ah ... leaves behind, ah ... a certain happiness in that boy or in that girl. Also, ah ... they will have reminded him of many things. Ah ... and also, ah ... as we said, ah ... the song has, ah ... the expression of a lot of issues. I will examine some of the lyrics from the ... the lyrics present in the region of, ah ... the *jarari* or the region, I mean, where they practice the *jarari*. The *jarari*, everyone, is a kind of singing similar to ... the dance is similar to the gait of a camel. This kind of singing is mostly found in the region which ... the desert region or the semi-desert region. I'll try to present an example of the *jarari* song:

Ah ... I have presented

the branch that sways

Greet our family.

If they say we've been away too long,

The land of Upper Egypt is paradise.

And also:

We meet, we meet
On the powdery sand.
How my soul is longing!
How it wants a meeting
With the one who left and has not met us!

I mean, when we consider folk singing in central Sudan and in west ... and in the south and the north and the east, we find, I mean, there are the *banina* songs, in the region of the Ja'ali. In my estimation the ... the ... the ... ah ... *banina* songs, ah ... have not found, ah ... I mean, people who shed light on them in a way that is sufficient ... because any woman, ah ... who has a son, for example, ah ... who has reached, that, the stage of getting married or the stage of getting circumcised, you find that his grandmother or his mother has become a poet who has composed a *banina*. This *banina*, when we consider it, the best example of it would be:

Tonight, the one who is good and handsome

We find that here there are the values of a good upbringing present in these words, "I want you to help your neighbor and to support the weak. You are the bright light of the tribe" and so on. Thus ... we find that the ... the folksong, as we said, that it ... carries messages. I mean, not only the songs of Kordofan, but all existing folksongs carry messages. They carry, ah ... things that add quite a lot to ... ah ... existing values, ah ... of this people. Therefore, I mean, one can say that we carry within us great treasures which must be made visible to the world. By means of these folk practices and by means of our singing and our culture we will be able to accomplish a lot, ah ... and a lot.

# Glossary

# Glossary Introduction

Entries are given in alphabetical order, rather than root order as in some Arabic reference works. Alphabetical order is based on the Arabic alphabet. Changes to the conventional order of the Arabic alphabet accomodate the sound system of SA. The table that follows lists IPA symbols in order.

Please note that the definite article /al-/ in proper names does affect alphabetical order. For example, a proper name such as **/assuudaan/** 'Sudan' appears under /s/, not /a/.

| Latin | Arabic |
|---|---|
| aa | اَ |
| ee | َيْ |
| oo | َوْ |
| aw | َوْ |
| a | َ |
| b | ب |
| p | پ |
| t | ت |
| θ | ث |
| j | ج |
| ḥ | ح |
| x | خ |
| d | د |
| ð | ذ |
| r | ر |
| z | ز |
| s | س |
| ʃ | ش |
| ṣ | ص |
| ḍ | ض |
| ṭ | ط |
| ẓ | ظ |
| ð̣ | ظ |
| ʕ | ع |
| ɣ | غ |
| f | ف |
| g | ق |
| q | ق |
| k | ك |
| l | ل |
| ḷ | ل |
| m | م |
| n | ن |
| h | ه |
| uu | ُو |
| u | ُ |
| w | و |
| ii | ِي |
| i | ِ |
| y | ي |

**aa**

**aa-** آ **[yaa-]** *particle, takes suffixed pronoun* he/she/it is, they are {*ms:* **aahuu**, *fs:* **aahaa**, *mpl:* **aahum**, *fpl:* **aahin**} 8

**oo**

**ooʕaa** أوْعَى **[awʕaa]** *vi used in imperative* let it not be that (preceding imperfect of /**kaan**/); do not do s.t. (preceding simple imperfect); watch out (without following verb) {*fs:* **ooʕii**, *mpl:* **ooʕuu**, *fpl:* **ooʕan**} 26

**a**

**abadan** أبَدًا *adv* never; not at all 26

**abahaan** أبَهَانْ **[abahaat]** *nmpl not conventional* parents {*nms:* **ab**, *nms:* **abuu**} 9

**abriil** أبْرِيلْ *nms* April

**abuu** أبُو **[ab]** *nms* souce, origin 19; elderly person; ancestor; father, parent {*pl:* **abahaat**}

**ajur** أجُرْ *nms* recompense; wages 24

**axad** أخَدْ *vt* to take, spend (time) 3; to take up to use 10; to take, receive 23 {*imperf:* **yaaxud**, *vn:* **axid**}

**adbaxaana** أدْبَخَانَةْ *nfs* toilet, restroom {*pl:* **adbaxaanaat**}

**addaa** أدَّى *vt* to give {*imperf:* **yaddii**, *vn:* **iddeey**} 5

**areet** أرَيْتْ **[yaa reet]** *disc marker* would that, if only (indicates contrary-to-fact wish) 22

**areet- samaaḥt albannuut li-ḥaddihin** أرَيْت سَمَاحَةْ اَلْبَنُوت لحَدَّهِنْ if only the other girls were so pretty (used proverbially by women) *(lit. if only the beauty of the little girls [was] to their limit)* 22

**araḥ** أرَحْ *particle, suffix of imperative verb* adds inclusive meaning (with me, you, etc.) 12

**arbaʕa** أرْبَعَةْ *nfs invariable* four

**arbaʕṭaaʃar** أرْبَعْطَاشَرْ *nfs invariable* fourteen; fourteenth

**arbaʕiin** أرْبَعِينْ *nfs invariable* forty; fortieth

**azaa**[1] أزَى *nms* hurt; harm 12

**azaa**[2] أزَى *vt* to hurt, harm {*imperf:* **yaazii**, *vn:* **azaa**} 26

**azzeey** أزَّيْ **[azzayy]** *interrog* how is, how are 8

**asaasan** أسَاسًا *adv* basically, fundamentally 15

**aswad**[1] أسْوَدْ *adj* black in color {*fs:* **soodaa**, *pl:* **suud**}

**aswad**[2] أسْوَدْ *nms* eggplant (collective noun)

**aṣluu** أصْلُو *adv* the fact is 10

**aḍaan** أضَانْ *nfs* ear {*pl:* **iḍneen**}

**aʕuuzuu bi-llaah** أعُوزُ بِاللَّهْ God help me (pious response to sin or occasion of sin) *(lit. I seek refuge in God)* 19

**aɣuṣṭus** أغُصْطُسْ *nms* August

**akiid** أكيدْ *adj* certain; *adv* for sure, certainly {*fs:* **akiida**, *mpl:* **akiidiin**, *fpl:* **akiidaat**} 8

**al-** ألْ *pron, invariable relative pronoun* who, which, that 3

**aleetuu** أَلَيْتُهْ *particle, invariable; poetic or non-Khartoum usage* would that, if only (indicates contrary-to-fact wish) 27

**alf** ألْفْ *nfs, invariable* thousand; thousandth {*pl:* **aalaaf**}

**allii huu** اَلّلي هُو **[allii huwa]** *disc marker, also invariable* that is;

namely; that would be (precedes and indicates explanatory comment) {*fs:* **allii hiya**, *mpl:* **allii hum**, *fpl:* **allii hin**} 2

**aḷḷaa yabaarik fiik** اَللّٰهْ يَبَارِكْ فِيكْ thank you (possible response to /mabruuk/ 'congratulations') *(lit. may God bless you)*

**aḷḷaa yadoowim allinbisaaṭ** اَللّٰهْ يَدَوِّمْ اَلاَنْبِسَاطْ God keep s.o. happy *(lit. may God make the happiness continue)* 18

**aḷḷaa yaddii- alʕaafiyya** اَللّٰهْ يَدِّي اَلْعَافِيَّهْ may God grant s.o. good health (request or thanks for act of physical exertion)

**aḷḷaa yasallim-** اَللّٰهْ يَسَلِّم may God keep s.o. safe (possible response to /ḥamdi llaa ʕa ssalaama/ 'thank God for s.o.'s safety') 7

**aḷḷaa yakfiinaa ʃarr-** اَللّٰهْ يَكْفِينَا شَرّ God help us (where s.o. is concerned) *(lit. God protect us from s.o.'s evil)* 26

**aḷḷaa yilʕan abuu dii ʕiiʃa dii** اَللّٰهْ يِلْعَنْ اَبُو دي عيشَهْ دي **[aḷḷaa yalʕan abuu dii ʕiiʃa dii]** God curse this life *(lit. God curse the source of this life)* 19

**amriikii** اَمْرِيكِي *adj* American {*fs:* **amriikiyya**, *mpl:* **amriikaan**, *fpl:* **amriikiyyaat**} 14

**amma** اَمَّا *conj* but, however

**amis** اَمِسْ *adv* yesterday

**aha** اَهَهْ *nfs* sigh {*pl:* **ahaat**} 4

**ahal** اَهَلْ *nmpl* family, relatives, kin *(lit. people)* {*pl:* **ahaalii**} 3

**awʕaa** أَوْعَى **[ooʕaa]** *vi, used in imperative* let it not be that (preceding imperfect of /kaan/); do not do s.t. (preceding simple imperfect); watch out (without following verb) {*fs:* **awʕii**, *mpl:* **awʕuu**, *fpl:* **awʕan**} 18

**awwal** اَوَّلْ *adj* first {*fs:* **uulaa**}

**awwalaanii** اَوَّلاَنِي *adj* first {*fs:* **awwalaaniyya**, *mpl:* **awwalaaniyyiin**, *fpl:* **awwalaaniyyaat**}

**awwal maa** اَوَّلْ مَا *conj* as soon as

**awwal umbaariḥ** اَوَّلْ اُمْبَارِحْ day before yesterday

**ay** اَيْ **[ayya; aywa; iywa]** *interj* yes 5

**aywa** اَيْوَهْ **[iywa; ay; ayya]** *interj* yes 7

**ayy** اَيّ **[eey]** *adj, invariable, precedes noun* every; any 10

**ayya** اَيَّ **[ay; aywa; iywa]** *interj* yes 18

**b**

**baaẓ** بَاظْ *vi* to break down; to be out of order {*imperf:* **yabuuẓ**, *vn:* **bawaẓaan**}

**baagii leek** بَاقِي لَيْكْ do you think, would you say 26

**baakir** بَاكِرْ *adv* tomorrow

**baal** بَالْ *nms* intention; mind 22

**baalaɣ** بَالَغْ *vi* to be absent for too long (used jokingly); to go overboard *(lit. to do s.t. too much or too long; to exaggerate)* {*imperf:* **yabaaliɣ**, *vn:* **mubaalaɣa**} 22

**baayiẓ** بَايِظْ *adj* broken, out of order {*fs:* **baayẓa**, *mpl:* **baayẓiin**, *fpl:* **baayẓaat**}

**baayin ʕalaa** بَايِنْ عَلَى *invariable* it seems that, it appears that 7

**been** بَيْنْ *prep* between, among

**beenaat-** بَيْنَاتْ **[been]** *prep, with plural noun or suffixed pronoun* between, among 12

**baḥar** بَحَرْ *nms* river; ocean {*pl:* **buḥuur**} 14

**baḥr alɣazaal** بَحْرْ اَلْغَزَالْ *prop* Bahr al-Ghazal (region and river of southwestern Sudan) 14

**badal** بَدَلْ *conj, also prep* instead of 6

**badrii** بَدْرِي *adv* early 18

**baraa-** بَرَا *prep* alone, by oneself; oneself 18

**barðuu** بَرْظُهْ **[barḍuu; barduu]** *adv* also, too 3

**barraa** بَرَّا *prep* outside of 17

**b-arraaḥa** بَالرَّاحَهْ carefully; slowly *(lit. with relaxation)*

**barḍ-** بَرْضْ *adv with suffixed pronoun* nevertheless, even so; also, too {*ms:* **barḍuu**, *fs:* **barḍaa**, *mpl:* **barḍum**, *fpl:* **barḍun**} 12

**barḍuu** بَرْضُهْ **[barðuu; barduu]** *adv* also, too 2; nevertheless, even so 11

**barlamaan** بَرْلَمَانْ *nms* parliament {*pl:* **barlamaanaat**}

**barmiil** بَرْمِيلْ *nms* barrel, cask {*pl:* **baraamiil**} 18

**bass** بَسّ *conj* but 2; only, solely 3

**basiiṭ** بَسِيطْ *adj* small (in amount) 15; of humble origin, of modest social position 17; simple {*fs:* **basiiṭa**, *mpl:* **busaṭa**, *mpl:* **basiiṭiin**, *fpl:* **basiiṭaat**}

**baṭṭaal** بَطَّالْ *adj* bad; evil; spoiled (of food) {*fs:* **baṭṭaala**, *mpl:* **baṭṭaaliin**, *fpl:* **baṭṭaalaat**} 7

**baʕad** بَعَدْ *prep* after

**baʕad maa** بَعَدْ مَا *conj* after

**baʕaḍ** بَعَضْ *nms invariable* each other, one another (indicates reciprocity) 20

**baʕdeen** بَعْدَيْنْ *adv* afterwards, then, next; too, also 10

**bagaa** بَقَى *adv invariable* so, then, now 18

**baggaa** بَقَّى *vt* to cause s.t. to happen {*imperf:* **yabaggii**, *vn:* **tabgiyya**} 16

**albaggaara** اَلْبَقَّارَهْ *prop* the Baggara, the Baqqara (general term for cattle-herding nomads of Sudan) *(lit. cowherders)* 27

**bakaan** بَكَانْ *nms* **[makaan]** place, location {*pl:* **bakaanaat**}

**balaa** بَلَا *disc marker* enough of, forget about (indicates disapproval or disagreement) 19

**balad** بَلَدْ *nfs, also nms* country, nation {*pl:* **bilaad**} 2

**baladii** بَلَدِي *adj, also invariable* traditionally Sudanese, authentically Sudanese; rural {*fs:* **baladiyya**, *mpl:* **baladiyyiin**, *fpl:* **baladiyyaat**}

**balwa** بَلْوَهْ *nfs* calamity, misfortune {*pl:* **balaawii**} 19

**bambay** بَمْبَي *nms collective* sweet potatoes

**banṭaloon** بَنْطَلُونْ *nms* pair of pants, pair of trousers {*pl:* **banaaṭliin**} 24

**b-annabii** بَالنَّبِي by the Prophet (oath or exclamation) 19

**banii ʔaadam** بَنِي آدَمْ *nms* human being *(lit. son of Adam)* {*fs:* **banii ʔaadma**, *mpl:* **banii ʔaadmiin**, *fpl:* **banaat ḥawwaa**} 19

**baniina** بَنِينَهْ *nfs* <u>banina</u> (a kind of Sudanese folksong) 27

**buuliis** بُولِيسْ *nms singular and plural* police 19

**bulbula** بُلْبُلَهْ *nfs* female

nightingale {*pl:* **bulbulaat**}

**bi-**[1] ب **[b-; bii-]** *particle* prefix of imperfect verb indicating simple present, habitual present, or future, depending on context 3

**bi-**[2] ب **[ba-; bee-]** *prep* with, by means of

**bitaaʕ**[1] بِتاعْ *adj* of, belonging to (possessive adjective) 2; about, approximately {*fs:* **bitaaʕa**, *mpl:* **bitaaʕiin**, *fpl:* **bitaaʕaat**}

**bitaaʕ**[2] بِتاعْ *nms* thing, what's-its-name {*fs:* **bitaaʕa**, *mpl:* **bitaaʕiin**, *fpl:* **bitaaʕaat**} 17

**biteen** بِتَيْنْ **[miteen]** *interrog* when

**bitt** بِتّ **[bint]** *nfs* daughter; girl; unmarried woman {*pl:* **banaat**} 18

**albirka** اَلْبِرْكَة *prop* Birka (district in Northern Province) 13

**bi-zzaat** بِالزّات **[bii-zaat]** especially, in particular 14

**bi-ssaahil** بِالسّاهِلْ easily 14

**biskawiit** بِسكَويتْ *nms collective* cookies {*fs:* **biskawiita**, *pl:* **biskawiitaat**} 24

**bi-ẓẓabṭ** بِالظّبْطْ **[bi-ð̣ð̣abṭ; bi-ḍḍabṭ]** exactly, precisely 2

**bigaa** بِقَى *vt, pre-verb* to get to the point that 5; to begin (inchoative action) 5; to be 6; to become 9 {*imperf:* **yabgaa**, *vn:* **bagayaan**}

**bi-lḥeel** بِالْحَيْلْ indeed, certainly 18

**bi-lkaamil** بِالْكامِلْ completely, entirely 10

**bi-llaahii** بِاللّه by God (oath or exclamation) 19

**biniyya** بِنيّة **[biiniyya]** *nfs diminutive* little girl {*pl:* **biniyyaat**, **bannuut**} 22

**t**

**taasiʕ** تاسِعْ *adj* ninth {*fs:* **taasiʕa**}

**taalit** تالِتْ *adj* third {*fs:* **taalta**}

**taamin** تامِنْ *adj* eighth {*fs:* **taamna**}

**taanii**[1] تاني *adj* next 2; second; another {*fs:* **taanya**, *mpl:* **taanyiin**, *fpl:* **taanyaat**}

**taanii**[2] تاني *adv* again, another time 3; also, as well 8

**taaniyyan** تانِيّاً *adv* also, additionally

**taah (tuhta)** تاهْ (تُهْتَ) *vi* to get lost, go astray {*imperf:* **yatuuh**, *vn:* **tawahaan**} 4

**toob** تَوْبْ *nms* traditional Sudanese wrap worn by women and men {*pl:* **tiyaab**, **teebaan**} 20

**toob assurratii** تَوْبْ اَلسُّرَّتي Sudanese bridegroom's traditional wrap of white fabric

**tabbaara** تَبّارَة *nfs* admirable woman; (a kind of) flower 22

**tajruba** تَجْرُبَة **[tajriba]** *nfs* experience, background {*pl:* **tajrubaat**, **tajaarib**} 16

**taʕaal** تَعال *vi imperative of* /jaa/ *'to come'* come one, let's (do s.t.); come, come here {*fs:* **taʕaalii**, *pl:* **taʕaaluu**} 1

**taʕbaan** تَعْبانْ *adj* tired; sick, ill; of poor quality {*fs:* **taʕbaana**, *mpl:* **taʕbaaniin**, *fpl:* **taʕbaanaat**}

**taksii** تَكْسي *nms* taxi {*pl:* **takaasii**} 25

**talaata** تَلاتَة *nfs invariable* three

**talaatiin** تَلاتينْ *nfs invariable* thirty; thirtieth

**talaṭṭaaʃar** تَلَطّاشَرْ *nfs invariable* thirteen; thirteenth

**tallaaja** تَلاّجَهْ *nfs* refrigerator {*pl:* **tallaajaat**} 18

**tamaam** تَمَامْ *adj invariable* complete, perfect; *adv* completely 22

**tamaam attamaam** تَمَامْ اَلتَّمَامْ absolutely perfect 22

**tamaaniin** تَمَانين *nfs invariable* eighty; eightieth

**tamanya** تَمَنْيَهْ **[tamaanya]** *nfs invariable* eight

**tamma** تَمّ *vt* to complete, finish {*imperf:* **yatimm**, *vn:* **tamaam**} 20

**tannaa** تَنَّى *vi* to walk with a swaying motion {*imperf:* **yatannaa**, *vn:* **tineey**} 27

**tawaaṣul** تَواصُلْ *nms* social interaction 10

**tawwaaq** تَوّاقْ *adj* yearning for, longing for {*fs:* **tawwaaqa**, *mpl:* **tawwaaqiin**, *fpl:* **tawwaaqaat**}

**turkwaazii** تُرْكْوازي *adj* turquoise in color {*fs:* **turkwaaziyya**, *mpl:* **turkwaaziyyiin**, *fpl:* **turkwaaziyyaat**}

**tusʕumiyya** تُسْعُمِيَّهْ *nfs invariable* nine hundred; nine-hundredth

**tultumiyya** تُلْتُمِيَّهْ *nfs invariable* three hundred; three-hundredth

**tumnumiyya** تُمْنُمِيَّهْ *nfs invariable* eight hundred; eight-hundredth

**tiḥit** تِحِتْ *prep* below, under

**tisʕa** تِسْعَهْ **[tizʕa]** *nfs invariable* nine

**tisʕaṭaaʃar** تِسْعَطاشَرْ *nfs invariable* nineteen; nineteenth

**tisʕiin** تِسْعِينْ *nfs invariable* ninety; ninetieth

**tilif** تِلِفْ *vi* to be destroyed {*imperf:* **yitlaf**, *vn:* **talaf**}

**θ**

**θaanawii ʕaalii** ثانَوي عَالي **[saanawii ʕaalii]** *nms* high school 5

**j**

**jaa** جَا *vt irregular conjugation* to come, arrive {*imperf:* **yajii**, *vn:* **jayya**} 2

**jaab (jibta)** جَابْ (جِبْتَ) *vt* to bring {*imperf:* **yajiib**, *vn:* **jayabaan**} 15

**jaaluun** جَالُونْ *nms* gallon {*pl:* **jaaluunaat, jawaaliin**}

**jaamiʕ** جَامِعْ *nms* mosque {*pl:* **jawaamiʕ**} 25

**jaahiz** جَاهِزْ *adj* ready, ready-made {*fs:* **jaahza**, *mpl:* **jaahziin**, *fpl:* **jaahzaat**}

**jaay**[1] جَايْ *adj* coming; having arrived {*fs:* **jaaya**, *mpl:* **jaayiin**, *fpl:* **jaayaat**} 4

**jaay**[2] جَايْ *adv* here; this side, this end 11

**ajjabha lʔislaamiyya** الجَّبْهَه الإسْلامِيَّهْ *prop* the National Islamic Front (NIF) 15

**jabhajii** جَبْهَجي *nms, stress on second (penultimate) syllable* supporter of */ajjabha alʔislamiyya/* 'the National Islamic Front' (NIF) {*fs:* **jabhajiyya**, *mpl:* **jabhajiyya**, *fpl:* **jabhajiyyaat**} 15

**jaraarii** جَراري *nms* jarari (a kind of Sudanese folksong) 27

**jartag** جَرْتَقْ *vt* to hold the third night ceremony of a traditional Sudanese wedding ritual; to make cosmetic preparations for this ceremony {*imperf:* **yajartig**, *vn:* **jirtig**}

**jazma** جَزْمَة *nfs* pair of shoes {*pl:* **jizam**} 20

**jaziira** جَزِيرَة *nfs* island {*pl:* **juzur, jazaayir**} 5

**ajjaziira** اَلجَّزِيرَة *prop* al-Jazira (region and province of Sudan) 5

**jaʕalii** جَعَلي *prop* Ja'ali (member of group of farmers and sedentary herders living along the Nile from Dongola to south of Khartoum) {*fs:* **jaʕliyya,** *mpl:* **jaʕliin,** *fpl:* **jaʕliyyaat**} 27

**jaglab** جَقْلَب *vi* to lose one's nerve {*imperf:* **yajaglib,** *vn:* **jaglaba**} 26

**jallaabiyya** جَلاَّبِيَّة *nfs* galabia (traditional male garment) {*pl:* **jalaaliib**}

**jamaaʕa** جَمَاعَة *nfs may take MP agreement* group, people {*pl:* **jamaaʕaat**} 17

**jamra** جَمْرَة *nfs* burning coal {*pl:* **jamraat**}

**ajjamʕiyya ttaʔsiisiyya** اَلجَّامْعِيَّة التَّأسِيسِيَّة constituent assembly (governmental group charged with drafting a constitution) 16

**janaa** جَنَى *nms* child (term of endearment); embryo {*pl:* **jiniyaat**} 21

**januub kurdufaan** جَنُوبْ كُرْدُفَان *prop* Janub Kordofan, Southern Kordofan Province 3

**jahjaha** جَهْجَهَة *nfs* aggravation; worry; confusion 9

**juubaa** جُوبَا *prop* Juba (capital of Bahr al-Jabal Province) 5

**juul** جُول **[jull]** *nms* majority; entirety 27

**juzuu** جُزُو **[juzuʔ]** *nms* <u>juzuʔ</u> (one-thirtieth portion of the Qur'an); part, portion {*pl:* **ajzaa**} 6

**juzuu ʕamm** جُزُو عَمّ <u>juzuʔ ʕamm</u> (last portion of the Qur'an, first portion learned by heart) 6

**jidaad** جِدَاد *nms collective* chickens

**jidla** جِدْلَة *nfs* bride's traditional headdress {*pl:* **jidlaat**}

**jirtig** جِرْتِق *nms* third night ceremony of traditional Sudanese wedding

**jiziirat ʔartimiirii** جِزِيرَة أَرْتِمِيرِي **[jiziirat ʔartiimiirii; jiziirat ʔartimirii]** *prop* Artimiry Island (near Wadi Halfa in Northern Province) 1

**jineeh** جِنَيْه *nms in number-counted noun structures, singular may be used for numbers 2-10* Sudanese pound (unit of Sudanese currency) {*pl:* **jineehaat**} 17

**jinis** جِنِس *nms in structure (adjective - /jinis/ cognate verbal noun)* some kind of, really, very

**jiha** جِهَة **[jiiha]** *nfs* location {*pl:* **jihaat**}

**jihiz** جِهِز *vi* to be prepared, be ready {*imperf:* **yajhaz,** *vn:* **jahazaan**}

## ḥ

**alḥaaj yuusif** اَلحَاجْ يُوسِف *prop* al-Hajj Yousif (neighborhood in Khartoum region) 26

**ḥaaja** حَاجَة *nfs* thing, something {*pl:* **ḥaajaat**} 2

**ḥaaja kidaa** حَاجَة كِدَا something (difficult to describe) 6

**ḥaajj** حَاجّ *nms* hajj; sir (respectful form of address to an older man) {*fs:* **ḥaajja,** *mpl:* **ḥujjaaj,** *fpl:*

**ḥaajjaat**} 12

**ḥaaḍir** حَاضِرْ *interj invariable* at your service, will do (used when agreeing to request or order) *(lit. present, here)* 26

**ḥaagid** حَاقِدْ *adj* vicious {*fs:* **ḥaagda**, *mpl:* **ḥaagdiin**, *fpl:* **ḥaagdaat**} 19

**ḥooʃ** حَوْشْ *nms* yard, courtyard {*pl:* **ḥeeʃaan**}

**ḥa-** حَ *particle* will (future marker) 14

**ḥabbooba** حَبُّوبَهْ *nfs* grandmother {*fpl:* **ḥabboobaat**}

**ḥabba** حَبّ *vt* to want, like, love {*imperf:* **yaḥibb**, *vn:* **ḥubb**} 15

**ḥajwaa** حَجْوَى *nfs* riddle {*pl:* **ḥajaawii**, **ḥajwaat**}

**ḥaddad** حَدَّدْ *vt* to determine, set {*imperf:* **yaḥaddid**, *vn:* **taḥdiid**} 20

**ḥassas** حَسَّسْ *vt* to make s.o. feel {*imperf:* **yaḥassis**, *vn:* **taḥsiis**} 24

**ḥaṣṣal** حَصَّلْ *vt* to catch up to, reach {*imperf:* **yaḥaṣṣil**, *vn:* **taḥṣiil**} 7

**ḥaṭab** حَطَبْ *nms collective* firewood {*fs:* **ḥaṭaba**, *pl:* **ḥaṭabaat**}

**ḥaffaẓ** حَفَّظْ *vt* to cause s.o. to memorize; to teach s.o. (through memorization) {*imperf:* **yaḥaffiẓ**, *vn:* **taḥfiiẓ**} 23

**ḥagg**[1] حَقّ *adj possessive* of, belonging to {*fs:* **ḥaggat**, *mpl:* **ḥaggiin**, *fpl:* **ḥaggaat**} 18

**ḥagg**[2] حَقّ *nms* share, right, legal claim; right, truth {*pl:* **ḥuguug**} 14

**ḥaggi ḥaggak** حَقِّي حَقَّكْ what is mine is yours

**alḥagg li-llaahi** اَلْحَقّ لِلَّه as God is my witness (in self-validation); to tell the truth, to be fair (in support of statement with which one does not agree) *(lit. truth belongs to God)* 22

**ḥagiiga** حَقِيقَهْ **[alḥagiiga]** *disc marker* truly, the fact is that (softens opinion or correction) 8

**ḥakaa** حَكَى *vt* to tell, narrate (a story, joke, etc.) {*imperf:* **yaḥkii**, *vn:* **ḥakii**} 11

**ḥalaawa** حَلاوَهْ *nfs* sweetness, pleasurableness; candy, sweet treat; paste made of sugar and lemon juice (used for hair removal)

**ḥalla ʕalaa** حَلّ عَلَى *vi* to befall {*imperf:* **yaḥill**} 19

**ḥamaa** حَمَى *vt* to prevent; to forbid {*imperf:* **yaḥmii**, *vn:* **ḥimaaya**} 25

**alḥamar** اَلْحَمَرْ *prop* Hamar (group in western Sudan) 27

**alḥamdi li-llaa** اَلْحَمْدْ لِلَّه **[alḥamdi li-llaa; lḥamdi llaa ; ḥamdi llaah]** thank God *(lit. praise belongs to God)* 6

**ḥammal** حَمَّلْ *vt* to blame {*imperf:* **yaḥammil**, *vn:* **taḥmiil**} 15

**ḥannas** حَنَّسْ *vt* to insist on asking; to plead {*imperf:* **yaḥannis**, *vn:* **taḥniis**}

**ḥudaa-** حُدَا *prep* next to, beside

**ḥurga** حُرْقَهْ *nfs* agony {*pl:* **ḥurgaat**} 4

**ḥitta** حِتَّهْ *nfs* place, locale 3; situation, condition 11; portion, piece {*pl:* **ḥitat**}

**ḥidaaʃar** حِداشَرْ *nfs invariable* eleven; eleventh

**ḥirig** حِرِقْ *vi* to be burned, burnt down {*imperf:* **yiḥrag**, *vn:* **ḥariig**, *vn:* **ḥaragaan**}

**ḥiṣṣa** حصّة *nfs* class period, class session {*pl:* **ḥiṣaṣ**}

**ḥikaaya** حكاية *nfs* story, tale 17; affair, matter 26 {*pl:* **ḥakaawii**}

**ḥilla** حلّة *nfs* village; neighborhood {*pl:* **ḥallaal, ḥilal**} 9

**ḥilwa** حلو *adj* nice; pretty; sweet {*fs:* **ḥilwa**, *mpl:* **ḥilwiin**, *fpl:* **ḥilwaat**} 2

**ḥinna** حنّة *nfs* henna (traditional dye made from dried leaves)

**ḥiwaar** حوار *nms* disciple, follower {*pl:* **ḥawaariin, ḥeeyraan**} 25

**x**

**xaattii** خاتّي *adj* putting; having put {*fs:* **xaatta**, *mpl:* **xaattiin**, *fpl:* **xaattaat**} 11

**xaaliṣ** خالص *adv* very, extremely 5

**xaamma** خامّ *adj invariable* great, terrific 8

**xaamis** خامس *nfs* fifth {*fs:* **xaamsa**}

**xoor** خور *nms* streambed (of seasonal stream) {*pl:* **xeeraan**}

**xataa** ختى *vt* to avoid {*imperf:* **yaxtaa**, *vn:* **xatayaan**} 26

**xatta** خت *vt* to put, place 11; to set up, implement 15 {*imperf:* **yaxutt**, *vn:* **xatta**, *vn:* **xatataan**}

**xatta baal- ʕalaa** خت بال على to have an eye on; to be preoccupied by; to care about {*imperf:* **yaxutt baal- ʕalaa**, *vn:* **xatt baal- ʕalaa**, *vn:* **xatataan baal- ʕalaa**} 22

**xattahuu garaḍ** ختّه قرض *verb takes invariable 3ms suffixed pronoun* to fight bitterly *(lit. to put it [like] /garaḍ/)* {*imperf:* **yaxattuu garaḍ**, *vn:* **xattuu garaḍ**}

**xaddaam** خدّام *nms* servant {*pl:* **xaddaamiin**, *pl:* **xadaadiim**}

**xaʃam** خشم **[xaʃum]** *nms* mouth; entrance {*pl:* **xuʃuum**} 20

**xaʃʃa** خشّ *vt* to enter {*imperf:* **yaxuʃʃ**, *vn:* **xaʃaʃaan**} 5

**xaṭab** خطب *vt* to ask for a woman's hand in marriage {*imperf:* **yaxṭub**, *vn:* **xuṭuuba**} 20

**xaṭiir** خطير *adj* great, terrific *(lit. dangerous)* {*fs:* **xaṭiira**, *mpl:* **xaṭiiriin**, *fpl:* **xaṭiiraat**}

**xalaa** خلا *nms* open country, countryside

**xalaaṣ** خلاص *interj* that's it, that's the end of it; *adv* finally, once and for all 16

**xalaf-** خلف **[xalfa]** *prep* besides, over and above, in addition to 15

**xalag** خلق *vt* to create {*imperf:* **yaxalig**, *vn:* **xalag**} 26

**xallaa** خلّى *vt* to cause to be 5; to let, allow 5; to leave alone, let be 19; to leave (behind) 10; {*imperf:* **yaxallii**, *vn:* **xilleey**}

**xallaṣ** خلّص *vt* to settle (account, debt, etc.) {*imperf:* **yaxalliṣ**, *vn:* **taxliiṣ**}

**xalwa** خلوة *nfs* xalwa, Qur'an school {*pl:* **xalaawii**} 6

**xamasṭaaʃar** خمسطاشر *nfs invariable* fifteen; fifteenth

**xamsa** خمسة *nfs invariable* five

**xamsiin** خمسين *nfs invariable* fifty; fiftieth

**xawaaja** خواجة *nms* foreigner {*fs:* **xawaajiyya**, *mpl:* **xawaajaat**, *fpl:* **xawaajaat**}

**xuuxa** خوخة **[xooxa]** *nfs* xuuxa (a kind of traditional Sudanese woman's cosmetic)

**alxurṭuum** اَلْخُرْطُوم **[alxarṭuum]** *prop* Khartoum (capital of Sudan) 1

**xuṣla** خُصْلَة *nfs* lock of hair {*pl:* **xuṣlaat**} 4

**xumsumiyya** خُمْسُمِيَّة *nfs invariable* five hundred; five-hundredth

**d**

**daa** دَا *pron ms* this, near demonstrative {*fs:* **dii**, *pl:* **deel**} 2

**daab (dubta)** دَاب (دُبْت) *vi* to dissolve {*imperf:* **yaduub**, *vn:* **dawabaan**} 4

**daa... daa** دَا ... دَا *disc marker with indef. noun or noun phrase* indicates positive or negative emotion toward noun phrase {*fs:* **dii... dii**, *mpl:* **dool ... dool**, *fpl:* **deelaa ... deelaa**} 11

**daar**[1] دَار *nfs* region, area; house, home {*pl:* **diyaar**} 27

**daar**[2] **(durta)** دَار (دُرْت) *vt* to want {*imperf:* **yaduur**, *vn:* **door**} 22

**daarfuur** دَارْفُور *prop* Darfur (region of western Sudan) 27

**daak** دَاك **[daaka]** *pron ms* that, far demonstrative {*fs:* **diik**, *pl:* **deelak**} 3

**daaka** دَاكَ **[daak]** *pron ms* that, far demonstrative {*fs:* **diik**, *pl:* **deelak**} 2

**daa maa kalaam daa** دَا مَا كَلَام دَا this does not make sense; this is not acceptable *(lit. this is not speech this)*

**daayman** دَايْمًا *adv* always, constantly 7

**daayir** دَايِر *adj, pre-verb* wanting, desiring 9; needing 18; intending to, going to {*fs:* **daayra**, *mpl:* **daayriin**, *fpl:* **daayraat**}

**deel** دَيْل *pron mp* these, near demonstrative {*ms:* **daa**, *fs:* **dii**, *pl:* **deel**} 6

**doowam** دَوَّم **[dawwam]** *vt* to prolong s.th. {*imperf:* **yadoowim**, *vn:* **tadwiim**} 18

**daraja** دَرَجَة *nfs* point, degree (of measurement) {*pl:* **darajaat**}

**dassa** دَسّ *vt* to hide, conceal {*imperf:* **yadass**, *vn:* **dassa**} 12

**dalluuka** دَلُّوكَة *nfs* dalluka (a kind of traditional Sudanese drum); music played on a dalluka {*pl:* **dalaaliik**}

**damm xafiif** دَمّ خَفِيف nice, easy to get along with 22

**duxxaan** دُخَّان *nms* smoke; smoke bath {*pl:* **daxaaxiin**}

**dukkaan** دُكَّان *nms* store, shop {*pl:* **dakaakiin**}

**dii** دي **[diyyat; diyya; dih]** *pron fs* this, near demonstrative {*ms:* **daa**, *fs:* **dii**, *pl:* **deel**} 3

**diisambar** دِيسَمْبَر *nms* December

**diik** دِيك *pron fs* that, far demonstrative {*ms:* **daak**, *fs:* **diik**, *pl:* **deelak**} 6

**diin** دِين *nms* religion (specifically Islam) {*pl:* **adyaan**} 23

**dilka** دِلْكَة *nfs* dilka (a kind of aromatic paste used as traditional Sudanese cosmetic)

**diyyat** دِيَّت **[deeya; dii; dayya]** *pron fs* this, near demonstrative {*ms:* **daa**, *fs:* **diyyat**, *pl:* **deel**} 13

r

**raabiṭa** رَابِطَة *nfs* association, group (in urban centers, organized on basis of village or regional origin and possessing legal identity) {*pl:* **rawaabiṭ**} 13

**raabiʕ** رَابِع *adj* fourth {*fs:* **raabiʕa**}

**raajil** رَاجِل *nms* man {*pl:* **rujaal**} 7

**raajil arbaab** رَاجِل أرْبَاب prince of a guy (generous and well-liked) *(lit. man of the lords)* {*pl:* **rijaal arbaab**}

**raad (ridta)** رَاد (رِدْت) *vt* to like, love {*imperf:* **yariid**, *vn:* **reed**} 7

**raadyo** رَادْيُو **[raadii]** *nms* radio {*pl:* **raadyoohaat, rawaadii**}

**raahin** رَاهِن *adj* current; present {*fs:* **raahna**, *mpl:* **raahniin**, *fpl:* **raahnaat**} 15

**reed** رِيْد *nms* love 4

**rabba** رَبّ *vi* to host a good party; to be a good party {*imperf:* **yaribb**, *vn:* **rabba**}

**rabbanaa yatammim ʕalaa xeer** رَبَّنَا يَتَمِّمْ عَلَى خَيْر may our Lord bring s.t. to a successful conclusion (used of upcoming wedding)

**rabnaa** رَبْنَا **[rabbanaa]** God, our Lord 18

**rajaa** رَجَا *vt* to beg, implore {*imperf:* **yarjuu**, *vn:* **rajaa**}

**ragiba** رَقَبَة *nfs* person, self; neck {*pl:* **ragibaat, rigaab**} 19

**rahiib** رَهِيب *adj* great, terrific *(lit. dreadful, terrible)* {*fs:* **rahiiba**, *mpl:* **rahiibiin**, *fpl:* **rahiibaat**}

**rawʕa** رَوْعَة *nfs* beauty; splendor 4

**rayyaḥ** رَيَّح *vt* to give ease, give relief; to give peace of mind to; to satisfy {*imperf:* **yarayyiḥ**, *vn:* **raaḥa**}

**rayyis** رَيِّس *nms* boss, chief, leader {*pl:* **ruyasa**} 26

**ruṭaana**[1] رُطَانَة *nfs* rutana, any non-Arabic language variety spoken in Sudan *(lit. dialect; jargon)* {*pl:* **ruṭaanaat**} 13

**ruṭaana**[2] رُطَانَة *prop* Rutana (a tribe in eastern Sudan)

**rufaaʕa** رُفَاعَة *prop* Rufaa (town southeast of Khartoum on the Blue Nile) 23

**riiḥa** رِيحَة *nfs* perfume, cologne {*pl:* **aryaaḥ**} 20

**riif** رِيف *nms* countryside {*pl:* **aryaaf**} 27

**rijaa** رِجَا *vi* to wait {*imperf:* **yarjaa**, *vn:* **rijaa**}

**rijil** رِجِل *nfs* foot {*pl:* **rujuul**}

**rimiʃ** رِمِش *nms* eyelash {*pl:* **rumuuʃ**} 4

z

**zaat**[1] زَات *disc marker, takes suffixed pronoun* oneself (adds emphasis or prominence to preceding noun phrase) 11

**zaat**[2] زَات *nfs* self 6

**zaag (zugta)** زَاق (زُقْت) *vi* to get away; to escape undetected {*imperf:* **yazuug**, *vn:* **zawagaan**} 26

**azzaayir** اَلزَّايِر **[aẓẓaahir]** it seems that *(lit. the appearing thing)*

**zeen**[1] زَيْن *adj* beautiful {*fs:* **zeena**, *mpl:* **zeeniin**, *fpl:* **zeenaat**}

**zeen**[2] زِيْن *nms* beauty 27

**zeey** زَيّ **[zayy]** *prep* approximately, about 3

**zool** زُوْل *nms* individual, person 2; friend, pal, buddy 12 {*fs:* **zoola**, *pl:* **naas**} 2

**zabaadii** زَبَادي *nms* yoghurt

**zaʕlaan** زَعْلان *adj* upset, angry {*fs:* **zaʕlaana**, *mpl:* **zaʕlaaniin**, *fpl:* **zaʕlaanaat**} 18

**zaɣrad** زَغْرَد *vi* to produce a high trilling sound (by women on happy occasions) {*imperf:* **yazaɣrid**, *vn:* **zaɣrada**} 20

**zafaaf** زَفاف *nms* wedding

**zalaabiya** زَلابيَة *nfs* zalabiya (a kind of pastry fried and soaked in syrup) 24

**zamaan** زَمان *adv* long ago 6

**zahabii** زَهَبي *adj* gold in color; made of gold {*fs:* **zahabiyya**, *mpl:* **zahabiyyiin**, *fpl:* **zahabiyyaat**}

**zayy-** زَيّ **[zeey]** *prep* about, approximately 2, something like 3; like, as

**zayy alḥaal** زَيّ اَلْحال how are you 8

**zayy maa** زَيّ ما **[zeey maa]** *conj* as 3

**zayy maa taguul** زَيّ ما تَقُول as they say *(lit. as you would say)* 3

**ziik** زِيك *nms* edge, border {*pl:* **azyaak**}

**ziyaada** زِيادة *nfs* increase; *adv* more {*pl:* **ziyaadaat**} 12

**ziyaara** زِيارة *nfs* pilgrimage, visit to holy place; visit (in general) {*pl:* **ziyaaraat**} 25

**s**

**saab (sibta)** (سِبْت) ساب *vt* to leave behind; to leave alone {*imperf:* **yasiib**, *vn:* **sayabaan**} 4

**saabiʕ** سابِع *adj* seventh {*fs:* **saabiʕa**}

**saaḥa** ساحَة *nfs* city square; open space in or near village, town, or city {*pl:* **saaḥaat**} 24

**saadis** سادِس *adj* sixth {*fs:* **saatta**}

**saariḥ** سارِح *adj* distracted; absent-minded {*fs:* **saarḥa**, *mpl:* **saarḥiin**, *fpl:* **saarḥaat**} 12

**saakit** ساكِت **[saay]** *adv* just, only 9

**saay** ساي **[saakit]** *adv* just, only

**saʔal min-** سَأل مِن *vi* to check on, ask after s.o. {*imperf:* **yasʔal min-**, *vn:* **suʔaal min-**} 22

**sabʕa** سَبْعَة *nfs invariable* seven

**sabʕaṭaaʃar** سَبْعَطاشَر *nfs invariable* seventeen; seventeenth

**sabʕiin** سَبْعين *nfs invariable* seventy; seventieth

**sadda** سَدّ *vt* to pay (debt, bill, etc.); to close, shut {*imperf:* **yasidd**, *vn:* **sadd**} 20

**sadd almaal** سَدّ اَلْمال **[sidd almaal]** sadd almaal (payment or delivery of the entire mahar) 20

**sarra** سَرّ *vt* to please, make happy {*imperf:* **yasurr**, *vn:* **suruur**} 13

**sariiʕ** سَريع *adj* quick; *adv* quickly {*fs:* **sariiʕa**, *mpl:* **suraaʕ**, *fpl:* **sariiʕaat**} 21

**saʕaa** سَعَى *vi* to try, attempt {*imperf:* **yasʕaa**, *vn:* **saʕii**} 8

**samaaḥa** سَمَاحَة *nfs* beauty 22

**samiḥ** سَمِح *adj* pretty, beautiful; pleasant; good {*fs:* **samḥa**, *mpl:* **samḥiin**, *fpl:* **samḥaat**} 22

**sawwaa** سَوَّى *vt* to do, make {*imperf:* **yasawwii**, *vn:* **suwaa**} 19

**sawwaa ʕalaa** سَوَّى عَلَى *vt* to set s.o. up, entrap s.o. *(lit. to do against s.o.)* {*imperf:* **yasawwii ʕalaa**, *vn:* **suwaa ʕalaa**} 19

**assuudaan** اَلسُّودَان *prop nms* Sudan 2

**subʕumiyya** سُبْعُمِيَّة *nfs invariable* seven hundred; seven-hundredth

**suttumiyya** سُتُّمِيَّة *nfs invariable* six hundred; six-hundredth

**surratii** سُرَّتِي *adj* a type of fabric

**sukkariyyaat** سُكَّرِيَّات *nfpl* sweets, candies 24

**sumʕa** سُمْعَة *nfs* good name, reputation {*pl:* **sumʕaat**} 19

**siid** سِيد *nms* master; possessor, owner {*pl:* **asyaad**} 4

**sibtambir** سِبْتَمْبِر *nms* September

**sibḥa** سِبْحَة *nfs* prayer beads, rosary {*pl:* **sibaḥ**}

**sitt** سِتّ *nfs* lady; married woman {*pl:* **sittaat**} 22

**sitta** سِتَّة *nfs invariable* six

**sittiin** سِتِّين *nfs invariable* sixty; sixtieth

**sirig** سِرِق *vi* to be stolen {*imperf:* **yisrag**, *vn:* **sirga**}

**siṭṭaaʃar** سِطَّاشَر *nfs invariable* sixteen; sixteenth

**sikka ḥadiid** سِكَّة حَدِيد railway

**silʕii** سِلْعِي *adj* of commodities {*fs:* **silʕiyya**, *mpl:* **silʕiyyiin**, *fpl:* **silʕiyyaat**}

**simuuta** سِمُوتَة *nfs* ceremonial bracelet made of beads used in the jirtig

## ʃ

**ʃaaf (ʃufta)** (شُفْت) شَاف *vt* to see 3; to find, get 17; to understand, get, see {*imperf:* **yaʃuuf**, *vn:* **ʃoof**}

**ʃaal (ʃilta)** (شِلْت) شَال *vt* to carry; to take {*imperf:* **yaʃiil**, *vn:* **ʃeel**, *vn:* **ʃeyalaan**} 4

**ʃaahad** شَاهَد **[ʃaahid]** *vt* to experience, witness {*imperf:* **yaʃaahid**, *vn:* **muʃaahada**} 3

**ʃaahii** شَاهِي *nms* tea {*pl:* **ʃawaahii**} 24

**ʃeex** شَيْخ *nms* sheikh, religious authority {*pl:* **ʃuyuux**} 21

**ʃeela** شَيْلَة *nfs* sheela (bride's clothing, cosmetics, and basic foodstuffs for wedding celebrations, given to the bride's family by the bridegroom's family before the wedding) {*pl:* **ʃeelaat**} 20

**ʃabah** شَبَه *vt* to resemble {*imperf:* **yaʃbah**, *vn:* **ʃabah**} 11

**ʃadiid** شَدِيد *adv* very, extremely; frequently; a lot 2

**ʃariiḥa** شَرِيحَة *nfs* section, division, sector {*pl:* **ʃaraayiḥ**} 5

**ʃaṭaara** شَطَارَة *nfs* cleverness 10

**ʃaʕbiyyaat** شَعْبِيَّات *nfpl* folklore, popular culture

**ʃaɣalaaniyya** شَغَلَانِيَّة *nfs* job; task; problem, headache {*pl:* **ʃaɣalaaniyyaat**} 17

**ʃaɣala** شَغَلَة *nfs* concern, interest; task, work {*pl:* **ʃaɣalaat**} 19

**ʃaɣɣaal** شَغَّال *adj* working {*fs:* **ʃaɣɣaala**, *mpl:* **ʃaɣɣaaliin**, *fpl:*

**ʃayɣaalaat**} 3

**ʃafaxaana** شَفَخَانَةْ *nfs* clinic {*pl:* **ʃafaxaanaat**} 3

**ʃagalap** شَقَلاَبْ *nms* shagalab (a kind of Sudanese folksong) 27

**ʃakal** شَكَلْ *nms* fighting; quarreling

**ʃakkar fii** شَكَّرْ في *vt* to speak highly of {*imperf:* **yaʃakkir**, *vn:* **taʃkiir**} 19

**ʃakil** شَكِلْ *nms* type, form, way; outward appearance, form, shape {*pl:* **aʃkaal**} 6

**aʃʃamaaliyya** اَلشَّمَالِيَّةْ **[aʃʃimaaliyya]** *prop* al-Shamaliyya, Northern Province 13

**ʃamiʃ** شَمِش **[ʃamis]** *nfs* sun {*pl:* **ʃamsaat**} 20

**ʃanṭa** شَنْطَةْ *nfs* suitcase; handbag {*pl:* **ʃunaṭ**} 20

**ʃahaada** شَهَادَةْ **[ʃihaada]** *nfs* diploma, degree {*pl:* **ʃahaadaat**} 5

**ʃahr arbaʕa** شَهْرْ اَرْبَعَةْ April (*lit. month four)*

**ʃahr alʕasal** شَهْرْ اَلْعَسَلْ honeymoon *(lit. month of honey)*

**ʃahri talaata** شَهَر تَلاَتَةْ March *(lit. month three)*

**ʃahri tamaanya** شَهَر تَمَانْيَةْ **[ʃahri tamanya]** August *(lit. month eight)* 2

**ʃahri tamanya** شَهَر تَمَنْيَةْ **[ʃahri tamanya]** August *(lit. month eight)*

**ʃahr itneen** شَهْرْ اتْنَيْنْ February *(lit. month two)*

**ʃahri tisʕa** شَهَر تِسْعَةْ September *(lit. month nine)*

**ʃahri ḥidaaʃar** شَهَر حِدَاشَرْ November *(lit. month eleven)*

**ʃahri xamsa** شَهَر خَمْسَةْ May *(lit. month five)*

**ʃahri sabʕa** شَهَر سَبْعَةْ July *(lit. month seven)*

**ʃahri sitta** شَهَر سِتَّةْ June *(lit. month six)*

**ʃahri ʕaʃara** شَهَر عَشَرَةْ October *(lit. month ten)*

**ʃahri waaḥid** شَهَر وَاحِدْ January *(lit. month one)*

**ʃahri iṭnaaʃar** شَهَر اِطْنَاشَرْ December *(lit. month twelve)*

**ʃnuu** شْنُو **[ʃinuu]** *interrog invariable* what 7

**ʃuraap** شُرَابْ *nms* shurab (a kind of Sudanese folksong) 27

**ʃufta keef** شُفْتَ كَيْفْ do you understand, do you agree *(lit. you see how)* {*fs:* **ʃuftii keef**, *mpl:* **ʃuftuu keef**, *fpl:* **ʃuftan keef**}

**ʃwayya**[1] شْوَيَّةْ **[ʃwiyya, ʃiwayya]** *adv* somewhat, a bit 2

**ʃwayya**[2] شْوَيَّةْ **[ʃiwayya, ʃwiyya]** *nfs* a short period of time; *adv* for a little while {*pl:* **ʃwayyaat**} 10

**ʃwiyya** شْوِيَّةْ **[ʃiwayya, ʃwayya]** *adv* somewhat, a bit 8

**ʃii** شي *nms* thing; something {*pl:* **aʃyaaʔ**} 6

**ʃidar** شِدَرْ **[ʃijar]** *nms collective* trees

**ʃiʕiriyya** شِعِرِيَّةْ *nfs* shiʕiriya (a kind of sweet made of fine spaghetti) 24

**aʃʃimaaliyya** اَلشِّمَالِيَّةْ **[aʃʃamaaliyya]** *prop* al-Shamaliyya, Northern Province 12

**ʃin-** شِنْ *interrog, takes suffixed pronoun* what {*ms:* **ʃinuu**, *fs:* **ʃinaa**, *pl:* **ʃinum**} 7

ṣ

**ṣaaḥii** صَاحي *adj* awake {*fs:* **ṣaaḥya**, *mpl:* **ṣaaḥyiin**, *fpl:* **ṣaaḥyaat**} 24

**ṣaaḥib** صَاحب *nms* friend {*fs:* **ṣaaḥba**, *mpl:* **aṣḥaab**, *fpl:* **ṣaaḥbaat**} 18

**ṣaḥḥ** صَحّ *adj invariable* correct 5

**ṣaḥḥii** صَحّي *interj* really, is that so

**aṣṣaʕiid** الصَّعيد *prop* al-Sa'id, Upper Egypt (the region from south of Cairo to Lake Nasser) 27

**ṣalaa** صَلاه *nfs* prayer {*pl:* **ṣalawaat**} 24

**ṣuufii** صُوفي *adj* of Sufism, Islamic mysticism {*fs:* **ṣuufiyya**, *mpl:* **ṣuufiyyiin**, *fpl:* **ʃuufiyyaat**} 23

**ṣubaaɣ** صُبَاغ *nms collective* subaɣ (a kind of tree with aromatic wood) {*nfs:* **ṣubaaɣa**, *pl:* **ṣubaaɣaat**}

**ṣiḥaa** صِحي *vi* to awaken {*imperf:* **yaṣḥaa**, *vn:* **ṣaḥayaan**} 24

**ṣirṣaar** صرصَار *nms* cockroach {*pl:* **ṣaraaṣiir**}

**ṣiɣayyir** صغيَّر *adj* small {*fs:* **ṣaɣayyira**, *mpl:* **ṣaɣayyiriin**, *mpl:* **ṣuɣaar**, *fpl:* **ṣaɣayyiraat**}

ḍ

**ḍarab li- taliifuun** ضَرَب ل تَليفُون *vt* to phone, call s.o. on the telephone (*lit. to hit to s.o. a telephone)* {*imperf:* **yaḍrub li- taliifuun**, *vn:* **ḍarib li- taliifuun**} 11

**ḍaruurii** ضَرُوري *adj* imperative, necessary; *adv* urgently {*fs:* **ḍaruuriyya**, *mpl:* **ḍaruuriyyiin**, *fpl:* **ḍaruuriyyaat**} 26

**ḍufur** ضُفُر *nms* toenail; fingernail {*pl:* **ḍufuur**} 22

**ḍuhur** ضُهُر **[ḍuhuur]** *nms* afternoon 2

**ḍiḥaa** ضِحى **[ḍaḥaa]** *nms* morning; late morning 24

ṭ

**ṭaar fii ssamaa** طَار في السَّما to get lost *(lit. to fly in the sky)* {*imperf:* **yaṭiir fii ssamaa**, *vn:* **ṭayaraan fii ssamaa**} 19

**ṭaaliʕ** طَالع *adj* going out, leaving; getting up, standing up; turning out to be; going up, ascending {*fs:* **ṭaalʕa**, *mpl:* **ṭaalʕiin**, *fpl:* **ṭaalʕaat**} 24

**ṭarabeeza** طَرَبيزَه *nfs* table {*pl:* **ṭarabeezaat**}

**ṭariiga** طَريقَه *nfs* Sufi brotherhood, Sufi order; way, method {*pl:* **ṭurug**} 23

**ṭagg** طَقّ *adv* completely, absolutely 18

**ṭalaʕ** طَلَع *vt* to go out, leave 2; to turn out to be 18; to get up, stand up; to go up, ascend {*imperf:* **yaṭlaʕ**, *vn:* **ṭuluuʕ**}

**ṭaliḥ** طَلح *nms collective* talih (a kind of tree with aromatic wood) {*fs:* **ṭalḥa**, *pl:* **ṭalḥaat**}

**ṭamaaṭim** طَمَاطم *nms collective* tomatoes

**ṭamanṭaaʃar** طَمَنْطَاشَر *nfs invariable* eighteen; eighteenth

**ṭahhaar** طَهَّار *nms* circumciser {*mpl:* **ṭahhaariin**} 27

**ṭawwaalii** طَوَّالي *adv* immediately, right away 3; always, continuously 12

**ṭawwal** طَوَّلْ *vi* to take a long time (doing s.t.); to be away for a long time {*imperf:* **yaṭawwil**, *vn:* **taṭwiil**} 4

**ṭawwal ruuḥ-** طَوَّلْ رُوح- to be patient; to put up (/li-/ 'with s.o.') {*imperf:* **yaṭawwal ruuḥuu**, **taṭwiil ruuḥ-**} 26

**ṭawiil** طَويلْ *adj* long; *adv* for a long time; for a long distance {*fs:* **ṭawiila**, *mpl:* **ṭuwaal**, *fpl:* **ṭawiilaat**} 25

**ṭayyar** طَيَّرْ *vt* to start (a fight) *(lit. to launch, let fly)* {*imperf:* **yaṭayyir**, *vn:* **taṭyiir**}

**ṭayyar ʃakal-** طَيَّرْ شَكَلْ to start a fight with s.o. *(lit. to launch s.o.'s fight)* {*imperf:* **yaṭayyir ʃakal-**, *vn:* **taṭyiir ʃakal-**}

**ṭayyib** طَيِّبْ *adj* good, well; all right {*fs:* **ṭayyiba**, *mpl:* **ṭayyibiin**, *fpl:* **ṭayyibaat**} 1

**ṭayyib aʃʃeex ʕabd albaagii** طَيِّبْ اَلشَّيْخ عَبْد اَلْبَاقي *prop* Tayyib al-Shaykh Abd al-Bagi (place in al-Jazira) 9

**ṭuub** طُوبْ *nms collective* bricks {*fs:* **ṭuuba**, *pl:* **ṭuubaat**} 25

**aṭṭunḍub** اَلطُّنْضُبْ *prop* Tundub (village east of Khartoum) 25

**ẓ**

**ẓabbaṭ** ظَبَّطْ *vt* to control; to adjust, regularize {*imperf:* **yaẓbuṭ**, *vn:* **taẓbiiṭ**}

**ẓariif** ظَريفْ *adj* nice; elegant {*fs:* **ẓariifa**, *mpl:* **ẓurafa**, *fpl:* **ẓariifaat**} 7

**ẓuruuf** ظُرُوفْ *nmpl* unfortunate circumstances 8

**ʕ**

**ʕaad** عَادْ *adv* actually; if you ask me; as a matter of fact 22

**aʕuuzuu bi-llaah** اَعُوزُ بِاللّهْ God help me (pious response to sin or occasion of sin) *(lit. I seek refuge in God)* 19

**ʕaaʃ alʔisim** عَاشْ اَلإسِمْ polite response to meeting s.o. who shares the same name, or meeting s.o. named after a major religious figure *(lit. may the name live)* {*mpl:* **ʕaaʃat alʔasaamii**}

**ʕaaʃir** عَاشِرْ *adj* tenth {*fs:* **ʕaasra**}

**ʕaafiyya** عَافيَّهْ *nfs* good health, strength

**ʕaawiz** عَاوِزْ **[ʕaayiz]** *adj pre-verb* wanting, desiring {*fs:* **ʕaawza**, *mpl:* **ʕaawziin**, *fpl:* **ʕaawzaat**} 5

**ʕaayan li-** عَايَنْ لِ *vi* to look at; to stare at {*imperf:* **yaʕaayin**, *vn:* **muʕaayana**} 7

**ʕaayiz** عَايِزْ **[ʕaawiz]** *adj pre-verb* wanting, desiring {*fs:* **ʕaayza**, *mpl:* **ʕaayziin**, *fpl:* **ʕaayzaat**} 7

**ʕeeʃ** عيْشْ *nms* bread

**ʕa-** عَ **[ʕalaa; ʕalee]** *prep* for, about (object of reference or concern) 7

**ʕajab** عَجَبْ *vt impersonal construction* to please s.o. {*imperf:* **yaʕjib**, *vn:* **ʕajab**} 10

**ʕajiib** عَجيبْ *adj* strange, odd {*fs:* **ʕajiiba**, *mpl:* **ʕajaayiib**, *fpl:* **ʕajiibaat**} 18

**ʕadiil** عَديلْ *adj* good; agreeable; morally upright *(lit. straight)* {*fs:* **ʕadiila**, *mpl:* **ʕadiiliin**, *fpl:* **ʕadiilaat**} 27

**ʕarooka** عَرَوْكَهْ *nfs* ʕarooka (a kind

of traditional Sudanese cosmetic)

**ʕarabiyya** عَرَبِيَّة *nfs* automobile {*pl:* **ʕarabaat, ʕarabiyyaat**} 9

**ʕaruus** عَرُوس *nfs* bride {*nfpl:* **ʕaruusaat**} 20

**ʕasaa wa-laʕalla** عَسَى وَلَعَلَّ perhaps, maybe 21

**ʕaʃaan** عَشَان *conj* because, because of 3; to, in order to 5

**ʕaʃara** عَشَرَة *nfs invariable* ten

**ʕaẓiim** عَظِيم *adj* great, terrific {*fs:* **ʕaẓiima,** *mpl:* **ʕuẓamaa,** *mpl:* **ʕaẓiimiin,** *fpl:* **ʕaẓiimaat**}

**ʕafaʃ** عَفَش **[ʕafiʃ]** *nms collective* furniture, furnishings; luggage

**ʕagad aamaal** عَقَد آمال to set one's hopes on {*imperf:* **yaʕgid aamaal,** *vn:* **ʕagda aamaal**} 10

**ʕagad ʕalaa** عَقَد عَلَى to sign a contract of marriage for (the woman one marries) {*imperf:* **yaʕgid ʕalaa,** *vn:* **ʕagad ʕalaa**} 20

**ʕalaa** عَلَى **[ʕa; ʕalee]** *prep* for, about (object of reference or concern) 7; of duty, obligation 11; according to 12; on, atop

**ʕalaa- aḷḷaa** عَلَى اللّٰه for God's sake, for the love of God (adds emphasis to requests and questions); *(lit. by s.o.'s oath to God, on s.o. is the oath "by God")* 19

**ʕalaa raaḥat-** عَلَى رَاحَة **[ʕalee raaḥat-]** take your time; take it easy; whenever (as deadline) *(lit. at s.o.'s convenience)* 12

**ʕalaa keef-** عَلَى كَيف **[ʕalee keef-]** whatever s.o. wants, as s.o.wishes *(lit. according to s.o.'s preference)* 12

**ʕalaa kulla ḥaal** عَلَى كُلّ حَال in any case 18

**ʕamaliyya** عَمَلِيَّة *nfs* matter, affair, business; process; operation {*pl:* **ʕamaliyyaat**} 9

**ʕamla** عَمْلَة *nfs* deed, act (usually bad) {*pl:* **ʕamaayil**} 19

**ʕamil ʕamla** عَامِل عَمْلَة to do something (usually bad) *(lit. to do a deed)* {*imperf:* **yaʕmil ʕamla,** *vn:* **ʕamal ʕamla**}

**ʕamil fiihaa** عَامِل فِيهَا to be pretentious *(lit. to do with relation to it)* {*imperf:* **yaʕmil fiihaa,** *vn:* **ʕamal fiihaa**}

**ʕamil naayim** عَامِل نَايِم to pretend to sleep; to be unresponsive *(lit. to make sleeping)* {*imperf:* **yaʕmil naayim,** *vn:* **ʕamal naayim**}

**ʕan** عَن *prep* in comparison with; from

**ʕawaja** عَوَجَة *nfs* harm, damage {*pl:* **ʕawajaat**} 12

**ʕawwag** عَوَّق *vt* to harm, damage {*imperf:* **yaʕawwig,** *vn:* **taʕwiig**} 26

**ʕaynii** عَينِي *adj* in kind, consisting of goods or materials (rather than money) {*fs:* **ʕayniyya,** *mpl:* **ʕayniyyiin,** *fpl:* **ʕayniyyaat**}

**ʕayyaan** عَيَّان *adj* sick, ill {*fs:* **ʕayyaana,** *mpl:* **ʕayyaaniin,** *fpl:* **ʕayyaanaat**}

**ʕuu** عُو *interj* hey (used mainly by older persons) 18

**ʕugbaal** عُقْبَال *interj* may it be the same for s.o. (conventional response to congratulations from s.o. not yet in same situation)

**ʕiʃriin** عِشرِين *nfs invariable* twenty; twentieth

**ʕind-** عِنْد **[ʕinn-]** *prep* at (place or

person's home)

**ʕinn-** عِنّ *prep* at (place or person's home)

**ɣ**

**ɣaab u-jaab** غَابْ أُجَابْ he traveled and brought wealth back (proverbial)

**ɣaatal** غَاتَلْ *vt* to carry on a fight with, carry on a struggle with {*imperf:* **yaɣaatil**, *vn:* **muɣaatala**} 23

**ɣaadii** غَادِي *adv* there; that side, that end

**ɣaas (ɣista)** غَاسْ (غِسْتْ) *vt* to help {*imperf:* **yaɣiis**, *vn:* **ɣaws**} 14

**ɣaafir** غَافِرْ *nms* guard {*mpl:* **ɣufaraa**}

**alɣaahira** اَلْغَاهِرَهْ *prop* Cairo (capital of Egypt)

**ɣaaytuu** غَايْتُهْ *adv* to the utmost; very much 8

**ɣaṣbaan ʕan** غَصْبَانْ عَنْ **[ɣaẓbaan ʕan]** against s.o.'s will 7

**ɣannaaya** غَنَّايَهْ *nfs* professional singer {*fpl:* **ɣannaayaat**}

**alɣurʔaan** اَلْغُرْآنْ *prop* the Qur'an (scripture of Islam) 23

**ɣilib** غلبْ *vi* to be conquered, defeated {*imperf:* **yiɣlab**, *vn:* **ɣulub**, *vn:* **ɣalabaan**}

**f**

**faat (futta)** فَاتْ (فُتّ) *vt* to have passed in time, be in the past {*imperf:* **yafuut**, *vn:* **fawataan**} 4

**faatuura** فَاتُورَهْ *nfs* bill, receipt {*pl:* **fawaatiir**} 18

**faaḍii** فَاضِي *adj* unoccupied, having free time; empty {*fs:* **faaḍya**, *mpl:* **faaḍyiin**, *fpl:* **faaḍyaat**} 22

**feen** فَيْنْ *interrog* where 9

**foog** فَوْقْ *prep* above; on top of

**fabraayir** فَبْرَايِرْ *nms* February

**fattaʃ fi-** فَتَّشْ فِي *vt* to search for {*imperf:* **yafattiʃ fii-**, *vn:* **taftiiʃ fii-**} 7

**fatḥat alxaʃam** فَتْحَةْ اَلْخَشَمْ **[fatḥat alxaʃum]** opening of negotiations for marriage *(lit. opening the mouth)* 20

**fatraan** فَتْرَانْ *adj* tired {*fs:* **fatraana**, *mpl:* **fatraaniin**, *fpl:* **fatraanaat**}

**faddaan** فَدَّانْ *nms* <u>feddan</u> (land measure of approximately one acre or one-half hectare) {*pl:* **fadaadiin**, **afdina**} 13

**farraʃ** فَرَّشْ *vt* to put fresh covers on cushions and beds; to furnish; to set up, set out s.t. {*imperf:* **yafarriʃ**, *vn:* **faraʃ**} 24

**faṭuur** فَطُورْ *nms* breakfast 24

**fakk aʃʃaariʕ** فَكّ اَلشَّارِعْ to leave the road, drive off the road *(lit. to let go of the road)* {*imperf:* **yafikk aʃʃariiʕ**, *vn:* **fakk aʃʃariiʕ**} 25

**fakii** فَكي *nms* religious authority {*pl:* **fukayaa**} 25

**fawḍaa** فَوْضَى *nfs* chaos, utter disorder

**fustaan** فُسْتَانْ *nms* woman's dress, frock {*pl:* **fasaatiin**} 20

**fusḥa** فُسْحَهْ *nfs* outing; stroll, walk {*pl:* **fusaḥ**}

**fulaan** فُلَانْ *nms* so and so, what's-his-name {*fs:* **fulaana**} 20

**fulaan alfartakaanii** فُلَانْ اَلْفَرْتَكَانِي so-and-so, John Doe, what's his name (full name)

**fulaanii** فُلانـي *adj* so-and-so, what's his name (family name) {*fs:* **fulaaniyya**, *mpl:* **fulaaniyyiin**, *fpl:* **fulaaniyyaat**} 20

**fii**[1] فـي *particle invariable* there is, there are (existential) 5; to be going on, be wrong, be a problem 12

**fii-**[2] فـي *prep* for (amount of time) 15; of (partitive relationship) 26; at; on

**fii rajaa-** فـي رَجا begging s.o. (strong request or admission of weakness) *(lit. in urgent request of)* 26

**fii ʃnuu** فـي شْنُو **[fii ʃinuu]** what's going on, what's up, what's wrong *(lit. there is what)* 19

**fiɣra** فـغْرَه *nfs* period of study, phase of study; paragraph {*pl:* **fiɣaraat**} 1

q

**quṭur** قُطُر *nms* diameter {*pl:* **aqṭaar**}

g

**gaadir** قَادِر *adj pre-verb* able to {*fs:* **gaadra**, *mpl:* **gaadriin**, *fpl:* **gaadraat**} 7

**gaaṭiʕ alkalaam** قَاطِعْ اَلْكَلام the last word, the living end, the ultimate (high praise) *(lit. cutting off speech)* {*fs:* **gaaṭʕa lkalaam**, *mpl:* **gaaṭʕiin alkalaam**, *fpl:* **gaaṭʕaat alkalaam**} 22

**gaaʕid** قَاعِد *adj pre-verb* keeping on, continuing (continuous action) 11; staying, remaining 17; staying, remaining 25; sitting, sitting down {*fs:* **gaaʕda**, *mpl:* **gaaʕdiin**, *fpl:* **gaaʕdaat**}

**gaal (gutta)** (قُتَّ) قَال *vt* to think; to say {*imperf:* **yaguul**, *vn:* **gool**} 12

**gaam** قَامْ *disc marker invariable* so, anyway (resumes narrative after interruption or digression) 25

**gaam (gumta)** (قُمْتَ) قَامْ *vi pre-verb, agrees in number, gender, and tense with main verb* to up and (do s.t.), suddenly (do) 3; to get up (in order to do s.t.) 12; to do, go ahead and do (as a consequence or result of previously described event) 20; to wake up, get up 24; to get up, stand up {*imperf:* **yaguum**, *vn:* **goom**} 3

**gaayil** قَايِل *adj* thinking; saying {*fs:* **gaayla**, *mpl:* **gaayliin**, *fpl:* **gaaylaat**} 19

**gool** قَوْل **[guul]** *nms* opinion; act of speaking {*pl:* **agwaal**} 22

**gabbal** قَبَّل *vi* to turn toward *(lit. to turn or go south)* {*imperf:* **yagabbil**, *vn:* **tagbiil**} 19

**gabli maa** قَبْلِ ما *conj* before

**gaddam** قَدَّمْ *vt* to submit, present, turn in {*imperf:* **yagaddim**, *vn:* **tagdiim**} 8

**gadur** قَدُرْ *prep* as much as

**gadur maa** قَدُرْ ما **[gadru maa]** *conj* as much as, the more that 26

**garaa** قَرَا *vt* to study; to get an education {*imperf:* **yagraa**, *vn:* **giraaya**} 5

**garaḍ** قَرَضْ *nms collective* ugly fight *(lit. bitter pods of the sunt tree)* {*fs:* **garaḍa**, *pl:* **garaḍaat**}

**garraa** قَرَّا *vt* to teach; to teach s.o. to read {*imperf:* **yagarrii**, *vn:* **girreey**}

**garraaʃ** قَرَّاش *nms* garage {*pl:*

**garraaʃaat**}

**garrab** قَرَّبْ *vi pre-verb* to be at the point of (doing s.th.) {*imperf:* **yagarrib**, *vn:* **tagriib**} 9

**gariib** قَرِيبْ *prep* about, approximately; *adj* near, close 8

**gaʃʃa** قَشّ *vt* to sweep {*imperf:* **yaguʃʃ**, *vn:* **magʃaaʃa**}

**gaṣṣar** قَصَّرْ *vi* to run out, fall short {*imperf:* **yagaṣṣir**, *vn:* **tagṣiir**} 25

**gaʕad** قَعَدْ *vi* to stay, remain; to sit {*imperf:* **yagʕud**, *vn:* **guʕaad**} 2

**gaʕʕad** قَعَّدْ *vt* to cause s.o. to sit, cause s.o. to stay {*imperf:* **yagaʕʕid**, *vn:* **gaʕʕeed**} 23

**galab** قَلَبْ *vt* to change, convert s.t. {*imperf:* **yaglib**, *vn:* **galab**} 16

**gamiiṣ** قَمِيصْ *nms* shirt {*pl:* **gumṣaan**} 24

**gannab** قَنَّبْ *vt* to begin to; to sit down {*imperf:* **yagannib**, *vn:* **ginneeb**} 17

**guul** قُولْ **[gool]** *nms* opinion; act of speaking {*pl:* **agwaal**} 22

**guulat xeer** قُولَةْ خَيْرْ guulat xeer (good-faith offering, small gift from man's family to woman's family that begins negotiations for marriage) *(lit. a speaking of goodness)* 20

**gubbaal** قُبَّالْ *prep* before

**gubbaal maa** قُبَّالْ مَا *conj* before

**gubba** قُبَّةْ **[kubba]** *nfs* domed tomb {*pl:* **gubab**} 25

**guruuʃ** قُرُوشْ *nfpl* money (collective) {*nms:* **giriʃ**} 11

**guṣaad** قُصَادْ *prep* opposite; across from

**giibaalik** قِيبَالِكْ *adv* for a while 7

**giddaam** قِدَّامْ *prep* in the future, the time to come; ahead, forward 8

**gidir** قِدِرْ *vi pre-verb* to be able to {*imperf:* **yagdar**, *vn:* **gudra**} 2

**giriṣ** قِرِصْ *vi* to be bitten by a snake {*imperf:* **yigraṣ**, *vn:* **garaṣ**}

**girif** قِرِفْ *vi* to be disgusted, be sickened {*imperf:* **yigraf**, *vn:* **garaf**, *vn:* **garafaan**}

**gizaaz** قِزَازْ *nms collective* glass (material); window pane {*fs:* **gizaaza**, *pl:* **gizaazaat**} 25

## k

**kaaduglii** (كَادُجْلِي) كَادُقْلِي *prop* Kadugli (city in Southern Kordofan Province) 3

**kaadir** كَادِرْ *nms* work force {*pl:* **kawaadir**}

**kaas ʕalaa (kusta)** (كُسْتَ) كَاسْ عَلَى *vi* to look for, search for {*imperf:* **yakuus ʕalaa**, *vn:* **kawasaan**} 26

**kaan** كَانْ *particle invariable conditional* if 8

**keef**[1] كَيْفْ *interrog* what, I'm sorry, what did you say (requests repetition or indicates surprise) 11; how

**keef**[2] كَيْفْ *nms* wish, desire, preference; enjoyment of life's simple pleasures (especially tea, coffee, and cigarettes) 12

**keef aḥwaal** كَيْفْ اَحْوَالْ how is, how are 8

**keefinn-** كَيْفِنْ *interrog form of /keef/ 'how' used with suffixed pronouns* how is, how are

**ka-** كَ *prep* in the capacity of 3; like, as

**kabbar** كَبَّرْ *vi* to praise God by saying /aḷḷaahu ʔakbar/ (i.e, 'God is great') {*imperf:* **yakabbir**, *vn:* **takbiir**} 24

**kattal** كَتَّلْ *vt* to massacre, slaughter {*imperf:* **yakattil**, *vn:* **katteel**} 14

**katiir** كَتِيرْ *adv* a lot; very much; *adj* much, many 8

**kadaa** كَدَا *adv* thus, in such a way 21

**kadii** كَدِي **[kidaa]** *adv* sort of, more or less

**kadiis** كَدِيسْ *nms* cat {*mpl:* **kadaayis**}

**karaama** كَرَامَةْ *nfs* extraordinary action performed by a wali, saint's miracle {*pl:* **karaamaat**} 25

**karrab** كَرَّبْ *vt* to tighten {*imperf:* **yakarrib**, *vn:* **takriib**}

**kasalaa** كَسَلَا *prop* Kassala (city in eastern Sudan, a popular destination for honeymooners)

**kaʕab** كَعَبْ *adj* bad {*fs:* **kaʕba**, *mpl:* **kaʕbiin**, *fpl:* **kaʕbaat**}

**kafaa** كَفَى *interj invariable* enough; stop that 19

**kalaam** كَلَامْ *nms* situation; event 6; talking, speech {*pl:* **kalaamaat**}

**kalaam ɣariib** كَلَامْ غَرِيبْ what a strange thing; that's unbelievable *(lit. strange talk)*

**kalaam faariɣ** كَلَامْ فَارِغْ nonsense *(lit. empty talk)* 19

**kam** كَمْ *particle* so many (unspecified number) *(lit. how much, how many)* 16

**kamaan** كَمَانْ *adv* also, as well 18

**kahrab** كَهْرَبْ *vt* to install electricity in or at, electrify; to give s.o. a hard time; to make a situation tense {*imperf:* **yakahrib**, **kahrabaa**}

**kahrabaa** كَهْرَبَا *nfs* electricity; lamp {*pl:* **kahaarib**} 18

**kubba** كُبَّةْ **[gubba]** *nfs* domed tomb {*pl:* **kubab**} 25

**kurdufaan** كُرْدُفَانْ *prop* Kordofan (region of central Sudan) 27

**kur ʕalaa-** كُرْ عَلَى poor dear s.o. (used by women in response to unpleasantness or pain) 19

**kulfa** كُلْفَةْ *nfs* formality; fuss 12

**kulla maa marra** كُلَّ مَا مَرَّةْ each time, every time, each and every time 22

**kulluu kulluu** كُلُّهْ كُلُّهْ at all, completely (also negative) 12

**kwayyis** كُوَيِّسْ *adj* good, nice {*fs:* **kwayyisa**, *mpl:* **kwayyisiin**, *fpl:* **kwayyisaat**} 6

**kiima** قِيمَةْ **[giima]** *nfs* value, worth {*pl:* **kiyam**} 6

**kitil** كِتِلْ *vi* to be killed {*imperf:* **yiktal**, *vn:* **gatal**}

**kidaa** كِدَا **[kadii]** *adv* sort of, more or less 2

**kidaa** كِدَا *pron* this, that 3

**kidaa** كِدَا *interrog* is that so, really 7

**kidaa kidaa** كِدَا كِدَا so-and-so; so-so, not so great; either …or … 20

**l**

**laaʔ** لَاءْ **[laaʔa; laa]** *interj* no 6

**laa ʔilaaha ʔillaa llaah** لَا إِلَاهَ إِلَّا اللّٰهْ God rest s.o.'s soul (first response upon hearing of a death); Muslim profession of faith *(lit. there is no god but God)* 19

**laaffii** لَافِّي *adj* going around, going about; turning, making a turn {*fs:*

**laaffa**, *mpl:* **laaffiin**, *fpl:* **laaffaat**} 26

**laakin** لَكِنْ *conj stress on second syllable* but, however

**leed** لِيدْ **[wileed]** *nms* little boy (diminutive of /wad/) {*pl:* **leedaat**} 27

**alleela** اَللَّيْلَة *adv* today; now 14

**leeh** لِيهْ *interrog* why 4

**leeyin** لَيِّنْ *adj* wet {*fs:* **leeyna**, *mpl:* **leeyniin**, *fpl:* **leeynaat**}

**loo** لَوْ **[law]** *conj* if 5

**laffa** لَفّ *vi* to go around, go about; to turn, make a turn {*imperf:* **yaliff**, *vn:* **laff**, *vn:* **liff**} 26

**lammaa** لَمّا **[lamman]** *conj* when 10

**lamma** لَمّ *vt* to gather up, gather in {*imperf:* **yalimm**, *vn:* **lamm**, *vn:* **limm**} 19

**lamma fii** لَمّ فِي *vi* to get together with 11; to put s.o. in touch with s.o. 26; to find, encounter, meet {*imperf:* **yalimm fii**, *vn:* **lamm fii**, *vn:* **limm fii**}

**lamman** لَمَّنْ **[lammaa]** *conj* when 5

**luuḥ** لُوحْ *nms* tablet (piece of wood for reading and writing practice in a xalwa); wooden board, panel {*pl:* **alwaaḥ**} 23

**li-** لِ **[la-; lee-; lii-]** *prep* to, for 2; to have been for (amount of time) 9

**liʔannuu** لأَنُّه **[liyannuu; liʔinnuu; laʔannuu]** *conj invariable* because, on account of; so that 2

**liʔinnuu** لأِنُّه **[laʔannuu; liʔannuu]** *conj invariable* because, on account of; so that 15

**li-ḥaddi** لِحَدّ **[la-ḥaddii]** *conj* until, up to 3

**li-ḥaddi maa** لِحَدّ ما *conj* until

**lidiɣ** لِدِغْ *vi* to be stung (by an insect) {*imperf:* **yildaɣ**, *vn:* **ladaɣ**, *vn:* **ladaɣaan**}

**lista** لِسْتَة *nfs* menu; list {*pl:* **listaat**}

**lissa** لِسّه *adv* not yet 8; still 12

**ligaa** لِقَى *vt* to find, discover {*imperf:* **yalgaa**, *vn:* **lagayaan**} 5

**li-ghayat maa** لِغايَة ما *conj* until

**m**

**maa**[1] ما *disc marker* come on, but (adds emphasis or prominence to following phrase) 11

**maa**[2] ما *particle* not 2

**maaxud** ماخُد **[maaxid]** *adj* taking, getting, obtaining; taking up to use {*fs:* **maaxda**, *mpl:* **maaxdiin**, *fpl:* **maaxdaat**} 10

**maaxid** ماخِد **[maaxud]** *adj* taking up to use; taking, getting, obtaining {*fs:* **maaxda**, *mpl:* **maaxdiin**, *fpl:* **maaxdaat**} 23

**maaris** مارِس *nms* March

**maasuura** ماسُورَة *nfs* pipe; faucet; water hydrant {*pl:* **mawaasiir**, **maasuuraat**} 18

**maa ʃaa ʔaḷḷah** ما شا اَللّه my goodness (used alone as expression of admiration or with another such expression) *(lit. what God wills)* 18

**maa fii ʕawaja** ما فِي عَوَجَة everything's OK; there is no problem; no harm done 12

**maa fii- gool** ما فِي قَوْل there is nothing bad to say about s.o., there is nothing to say against s.o. 22

**maa kadii** ما كَدِي **[miʃ kidaa]** right,

isn't that so 22

**maal-** مَال *interrog takes pronoun suffix* what about s.o., what's wrong with s.o. 7

**maaliḥ** مَالِح *adj* salty {*fs:* **maalḥa**, *mpl:* **maalḥiin**, *fpl:* **maalḥaat**}

**maa li- daaʕii** مَا لِ دَاعِي there's no need for s.t. 12

**maamaa** مَامَا *nfs* mamma; affectionate form of address to young woman 22

**maahuu** مَاهُ *adv* but, the fact is 18

**maahiya** مَاهِيَة *nfs* salary, wages {*pl:* **mawaahii**}

**maa wakit-** مَا وَكِت this is not the time for s.t. or s.o. 12

**maayuu** مَايُو *nms* May

**mooruus** مَوْرُوس *adj* traditional, inherited {*fs:* **mooruusa**, *mpl:* **mooruusiin**, *fpl:* **mooruusaat**} 16

**moos** مَوْس **[muus]** *nms* razor; blade {*pl:* **amwaas**} 27

**mooya** مَوْيَة *nfs* water 18

**mabruuk ʕalaa-** مَبْرُوك عَلَى *invariable* congratulations to s.o. (or for s.t.) *(lit. blessed for s.o. or s.t.)*

**mabsuuṭ** مَبْسُوط *adj* happy, glad {*fs:* **mabsuuṭa**, *mpl:* **mabsuuṭiin**, *fpl:* **mabsuuṭaat**} 18

**matmuum** مَتْمُوم *adj* completed {*fs:* **matmuuma**, *mpl:* **matmuumiin**, *fpl:* **matmuumaat**} 25

**majlis assayaada** مَجْلِس اَلسِّيَادَه *prop* Revolutionary Command Council (following coups in 1969 and 1989, coup leaders established governing bodies under this name)

**almaḥas** اَلْمَحَس *prop* Mahas (region of northern Sudan) 13

**maḥalla** مَحَلَّة *nfs* place; location; seat {*pl:* **maḥallaat**} 5

**maḥalla maa** مَحَل مَا *conj* wherever

**maḥalliyya** مَحَلِّيَّة *nfs* district, region; municipality {*pl:* **maḥalliyyaat**} 13

**maḥmuul** مَحْمُول *adj* overloaded with responsibilities {*fs:* **maḥmuula**, *mpl:* **maḥmuuliin**, *fpl:* **maḥmuulaat**}

**mara** مَرَاه *nfs* married woman; woman (in general) {*nfpl:* **niswaan**} 21

**marag** مَرَق *vt* to release, set free 12; to go out, exit 24 {*imperf:* **yamrug**, *vn:* **muruug**}

**marraat** مَرَّات *adv* at times, sometimes 21

**marra** مَرَّة *nfs* time, occasion {*pl:* **marraat**} 6

**markaz** مَرْكَز *nms* center, hub; police station {*pl:* **maraakiz**}

**masʔala** مَسْأَلَة *nfs* matter, affair {*pl:* **masaaʔil**} 10

**masaafa** مَسَافَة *nfs* a long time; a long distance {*pl:* **masaafaat**} 2

**masiid** مَسِيد *nms* mosque {*pl:* **masaayid**} 23

**maʃaa** مَشَى *vt* to go; to go to; to leave {*imperf:* **yamʃii**, *vn:* **maʃii**} 2

**maʃaa li-** مَشَى لِ *vi* to take s.o. or s.t. {*imperf:* **yamʃii**, *vn:* **maʃii**} 21

**maʕaa** مَع *prep* with, accompanying

**maʕa- ḥagg** مَع حَقّ s.o. is right, what s.o. says is right *(lit. with s.o. is right)* 10

**maʕruuf** مَعْرُوف *adj* known; it is known that {*fs:* **maʕruufa**, *mpl:* **maʕruufiin**, *fpl:* **maʕruufaat**} 13

**maʕleeʃ** مَعْلَيْش **[maʕliiʃ]** *interj* never mind, I'm sorry, don't worry 12

**maʕliiʃ** مَعْلِيش **[maʕleeʃ]** *interj* never mind, I'm sorry, don't worry 7

**maɣarr** مَقَرّ *nms* site, place; headquarters {*pl:* **maɣaar, maɣarraat**} 3

**maɣar ʕamal** مَقَر عَمَل work place {*pl:* **maɣaar ʕamal, maɣaaraat ʕamal**} 3

**maɣlag** مَغْلَق *nms* hardware store {*pl:* **maɣaalig**} 12

**mafruuḍ** مَفْرُوض *adj invariable; pre-verb* should, ought to 5

**mafhuum** مَفْهُوم *nms* conception, notion, what is understood {*pl:* **mafaahiim**} 23

**makaan** مَكَان *nms* **[bakaan]** place, location {*pl:* **makaanaat** }

**makaroona** مَكَرُونَة *nfs* pasta 24

**mallas** مَلَّس *vt* to be overly nice to; to stroke, caress {*imperf:* **yamallis**, *vn:* **timillis**}

**mahar** مَهَر **[muhar]** *nms* mahar (gift from groom to bride consisting of money or property; dowry) {*pl:* **muhuur**} 20

**mahrajaan** مَهْرَجَان *nms* festival, fair {*pl:* **mahrajaanaat**} 24

**mawjuud** مَوْجُود **[moojuud]** *adj* present; alive; available {*fs:* **mawjuuda**, *mpl:* **mawjuudiin**, *fpl:* **mawjuudaat**} 3

**maydaan** مَيْدَان **[meedaan]** *nms* city square; playing field {*pl:* **mayaadiin**} 24

**mutaabaʕa** مُتَابَعَة *nfs* follow-up {*pl:* **mutaabaʕaat**}

**mutjaawib maʕa** مُتْجَاوِب مَع *adj* to be in harmony with, be in agreement with {*fs:* **mutjaawba maʕa**, *mpl:* **mutjaawbiin maʕa**, *fpl:* **mutjaawibaat maʕa**} 15

**mujarrad** مُجَرَّد *adv* merely, solely 10

**mujarrad maa** مُجَرَّد مَا *conj* as soon as, no sooner than 20

**muḥaafaẓa** مُحَافَظَة *nfs* administrative district {*pl:* **muḥaafaẓaat**} 13

**muxmal** مُخْمَل *nms* velvet {*pl:* **maxaamil**}

**muduun-** مُدُون **[biduun; muuduun]** *prep* without

**murtaaḥ** مُرْتَاح *adj* prosperous, well-off; relaxed, at ease {*fs:* **murtaaḥa**, *mpl:* **murtaaḥiin**, *fpl:* **murtaaḥaat**} 9

**musaɣɣaf** مُسَقَّف *adj* educated; cultured; intellectual {*fs:* **musaɣɣafa**, *mpl:* **musaɣɣafiin**, *fpl:* **musaɣɣafaat**} 16

**muʃ** مُش **[miʃ]** *particle* not 6

**muʕaaraḍa** مُعَارَضَة *nfs* opposition {*pl:* **muʕaaraḍaat**} 17

**muʕaayana** مُعَايَنَة *nfs* interview; inspection {*pl:* **muʕaayanaat**} 8

**muɣarraraat** مُقَرَّرَات *npl* curriculum 6

**mufattiʃ** مُفَتِّش *nms* inspector (one who carries out inspections or searches) {*pl:* **mufattiʃiin**}

**mulaaḥ** مُلَاح *nms* stew

**mumkin** مُمْكِن *adj, also pre-verb* possible {*fs:* **mumkina**, *mpl:* **mumkiniin**, *fpl:* **mumkinaat**} 6

**munzuu-** مُنْزُو *prep* since 14

**muhar** مُهَر **[mahar]** *nms* mahar (gift from groom to bride consisting of money or property; dowry) {*pl:*

**muhuur**} 20

**almuhim** اَلْمُهِمْ **[(al)muhim(ma); (al)mihimm]** *disc marker* the important thing is; the fact is (indicates return to topic after digression; precedes and indicates evaluative comment) 3

**miiteen** ميتَيْنْ *nfs invariable* two-hundredth; two-hundredth

**miinaa** مينَا *nfs* port, harbor {*pl:* **mawaanii**} 25

**miteen** متَيْنْ **[biteen]** *interrog* when 9

**miteen ma** متَيْنْ ما *conj* whenever

**mitil-** متِلْ *prep* like, as

**mitil maa** متِلْ ما *conj* like, as

**miʃ** مِشْ **[muʃ]** *particle* not 7

**miʃ kidaa** مِشْ كِدَا isn't that so, right 7

**mimmaa** ممَّا *conj* from the time that; as soon as 9

**min**[1] مِنْ *conj* since the time that 26; when, at the time of

**min-**[2] مِنْ *interrog takes suffixed pronoun* who {*ms:* **minuu**, *fs:* **minaa**, *pl:* **minum**} 7

**minuu** منُو **[mnuu]** *interrog invariable* who 7

**miyya** مِيَّةْ *nfs* one hundred; one-hundredth {*pl:* **miyyaat**}

**miyya lmiyya** مِيَّةْ الْمِيَّةْ one hundred percent

**n**

**naas** نَاسْ *nmpl* a person's social circle (non-familial friends, neighbors, colleagues, and acquaintances) 10; people

**naam (numta)** نَامْ (نُمْتْ) *vi* to sleep; to go to sleep {*imperf:* **yanuum**, *vn:* **noom**}

**noota** نَوْتَةْ *nfs* notebook {*pl:* **nuwat**}

**nabaḍ** نَبَضْ *nms* pulse, heartbeat {*pl:* **nabḍaat**} 4

**natiija** نَتيجَةْ *nfs* grade, result {*pl:* **nataayij**, **nataa?ij**} 5

**najjaḍ** نَجَّضْ *vt* to cook {*imperf:* **yanajjiḍ**, *vn:* **najeeḍ**}

**naṣar** نَصَرْ *vt* to side with, take sides with {*imperf:* **yanṣur**, *vn:* **naṣar**} 16

**naṣiib** نَصيبْ *nms* fate, destiny; share, portion {*pl:* **naṣaayib**} 23

**naṣiiba** نَصيبَةْ **[maṣiiba]** *nfs* calamity, disaster (used by women; euphemism for /maṣiiba/ 'calamity, disaster') {*pl:* **naṣaayib**} 19

**naḍam** نَضَمْ *vt* to speak {*imperf:* **yanḍum**, *vn:* **naḍam**} 4

**naẓra** نَظْرَةْ *nfs* look in s.o.'s eyes {*pl:* **naẓraat**, **naẓaraat**} 7

**nuura** نُورَةْ *nfs* beautiful glow 22

**nuufimbir** نُوفِمْبِرْ *nms* November

**nuṣṣ** نُصّ *nms* half {*pl:* **anṣaaṣ**} 2

**niḥnaa** نِحْنَا *pron* we 4

**niswaan** نِسْوَانْ *nfpl* married women; women (in general) {*fs:* **mara**} 20

**nimra** نِمْرَةْ *nfs* number {*pl:* **nimar**}

**h**

**haadaak** هَدَاكْ *pron ms* that, far demonstrative {*fs:* **haadiik**, *mpl:* **haadoolak**, *fpl:* **haadeelak**} 7

**alhabbaaniyya** اَلْهَبَّانيَّةْ *prop* Habbaniyya (ethnic group in western Sudan) 27

**habuub** هَبُوبْ *nms* wind; dust storm {*pl:* **habaayib**}

**hassa** هَسَّهْ **[hassaʕ; hassii]** *adv* now; just now 2

**hassaʕ** هَسَّعْ **[hassii; hassaa]** *adv* now; just now 10

**hassii** هَسِّي **[hassaʕ; hassa]** *adv* now; just now 3

**hallal** هَلَّلْ *vi* to praise God by saying /laa ʔilaaha ʔillaa ḷḷaah/ 'there is no god but God' {*imperf:* **yahallil,** *vn:* **tahliil**} 24

**haybaan** هَيْبَانْ *prop* Hayban (town in Southern Kordofan Province) 3

**huu kaan maa saakit** هُو كَانْ مَا سَاكِتْ who would believe it (ironic question) *(lit. but if it isn't nonsense)* 18

**hii** هِي **[hiya]** *pron* she 5

**hiduum** هِدُومْ *nms* clothes, clothing

**hilaal** هِلَالْ *nms* hilal (bridegroom's traditional headband adorned with a crescent) {*pl:* **hilaalaat**}

**hinaa** هِنَا *adv* here 8

**hinaak** هِنَاكْ *pron* there 3

**hinaay** هِنَايْ *nms* thingamabob, what do you call it; what's his name; etcetera {*fs:* **hinaaya**, *pl:* **hinaayaat**} 3

**u**

**alʔubayyiḍ** اَلأُبَيِّضْ *prop* al-Ubayyid (capital of Northern Kordofan Province) 3

**urbuʕmiyya** أُرْبُعْمِيَّهْ **[rubʕumiyya]** *nfs invariable* four hundred; four-hundredth

**urneek** أُرْنِيكْ *nms* official form; template; pattern {*pl:* **araaniik**}

**uktoobir** أُكْتُوبِرْ *nms* October

**umbaariḥ** أُمْبَارِحْ *adv* yesterday 12

**um baddaa** أُمْ بَدَّا **[umm badda]** *prop* Ombadda (town in Omdurman region) 18

**um jiriis** أُمْ جِرِيسْ **[umm jirees]** *prop* Umm Jurays (village east of Khartoum) 9

**umm addunyaa** أُمّ اَلدُّنْيَا the greatest place *(lit. mother of the world)* 10

**umm durmaan** أُمّ دُرْمَانْ *prop* Omdurman (city across Nile River from Khartoum) 1

**umm ʃinaaʃin** أُمّ شِنَاشِنْ *prop* Umm Shinashin (village east of Khartoum) 25

**w**

**waaḥid**[1] وَاحِدْ *adj* single, sole {*fs:* **waaḥda,** *mpl:* **waaḥdiin,** *fpl:* **waaḥdaat**} 5

**waaḥid**[2] وَاحِدْ *nfs* one (number) {*fs:* **waaḥda**}

**waaḥid**[3] وَاحِدْ *nms* someone, a person 8

**waadii ḥalfaa** وَادِي حَلْفَا *prop* Wadi Halfa (city and district in northern Sudan) 13

**waaṭaa** وَاطَا *nms* ground, floor; piece of land {*pl:* **waaṭaat**}

**ween** وِيْنْ *interrog may take suffixed pronoun* where 7

**ween maa** وَيْنْ مَا **[weem maa]** *conj* wherever

**ween u-ween** وَيْنْ أُوَيْنْ where exactly *(lit. where and where)* 8

**wa-** وَ **[w-; u-]** *conj* and; but

**wa-ḥaat-** وَحَاتْ by the life of s.o.

(oath or exclamation) 4

**wad** وَدْ **[walad]** *nms* boy; child {*pl:* **oolaad**} 19

**wad ʔummii** وَدْ أُمِّي **[wid ummii]** my brother *(lit. son of my mother)* 19

**waddaa** وَدَّى *vt* to send 6; to take (s.o. or s.t. to a place), convey 11; to put, place 19 {*imperf:* **yawaddii,** *vn:* **widdeey**}

**waddaa wiʃʃ- min- feen** وَدَّى وِشّ مِنْ فِيْنْ to be able to face s.o. (used in embarrassing situations) *(lit. to put one's face with respect to s.o. else)* {*imperf:* **yawaddii,** *vn:* **widdeey**} 19

**waddar** وَدَّرْ *vt* to lose (s.t.) {*imperf:* **yawaddir,** *vn:* **widdeer**}

**waddaʕ aḷḷaa** وَدَّعْ اَللّه *used in perfect* to say goodbye, bid farewell *(lit. I entrust s.o. to God)* 18

**waraa** وَرَا *prep* behind

**warad** وَرَدْ *vi* to get water (from a well, stream, pump, etc.) {*imperf:* **yarid,** *vn:* **wuruud**}

**warraa** وَرَّى *vt* to tell; to show {*imperf:* **yawarrii,** *vn:* **warraa**} 12

**wasaɣ** وَسَغْ *vi* to have confidence, trust {*imperf:* **yasiɣ,** *vn:* **siɣa**} 15

**waʃʃ** وَشّ *nms* face {*pl:* **wuʃuuʃ**}

**waṣiyya** وَصِيَّة *nfs* advice {*pl:* **waṣaayaa**} 10

**waʕii** وَعي *nms* consciousness; attention 23

**wakit** وَكِتْ *nms* time; period of time; point in time {*pl:* **awkaat**} 3

**wakit** وَكِتْ *conj* when, at the time that 4

**wa-kidaa** وَكِدَا and so on, etcetera 5

**wa-kidaa daa** وَكِدَا دَا **[wa-kidaa dayya; wa-kidaa]** *invariable* and so on, etcetera 2

**wa-kidaa dayya** وَكِدَا دَيّ **[wa-kidaa daa; wa-kidaa]** *invariable* or so, something like that 2

**wallaa** وَلاَّ *conj* or 5

**wallaa kidaa** وَلاَّ كِدَا or something like that 5

**walii** وَلي *nms* man known for his piety, holy man {*pl:* **awliyaa**} 25

**w-aḷḷaahii** وَاللّه **[w-aḷḷaah]** really and truly, by God (oath or exclamation) 8

**wiḥda** وِحْدَة *nfs* region center, local center; unit, basic unit {*pl:* **wiḥdaat**} 3

**wiʃʃ** وِشّ **[waʃʃ]** *nms* face {*pl:* **wuʃuuʃ, awʃaaʃ**} 19

**wilaaya** وِلاَيَة *nfs* province {*pl:* **wilaayaat**} 13

**i**

**itʔassar** اِتْأَسَّرْ *vi* to be emotionally moved; to be affected, be touched {*imperf:* **yitʔassar,** *vn:* **taʔassur**} 17

**itta** اِتّ **[inta; itt]** *pron ms* you 9

**ittan** اِتَّنْ *pron fp* you 22

**ittuu** اِتُّو **[intuu]** *pron mp* you 18

**ittii** اِتِّي **[intii]** *pron fs* you 15

**itḥaakam** اِتْحَاكَمْ *vi* to be prosecuted, put on trial {*imperf:* **yitḥaakam,** *vn:* **maḥaakama**} 19

**itḥarrak** اِتْحَرَّكْ *vi* to depart, leave; to go; to move {*imperf:* **yitḥarrak,** *vn:* **ḥaraka**} 2

**itxatta** اِتْخَتّ *vi* to be placed {*imperf:* **yitxatt,** *vn:* **xatt**}

**itxamma** اِتْخَمّ *vi* to be fooled {*imperf:* **yitxamm,** *vn:* **xamm**}

**itxayyal li-** اتْخَيَّل ل *vi impersonal construction* to imagine (where logical subject is object of preposition) *(lit. to be or become the object of imagination for s.o.)* {*imperf:* **yitxayyal li-**, *vn:* **taxayyul**} 10

**itsabbab fii-** اتْسَبَّب في *vi* to be the cause of {*imperf:* **yitsabbab**, *vn:* **tasabbub**} 12

**itʃarbak fii** اتْشَرْبَك في *vi* to hold on to, stick to; to insist on *(lit. to become ensnared, embroiled, tangled in)* {*imperf:* **yitʃarbak**, *vn:* **ʃarbaka**} 26

**itʃanag** اتْشَنَق *vi* to be hanged, be executed by hanging {*imperf:* **yitʃanig**, *vn:* **ʃanig**} 19

**itṣadam** اتْصَدَم *vi* to be hit, be in a collision; to be deeply shocked {*imperf:* **yitṣadim**, *vn:* **ṣadim**} 22

**itʕaṭṭal** اتْعَطَّل *vi* to be late; to not work, be idle; to break down. be out of order {*imperf:* **yitʕaṭṭal**, *vn:* **taʕṭiil**} 12

**itʕawwag** اتْعَوَّق *vi* to be injured {*imperf:* **yitʕawwag**, *vn:* **ʕawaga**} 12

**itfataḥ** اتْفَتَح *vi* to be opened, opened up {*imperf:* **yitfatiḥ**, *vn:* **fatiḥ**} 3

**itfataḥ fii ddunya** اتْفَتَح في الدُّنْيا to grow up; to become aware of the world around one *(lit. to open up to the world)* {*imperf:* **yitfatiḥ fii ddunya**, *vn:* **fatiḥ fii ddunya**} 3

**itfarraɣ** اتفَرَّغ **[yitfarrig; yitfarraɣ]** *vi* to have leisure; to take time, set aside time {*imperf:* **yitfarraɣ**, *vn:* **tafarruɣ**} 12

**itfaḍḍal** اتْفَضَّل *vt used in imperative* please, go ahead {*fs:* **itfaḍḍalii**, *pl:* **itfaḍḍaluu**} 1

**itfagad** اتْفَقَد *vi* to be lost, have been lost {*imperf:* **yitfagid**, *vn:* **fugdaan**} 21

**itgabaḍ** اتْقَبَض *vi* be arrested, seized {*imperf:* **yitgabiḍ**, *vn:* **gabiḍ**} 19

**itneen** اتْنَيْن *nfs invariable* two

**itnasnas fii** اتْنَسْنَس في *vi* to poke into, snoop {*imperf:* **yitnasnas**, *vn:* **nasnas**} 22

**itnagal** اتْنَقَل *vi* to be transferred, moved {*imperf:* **yitnagil**, *vn:* **nagliyya**} 3

**itwarraṭ** اتْوَرَّط *vi* to become embroiled or entangled in difficulties or problems {*imperf:* **yitwarraṭ**, *vn:* **tawarruṭ**, *vn:* **warṭa**} 26

**itwaswas** اتْوَسْوَس *vi* to whisper; to gossip, talk about s.o. behind s.o.'s back {*imperf:* **yitwaswas**, *vn:* **tawaswus**} 22

**itwalad** اتْوَلَد *vi* to be born {*imperf:* **yitwalid**, *vn:* **wilaada**} 3

**itwannas** اتْوَنَّس *vi* to chat {*imperf:* **yitwannas**, *vn:* **wanas**}

**iḥtimaal** احْتِمال *nms* possibility; *adv* probably {*pl:* **iḥtimaalaat**} 24

**izaa kaan** إذا كان *conj invariable or conjugated* whether s.t. be ... or ..., be s.t .... or ... 15

**izaa ... wa ʔizaa ...** إذا ... وَ إذا ... *conj* either ... or ...

**izan** إذاً *conj* so, therefore 17

**isbitaaliya** اسْبِتالِيَة **[istibaaliya]** *nfs* hospital {*pl:* **isbitaalyaat**} 22

**istaad** اسْتاد *nms* stadium {*pl:* **istaadaat**}

**istamtaʕ** اسْتَمْتَع *vt* to enjoy {*imperf:* **yistamtaʕ**, *vn:* **istimtaaʕ**} 2

**istibaaliya** اَسْتبـاليَهْ **[istibaaliya]** *nfs* hospital {*pl:* **istibaalyaat**} 22

**ism- minnuu** اسْـمْ مـنُّو what is s.o.'s name *(lit. s.o.'s name is where)*

**iḍḍaayag** اضَّايَقْ *vi* to become annoyed {*imperf:* **yiḍḍaayig**, *vn:* **ḍiig**} 25

**iṭṭarra** اطَّرّْ *vt* to force (s.o. to do s.th.) {*imperf:* **yiṭṭarr**, *vn:* **iṭṭiraar**} 3

**iṭnaaʃar** اطْنَاشَرْ *nfs invariable* twelve; twelfth

**iʕtaraḍ** اعْتَرَضْ *vt* to protest, object {*imperf:* **yiʕtariḍ**, *vn:* **iʕtiraaḍ**} 19

**illaa**[1] الاّ *conj* but, however; *prep* except, unless 18

**illaa**[2] الاَّ *particle* of all things, imagine (of a sudden or unexpected development); come on, you can't be serious (introduces skeptical question) 22

**illii** اللِّي *pron invariable relative pronoun* who, which, that 3

**imtaḥan** امْتَحَنْ *vt* to take an exam (in a field or at a level); to give an exam (in a field or at a level) {*imperf:* **yimtaḥin**, *vn:* **imtiḥaan**} 5

**inta**[1] انْتَ **[itta; itt]** *pron ms* you 4

**inta**[2] انْتَ *disc marker invariable* you (device to get listener's attention and underscore urgency of question or request) 7

**intahaa min** انْتَهَى مِنْ *vi* to finish, put an end to {*imperf:* **yintahii**, *vn:* **intihaaʔ**, *vn:* **nihaaya**} 26

**intuu** انْتُو **[ittuu]** *pron mp* you 17

**intii** انْتِي **[ittii]** *pron fs* you 8

**intiɣaalii** انْتِغَالي *adj* transitional {*fs:* **intiɣaaliyya**, *mpl:* **intiɣaaliyyiin**, *fpl:* **intiɣaaliyyaat**} 15

**inʃaal** انْشَالْ *vi* to be removed, taken {*imperf:* **yinʃaal**, *vn:* **ʃeel**, *vn:* **ʃeyalaan**} 16

**in ʃaa ḷḷaa** انْ شَا اللَّهْ God willing (conventionally used when discussing the future) *(lit. if God wills)* 12

**in ʃaa ḷḷaa xeer** انْ شَا اللَّهْ خَيْرْ I hope that everything is ok *(lit. if God will, it is [was; will be] good)* 26

**innuu** انّهْ *conj invariable* that 2

**iywa** ايْوَهْ **[aywa; ay; ayya]** *interj* yes

**y**

**yaa-**[1] يَا **[aa-]** *particle takes suffixed pronoun* he/she/it is, they are {*ms:* **yaahuu**, *fs:* **yaahaa**, *mpl:* **yaahum**, *fpl:* **yaahun**} 6

**yaa**[2] يَا *interj* how; oh (adds exclamatory quality to following word) 27

**yaa ʔaḷḷaa yaamiin** يَا أَللَّهْ يَامِينْ barely; by the skin of one's teeth *(lit. either God or amen)* 9

**yaa jamaaʕa** يَا جَمَاعَهْ hey everyone *(lit. o group)* 17

**yaa ḥileel** يَا حلَيْلْ oh for s.o. or s.t. (expression of regret)

**yaax** يَاخْ brother, friend, buddy (polite term of address to male of same or lesser status) 17

**yaa xaṣaara** يَا خَصَارَهْ what a pity, too bad *(lit. o loss!)* 7

**yaa xii** يَا اخي my brother (informal term of adddress to male of same status) 11

**yaadaab** يَادَابْ **[yaadoob]** *adv*

barely, just

**yaadoob** يَادُوبْ **[yaadaab]** *adv* barely, just 5

**yaa salaam** يَا سَلَامْ my goodness (exclamation of amazement) 25

**yaa ... yaa** يَا...يَا *conj* either ... or 9

**yoom** يَوْمْ *nms* day {*pl:* **ayaam**} 2

**yoom attalaata** يَوْمْ اَلتَّلَاتَهْ Tuesday

**yoom ajjumʕa** يَوْمْ اَلجُّمْعَهْ Friday

**yoom assabit** يَوْمْ اَلسَّبِتْ Saturday

**yoom alxamiis** يَوْمْ الْخَمِيسْ Thursday

**yoom allaḥad** يَوْمْ اَلأَّحَدْ Sunday

**yoom allarbaḥa** يَوْمْ الأَّرْبَحَهْ Wednesday

**yoom allitneen** يَوْمْ الأِّتْنَيْنْ Monday

**yaʕnii** يَعْنِي *interj invariable* you know, I mean, that is *(lit. it means)* 2

**yaḷḷaa** يَلاَّ *interj invariable* come on, move; let's go 12

**yammaa** يَمَّا *interj* o mamma (exclamation used by women) 22

**yanaayir** يَنَايِرْ *nms* January

**yannuu** يَنَّهْ **[annuu; ʔannuu]** *conj* that 5

**yeh** يَهْ *interj* my, goodness (with exaggerated intonation, an expression of admiration) 22

**yuulya** يُولْيَه *nms* July

**yuunya** يُونْيَهْ *nms* June

**yibgaa** يِبْقَى *adv invariable* then, that's it 5

**yimkin** يِمْكِنْ *disc marker invariable; also variable pre-verb* maybe *(lit. it is possible)* 3